Using Microsoft® Word:
Macintosh Version

Steve Lambert
Marsha L. Miliman

Que™ Corporation
Carmel, Indiana

Dedication

To Joan

Product Director
David F. Noble, Ph.D.

Acquisitions Editor
Pegg Kennedy

Editors
Barbara Potter
Sandra Blackthorn
Gail Burlakoff
Jeannine Freudenberger, M.A.
Rebecca Whitney

Manuscript preparation provided by Online Press Inc.

Technical Editor
Bryan Pfaffenberger

Book Design and Production
Dan Armstrong
Sharon Hilgenberg
Jennifer Matthews
Cindy Phipps
Dennis Sheehan
Carrie Torres

Using Microsoft Word: Macintosh Version is based on
Microsoft Word, Version 3, and earlier Versions.

About the Authors

Steve Lambert

Well known as a writer in the computer field, Steve Lambert is the author of two books about products for the Apple Macintosh (*Presentation Graphics on the Apple Macintosh* and *Creative BASIC on the Apple Macintosh*) as well as books and articles about IBM PC products. He also has compiled two books about emerging optical-media technologies (CD-ROM and CD-I).

The challenge of finding solutions to new and different problems has led Steve Lambert to work in fields as diverse as high-rigging, electronic security, photography, and computer programming. As former president of Info Express Inc., he guided the development of a highly acclaimed image-processing system that produces real-time screen displays of the bottom of the ocean. Steve Lambert recently co-founded Online Press Inc., a company dedicated to the design, preparation, and publication of full-text and relational-database information on paper, magnetic, and optical media.

Marsha L. Miliman

Marsha Miliman, a native of Los Angeles, California, has been a technical and marketing writer for more than 17 years. She has written on such diverse subjects as economic development, energy and natural resources, biomedical research, artificial intelligence, planetary exploration, and other areas of high technology. She graduated from the University of California, Berkeley, and studied economics at the University of Massachusetts, Amherst, focusing on problems of economic development.

Working as a technical writer for the Jet Propulsion Laboratory in the late 1970's, Marsha Miliman wrote several award-winning publications on NASA's Voyager mission to the outer planets. She moved to Seattle in 1980 and started COMMUNICORPS, a consulting firm that provides documentation, presentation, and conference planning services for corporations and associations throughout the country.

Contents at a Glance

Table of Contents

I Starting with the Basics

4   Fabulous Formatting 81

II Adding to Your Repertoire

III Using Advanced Features for Long Documents

19   Creating a Table of Contents 433

20   Creating Footnotes 441

A   Using the Apple Extended Keyboard 457

Index 459

Quick Reference Guide

Acknowledgments

Our thanks to Dale Callison, who burned the midnight oil with us. Thanks also to Microsoft's Product Support team, who helped us unravel some of the mysteries of Word.

Trademark Acknowledgments

Introduction

Microsoft® Word, Version 3, for the Macintosh® transforms word-processing power into publishing power. With Version 3 you can make documents more professional-looking than those created with previous versions of Word. You can integrate text and graphics, create side-by-side or snaking columns, box both text and graphics, and preview your page layout to make formatting adjustments or to add finishing touches. You also can customize Word's menus and switch instantly between Word and other Macintosh applications, such as Microsoft® Excel, MacDraw®, MacPaint®, Adobe™ Illustrator, and PageMaker®.

Using Microsoft Word: Macintosh Version does not pretend to be an exhaustive guide to the Word program. Throughout the book, we give you enough information to enable you to use a particular Word feature, and we offer one or two examples to guide you. However, the Macintosh was designed to be easy to use, and Word was designed to take advantage of all the capabilities of the Macintosh. You do not need volumes of information to be able to integrate Word smoothly into your working environment. All you need is a little time, a little patience, this book, and your own imagination.

About Word's Users and Their Computers

Using Microsoft Word: Macintosh Version is written for all Word users. Whether you're a first-time user who is nervous about working with such a powerful program or an experienced user who can't wait to test Word's newest features, you'll find this book packed with the information you need. What's more, as you follow along with the examples in the book, we hope that you will find that you're actually having fun.

Microsoft Word, Version 3, runs on all Macintosh computers, including the original Macintosh 512K; the Macintosh® Plus; the Macintosh® SE; and the new, open-architecture Macintosh® II. However, we found we couldn't work efficiently with a Macintosh® 512K. The smallest system powerful enough to take advantage of all of Word's features and speed is a Macintosh Plus with an external drive. Working with a hard disk, of course, enhances the program's speed.

Whether you use the mouse or the keyboard is largely a matter of preference and circumstance, so we encourage you to experiment with both methods to discover which method feels most comfortable for you. Almost all of Microsoft Word's commands can be duplicated on the keyboard, and we point out these keyboard shortcuts as we go along. Although most keyboard actions are the same on the Macintosh Plus keyboard and the extended keyboard, some differences exist. (These differences are summarized in Appendix A.)

About This Book

Using Microsoft Word: Macintosh Version is divided into three sections so that you easily can find the information you need. The first section provides information about how your Macintosh works with the Word program. You then explore the basic functions of the program, such as editing, formatting, printing, and so on. In the second section, you learn some timesaving techniques that help you turn Word from a word-processing program into a desktop-publishing program. And finally, the last section shows you how to make working with long or technical documents easy by introducing you to Word's outline, table of contents, and footnote functions.

Part I: Starting with the Basics

If you're new to Microsoft Word for the Macintosh, we suggest that you start at the beginning of the book with the first seven chapters.

Chapter 1 covers basic Macintosh housekeeping techniques. We guide you through the process of preparing Word to run on your computer and then give you a sneak preview of some of Word's powerful features.

In Chapter 2, you learn how to get into and out of Word and how to use the mouse and the keyboard to choose commands. Then you apply this information to create and save two simple documents.

Chapter 3 covers the basic Word editing commands—Cut, Copy, Paste, and Undo from the Edit menu. You learn how to select, delete, and rearrange your text. You also review how to use the scroll bars and keyboard commands to move through a document.

In Chapter 4, you first see how to use Word's paragraph formatting options to position various elements of text for greater emphasis, how to vary line spacing, and how to set tab stops. Then you learn how to color the words within the text by using character formatting to change the style, size, and font of the characters.

In Chapter 5, you explore the page layout options in the Page Setup dialog box. Then you take a look at the additional page layout options available with the new Section command. Finally, you practice using the Page Setup and Section commands to prepare a document for printing.

Chapter 6 shows you how to activate the Page Preview window, which gives you a bird's-eye view of your document's pages. You also learn how to magnify an area of a page preview page to see the area more clearly and how to use page preview tools to make formatting changes that would otherwise require setting Paragraph, Page Setup, and Sections options.

Chapter 7, the last chapter in Part I, covers printing. You first learn how to prepare your Macintosh to print Word documents. Then you see how to print a document from within Word and from the Macintosh Finder™. By the end of this chapter, you know enough to create straightforward but elegant documents that will meet most of your printing needs.

Part II: Adding to Your Repertoire

When you have had a chance to practice the basic skills in Part I and you feel comfortable with the program, move on, at your leisure, to Part II. It covers many of the timesaving features offered by Word, Version 3.

Chapter 8 begins by explaining the basic concept of glossaries and briefly touring the Glossary command's dialog box. You are introduced to the Standard Glossary and learn two methods for inserting a glossary entry into a document. Next, you create a simple glossary entry so that you will know how to name, add, change, and delete your own entries. Finally, you learn how to create specialized glossaries and how to merge, switch between, delete, and print these glossaries while you work with a document.

In Chapter 9, you learn about style sheets. After becoming acquainted with the basic styles in Word's default style sheet, you learn how to add, change, and delete styles of your own. Finally, you see how to merge style sheets and how to print the contents of a style sheet for reference.

Chapter 10 shows you how to split a single window into two sections to view two portions of the same document, how to view the same document in several windows, and how to open and close several documents in different windows. You see how to transfer information between two documents displayed simultaneously in different windows and how to access documents through the Window menu.

Customizing menus is the topic covered in Chapter 11. You learn how to tailor to your own needs the Format and Font menus and how to create a Work menu by adding and deleting menu items. The chapter also discusses specific techniques for working with commands, documents, glossary entries, and styles from custom menus.

In Chapter 12, you learn how to insert into a Word document a graphic created in another application, such as MacDraw, MacPaint, SuperPaint™, Microsoft® Chart, or Microsoft Excel. You also learn how to position graphics, how to change their size and shape, and how to combine text and graphics so that they function as single elements.

Chapter 13 begins with a discussion of uses and designs for headers and footers and then introduces the set of headers and footers available for various parts of a document. You then learn how to create, position, and format headers and footers and how to view and adjust them in the Page Preview window.

In Chapter 14, you first learn the basic procedure for checking your spelling. After taking a tour of the Spelling dialog box, you find out more about Word's dictionaries, including when and how to create, open, and close your own user dictionaries. Finally, you work through a spelling check with a sample document.

Hyphenation is the topic covered in Chapter 15, in which you see how Word can help you improve the appearance of a document by breaking lines to eliminate unnecessary or distracting white space.

Chapter 16, the last chapter in Part II, first shows you the basic techniques for using Word's print merge feature. You then see how to use conditional instructions to vary the contents of a form letter. Finally, you apply these techniques to the task of printing mailing labels.

Part III: Using Advanced Features for Long Documents

Part III takes you through some of the features Word offers for creating long or technical documents.

In Chapter 17, you are introduced to the two ways of viewing an outlined document, and you learn basic outlining techniques. Then you outline a sample document while setting and changing heading levels and adding text. You learn how to collapse and expand subheadings and text so that you can move easily through a document, and you learn how to move large sections of the document simply by moving a heading. You also see how to edit a document by editing its outline and how to apply styles to the document by applying them to its outline. Finally, you learn how to number headings and how to print the outline.

Word offers both speed and efficiency for making use of your documents by giving you the tools first to record information and then to access the information through detailed and accurate indexes. In Chapter 18, you learn how to use the Index command in the Document menu to index your documents.

Chapter 19 shows you how to create a table of contents. Word can compile the table from either outline headings (if the document has been outlined) or coded entries.

Finally, Chapter 20 shows you how to create footnotes and how to revise them as you change a document. The chapter then demonstrates some of the finer points of formatting footnotes so that you can give your footnotes a professional look.

Appendix A and the tear-out Quick Reference Guide complete the book. Appendix A briefly describes how Word takes advantage of the extra keys on the Apple® Extended Keyboard, which some of you may be using with the Macintosh II. The Quick Reference Guide puts the Word commands at your fingertips for easy reference. Tear out the guide and post it by your computer or carry it in your briefcase so that you will have the commands to refer to whenever you need them.

You gain more insight into Word if you follow along on your Macintosh with the examples presented in each chapter. The examples enable you to "feel" how each feature or command works. However, we've sprinkled pictures of the screen liberally throughout the book to allow you to follow along just as easily when you are riding the bus or lounging at home in your most comfortable chair. In many of the exercises, we provide sample documents for those of you who want to make sure you've mastered a particular technique before trying it on one of your own documents. If you prefer to work with your own documents, you will find that the step-by-step instructions are general and easily can be adapted to your specific needs.

We don't expect you to read *Using Microsoft Word: Macintosh Version* from cover to cover in just a few sittings. We do hope that you will find the book a handy reference source, worthy of the little space it takes up on your desk. And we know that, once you learn how to use this powerful program, your documents will never look the same again. You will have had a taste of the exciting new world of desktop publishing, and you will never look back.

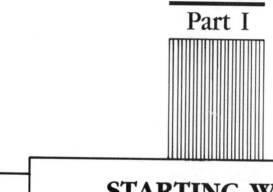

Part I

STARTING WITH THE BASICS

Includes:

Setting Up Word

Getting Started

Quick and Easy Editing

Fabulous Formatting

Laying Out Pages

Previewing Pages

No-Fuss Printing

Setting Up Word

Microsoft Word has been the leading word-processing program for the Macintosh since Apple® released the machine in 1984. For each new Macintosh upgrade, Microsoft has updated Word to take advantage of the machine's added speed and power and to offer additional features. And with Version 3 of Word, Microsoft began bridging the gap between conventional word processing and desktop publishing. As you get to know Version 3 of Word, you will find that it can take care of all your word-processing needs. You also will discover that the program has the power and flexibility to perform most desktop-publishing tasks without the slowness and other limitations normally associated with desktop-publishing programs.

If you are already familiar with your Macintosh, installing and learning to use Microsoft Word will be relatively quick and easy, and you may need to do no more than skim this chapter. If you have just purchased your Macintosh and are still unfamiliar with basic housekeeping techniques, this chapter will guide you through the process of preparing Word to run on your computer and then give you a sneak preview of some of Word's powerful features.

Making Sure That You Have the Right Equipment

To run Word, Version 3, you need the following:

- An Apple Macintosh system with a minimum of 512K of memory. One megabyte of memory is preferred because it provides faster operation.

With the exception of the original "slim" Mac® (the first Macintosh, with a limited memory of 128K), any Macintosh model will do—including a "fat" Mac (a 512K Macintosh), Macintosh Plus, Mac II, or Macintosh SE. We used a Macintosh Plus with 1M of memory when developing the examples in this book.

- An internal or external double-sided 800K disk drive; two single-sided 400K disk drives; or a hard disk and a single- or double-sided disk drive

Word, Version 3, is available on 400K disks for use on a 512K Macintosh, but that configuration doesn't fully take advantage of Word's speed and leaves little disk space for your documents. Unless otherwise stated, the instructions in this book are for a system with two 800K disk drives.

- A copy of Microsoft Word 3.0 or above, including the Program and Utilities disks

The Program disk contains the Macintosh System and Finder files as well as the Word program, so you can start the Macintosh directly from the Program disk.

- Two blank double-sided disks for making copies of the original Program and Utilities disks

- Blank disks, called *data disks* in this book, for storing the documents you create

- A Macintosh-compatible printer—for example, an Apple ImageWriter®, an Apple LaserWriter®, or an Apple LaserWriter® Plus with downloadable fonts; a daisywheel printer, such as a Diablo 630®, a NEC® 7710, or an Apple daisywheel printer. (All these printers need a serial interface to work with the Macintosh.)

Mastering Basic Macintosh Skills

If you are a new Macintosh user and don't yet feel entirely at home in the desktop environment—a temporary state, we assure you—we recommend that you spend some time reading your Macintosh owner's guide before trying to learn Word. In particular, you should know how to do the following:

- Turn your system on and off

- Insert and eject disks

- Click, double-click, and drag the mouse

- Use the mouse to open, close, copy, and transfer documents and disks in the Finder

- Pull down and choose commands from the program's menus—Apple, File, Edit, View, and Special (We'll explain the menu commands in later chapters.)

- Open, close, and move windows on your desktop

If you aren't familiar with these operations, please take the time to review them in your owner's guide. This preparation will enable you to explore Word's many exciting features without worrying about mastering the basics at the same time.

If you have a system with two disk drives, read the following section. If you have a hard disk system, skip to "Setting Up Word on a System with a Hard Disk."

Making Backup Copies of Your Word Disks on Two Disk Drive Systems

You need to make a backup copy of your Program and Utilities disks and use the backup copies as your working disks. Store the originals in a safe place in case you lose or damage the copies. Because the Word disks are not copy protected, you can make your backups by using any of the disk-copy programs available for the Macintosh, or you can use the program included in the Macintosh Finder.

To make a backup copy of your Word Program disk, using the Finder, do the following:

1. Turn on your Macintosh and insert the Word Program disk in the internal drive (with the metal tab inserted first and the label up).

Actually, using either the internal or the external drive makes no difference, but keeping track of your disks is easier if you always put the Program disk (which includes the Macintosh operating system) in the internal drive, and your data disk in the external drive.

After a few seconds, a window containing a number of icons opens on the desktop, similar to the window shown in figure 1.1. (You'll explore these icons shortly, in the section titled "Exploring the Program and the Utilities Disks.") You also see a disk icon, labeled Word Program, on the upper right corner of the desktop. If only the icon appears, double-click it, and the window opens.

Fig. 1.1

The open window that appears after you insert Word's Program disk.

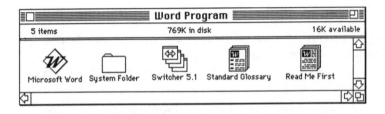

2. Insert a blank disk in the external drive.

If the disk is already *initialized*—prepared for use on the Macintosh—skip to Step 5. If not, a dialog box like the one in figure 1.2 asks whether you want to initialize the disk and, if the disk is in an 800K drive, offers three choices: Eject (to cancel the operation), One-Sided, and Two-Sided.

Fig. 1.2

The dialog box that appears when you insert an uninitialized disk.

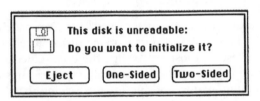

3. Click **One-Sided** or **Two-Sided** to start the initialization
   process. If you have a 400K drive and a single-sided disk, click
   One-Sided; if you have an 800K drive and a double-sided disk,
   click **Two-Sided**.

When the disk is initialized, a new dialog box tells you to name the disk.
What you type is inserted character by character at the *insertion point*,
the flashing vertical bar.

4. Type a name for the backup disk (such as *Copy of Word* or
   Word-2). If you make a typing mistake, press the Backspace key
   to delete the error and type the name again. When you finish,
   press **Return** or click **OK**.

The dialog box closes, and a disk icon bearing the name that you have
given your disk appears on-screen.

5. To copy all the files on your Word Program disk to the new
   disk, drag the Program disk icon until it rests on top of the
   new disk icon.

Word asks you to confirm your desire to replace the contents of the
disk in the external drive with the contents of the disk in the internal
drive.

6. Click **OK**.

The Mac starts copying Word Program files to the blank disk. As the
Mac copies the disk, the computer displays a status box telling you how
many files remain to be copied.

7. When copying is complete, choose **Eject** from the File menu
   (or press **Command-E**) to eject the selected disk.

The Macintosh ejects the selected (highlighted) disk—in this case the
backup disk.

8. Select the **Program** disk and choose **Eject** again.

The Mac ejects the Program disk.

A shortcut for ejecting a disk that is not selected is to press the Shift,
Command (labeled ⌘), and 1 keys simultaneously; press Shift-
Command-2 to eject a disk from the external drive. Or, provided the
disk you're working with does *not* contain the operating system, you
can eject the disk by dragging the disk icon to the trash can. Dragging
the icon to the trash causes the Finder to "forget" the disk so that its
icon disappears from the screen.

Using this shortcut when your screen gets cluttered with icons of disks you no longer use is a good idea because the Finder frequently needs to update information on all the disks displayed with icons. If too many disks are displayed, you will have to switch disks before processing can resume.

Next, make a copy of the Word Utilities disk by repeating the same steps:

1. Insert the Utilities disk in the internal drive.

An icon labeled Word Utilities appears on the right side of the desktop, just below the other disk icons.

Notice that using the File menu's Eject command to pop disks out of your Macintosh does not close their windows or remove their icons from the desktop. These windows and icons normally don't interfere with the copying of the Utilities disk. However, if a window does obscure the Utilities disk icon, you can click the close box in the window's upper left corner to close the window. To remove from the screen any icon except the one for the disk containing the operating system, you can drag the icon to the trash can.

2. Insert a blank disk in the external drive and initialize it as you did the disk for the Program files.

3. Name the new backup disk when the dialog box prompts you to do so.

4. Drag the Utilities disk icon on top of the new disk icon to begin copying the Utilities files.

5. When copying is complete, eject both disks.

When you finish, store the original Program and Utilities disks in a safe place.

The next section is for those of you who have hard disks. The rest of you can skip to the section titled "Exploring the Program and the Utilities Disks."

Setting Up Word on a System with a Hard Disk

If you have a hard disk, you undoubtedly have already copied the Macintosh operating system onto the hard disk and know how to transfer programs to it. Do the following procedure to copy the necessary Word files to the hard disk.

To copy the Word Program and Utilities disks to your hard disk, do the following:

1. Insert the Word Program disk in the internal disk drive.

2. Create a folder for Word on the hard disk by choosing **New Folder** from the File menu. When the Mac displays a folder labeled New Folder, type **Word** to name the folder. (If you make a mistake, press the Backspace key to rub out the error.) Press **Return** when you're done.

3. If the Word Program disk window isn't open, open it now by double-clicking the Word Program disk icon. Position the window so that you can see the Word folder in the hard drive window. Select everything except the System Folder in the Word Program window by positioning the pointer to one side of the group of file icons and dragging across them.

4. To copy the selected files, position the pointer over one of the selected file icons and drag the icon to the Word folder icon in the hard disk window. The Word folder icon becomes black when the icon you are moving touches the folder icon.

All the selected file icons move with the one you are dragging. The Mac then copies the files one by one to the hard disk.

5. After the files are copied, eject the Word Program disk and insert the Word Utilities disk in the internal disk drive.

6. Drag the Utilities disk icon on top of the Word folder icon to copy the Utilities disk's contents to the hard disk.

7. Choose **Eject** from the File menu to eject the Utilities disk from the internal drive.

You can avoid swapping disks by putting the Program disk in the internal drive and the Utilities disk in the external drive, or vice versa.

Exploring the Program and the Utilities Disks

Now that you've copied the Program and the Utilities disks, you need to know exactly what's on them.

The Program Disk

As you probably know, the Macintosh has its own unique operating system, a complex program that monitors and controls the operations of the Mac and any devices connected to it. Most of this operating system is called the *System* and is normally stored in the System Folder along with other System programs. The operating system's *user interface*, the part that handles communication with you, the user, is contained in a system program file called the *Finder*. Other System Folder files include the Clipboard and ImageWriter, a file that contains information Word needs in order to use the ImageWriter printer.

Even though the Mac's System disk contains this operating system, the system's essential elements also are included with Word—and with most other Macintosh application programs. Thus, you are able to use the Word Program disk as a startup disk instead of having to insert a separate System disk. (If you don't have a hard disk, turning on your computer and inserting a disk that doesn't have the Macintosh operating system on it displays a Macintosh icon with a frowning face. The frowning face lets you know that you can't start up your computer with that disk because the disk doesn't have the System file on it.)

To look at the other files your Word Program disk contains, make sure that the Program disk window is open on your screen. Several icons, each representing a file or group of files, tell you which files are on the disk. You also can ask Word to list the files by name, by date of creation or revision, by size, by kind, or with smaller icons. (Listing by smaller icons is handy if your disk contains many files.) The View menu, shown in figure 1.3, lists the ways you can display the files. Go ahead and choose these commands, one after another, to see the different views.

When you start creating documents, you'll probably prefer to use the Name and Date views, shown in figures 1.4 and 1.5 respectively, which help you find the latest version of your work. The Name view lists files in alphabetical order, and the Date view lists your files in order of most recent modification.

The only information you can change in any of these views is the document or file name. If you want to change a name, just select it by pointing anywhere in its icon and clicking the mouse button, and then start typing. We don't recommend that you change the name of the System file or of Word's Program file, however, because you might forget the new names and have difficulty locating them later, particularly if you are using a hard disk that contains many files.

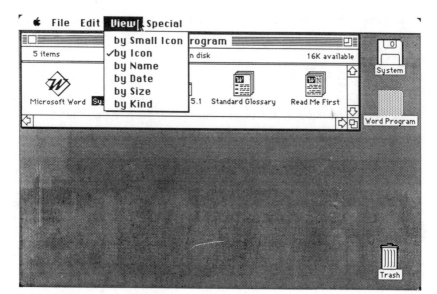

Fig. 1.3

The Program disk window with the View menu pulled down.

Name	Size	Kind	Last Modified	
Microsoft Word	332K	application	Thu, Feb 12, 1987	9:52 AM
Release Notes	5K	Microsoft Word d...	Tue, Feb 10, 1987	8:00 AM
Standard Glossary	1K	Microsoft Word d...	Sat, Jan 31, 1987	7:41 AM
System Folder	--	folder	Thu, Jun 25, 1987	3:24 PM

Fig. 1.4

The Name view, showing files in alphabetic order.

Name	Size	Kind	Last Modified	
System Folder	--	folder	Thu, Jun 25, 1987	3:24 PM
Microsoft Word	332K	application	Thu, Feb 12, 1987	9:52 AM
Release Notes	5K	Microsoft Word d...	Tue, Feb 10, 1987	8:00 AM
Standard Glossary	1K	Microsoft Word d...	Sat, Jan 31, 1987	7:41 AM

Fig. 1.5

The Date view, showing files in order of most recent modification.

You can obtain more information about a file by choosing Get Info from the File menu. To get information about the System file, for example, do the following:

1. Double-click the **System Folder**.

A second window opens, displaying icons for files in the System Folder: the System, the Finder, the ImageWriter printer driver, and the Clipboard file.

2. Click the **System** icon to select the file.

3. Choose **Get Info** from the File menu (or press **Command-I**).

A window appears, telling you what type of file is selected (in this case, a System document—other possibilities exist, such as an application or a document); how much disk space the file uses; which disk contains the file; when the file was created (equivalent of a version number); and when the file was last modified. Figure 1.6 shows how this window looks for Version 3.1 of the operating system.

Fig. 1.6

The Get Info dialog box.

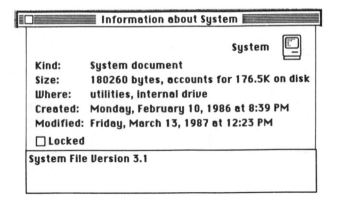

Notice the Locked check box below the Modified line. If you click this box, you won't be able to delete, modify, or change this file's name—and neither will anyone else—unless, of course, you return to this window and click the Locked check box again to toggle it off.

If you want, you can type a note about this file in the comment box at the bottom. (Some software manufacturers record the version number of the software in this box, but that shouldn't prevent you from adding your own notes.)

4. Click the close box in the upper left corner of the Information about System window to return to the System Folder window.

5. Click the close box on the System Folder window.

The System Folder is now closed.

You can use the Get Info command from the File menu to find basic information about each of the other files in the Program disk window, so we won't describe them in detail here. We will look a little more closely at a file called Read Me First or Release Notes. You may not recognize this file because it is unique to Word, Version 3. This document alerts you to any last-minute software changes that Microsoft was unable to incorporate in the reference manual, plus any updates or corrections to the manual.

To take a look at the Read Me First or Release Notes file, do the following:

1. Double-click the icon.

After a few seconds, Word displays a document.

2. Read the notes.

To page through the document, use the down- and up-arrows on the scroll bar. You also may use the Down- and Up-Arrow keys on the keyboard.

3. When you finish, click the close box in the document window.

You now see a blank window with Word's menu bar across the top. Why? This document is a Word document; and when you opened it, you automatically started the Word program.

4. To return to the Program disk window, choose **Quit** from Word's File menu.

Actually, you could have saved a little time by choosing Quit without first closing the document window, and even more time by using the Quit command's keyboard shortcut, Command-Q. You'll learn more about such shortcuts in Chapter 2.

The Utilities Disk

Before you actually start working with Word, look at some files on the Utilities disk. First, make sure that the Word Utilities window is open on your screen. The Utilities window looks like the one shown in figure 1.7. In the window's top row are several booklike icons emblazoned with the letter *W*, signifying their association with Version 3 of Word. The icons represent files, such as Main Dictionary, that you can attach to a document you're working on to help you in some way. Double-clicking one of these files opens a new Word document and attaches the selected file. You will learn more about these files as you use them.

Fig. 1.7

*The Word
Utilities window.*

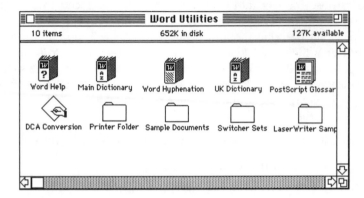

Several folders on the Utilities disk contain sample documents you can open and edit. To take a look at some LaserWriter samples by opening the LaserWriter Samples file, do the following:

1. Double-click the **LaserWriter Samples** icon.

Another window opens, containing icons representing three LaserWriter documents designed to show you what the Word-LaserWriter partnership can accomplish. Don't worry about the details you don't understand; they all will be discussed later in the book. For now, take a peek at the kinds of impressive documents you'll be producing in the near future.

2. Double-click the **Video/Dialog Script** icon.

A short two-column document containing the script for a video opens. The columns have been formatted with the Side-by-Side Paragraph menu option, explained in Chapter 4. At first glance, you may not realize the document has two columns because, as figure 1.8 shows, Word displays the columns offset, one lower than the other, instead of side by side.

You won't learn about two-column documents until later, but here's a sneak preview of one of Word's most sophisticated new features, Page Preview.

3. Choose **Page Preview** from the File menu.

The Script window closes, and a Page Preview window opens, displaying two miniature pages side by side, as shown in figure 1.9.

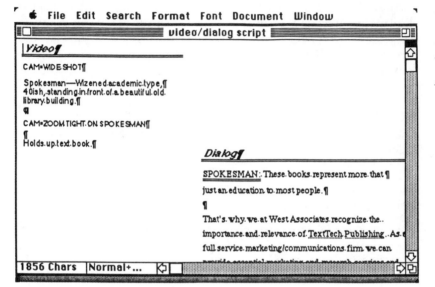

Fig. 1.8

A document formatted for side-by-side paragraphs.

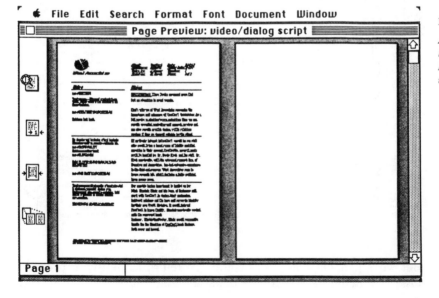

Fig. 1.9

A document in the Page Preview window.

Because the script document is only one page long, the document is displayed entirely on the left page. As you can see, the columns are, in fact, side by side rather than staggered. Page Preview is showing you exactly how the Script file will look when it's printed. To get a closer look at the page, go on to Step 4.

4. Click the uppermost icon on the left side of the screen—the icon of a page with a magnifying glass over it.

The pointer becomes the magnifying glass, and when you move the pointer away from the icon, the magnifying glass moves out of the icon.

5. Move the magnifying glass over the left page in the Page Preview window and click between the two columns under the first horizontal rule at the top.

Instantly, the miniature page zooms to full size, as shown in figure 1.10, revealing the same text you saw in the document when you first clicked the Video/Dialog Script icon.

Fig. 1.10

The magnified Page Preview window.

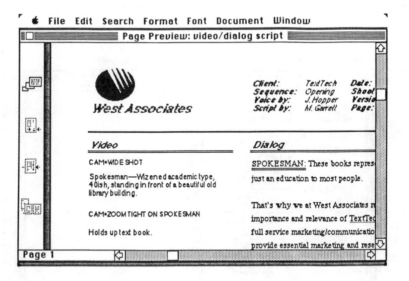

But we're jumping ahead of ourselves, so return to the Word Utilities disk window on the desktop by doing the following:

1. Click the close box in the Page Preview window.

2. Click the close box in the Video/Dialog Script window. (If you see a dialog box asking if you want to save changes to the document or save repagination before closing the window, click the **No** button.)

Now you see a blank Word window. When you opened the Video/Dialog Script window, the Macintosh automatically started Word.

3. Choose **Quit** from the File menu (or press **Command-Q**).

4. Close the LaserWriter Samples window.

Look at another item in the Utilities disk window. One folder you should know about and understand is the Printer Folder, shown in figure 1.11. Double-click the Printer Folder icon to open its window.

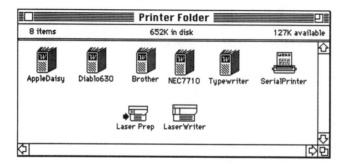

Fig. 1.11

The Utilities disk's Printer Folder.

The Printer Folder contains programs called *printer drivers*, each containing the information required by the Macintosh to communicate with a specific model of printer. At the bottom of the Printer Folder window are the LaserWriter and Laser Prep (short for preparation) icons, which together run the LaserWriter and LaserWriter Plus printers. The Utilities disk also contains the printer drivers for several other commonly used printers. If you have an ImageWriter, do nothing; the Word Program disk already contains the ImageWriter driver. If you want to use one of the other printers, copy its driver to the Word Program disk's System Folder.

In Chapter 7, we discuss more about the kinds of printers that can print Word documents.

You've learned a bit about the Word program in this chapter. The next chapter describes in detail how to start and quit Word, create and save new documents, and open and close existing documents. Also covered are basic techniques for working with Word on the Macintosh Plus, such as how to select text, move around within and among documents, and work with the keyboard and mouse. If you are familiar with these basic features of Word and the Macintosh Plus, you may want to skim Chapter 2 quickly and then move on to Chapter 3.

As you work along with us in the rest of Part I, you will learn first how to create and edit a document and then how to improve its appearance by applying Word's formatting and page layout options. Finally, you will be introduced to Word's powerful printing capabilities.

Getting Started

Now that you know how to use your Word disks, start Word and delve a little more deeply into its inner workings. As you work your way through Chapter 2, you learn how to get into and out of Word and how to use the mouse and the keyboard to select text and choose commands. We also introduce you to the special uses of some of the keys on the Macintosh keyboard. Those of you who have worked with other applications on the Macintosh may be able to skim most of this chapter, but do make sure that you create and save the two simple documents. You will use them in Chapter 3 to practice editing.

Starting Word

To start Word, do the following steps:

1. Turn on your system.

2. Insert the Program disk in the internal drive, and a disk with room for a small file (at least a few K) in the external drive.

Your Macintosh goes through its start-up process, ending with the Finder displayed on the screen. Each of the disks you insert is represented by a small icon at the upper right edge of the screen, and one or more windows may be open, displaying the contents of those disks. Whether windows open automatically when you start the Mac depends on their state when you last ejected the disks. If the windows were open when you ejected the disks, then they will be open now.

3. If the Word Program disk window in the Finder is not open, double-click the Word Program disk icon.

4. Double-click the **Microsoft Word** icon to load Word.

As your system loads the Word Program, your screen changes several times. First, a blank Microsoft Word window replaces the information in the Finder on the desktop. A few seconds later, the Word menu bar appears, and a blank document window opens with the words Microsoft Word in the title bar. The title quickly changes to Untitled1. Finally, a blinking *insertion point* appears in the window's upper left corner and hovers above a short horizontal line, called the *end mark*. Figure 2.1 shows how your screen looks when Word is loaded and ready for you to begin work.

Fig. 2.1

An untitled Microsoft Word window.

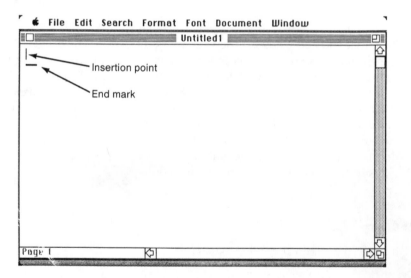

Just in case you get called away before you finish reading this chapter, we'll review how to quit Word.

Quitting Word

The steps for quitting Word are easy. The difficult part is leaving your work when you're having so much fun—right?

To quit Word from the Untitled1 window, do the following:

1. Choose **Quit** from the File menu or use the **Command-Q** keyboard shortcut.

Throughout this book, particularly with commonly used commands, you'll see references to keyboard shortcuts. Start using the shortcuts now so that you get used to them (see the Quick Reference Guide at the end of the book).

If you just couldn't wait and have gone ahead and entered text in the untitled window, Word displays a dialog box that asks whether you want to save the document. (We will discuss dialog boxes shortly.)

2. Click **No**.

You are returned to the desktop with the Word Program disk window open and the Finder's menu bar displayed.

Now that you know how to quit, start Word again so that you can learn more about the features of Word and of the Macintosh Plus. Double-click the Microsoft Word icon to return to the untitled document window.

One reason why working on the Macintosh is easy—and productive—is that the operating system and the applications written for the operating system share common features. All these programs use the mouse, the keyboard, menus, commands, and dialog and alert boxes. Also, in most programs, such actions as selecting text and opening, closing, and scrolling through documents are performed in the same way.

Your Macintosh owner's guide provides an excellent overview of these features. The following sections briefly review how Word and the Macintosh features work together.

Using the Mouse

Unlike the IBM® PC environment, where the mouse is optional, the mouse that comes with the Macintosh is an integral part of the system. Although Word now has keyboard equivalents for almost every command and mouse action, you still need to use the mouse to start Word and to move icons around on the Finder's desktop. Several actions require use of both the mouse and the keyboard.

When you are working with Word, you use the mouse most often to do the following:

- Open, copy, and close documents; move icons and windows; throw documents away in the trash; and perform other activities on the desktop

- Choose menus and commands from the Finder and within Word

- Select text and graphics (and tools, such as the painting and drawing tools in MacPaint and MacDraw)

- Move with ease within and among documents

Like all creatures great and small, the mouse needs room to move. But like its namesake, the Macintosh mouse doesn't need much room—an area about 8 inches square should be sufficient. Don't make the mouse stumble over pizza crumbs, paper clips, or its own tail; and don't allow the mouse to wade through little pools of seltzer on your desk. Any of these activities can interfere with the mouse's operation or even damage the mouse. In other words, when you use the mouse, make sure that the ball bearing on the bottom can slide along a flat, even, clean surface. If your desk or worktable is too slick or too rough to provide an even, smooth, and quiet surface for the mouse, you may want to buy one of the mouse pads available from your local computer store. Or, if your desk is too slippery for the mouse to get its footing, you can buy teflon pads (mouse feet) that help your mouse glide more easily.

The mouse, which you move with your hand, has a graphic counterpart on the screen. In most Macintosh applications, the mouse icon is a black arrow called the *pointer*. You usually use the pointer to choose menus and commands or to select graphics, icons, and certain kinds of text (such as the names of icons on the desktop). In Word, however, the mouse pointer changes shape when the pointer moves to different parts of the screen. The shape changes are important because they change the mouse's function. More information about that is provided later; for now, let's explore the shape changes.

Explore the screen with the mouse for a moment. Drag the pointer horizontally and then vertically across the screen. The black arrow becomes an I-beam as the pointer enters the document window. When the I-beam enters the invisible selection bar along the document window's left edge, the I-beam changes to a right-pointing arrow, which you can use to select blocks of text. As soon as you move the I-beam into one of the scroll bars along the right and bottom edges or up to the menu bar, it once again becomes the original pointer.

If you find that moving the mouse across your desk doesn't get the pointer all the way from one edge of the screen to the other, just pick up the mouse, move it back to where you started, and move the mouse again.

Meanwhile, the insertion point still is waiting for you to enter some text and is blinking in the upper left corner of the blank window. Before you create a new document, though, you need to review the parts of the keyboard. The keyboard has some new capabilities with Word, Version 3.

Using the Keyboard

The standard typewriter keyboard is a fairly straightforward piece of equipment. When you strike a typewriter key, the character, number, or punctuation mark on the key label is printed on your paper.

Figure 2.2 shows the Macintosh Plus keyboard and its special-function, direction, and numeric keys. The Mac II and SE keyboards have slightly different layouts and include extra special-function keys.

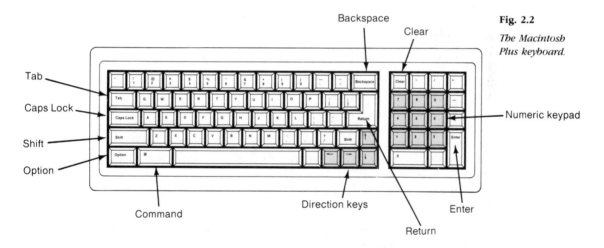

Fig. 2.2

The Macintosh Plus keyboard.

In addition to a typewriter's alphanumeric keys, the Macintosh keyboards have a number of other keys; some of the keys will be familiar to you, and some are new.

The Tab Key

Just as on a typewriter, pressing the Tab key on the Macintosh keyboard moves the insertion point from left to right across the page, stopping at intervals preset by Word (every 1/2 inch). (You can change the interval if you want; this procedure is discussed in Chapter 4.) Try pressing the Tab key now. Every time you press Tab, Word places an arrow in your document. If you delete the arrow, Word deletes the spaces.

In dialog boxes, the Tab key's function changes: the Tab key gives you a way to move from one option or text box to the next. See table 2.1 for ways to use the Shift and Command keys with the Tab key for even more flexible movement within a dialog box. Using the mouse to select the box you want usually is faster, though.

Table 2.1
Tabbing around a Dialog Box

Keys	*Action*
Tab	Moves to the next text box (where you enter information)
Shift-Tab	Moves to the preceding text box
Command-Tab	Moves to the next option
Command-Shift-Tab	Moves to the preceding option

The Shift Key

Pressing the Shift key produces uppercase letters as well as the upper symbols and punctuation marks on the keys. You also can use the Shift key to modify certain actions within Word. For example, you normally can select only one icon on the desktop at a time, but by holding down the Shift key while you click the mouse button, you can extend the selection to include additional icons.

You also can use the Shift key with the Command key or the Option key to perform a number of keyboard shortcuts, which we will discuss later, along with their corresponding commands.

The Caps Lock Key

By toggling on the Caps Lock key, you can type uppercase letters without holding down the Shift key. While the Caps Lock key is activated, however, you are still able to use all "lowercase" punctuation, such as the period, comma, and semicolon, so you do not have to deactivate the key in order to type common punctuation marks. The Caps Lock key affects only the letter keys; you need to use the Shift key to type the upper symbols and punctuation marks on the keys.

The Command Key

You can use the Command key (marked with ⌘) in combination with other keys to accomplish many functions with Word. Examples include entering special characters, choosing commands from Word menus, moving around in dialog boxes, scrolling through documents, moving the insertion point, performing certain editing actions, and formatting characters and paragraphs—as well as a host of other activities.

While you learn Word, your most common use of the Command key probably will be with various character keys as a shortcut for choosing commands from Word's menus. For example, you already may have used Command-Q to quit Word, rather than choosing Quit from the File menu. Other shortcuts will be pointed out as you go along. But for now, however, you might find these shortcuts useful: Command-O is a quick way to retrieve a document, and Command-S is the fastest way to save changes made to your documents.

Feel free, at any point in this book, to use the Command-key shortcut rather than the mouse in order to carry out a command: hold down the Command key and then press the second key.

The Option Key

People like to have options in their lives, and Word gives you many. Like the Shift key, the Option key, when used with other keys, produces an alternate set of characters, including characters with diacritical marks (accents).

To see Word's alternate character set, do the following:

1. Choose the **Key Caps** desk accessory from the Apple menu.

A window opens and displays a diagram of the keyboard.

2. Press **Option**.

Notice the change in the displayed keyboard.

3. Hold down the Option key and type a few of the stranger-looking characters. If you hold down the Option and the Shift keys together, you produce even more new characters.

When you type a character, its counterpart appears in the text box at the top of the Key Caps window, as shown in figure 2.3.

Fig. 2.3

*The Key Caps
window,
showing
characters typed
when you held
down the
Option key.*

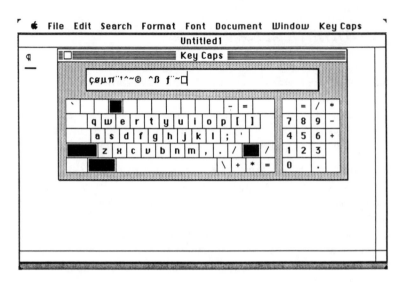

Once you know which key combination produces which character, you can type the characters directly into the document.

NOTE: You will not have access to all these characters if you have selected the New York or Venice fonts. If you plan to write technical or foreign-language manuscripts, choose a font, such as Chicago, Geneva, or Monaco, that makes available all these characters.

The Option key also carries out certain commands and actions when used with the Shift, Caps Lock, and/or Command key.

The Backspace Key

Pressing Backspace normally deletes the character that precedes the insertion point. However, you can delete any amount of selected text (or any size graphic) by pressing Backspace.

The Return Key

Unlike the return process on a traditional typewriter, you do not end each line of text by pressing the Return key on the Macintosh keyboard. Word, like most word-processing programs and many electronic typewriters, has a feature called wordwrap, which automatically wraps text around to the next line as you type.

For this reason, you should press Return only when you want to start a new paragraph. When you do press Return, Word inserts a paragraph marker (¶) in the text. You can see the marker if you select Show ¶ in the Edit menu. Pressing the Return key moves the insertion point to the beginning of the next line. You also can use Return, instead of clicking OK or some other confirmation button, to confirm a selection or setting you have made in a dialog box.

The Enter Key

The Enter key performs the same function as Return: it starts a new paragraph or initiates action in a dialog box.

The Clear Key

The Clear key lets you toggle the numeric keypad back and forth between entering numbers and either moving the insertion point or choosing commands. (We discuss the numeric keypad in more detail later.) When you press the Clear key, the message Num Lock appears on the message line (lower left) to show you that the numbers are active. Pressing Clear again turns the keypad back into a set of direction/command-choosing keys.

The Direction Keys

Word gives you a choice of direction keys. On the Macintosh Plus keyboard, you can move the insertion point by using the arrow keys in the main keyboard's lower right corner or by using certain numbered keys on the numeric keypad. The direction keys move the insertion point around the screen one character, line, or paragraph at a time, in fast succession. (Actually, dragging the mouse also moves the selection in increments, but you can't see these increments when you move the mouse quickly.) The direction keys also are useful for moving up and down list boxes and through groups of options in dialog boxes.

One of Word, Version 3's, new features is the capability to use the arrow keys—along with the period on the numeric keypad—to pull down menus and choose commands. Take a moment now to experiment with this feature.

Use the keyboard to pull down a menu and *highlight* (display in inverse video) a command by doing the following:

1. Press the **period** on the numeric keypad.

Pressing the period selects the entire menu bar. (If pressing the period doesn't work, press Num Lock and try again.) However, Word retains this selection for only a few seconds. Unless you choose a menu and command quickly, you have to press the period again.

2. Press the **Left-Arrow** or **Right-Arrow** key to pull down the File menu.

Pressing the arrow key cancels the selection of everything in the menu bar except the menu that is pulled down.

Notice that the menu stays pulled down. This feature can be convenient, especially when you're learning Word and want to study the keyboard shortcuts listed in a menu. When you use the mouse, the menu closes as soon as you release the mouse button.

3. Use the **Down-Arrow** key to move the highlight down the menu.

To choose a highlighted command, which you don't want to do right now, you press Return. Once you use a direction key to highlight a command, you have four ways to close the menu without choosing a command. You can move either forward or backward to another menu and then press Return while no command is highlighted; you can press the Backspace key; you can press Command-. (period); or you can click the menu name with the mouse.

The Numeric Keypad

The numeric keypad serves several purposes in Word. Using its keys, you can enter numbers, move around in your document, choose menus and commands, and carry out many other actions.

The Macintosh hosts a number of powerful spreadsheet programs, such as Microsoft Excel and Multiplan®; and the numeric keypad is designed to let you enter the numbers and mathematical symbols of these pro- grams more quickly than you can using the number keys on the main keyboard. Pressing the Clear key activates the keypad numbers. Otherwise, the keypad keys, like the keyboard's arrow keys, are used to move the insertion point and to choose Word commands.

Table 2.2 shows some of the ways you can use the numeric keypad with other keys to move around a document. You'll practice using these features in subsequent chapters.

Table 2.2
Swift Moves Using the Numeric Keypad

Keys	Action
8	Moves up one line
2	Moves down one line
4	Moves left one character
6	Moves right one character
7	Moves to the beginning of the line
1	Moves to the end of the line
9	Moves up one screen
3	Moves down one screen
Command-4	Moves left one word
Command-6	Moves right one word
Command-7	Moves to the preceding sentence
Command-1	Moves to the next sentence
Command-8	Moves to the preceding paragraph
Command-2	Moves to the next paragraph
Command-9	Moves to the beginning of the document
Command-3	Moves to the end of the document

Using Word's Menus and Commands

The cornerstone of any Macintosh application is its menu and command structure. Word, Version 3, has two sets of menus: *short menus*, containing the basic commands for creating and printing a simple document; and *full menus*, containing the basic commands as well as others for controlling Word's advanced features, such as style sheets and outlines.

Menus group similar types of actions or commands. For example, the File menu contains most of the commands for handling documents within your computer system—that is, for doing such things as opening, closing, saving, and printing the documents. The Format menu, on the other hand, contains the commands that affect how a document looks—the appearance of its characters, its paragraphs, and even whole sections.

Word also provides some commands that change their names in response to your actions. For example, if you watch the Undo command in the Edit menu while you're making changes to a document, you will see the Undo command change its name to reflect the type of edit you're performing: Undo Typing, Undo Cut, Undo Copy, Undo Formatting, or Undo Change (if you searched for and replaced text with the Change command). If you choose Undo to cancel your most recent edit, the command name changes to Redo, plus the type of edit (Redo Cut, for example).

Although working with menu options may appear to be a bit complex, you'll find that in practice the operation is fairly natural. The process of choosing commands is equally natural.

You can choose a command in one of two ways: with the mouse or with keyboard shortcuts. Before choosing a command that affects a part of your text, such as the editing commands Cut, Copy, and Paste, you must first select the text. Other commands, such as Save or Show ¶, don't require that you select text. These commands either affect the whole document or display a dialog box asking for more specific instructions.

Choosing Commands with the Mouse

While you are learning to use Word, choosing commands with the mouse may be easier than trying to memorize their keyboard shortcuts. Later, if you have to edit a document extensively, you still may find the mouse more convenient.

To choose a command with the mouse, do the following:

1. Point to the menu containing the command you want to choose.

2. Drag the mouse down through the commands until the one you want is highlighted.

3. Release the mouse button.

The pointer becomes a watch icon (⌚) to show you that you must wait while Word is working on your request.

Choosing Commands with the Numeric Keypad

The following exercises show you two ways to use keys on the numeric keypad to open menus and choose commands.

To choose commands using the keypad's period key and a letter key, do the following:

1. Press the **period** on the numeric keypad.

The menu bar becomes highlighted.

2. Press the first letter of the menu you want.

Press *F* this time around. Pressing *F* opens the File menu, as shown in figure 2.4. But what about the Format and Font menus, with names that also start with *F*? How do you open them? They're the exception to the rule and must be opened with the mouse or the arrow keys.

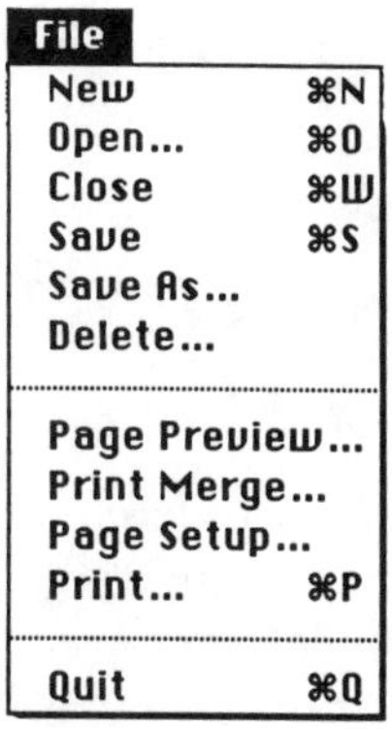

File	
New	⌘N
Open...	⌘O
Close	⌘W
Save	⌘S
Save As...	
Delete...	
Page Preview...	
Print Merge...	
Page Setup...	
Print...	⌘P
Quit	⌘Q

Fig. 2.4

Word's File menu.

3. Press the first letter of the command you want to choose in order to highlight it.

Highlight New by pressing *N*. If more than one command name starts with the same letter, as in the case of Save and Save As in figure 2.4, you can toggle back and forth between the two commands by repeatedly pressing the first letter.

4. Press **Return** or **Enter** to carry out the highlighted command.

Another way to open a menu with the numeric keypad is to press the keypad's period key and a keypad number from 0 through 7. Each of these keypad numbers corresponds to a position in the menu bar: 0 corresponds to the Apple menu; 1 corresponds to the File menu; and so on.

To choose commands using the keypad's period key and a keypad number, do the following:

1. Press the **period** on the numeric keypad.

2. Press the keypad number corresponding to the menu you want to choose.

Try pressing *5* to open the Font menu.

3. To highlight a command, press the first letter of the command's name; or move to the command by using the Up-Arrow or Down-Arrow keys, or the 8 and 2 keys on the keypad.

4. Press **Return** or **Enter** to carry out the highlighted command.

5. To close the command menu and move to another command menu, press the arrow keys or other number keys.

To close the menu without opening another one, press either the Backspace key or Command-. (period).

Choosing Commands with the Keyboard Shortcuts

Word, Version 3, is designed to make developing and changing documents as efficient as possible. When you're typing a new document, you'll probably experience the best results when you keep your hands on the keyboard as much as possible instead of jumping back and forth between the keyboard and the mouse. You just learned how you can choose almost any command by using the keyboard and the numeric keypad. In addition, Word provides keyboard shortcuts, as mentioned earlier. Getting used to some of these keyboard shortcuts, particularly those requiring that you press three or four keys at once, may take a little time. But you still may find the shortcuts more efficient than reaching for the mouse in the middle of typing. On the other hand, for tasks such as moving or reformatting large portions of text, the mouse can be handier.

Once you're comfortable with Word, you may find that choosing a command with a Command-key shortcut is the quickest approach. You were introduced to Command-Q, the shortcut for Quit, earlier in this chapter. Table 2.3 lists the Quit command and other shortcuts you'll use frequently.

Table 2.3
Command-Key Shortcuts

Command	Shortcut
Close	Command-W
Copy	Command-C
Cut	Command-X
New	Command-N
Open	Command-O
Paste	Command-V
Quit	Command-Q
Save	Command-S

Obviously, when several commands begin with the same letter, such as Close, Copy, and Cut, only one of the keyboard shortcuts can use the first letter. However, after using these shortcuts for a while, you'll find the correct keyboard character easy to remember.

Using Dialog and Alert Boxes

Sometimes Word needs more information before the program can carry out a particular command. A simple example is the Open command, which tells Word to open a document. Before Word can carry out your request to open a document, Word must know which document you want to open. Give Word this information in the Open dialog box, shown in figure 2.5.

Fig. 2.5

The Open dialog box.

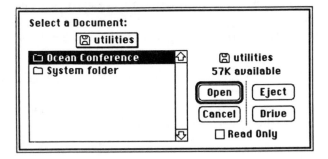

As you probably know, *dialog boxes* are small windows that open when you choose certain commands. An ellipsis (. . .) after a command name in the menu indicates that the command has a dialog box. Some dialog boxes have text boxes in which you can type text, and most have check boxes and buttons that you click to select or cancel an option. Sometimes an option is not available under all circumstances. Options that can't be chosen are shaded in the dialog box; available options are in bold.

An *alert box*—you've probably already encountered this, too—warns you about something Word can't do, or warns you when the command you've chosen can have drastic unforeseen results. The alert box usually gives you the choice of clicking a Yes or No button in response to the alert box's question or clicking a Cancel button to get out of a command. Figure 2.6 shows a typical alert box.

Fig. 2.6

A simple alert box.

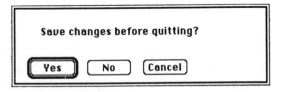

Throughout this book, whenever you choose a command that displays either a dialog or an alert box, you'll see an example of the box so that you'll know what to expect.

Creating a Simple Document

At this point, you know how to start and quit Word, move around using the mouse and keyboard, use the special-function keys, and choose menus and commands. Now you'll create a simple document to demonstrate some basic editing techniques. In Chapter 3, you'll learn more about Word's editing features, such as Edit menu commands for copying, moving, cutting, and pasting text.

The following sample document—a flyer—is the first in a series of small, related documents you will create as you work your way through this book. These documents all pertain to a hypothetical oceanographic conference being held at a fictitious convention center in a real place—Santa Barbara, California. Please do not write asking for more information about these meetings because they were never held. With that introduction out of the way, you can get to work.

NOTE: From this point on, we will provide both generic instructions that explain how to use a Word feature and instructions that are specific to the sample documents. We number the steps in the generic processes, following each step with the related sample-specific instructions.

As mentioned earlier, Word offers both short and full menus. The commands displayed in the short menus are all you'll be using in the first three chapters of this book. You may, at any time, use the full menus to experiment with more advanced features; but if you are following along with the examples, you won't need the full menus until Chapter 4.

Do the following to start a document in Word's short-menu mode:

1. Choose **Short Menus** from the Edit menu.

2. Choose **New** from the File menu.

A new document opens.

The insertion point should be in the upper left corner of the window. For now, you need to be in Show ¶ mode so that Word displays paragraph marks on the screen. If you're in the Show ¶ mode, you see a paragraph mark (¶) to the right of the insertion point. If not, switch to Show ¶ mode now.

3. Choose **Show ¶** from the Edit menu.

Word now displays the paragraph mark, and once you type something, Word also displays small dots representing spaces between words. Word displays these and other marks and symbols on your screen, but they do not appear in your document when you print it.

4. Type the text of your document.

Don't press Return at the end of each line; Word automatically wraps text around to begin the next line. Press Return twice at the end of each paragraph. The extra Returns create blank lines (actually, blank *paragraphs*) that separate the paragraphs, making the beginnings and endings of paragraphs easy to see.

To create the first sample document, type the following text, including anything you suspect is an error:

1987 International Pacific Oceanographic Conference

We're happy to have you join us this year for our tenth annual conference, and we look forward to meeting and working with each one of you during the coming week.

This year's conference is being sponsored by the International Society of Oceanographers, and is being held at the Oceanica Institute in Santa Barbera, California.

When you have finished typing the flyer, your screen looks like figure 2.7.

Fig. 2.7

The Conference Flyer document.

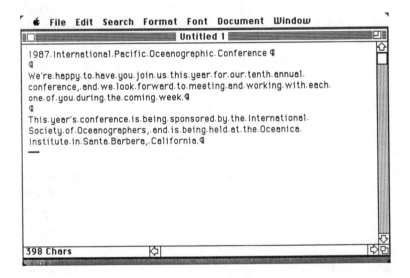

You know you need to go back and correct a few errors in this document, but for now you are just trying to get your thoughts on paper. (Besides, you want to save the errors so that we can correct them in Chapter 3.) What you've typed so far is a good start, but the words don't feel very welcoming. You'll improve the document in Chapter 3, but first you need to save the document.

Saving Documents

Unless you transfer your flyer from your computer's memory to your data disk or hard disk, you will lose the document when you turn off your Macintosh. Get in the habit of saving your work frequently, perhaps every 10 minutes or so. By saving your work every 10 minutes, you minimize the work that you can lose in the event of a power outage or because of the intervention of another person—such as your precocious five-year-old daughter, who has just discovered that the Macintosh is fun.

Word's File menu has two commands for saving your work. The Save command saves the current version of an existing document by overwriting the earlier version on the disk from which you opened the document; or the Save command lets you name and save a new document. The Save As command also lets you name and save a new document, or you can use the Save As command to make a duplicate of an existing document by saving it with a different name. By duplicating an existing document with a different name, you save a changed copy while preserving the original.

Saving New Documents

You can use either the Save or the Save As command to save a document that hasn't previously been saved. To see what happens when you save a new document using the Save command, do the following:

   1. Choose **Save** from the File menu.

The first time you save a document, Word displays the dialog box shown in figure 2.8. The disk or folder name appears at the top of the dialog box, next to a small disk icon. If you've been following along with this exercise, you will probably see the Word Program disk shown in figure 2.8. You need to save the document on a data disk, not the Word Program disk or the Utilities disk.

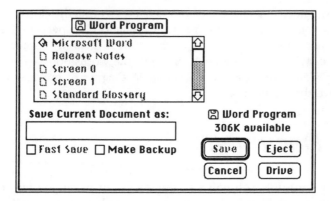

Fig. 2.8

*The Save
dialog box.*

2. Click the **Drive** button to change drives or click **Eject** to eject
   the current disk so that you can insert the data disk on which
   you want to save your document.

The list box beneath the disk or folder name shows the documents
stored on that disk. Just below the list box, to the right, is another disk
icon, the disk name, and a number telling how much disk space (or
volume, on a hard disk) is available. If you try to save a document on
a disk that is too full, the alert box shown in figure 2.9 tells you that
your disk has insufficient storage space available.

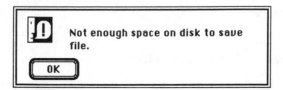

Fig. 2.9

*The Disk Full
alert box.*

The Save dialog box also has a text box containing the blinking insertion
point. You type the name you want to assign to your document here.
Beneath the text box is a check box labeled Fast Save. You can't select
the check box when you're working on a new document. The check
box is a shortcut for saving changes to a document after you have already
saved it once.

3. Type the name of your document in the text box.

4. Click **Save** or press **Return**.

Follow these instructions to save the sample document you have created.
Assign the document the name *Conference Flyer*.

As Word saves the document, Word displays, in the screen's lower left corner, the percentage of the document that has been saved. After the document is saved, the percentage changes to the number of characters the document contains or, if you've paginated the document, to the page number of the text currently displayed (see Chapters 5 and 6 for details on paginating). You may have noticed the character count in the bottom left corner of the Conference Flyer document displayed in figure 2.7. Saving a document this small takes only a couple of seconds, but the character information is helpful when your document is much larger.

Saving Existing Documents

After you've saved a document for the first time, Word performs each subsequent save of the document automatically when you choose the Save command. Word needs no additional instructions, so you don't see a dialog box. The process is simple and quick.

Do the following to update a retrieved document using Save:

1. Make your changes.

2. Choose **Save** from the File menu.

Just to see how saving an existing document works, try using the Save command again to update Conference Flyer.

Working with Folders

In the next few chapters, you'll create more documents about the hypothetical conference in Santa Barbara. To work easily with all the documents you'll be creating, you're now going to quit Word and create a folder to hold them all.

To quit Word from an open document window, do the following:

1. Click the close box in the window's upper left corner.

If the program asks whether you want to save any changes before closing the file, click your preference. Then the document window closes, and you return to the blank Microsoft Word window.

2. Choose **Quit** from the File menu.

Word returns you to the desktop. Your Data disk window, as well as the Word Program disk window, should be open.

To create a new folder, do the following:

1. Click the Data disk window, if it isn't already active, to make it active.

2. Choose **New Folder** from the File menu.

A blank document folder, appropriately called Empty Folder, appears in the Data disk window. Renaming the new folder is simple.

3. Type a new name.

For your exercise documents, create a folder called *Ocean Conference*.

Now you're ready to store the Conference Flyer document. To store a document in a folder, do the following:

1. Drag the document icon over the folder icon.

"File" the Conference Flyer document in the Ocean Conference folder by dragging the document icon over the folder icon.

2. To verify that filing is complete, double-click the folder icon.

A new window opens, displaying the document icon (in this case, the Conference Flyer icon).

Starting Word and Loading a Document at the Same Time

Now you have an opportunity to practice another way of starting Word. Earlier, you started Word by double-clicking the Microsoft Word icon in the Program disk window. Now that you have a document to play with, you can learn another way to start Word.

To load a document while starting Word, double-click the document icon. Double-clicking a document created in Word starts Word and opens the document. Try starting Word by opening the Conference Flyer document.

You won't be doing any more work with the Conference Flyer document just yet, but before we wind up Chapter 2, you need to create another document.

Creating a Document with the New Command

When you started Word by double-clicking the Microsoft Word icon in the Program disk window, Word opened a document window called Untitled1 in which you could, without further ado, begin typing. Creating a document with the New command is equally easy.

Do the following to create a document with the New command:

1. Choose **New** from the File menu.

That's all there is to getting started. The Conference Flyer window closes and a blank document window called Untitled1 opens, with the insertion point blinking in the upper left corner, ready for you to start entering text.

2. Type your document text.

3. Use the **Save** command to save your document.

If you want to continue working with the set of sample documents, type the following text into your new window to give you something to edit in the next chapter:

Conference Overview

Each year, the International Pacific Oceanographic Conference offers a variety of workshops featuring the scientific and commercial developments of the previous year. This year is no exception.

On the agenda are workshops that focus on general oceanographic issues, such as plate tectonics and developments in marine research. Additional workshops focus on new technologies used to map the ocean floor, to locate manganese nodules on the seabed, and to detect potential petroleum drilling sites. On a lighter note, a special session will review the attempts made over the past few years to find and recover the vast treasures believed to be scattered in sunken ships around the globe.

When you finish typing, save this document with the name *Conference Overview* and then quit Word.

On the desktop, the Conference Overview document should be in the Ocean Conference folder window. If it's not, either drag the document icon into the window or, if the window is closed, drag the document icon over the folder icon.

The Ocean Conference folder now contains two documents. You will use these documents again in Chapter 3 when you learn how to edit documents by selecting, inserting, and deleting blocks of text and by using the Edit menu's Cut, Copy, Paste, and Undo commands.

Taking a Break

If you want to stop reading for now—we realize that you have to eat and sleep—you need to get in the habit of properly shutting down your system.

To shut down your system, do the following:

1. Choose **Shut Down** from the Special menu.

The disks are ejected.

2. Turn off your system.

If you have a two-drive system, you can leave the disks perched in the internal and external disk drives if you plan to return to your work shortly. Otherwise, store the disks in a safe place each time you quit.

Quick and Easy Editing

Word, Version 3, cannot teach you how to think creatively, write correctly, or become a competent editor; however, Word can help you devote more time to achieving these goals instead of spending your time typing and retyping innumerable slightly revised versions of text. More important, with Word you can take giant steps beyond the basic chores of editing into the more artistic aspects of publishing. By allowing you more artistic freedom, Word enables you to create specially designed pages of text or to merge attractively text and graphics from different documents.

In Chapter 3, you lay the groundwork for using Word's advanced editing power by exploring Word's basic editing commands—Cut, Copy, Paste, and Undo from the Edit menu—and by learning how to select, delete, and rearrange your text. You also review how to use the scroll bars and the keyboard commands to get around in your documents.

You use only the commands available in the short menus for the following exercises, but if you are experienced—or inexperienced, but daring—feel free at any time to try using the more advanced commands. You can work at your own speed and, if you prefer, with your own document.

Duplicating Documents

Word, along with most other Macintosh applications, does not automatically make a backup copy of the document on which you are working, so if you may want to return to the original document for any reason, make a copy before changing anything. (Making a copy of your original is especially important if you are working with a "real" document of your own rather than one of the sample documents.) You can choose from among several of the following methods for making a duplicate of a document.

To duplicate a document from the Macintosh Finder, do the following:

1. Click the icon representing the file you want to duplicate.

2. Choose **Duplicate** from the File menu.

3. Type the name you want to assign to the duplicate.

The name you type appears beneath the icon.

To duplicate a document from within Word, do the following:

1. Choose **Save As** from the File menu.

Word displays the dialog box you saw when you first saved the documents you created in Chapter 2. This time the document's name is highlighted in the name box, and because the document has already been saved, the Fast Save check box is active (not shaded) and already checked. Fast Save speeds up the saving process but uses more space on a disk. At this point, your data disk should have plenty of space, so leave Fast Save checked.

2. Replace the document name with the name you want to assign to the duplicate.

3. Click **Save**.

Word returns to the document window, displaying the duplicate document's name in its title bar. The document now displayed is an exact copy of the original, which remains safely stored on your data disk.

Do the following to duplicate a document without leaving the original document:

1. Choose **Save As** from the File menu.

2. Click the **Make Backup** button.

3. Click **Save**.

Word saves a copy of the document under the name *Backup of [current document name]* but leaves the original document loaded. The backup document does not include any edits you have made since saving the displayed document.

If you haven't already done so, load the Conference Overview document you created in Chapter 2. You will use this document to practice various navigation techniques and editing commands. If you want, make a duplicate of the Conference Overview document for practice. If you are working on a document of your own, definitely make a duplicate so that you can follow the exercises in this chapter without "corrupting" the original document.

Moving around a Document

Word provides a variety of methods for quickly moving around your document: you can use the scroll bars, direction keys, keyboard commands, and the Find and Go To commands from the Search menu. With these tools, you can readily access any part of a document and find particular words, passages, or headings.

In Chapter 2, you learned how to use the arrow keys on the main keyboard and certain numbers on the numeric keypad to move around a document. And if you are a seasoned Mac user, you're probably also adept at using the scroll bars by now. But we'll review these techniques because you'll be using them often in the next few chapters.

Before beginning the editing exercises, however, you need to create a document large enough to scroll through. To create this large document, copy the text in Conference Overview four times. Farther along in the chapter, we explain the various methods for copying text. For now, just do the following procedure to enlarge the Conference Overview document.

To make multiple copies of a document's text, do the following:

1. Click an insertion point before the paragraph mark at the end of the document.

2. Press **Return** to insert a blank line.

3. Select the entire document by pressing **Command-Option-M**.

4. Choose **Copy** from the Edit menu or press **Command-C**.

5. Click an insertion point at the beginning of the document.

Your screen should look like the one in figure 3.1.

6. Choose **Paste** from the Edit menu or press **Command-V**.

Word inserts a duplicate of your document above the original and scrolls to the bottom of the inserted text. Until you copy or cut another piece

Fig. 3.1

The Conference Overview document.

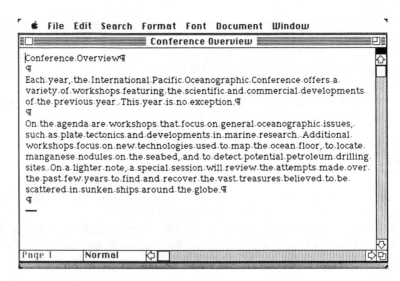

of text, you can paste this piece into your document as many times as you like.

7. Repeat Step 6 twice.

Now your Conference Overview document contains four copies of the original text.

Scrolling through a Document

Among all the impersonal, high-technology terms associated with computers—*dump, download, interface, enter,* and so forth—is the lovely word, *scroll*, which conjures up images of an ancient means of communication. The scribes of antiquity meticulously copied texts by hand onto long sheets of parchment, which were then rolled up for storage. These scrolls represent enormous human endeavor and remind us of the care and deliberation people once took when putting down their words of wisdom.

When you move through an electronic document, the document seems to unroll on your screen—hence the term *scrolling*, inspired by the way you "roll" and "unroll" a document to view its different parts. You may scroll up, toward the document's beginning, or down, toward its end. Note that scrolling doesn't affect the insertion point; it scrolls with the text and may scroll out of view. If the insertion point is out of view when you start typing, Word automatically scrolls the window so that you can see what you're doing.

Scrolling with the Keyboard

To scroll a document up or down without moving the insertion point, you can do either of the following:

- Press **Command-Option-[** to scroll the document up one line at a time.

- Press **Command-Option-/** to scroll the document down one line at a time.

Scrolling with the Mouse

Use the mouse and the two scroll bars along the right and bottom edges of the Macintosh screen (see fig. 3.1) to move the screen display up and down or left and right, respectively, within a document. Each scroll bar contains two arrows—one pointing toward each end of the bar—and a box. Clicking an arrow on the vertical scroll bar scrolls the document one line in the direction that the arrow is pointing, and dragging the box to a point in the scroll bar moves the display to a corresponding location in the document.

The following options are available to you when you scroll with the mouse:

- To move up or down one line at a time, click the up- or down arrow in the vertical scroll bar.

- To move continuously up or down one line, point to the up- or down arrow and hold down the mouse button.

- To jump to another area of the document, drag the scroll box in the vertical scroll bar to a point that approximates the relative position of the information you want to see in the document. For example, if the information is in the middle of the document, drag the scroll box to the middle of the scroll bar.

- To move up or down a screenful at a time, move the pointer to just above or just below the scroll box and click the mouse button.

You probably will scroll horizontally less often than vertically because most documents are narrow enough that you can see both the left and the right margins at once. Occasionally you may work with a document wider than the Mac's screen display. (In Word, you can create documents almost 22 inches wide.) In this case, use the arrows and scroll box in the horizontal scroll bar to view the areas of the document currently off the screen.

Using the Keyboard

As we noted in Chapter 2, during the keyboard-intensive work of creating a document, you may want to use the direction keys to move around in your document. These keys, unlike the scrolling commands just mentioned, move the insertion point, too. In table 3.1 we review how to move the insertion point in various increments, using the keyboard. (All the number keys mentioned here are on the numeric keypad.)

Table 3.1
Swift Moves with the Arrow Keys
and the Numeric Keypad

Keys	Insertion-Point Action
Left Arrow *or* 4	Moves left one character
Right Arrow *or* 6	Moves right one character
Command-Left Arrow *or* Command-4	Moves left one word
Command-Right Arrow *or* Command-6	Moves right one word
Up Arrow *or* 8	Moves up one line
Down Arrow *or* 2	Moves down one line
7	Moves to the beginning of a line

Keys	Insertion-Point Action
1	Moves to the end of a line
Command-7	Moves to the preceding sentence
Command-1	Moves to the next sentence
Command-Up Arrow or Command-8	Moves to the preceding paragraph
Command-Down Arrow or Command-2	Moves to the next paragraph
9	Moves up a windowful
3	Moves down a windowful
Command-9	Moves to the beginning of the document
Command-3	Moves to the end of the document

Practice moving around the document until you feel comfortable with each keyboard technique. As you become proficient with Word, you'll use the method of scrolling most appropriate to the type of work you are doing.

Using the Go To Command

The Search menu's Go To command takes you directly to a specific page in your document—without passing Go and without collecting $200 (for you Monopoly fans out there). To use the Go To command, however, you first must have Word number your document's pages. Word automatically numbers the pages when you print the document, or you can repaginate the document at any time by choosing the Document menu's Repaginate command.

Up to this point in your practice sessions, a shaded Page 1, indicating that the document has not yet been paginated, has been displayed in the lower left corner of the document window (see fig. 3.1). Had the document been paginated, Word would have displayed the correct page number in bold type. Conference Overview is now longer than one page, so you can use Conference Overview to experiment with the pagination procedure.

To paginate a document, choose Repaginate from the Document menu or press Command-J. Try either technique to paginate Conference Overview. When the Page 1 label becomes bold, the pagination process is finished.

You can scroll through a large document and watch the number in the page number box change. Watching the numbers change may be mildly interesting on a slow Saturday night, but it's nothing compared to the potential that pagination has opened up for you. Now you can not only scroll through those pages but also jump directly to any specific page. Going directly to a specific page is useful when you need to make minor changes on, say, pages 21, 37, 43, and 50 of a printed document.

To jump directly to a specific page, do the following:

1. Make sure that your document is paginated.

2. Choose **Go To** from the Search menu or press **Command-G**.

The dialog box shown in figure 3.2 opens, with the number 1 highlighted in the Page Number field.

Fig. 3.2

The Page Number dialog box.

3. Type the number of the page you want to display.

4. Click **OK** or press **Return**.

Experiment a little, using the Conference Overview document. Choose the Go To command and type the number *10* in the dialog box (even though Conference Overview couldn't possibly be 10 pages long). When you click OK, Word adjusts your screen to look like figure 3.3. If you type a page number higher than the last page of your document, Word moves the insertion point to the last page of your document.

The numbers that appear in the page number box are for Word's use in moving through the document. They don't appear on your printed

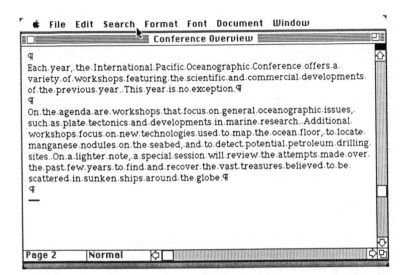

Fig. 3.3

When you specify a page number higher than the document's last page, Word jumps to the last page.

copy unless you specify that you want to print page numbers in one of the page-numbering formats discussed in Chapter 5. Word displays page breaks as a dotted line across the screen. *Page breaks* are places where the program starts a new page when you print your document. These page breaks are not active; in other words, if you add new text within a page, the page breaks may cease to be accurate. You must repaginate your document again before knowing exactly where the page breaks will occur.

This process may seem like a disadvantage, but it's not when you work on big editing projects. For example, suppose that you add a great deal of new text to page 41; you move elsewhere for a while and then want to go back. Typing *41* in the Go To dialog box returns you to the old page 41. This process is a convenience when you're editing from a marked-up, printed copy.

Using the Find Command

In a book or other printed document, some people can find certain subjects or specific text passages by looking in a table of contents or an index or by leafing through the pages until something looks familiar. These people have a particularly strong visual memory and have no trouble using this method to locate just the passage they are seeking. Then you have the rest of us, who retain only a vague recollection of what we're looking for and where it is. If you consider yourself a member of the latter group, then trying to find something specific in an electronic document can be particularly frustrating because only about one-third of a page appears at a time. Word helps compensate for this human weakness by providing commands in the Search menu with which you can locate and, optionally, change any or all instances of a specified piece of text.

The fastest way to find a specific word or phrase is to choose the Search menu's Find command and then type the desired word or phrase in the dialog box that appears. You can type as many as 255 characters in the text box—but typing only enough characters to distinguish the word, phrase, heading, or other text you want to find is usually best. (Fewer words mean fewer potential typos.)

With the Find command (and with the Change command, discussed later), you can specify either whole words or words that have certain characters in common. For example, if you type the word *work* and don't specify Whole Word in the dialog box, the program finds *workshop*, *working*, *workmanship*, or any other word containing the letters *w-o-r-k*.

You also can search for words that have only the exact upper- and lowercase letters you specify. For example, if you type *Workshop* and select the Match Upper/Lowercase option, Word locates *Workshop*, but not *workshop* or *WORKSHOP*.

Try using the Find command to locate the word *workshop* in the Conference Overview document. Because Word searches from the insertion point to the end of the document, move the insertion point to the top of the document before starting the search.

To find a word in your document, do the following:

1. Choose **Find** from the Search menu or press **Command-F**, to display the dialog box shown in figure 3.4.

To practice using the numeric keypad to choose menus and commands, press the period on the numeric keypad and the letter *S* to open the Search menu. Press *F* to highlight Find and then press Return.

2. In the Find What box, type the word you want to locate. If you make a typing error, backspace and type the correct letter(s).

Because you want to locate the whole word *workshop* regardless of the capitalization, click the Whole Word option but not the Match Upper/Lowercase option.

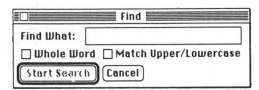

Fig. 3.4

*The Find
dialog box.*

3. Click **Start Search**.

Word locates and selects the first occurrence of the word (in this case, *workshop*).

4. Click **Find Next**.

The program moves to the next occurrence of the word.

5. Click **Cancel** or press **Command-.** (period), to stop the search and to close the Find dialog box.

Now you've learned the various methods for moving around a document. Once you get where you want to go, you need to know how to select text for editing.

Selecting Text

Almost every editing action in Word involves first selecting part of the document and then performing some action on the selection. You need to select text and graphics before you can move them or delete them from the document. You need also to select a place in the text before typing more text. The selection can be one or more characters, a word, a sentence, a paragraph, or the entire document. Word highlights the selected text and puts a box around the selected graphics. For now, just practice selecting segments of text. You'll learn how to select graphics in Chapter 12.

You can select text by dragging through it; but moving the I-beam into the selection bar at the screen's left edge, where the I-beam changes to a pointer, is often faster. You then can click, double-click, or drag to select a line, a paragraph, or your entire document.

Just as when you choose a command, you can use either the mouse or the keyboard to select text. The method you choose will depend on personal preference and the type of work you are doing. While typing, you probably will want to use the keyboard; when revising your work, however, using the mouse may be more convenient. In the following discussion, we describe both mouse and keyboard techniques for selecting various units of text. Try each method to see how it works, but don't attempt to memorize these techniques. After you use the techniques a few times, they'll come naturally. (For convenience, use the Quick Reference Guide at the end of the book to help you remember the keyboard shortcuts.)

NOTE: As elsewhere, if an instruction calls for the use of direction keys, you can use either the arrows on the keyboard or the numbers *2, 4, 6,* and *8* on the numeric keypad.

To select a character or series of characters, do the following:

1. Click an insertion point next to the character you want to select and press **Shift-Left Arrow** or **Shift-Right Arrow.**

   The Left Arrow selects the character to the left; the Right Arrow selects the character to the right.

2. To extend the selection character by character, simply hold down the Shift key and the appropriate arrow key until the selection is the desired length.

Or

1. Position the pointer next to the character you want to select and drag over the character.

2. Continue dragging to select a series of adjacent characters.

To select a word or series of words, do the following:

1. Double-click anywhere in the word you want to select.

2. Press **Shift-Command-Left Arrow** or **Shift-Command-Right Arrow** to extend the selection, one word at a time, to the left or right.

Or

1. Position the pointer at one end of the word and drag through it.

2. Continue dragging to select a series of adjacent words.

Do the following to select a sentence or series of sentences:

1. Hold down the Command key and click anywhere in the sentence you want to select.

2. To extend the selection one sentence at a time, hold down the Command key and drag up or down.

One peculiarity to watch for when you select sentences is Word's penchant for interpreting all periods, including decimal points and periods within abbreviations, as ending a sentence. For example, if you try to select the sentence *The gross national product of the U.S. in 1986 was $2.7 trillion*, Word stops after the *U*, the *S*, and the *$2*, as if each ends a different sentence. Therefore, if your sentence includes decimal points or abbreviations with periods, you may find that dragging through the sentence with the mouse is faster and more accurate than using the Command-click selection method.

To select a line or series of lines, do the following:

1. Click an insertion point at the beginning of the line and press **Shift-Up Arrow** or **Shift-Down Arrow**.

2. To extend the selection one line at a time, hold down the Shift key and the Up Arrow or Down Arrow until the selection includes the desired set of lines.

Or

1. Position the pointer in the selection bar next to the line you want to select, and click.

2. To extend the selection one line at a time, drag up or down.

The keyboard technique selects text before or after the insertion point, up to the insertion point's position in the line. For example, pressing Shift-Down Arrow, with the insertion point one inch from the left margin, selects the text between the insertion point and the point directly below it on the next line, as shown in figure 3.5.

Do the following to select a paragraph or series of paragraphs:

1. Double-click in the selection bar next to the paragraph.

2. Press **Shift-Command-Up Arrow** or **Shift-Command-Down Arrow**, to extend the selection one paragraph at a time.

Or

1. Double-click in the selection bar next to the paragraph, holding down the mouse button after the second click.

2. Drag up or down the page to extend the selection one paragraph at a time.

To select a large block of text, do the following:

1. Position the pointer where you want the selection to start.

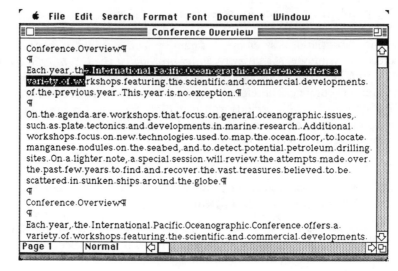

Fig. 3.5

*Using Shift-
Down Arrow to
select text
between the
insertion point
and the point
below it.*

2. Drag to the end of the text block you want to select.

   As your document scrolls up or down (forward or backward),
   Word selects one line at a time.

Or

1. Click an insertion point where you want the selection to start.

2. Position the pointer at the end of the text you want to select,
   using the scroll bars to bring the end into view, if necessary.

3. Hold down the Shift key and click the last character you want
   to select.

To select an entire document, do the following:

- Press **Command-Option-M**.

Or

- Hold down the Command key and click anywhere in the
  selection bar.

Or

1. Click an insertion point at the beginning (or end) of the
   document.

2. Hold down the Shift and Command keys, and press **3** (or **9**) on the numeric keypad.

If the insertion point is not at the beginning or end of the document, the third method selects the portion of the document between the insertion point and the document's beginning or end.

You can even select a column of text, which is handy when you're working with tables. Do the following to select a column:

1. Hold down the Option key.

2. Drag from one corner of the column to the diagonally opposite corner to produce a rectangular highlight.

To select a graphic or group of graphics, do the following:

1. Click inside the graphic or drag the pointer across the graphic.

2. To extend the selection to include more than one graphic, hold down the Shift key and click any number of graphics.

(You'll learn more about working with graphics in Chapter 12.)

Rearranging Text

The next sections cover the basic editing techniques of copying, cutting, and pasting text. By way of background for this discussion, the new Mac users among you need to get acquainted with the Clipboard.

Using the Clipboard

In Word, use the Copy and Cut commands with the Paste command, to move text in your document: Use Copy and Paste to duplicate text at another location; and use Cut and Paste to move the text, first cutting it out of its current location and then pasting it elsewhere. The difference between the two is that Copy preserves the text in its original location, whereas Cut removes the text. With these versatile commands, you can move graphics or blocks of text within a document, as well as transfer them between Word documents or even to documents in other applications.

Both Copy and Cut store selected text in a temporary area called the *Clipboard*, from which you can copy the text to as many locations as you like, using the Paste command. The most important thing to remember about the Clipboard is that it can hold only one item at a time.

Do the following to insert copied text from the Clipboard into an open document:

1. Click an insertion point where you want to begin the insertion.

In this case, move the insertion point to the bottom of the document by pressing Command-3.

2. Choose **Paste** from the Edit menu or press **Command-V**.

The text you copied to the Clipboard is inserted at the end of the document.

You can paste the same text into the document as many times as you like until you cut or copy something else to the Clipboard.

Using Command-Option-C

A quicker way to copy and insert text is to use the Command-Option-C keyboard shortcut, which eliminates the necessity of choosing the Paste command. You can choose between two Command-Option-C methods.

To copy text using the first Command-Option-C method, do the following:

1. Choose **Full Menus** from the Edit menu.

2. Select the text you want to copy.

3. Press **Command-Option-C**.

Notice that a Copy to message replaces the number in the page number box, as shown in figure 3.7.

4. Click an insertion point where you want to paste the copied text.

5. Press **Return**.

Word pastes the copied text at the insertion point.

Now, restore the Conference Overview document to its original state by choosing Undo Copy from the Edit menu so that you can practice the second method for using Command-Option-C. The second method is handy for inserting text where you are typing.

To copy text using the second Command-Option-C method, do the following:

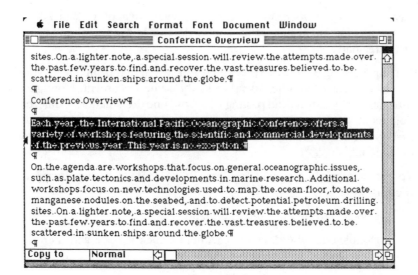

Fig. 3.7

*Pressing
Command-
Option-C
replaces the
page number
with* Copy to.

1. Click an insertion point where you want to insert the text and press **Command-Option-C**.

Notice that a Copy from message replaces the number in the page number box.

2. Select the text you want to copy.

The text is underscored with a dotted line, rather than highlighted.

3. Press **Return**.

Word pastes the selected text into the document at the insertion point.

If, while using either of the Command-Option-C methods, you change your mind about copying and inserting the selected text, cancel the process by pressing Command-. (period) before pressing Return. Word retains the selection in highlighted form.

Besides copying text and graphics, you can copy the formats of characters, paragraphs, or documents, and then apply the formats elsewhere (see Chapter 4).

Cutting and Pasting Text

Like the Copy command, the Cut command places text on the Clipboard and keeps the text there until you cut or copy something else. You can paste the text elsewhere in the same document, in another Word document, in a document in another application, or in the Scrapbook to use at a later date.

In the preceding exercises, you copied and pasted text from one location in a document to another location in the same document. Now get a little fancier by cutting and pasting text from one document to a different document. You are going to paste the contents of Conference Flyer, the first document you created, to the beginning of the Conference Overview document.

To open a second document and copy its contents to the Clipboard, do the following:

1. Choose **Open** from the File menu.

2. Double-click the document name, or click it once and then click Open.

In this case, double-click Conference Flyer.

3. Select the entire document by pressing **Command-Option-M**.

4. Choose **Cut** from the Edit menu.

Word cuts the entire contents of the document to the Clipboard.

5. Close the document window by clicking its close box.

6. When the Save Changes dialog box appears, click **No**.

Clicking No ensures that the previous version of the document remains safely stored on disk. Word closes the second document's window and redisplays the first document.

To insert the text from the Clipboard to the beginning of the first document, do the following:

1. Click an insertion point at the beginning of the document.

2. Choose **Paste** from the Edit menu.

In this case, Word inserts the Conference Flyer text at the beginning of the Conference Overview document.

Well, that was fun but not very practical. Recall that, when you created the Conference Flyer document at the end of Chapter 2, we commented that the document could be more welcoming. To that end, you are going to make a few adjustments to Conference Flyer.

Open the document now so that you can use the Cut and Paste commands to move a paragraph within the document. Farther along in this chapter, you will edit the paragraph to give it a lighter, more friendly tone.

To move text to a new location within the same document, do the following:

1. Select the text you want to move.

In this case, select the last paragraph of Conference Flyer by double-clicking in the selection bar adjacent to the paragraph (see fig. 3.8).

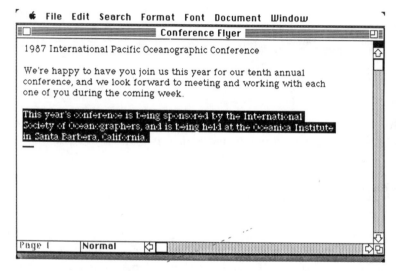

Fig. 3.8

The last paragraph of Conference Flyer, selected in preparation for moving.

2. Choose **Cut** from the Edit menu or press **Command-X**.

3. Click an insertion point in the location to which you want to move the text.

Click an insertion point in front of the first letter of the first word of the new last paragraph.

4. Choose **Paste** from the Edit menu or press **Command-V**.

Word copies the paragraph from the Clipboard, inserting the paragraph to the left of the insertion point. Figure 3.9 shows the document after the move.

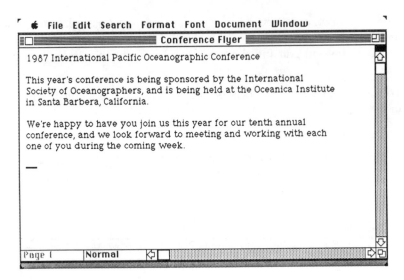

Fig. 3.9

The Conference Flyer document after you move the last paragraph.

The cut text still is stored on the Clipboard, so you could paste the text into other locations in the document if you wanted.

Deleting and Inserting Text

Using the Cut command is appropriate when you want to move text, but if you just want to get rid of the text, the fastest and simplest method is to select the text and then press Backspace—or the Delete key, if your keyboard has one. (Deleting a single character is the exception, because you do not need to select the character first. To delete a single character to the left of the insertion point, just press Backspace or Delete; press Command-Option-F to delete the character to the right of the insertion point.) Deleting text with the Backspace or Delete key, or by pressing Command-Option-F, does not store the deleted text on the Clipboard, so you can't subsequently paste the text elsewhere.

Remember the deliberate typo you introduced into *Santa Barbara* in the Conference Flyer document? You can use a delete/insert technique to correct this typo. Follow these steps to make a simple correction to your text:

1. Click an insertion point to the right of the character you want to delete.

For this example, click an insertion point between the *e* and the *r* in *Barbera* (see fig. 3.10).

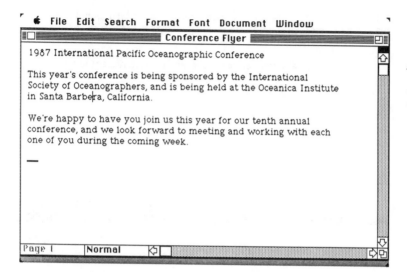

Fig. 3.10

The insertion point positioned to the right of a character to be deleted.

2. Press **Backspace** (or **Delete**).

3. Type the correct character.

In this case, type *a*.

Deletion and insertion are fundamental editing techniques, so to practice them, try making a few more changes to Conference Flyer. First, click an insertion point in front of *1987* in the first line and type *Welcome to the*. Then add an exclamation mark to the end of the first sentence (see fig. 3.11).

Now edit the second paragraph to make it more inviting. Click an insertion point between the *T* and the *h* of the first word and press Backspace (or Delete). Then, without moving the insertion point, type *As sponsors of t*. Next, select the space following the word *conference* and the words *is being sponsored by*, press Backspace, and type a comma. The results of these maneuvers are shown in figure 3.12.

Your changes have produced a nonsensical paragraph. You could finish editing the paragraph with more deletions and insertions, but instead, we'll show you another way to edit a document.

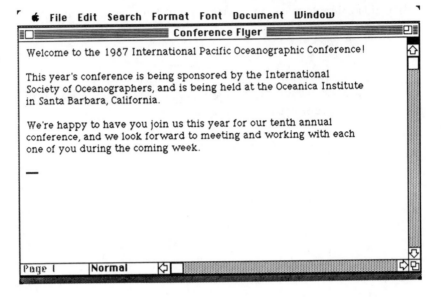

Fig. 3.11

Conference Flyer with a new opening.

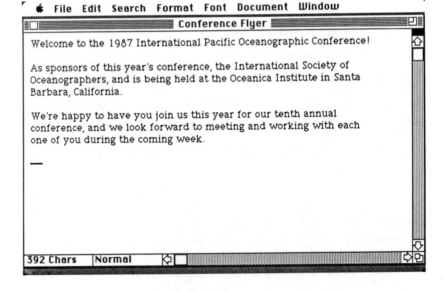

Fig. 3.12

Conference Flyer after you make some adjustments to the second paragraph.

Replacing Text

Sometimes you may want to replace an existing piece of text with new text. Rather than go through the two-step process of first deleting the existing text and then inserting the new, you can often save time by skipping the deletion step. In the following paragraphs, we show you several ways of replacing text without the deletion step.

Typing New Text over Old Text

The simplest way to replace a piece of text is to select the text you want to replace and then type the new text. When you type the first character, the selected text is automatically deleted to the scrap. The *scrap* is an area of memory that the program uses for temporary storage of text. The characters you then type are inserted in the old text's place.

To practice replacing old text with new, make another adjustment to the second paragraph of Conference Flyer. Select the comma following the word *Oceanographers* and extend the selection to include the words *and is being held at,* as shown in figure 3.13. Instead of pressing Backspace, simply type a space followed by the words *is pleased to welcome you to the campus of.* Word deletes the selected text when you type the first character, and the result is the grammatical and friendly paragraph shown in figure 3.14.

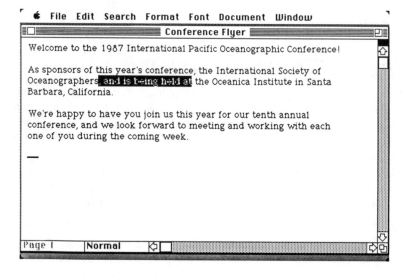

Fig. 3.13

Text selected in the second paragraph, ready for replacement.

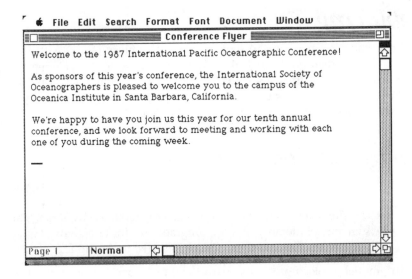

Fig. 3.14

*Conference
Flyer, edited to
make it more
welcoming.*

Using the Paste Command

When you paste text into a document, you usually position the new text before, after, or between existing paragraphs. However, sometimes you may want to replace a block of text with the text on the Clipboard. To make the replacement, simply select the text you want to replace instead of clicking an insertion point, and then choose Paste.

Using the Change Command

One of Word's most powerful and timesaving features is the program's capability to locate a particular piece of text and to replace it with another piece of text. The Change command from the Search menu gives you this power. With the Change command, you specify a word, phrase, or any other piece of text (including formatting characters) to be replaced; then you specify the text you want to substitute, and you can change all occurrences of the search text at once. Or, if you prefer, have Word stop at each occurrence so that you can decide whether you need to change it.

The Change command is similar to the related Find command, which we discussed earlier. The Change command accepts as many as 255 characters in the search string, and like the Find command, the Change command includes options for matching whole words or parts of words, for matching case, and for globally or selectively replacing occurrences of the string.

When you don't specify that Word match the pattern of upper- and lowercase that you type in the replacement string, Word finds all occurrences of the text, regardless of capitalization style, and maintains the capitalization style of the original in the replacement string. This process can be a real convenience. For example, if you instruct Word to replace all occurrences of the word *workshop* with the word *Session*, the program replaces *Workshop* with *Session*, and *workshop* with *session*, keeping the capitalization of the original words intact.

Now, put the Change command through its paces by changing the word *conference* to *convention* in the Conference Flyer document.

To replace one piece of text with another, using the Change command, do the following:

1. Click an insertion point at the top of the document.

2. Choose **Change** from the Search menu.

The Change dialog box opens, shown in figure 3.15. If you have searched for another piece of text with the Find command or used the Change command during this editing session, the previous Find What text remains in the Find What box.

Change
Find What: `workshop`
Change To:
☐ Whole Word   ☐ Match Upper/Lowercase
[Start Search] [Change]   [Change All]   [Cancel]

Fig. 3.15

The dialog box for the Change command.

3. In the Find What box, type the text you want to replace.

4. Tab to the Change To box and type the replacement text.

5. Select Whole Word if you want Word to find only the exact search text, not words that contain the search text in one form or another.

6. Select Match Upper/Lowercase if you want Word to find only the text that exactly matches the case of your search text, not all occurrences of the search text.

In the Conference Flyer document, type *conference* in the Find What box, and *convention* in the Change To box. Leave the Whole Word and the Match Upper/Lowercase check boxes unchecked.

7. Click Change All to replace all occurrences of the search text automatically, or click Start Search to have Word find the first occurrence and wait for further instructions.

If you click Change All in the Change dialog box, Word searches your document from the insertion point to the end of the document, automatically replacing all occurrences of the search text that meet your specifications. As Word searches, it displays, in the page number box in the window's lower left corner, the percentage of the document that has been searched, counting from 0 percent to 100 percent. When the search ends, this box shows the number of changes made. If Word cannot find the search text, Word displays the message No changes.

When the search reaches the end of the document, the alert box shown in figure 3.16 appears, offering you the opportunity to continue the search from the beginning of the document. Word searches from the insertion point's current location to the end of the document. If you forget to move the insertion point to the beginning of the document before starting a search, this alert box allows you to continue the search, ensuring that Word makes the specified changes throughout the document.

Fig. 3.16

The alert box for the Change command.

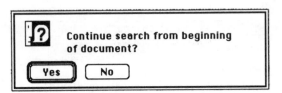

If you click Start Search without clicking Change All, Word highlights the first occurrence of the search text and waits for further instructions. The Start Search button changes to No Change; the Change button becomes available (no longer gray); and the Change All button changes to Change Selection, as shown in figure 3.17. Click No Change to leave the selected string unchanged and to select the next occurrence. Click Change Selection to replace the selected text without advancing to the next occurrence. Click Change to replace the selected text and to select the next occurrence of the search text.

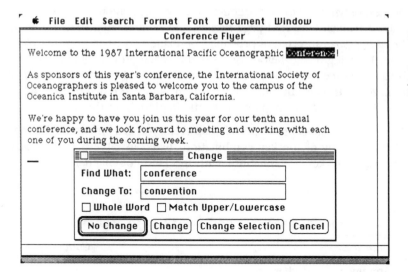

Fig. 3.17

*The Change
dialog box after
you click* Start
Search.

To replace all occurrences of *conference* with *convention*, click
Start Search, and then click Change for each occurrence that Word
finds, until you encounter the alert box in figure 3.16. (You could check
Change All, but then you would not have a chance to observe the search
process.)

The replacement text assumes the formatting of the text it replaces,
unless the replacement text is inserted from the Clipboard. For example,
if the search encounters the word *conference* in bold italic, the word
convention automatically assumes these two characteristics. However,
if you insert from the Clipboard a text block formatted in a different
manner than the document to which you insert the block, the text
block's original formatting is retained, not the document's.

Replacing Special Characters and Formatting Options

Besides looking for specific words and phrases, Word also can find special formatting symbols, such as paragraph, tab, and end-of-line marks;
mathematical symbols used in formulas; and even white space in your
document.

NOTE: *White space* is any combination of Space bar spaces (except the
one space entered with the Space bar to separate words in the normal

process of typing), tab marks, end-of-line marks, paragraph marks, section marks, manually inserted page breaks, and nonbreaking spaces. A *nonbreaking space*, inserted by pressing Command-Space bar, prevents Word from breaking a line before or after the space. You might use a nonbreaking space, for example, between the second period and the *J* of *E. L. Jones* to keep the initials *E. L.* from being stranded at the end of one line, while *Jones* is bumped to the beginning of the next.

To search for and replace special characters, you can type in the Change dialog box any of the key combinations listed in table 3.2. (You also can use these key combinations with the Find command.)

Table 3.2
Special Character Codes for Use in Searches

Character	Code
Any unspecified character	?
Question mark	^?
White space	^w
Nonbreaking space	^s
Tab mark	^t
Paragraph mark	^p
End-of-line mark	^n
Optional hyphen	^-
Section mark	^d
Caret or circumflex symbol	^^
Formula character	^\

Try replacing one formatting mark with another to see how this replacement works. For example, in the following exercise, you learn how to indent the first line of each paragraph in the Conference Flyer document by replacing the paragraph marks with a paragraph mark plus a tab mark.

To find and replace one string of formatting characters with another string throughout a document, do the following:

1. Click an insertion point at the top of the document.

2. Choose **Change** from the Search menu.

The Change dialog box appears, with the previous search text high-lighted in the Find What text box.

3. In the Find What field, type the characters you want to replace.

Type ^p (the symbol over the 6 on the main keyboard, and the lowercase p).

4. Tab to the Change To field.

5. Type the characters you want to substitute.

Your replacement characters in this case are ^p^t (representing a paragraph mark and a tab).

6. Make sure the Whole Word box is unchecked. Word cannot make the specified replacements if Whole Word is active.

7. Click **Change All**.

Within seconds, each paragraph after the first one is indented to the first tab stop. If you don't see the tab mark, choose the Edit menu's Show ¶ command. If you don't like the changes you've made, you can undo them by choosing Undo Change in the Edit menu.

Although we haven't yet told you anything about formatting, you doubtless can tell that the formatting you just applied to the text isn't a particularly attractive presentation of the text. (In Chapter 4, you'll learn how to turn a plain document into something unique by indenting paragraphs, altering line spacing, varying the text's type styles and sizes, and taking advantage of other formatting features.) You can eliminate the tabs quickly and painlessly by choosing Undo Change from the Edit menu. As you can see from this example, the Undo command is particularly useful when you're formatting a document. Having the command available frees you to take some daring steps without irrevocable consequences.

If you'd like to take a break at this point, quit Word without saving the work you've done in this chapter. You need to retain only the original Conference Overview document, already safely stored on disk.

Fabulous Formatting

When we speak, we infuse our words with meaning by changing the tone and inflection of our voices; by punctuating our thoughts with pauses; and by altering our stances, gestures, and facial expressions. These expressions convey to our listeners what is important—to us and to them—in the information we give them. For example, we gesticulate with our hands and strengthen our voices to convey enthusiasm to a large group of people. Or, to soothe someone who is hurt or afraid, we soften our voices and perhaps touch the person while we speak, to convey a sense of warmth and caring.

When we use written words to communicate, however, we distinguish individual waves of expression in an otherwise faceless sea of words only by varying, as much as possible, the visual presentation of our words. Formatting is the means we use to give printed words texture and life.

Extensive control of text formatting probably is Word's most powerful feature. One or two keystrokes or mouse movements can adjust both the texture and the alignment of a block of text or of the text throughout a document. If you change your mind after making a formatting change, you easily can return the affected text to its original appearance.

As you work with the Word program, you learn to think in terms of two basic types of text formatting: paragraph formatting and character formatting. Paragraph formatting affects all kinds of spacing within and between lines of text. Character formatting, on the other hand, affects the look of individual characters. In Chapter 4, you first learn how to use the program's paragraph formatting options to position text elements for greater emphasis. Then you learn how to color the words within the text, using character formatting.

When working with paragraph formatting, you learn how to use the formatting options available on the program's ruler in order to create various types of paragraphs, to vary line spacing, and to set tab stops. Then you are introduced to the Paragraph command, which, in addition to offering spacing and tab options, includes formatting options to help you get the page layouts you want without resorting to trial and error. After you are familiar with what can be done with paragraph formatting, you learn a few keyboard shortcuts so that you can format faster.

Next, you turn your attention to character formatting. You learn how to use the commands available from the Format and Font menus to change the style, size, and font of your text. Using the Character command, you tailor fonts to your needs—adjusting letter spacing, specifying superscript and subscript styles, and so forth. Then, you learn a few more shortcuts to speed up character formatting.

Preparing for the Formatting Exercises

All the basic formatting features are available from the program's short Format menu. But the more advanced features are present only in the full Format menu, which includes all the short menu's commands. Because you use the full menu as you follow the examples in this chapter and all subsequent chapters, choose Full Menus from the Edit menu now. If you quit and restart Word, you won't have to choose Full Menus again, because the program retains the selected menu mode from session to session.

Figure 4.1 shows the full Format menu; the options available on the short menu have been shaded.

You can format your document in two different ways. The first way, illustrated in figure 4.2, is to type the text first, select it, and format it. A second way, however, is to give a formatting command *before* you start typing; all the text you enter will conform to that format until you give another command. For now, try formatting your document the first way.

To learn how to use the program's formatting features and commands, create a sample registration packet for the fictitious oceanographic conference. Type the sample text exactly as you see it in figure 4.2. The

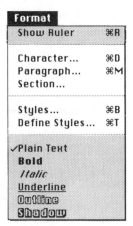

Fig. 4.1

*The full Format
menu (Shaded
options are
available on the
short menu.)*

text is unattractive, and finding where one paragraph ends and the next one begins is difficult. (To help you follow the text, we created figure 4.2 with the Show ¶ command selected, to display paragraph markers and spacing marks.) When you convert this ugly duckling into a graceful document, you will have mastered formatting options unheard of in the old days of typewriters.

Formatting Paragraphs

Formatting that affects the spacing of the lines of text on a page is known in word-processing jargon as *paragraph formatting*. In the text, you use paragraph formatting options to adjust left and right indents, tab settings and styles, line spacing, and paragraph alignment. You can use paragraph formatting tools also to control page breaks.

In Word, a *paragraph* simply is a block of text followed by a paragraph mark. The paragraph mark stores information about the formatting you have applied to the paragraph; therefore, you don't have to highlight an entire paragraph before you format it. Highlighting any portion of a paragraph or simply clicking an insertion point anywhere in the paragraph is adequate. To format adjacent paragraphs, you can select any portion of each paragraph. (However, if you want to format all the paragraphs in a document at one time, selecting the entire document is the fastest approach.)

When you apply basic paragraph formatting—setting indents, tab stops, line spacing, and alignment—to your documents, you probably will use the ruler most frequently. Before you learn more about the commands on the Format menu, you should master the ruler.

Fig. 4.2

The unformatted Registration Packet document.

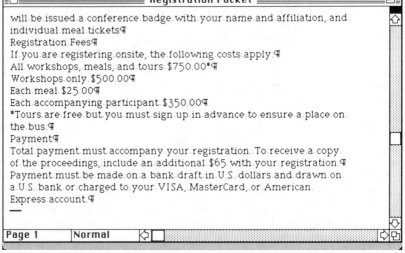

 File   Edit   Search   Format   Font   Document   Window

Registration Packet

Registration.Packet¶
Advance.Registration¶
If.you.registered.in.advance.but.did.not.receive.your.registration.
packet.in.the.mail,.come.to.the.Main.Hall.outside.the.Reef.Room.as.
soon.as.you.arrive..Your.registration.packet.will.include.your.hotel.
assignment.and.meal.and.tour.arrangements,.as.well.as.a.complete.
Conference.Program.¶
Onsite.Registration¶
If.you.have.not.preregistered.for.this.conference,.go.to.the.Emerald.
Cove,.next.to.the.Tidal.Gallery.in.the.Main.Hall,.at.least.30.minutes.
before.the.first.scheduled.conference..There.you.will.be.able.to.
register.for.all.workshops,.meals,.and.tours..If.you.have.not.already.
made.your.own.reservations,.you.also.will.be.able.to.arrange.for.
hotel.accomodations.¶
Please.fill.out.this.form.carefully.and.include.all.information.
requested..When.you.have.finished.filling.out.this.information,.
please.bring.your.complete.registration.packet.to.the.appropriate.
registration.table..After.you.pay.for.the.conference.and.hotel,.you.

Page 1   Normal

 File   Edit   Search   Format   Font   Document   Window

Registration Packet

will.be.issued.a.conference.badge.with.your.name.and.affiliation,.and.
individual.meal.tickets¶
Registration.Fees¶
If.you.are.registering.onsite,.the.following.costs.apply.¶
All.workshops,.meals,.and.tours.$750.00*¶
Workshops.only.$500.00¶
Each.meal.$25.00¶
Each.accompanying.participant.$350.00¶
*Tours.are.free.but.you.must.sign.up.in.advance.to.ensure.a.place.on.
the.bus.¶
Payment¶
Total.payment.must.accompany.your.registration..To.receive.a.copy.
of.the.proceedings,.include.an.additional.$65.with.your.registration.¶
Payment.must.be.made.on.a.bank.draft.in.U.S..dollars.and.drawn.on.
a.U.S..bank.or.charged.to.your.VISA,.MasterCard,.or.American.
Express.account.¶
—

Page 1   Normal

The Ruler

The program's *ruler*, similar to other rulers you have used, provides a horizontal scale that you use to measure or to line up items. One major difference, of course, is that you can't turn Word's ruler sideways or set it on end to use it.

Word's ruler has features that make up for its limitations, however. With the ruler, you can do the following:

- Select open or closed spacing between paragraphs
- Select line spacing—single, one-and-one-half, or double
- Align and indent paragraphs
- Set four varieties of tab stops
- Insert vertical lines in documents (between blocks of text or numbered columns, for example)

Later in the chapter, you will see examples of each of these formatting options. But for now, display the ruler by choosing Show Ruler from the Format menu or by pressing Command-R. At the top of your text window, Word displays the ruler and moves the text down to accommodate the ruler (see fig. 4.3). If you open the Format menu again, you see that the Show Ruler command has changed to the Hide Ruler command.

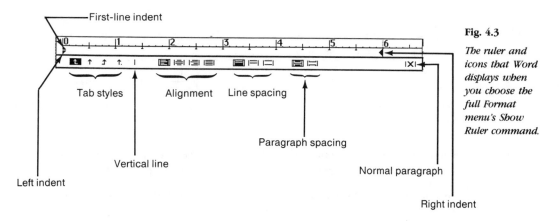

Fig. 4.3

The ruler and icons that Word displays when you choose the full Format menu's Show Ruler command.

Unless you have changed the ruler's unit of measure (with the Preferences command in the Edit menu, as discussed in the next chapter), the ruler is marked in 1/8-inch (0.125-inch) increments, with preset left tab markers every 1/2 inch (0.5 inch). Beneath the ruler is a bar that displays the formatting icons for tabs, vertical lines, alignment, line spacing, paragraph spacing, and normal paragraph. (If you display the ruler in short-menu mode, the only formatting icons displayed are the left-aligned tab, alignment, line spacing, and normal paragraph.) Clicking the X, known as the *normal paragraph icon*, at the right end of the bar instantly returns your document to the default paragraph formatting options: left-justified, single-spaced, and tabs every 0.5 inch. (You can adjust the default tab settings, as you see later in this chapter.)

In the following exercises, you use the ruler's formatting options in the order in which you might call on them when you build your own documents. A typical order is to choose line spacing, paragraph spacing, and first-line indents (if you plan to use them) for the entire document; then set the tabs and the alternate paragraph styles, such as hanging indents and nonindented headings, as required.

Changing Paragraph Spacing

The rightmost pair of icons on the ruler control the amount of space between the paragraphs you've selected (see fig. 4.4). The two options are *closed paragraph spacing*, which does not insert any extra space above paragraphs, and *open paragraph spacing*, which automatically inserts an extra line before each paragraph. When you choose open paragraph spacing, you don't have to press Return two times to separate paragraphs.

Fig. 4.4

The ruler's closed and open paragraph spacing icons.

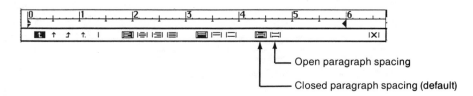

You now are ready for some actual formatting. Use open paragraph spacing to set off the paragraphs in the Registration Packet document.

To implement open paragraph spacing throughout a document, do the following:

1. Press **Command-Option-M** or use the mouse to select the entire document.

You easily can select the entire document with the mouse by moving the pointer into the left margin, where the pointer changes to a right-facing arrow, and then holding down the Command key while you click the mouse button.

2. Click the open paragraph spacing icon on the right side of the ruler or press **Shift-Command-O**.

Within a few seconds, the program displays an extra line before eacn paragraph (see fig. 4.5). Notice that these lines display no paragraph mark.

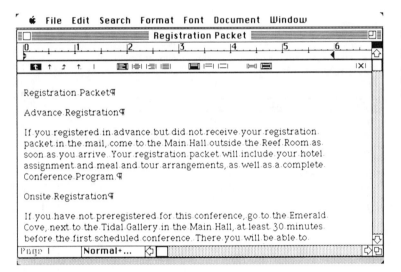

Fig. 4.5

The Registration Packet with open paragraph spacing.

Changing Line Spacing

The term *line spacing* refers to the amount of space between lines of text. Unless you specify otherwise, the program displays and prints text with single-spacing, indicated by the highlighted single-space icon (see fig. 4.6). By clicking the appropriate icon in the ruler, however, you can specify one-and-one-half-spacing or double-spacing. The paragraphs in figure 4.7 show the effects of the three formats.

To change a paragraph's line spacing, do the following:

1. Select the paragraph you want to format.

2. Click the icon for the line spacing you want.

In a few seconds, the paragraph spacing changes to reflect your choice.

Fig. 4.6

The ruler's line spacing icons.

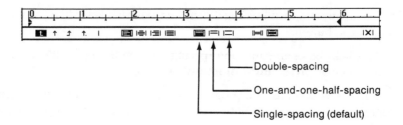

Fig. 4.7

A document showing single-spaced, one-and-one-half-spaced, and double-spaced text.

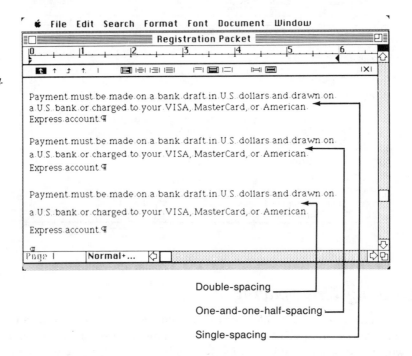

You also can change the line spacing from single to double by using a keyboard shortcut: press Shift-Command-Y. Or exercise even more control by using the Paragraph command (discussed in detail later in this chapter) to specify the exact amount of spacing.

Experiment by selecting a paragraph or two in the Registration Packet document and clicking the one-and-one-half-space icon. Choosing the one-and-one-half-space icon stretches the distance between the bottom of one text line and the bottom of the next line from 12 points to 18 points. (*Points* are a unit of measure used by typesetters; 72 points are in 1 inch.) Next, press Shift-Command-Y to implement double-spacing. The distance between text lines in the selected paragraph becomes 24 points. Finally, return the paragraph to the single-spaced format.

Changing Alignment

The ruler provides four types of paragraph alignment: left-aligned, centered, right-aligned, and justified. Each type is represented by an icon on the ruler (see fig. 4.8). The default alignment format is left-aligned (the flush-left and ragged-right alignment that you see in typed documents). When you type text on the Macintosh, the program automatically wraps the words around to the left margin at the beginning of the next line. Changing this default alignment is a simple process, as you can see from the next exercise.

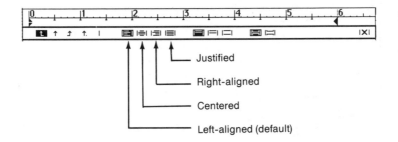

Fig. 4.8

The ruler's alignment icons.

To change a paragraph's alignment, do the following:

1. Select the paragraph you want to change.

2. Click the icon of the alignment you want.

The selected paragraph is realigned within the indents set for that paragraph.

In the Registration Packet document, select a paragraph that has several lines and experiment with the alignment options. Click the center-alignment icon or press Shift-Command-C. The program centers each line. Then click the right-alignment icon or press Shift-Command-R. This time, the paragraph is aligned along the right edge of the text, leaving a ragged left edge.

Continue changing your paragraph's alignment by clicking the justified-alignment icon or by pressing Shift-Command-J. Both the right and the left edges of the paragraph line up when Word inserts the spaces required to fill out each line (see fig. 4.9). In Show ¶ mode, only one dot appears between the words, but the sizes of the spaces surrounding the dot may vary. Notice the difference in the spacing of the second and fourth lines in the justified paragraph (see fig. 4.9). Return your selected text to its original state by clicking the left-alignment icon or by pressing Shift-Command-L.

Fig. 4.9

The justified text shows how Word adjusts the sizes of the spaces between words.

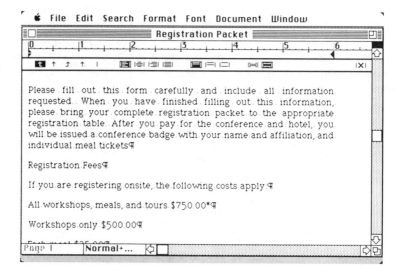

Indenting Paragraphs

Several settings in Word determine the position of the text on a page. The margin settings, which you specify with the File menu's Page Setup command (discussed in the next chapter), determine the usual boundaries of the print area. When you need to set apart text and distinguish among the ideas in your document, however, you use icons on the ruler to indent paragraphs or parts of paragraphs within these boundaries. Figure 4.10 shows the relationships between certain margins and indents.

Four margins—top, bottom, left, and right—set the distance from the edges of your paper to the outer edges of the print area. The *left indent* is the distance between the left margin and the left edge of the text

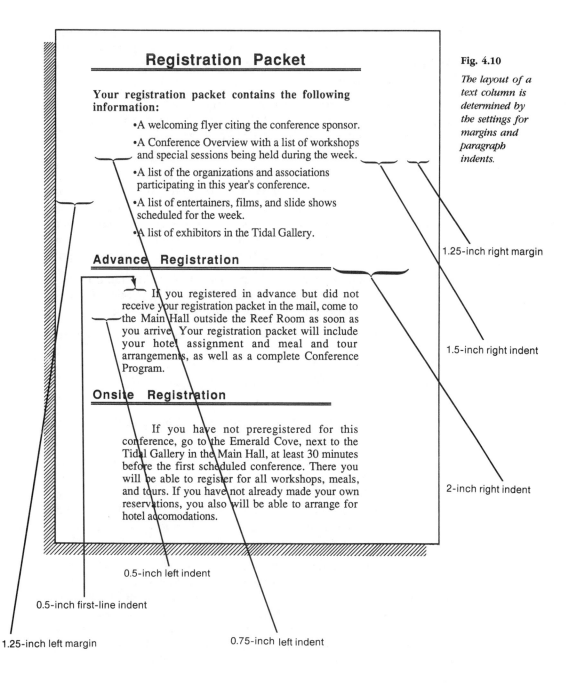

Registration Packet

Your registration packet contains the following information:

- A welcoming flyer citing the conference sponsor.
- A Conference Overview with a list of workshops and special sessions being held during the week.
- A list of the organizations and associations participating in this year's conference.
- A list of entertainers, films, and slide shows scheduled for the week.
- A list of exhibitors in the Tidal Gallery.

Advance Registration

If you registered in advance but did not receive your registration packet in the mail, come to the Main Hall outside the Reef Room as soon as you arrive. Your registration packet will include your hotel assignment and meal and tour arrangements, as well as a complete Conference Program.

Onsite Registration

If you have not preregistered for this conference, go to the Emerald Cove, next to the Tidal Gallery in the Main Hall, at least 30 minutes before the first scheduled conference. There you will be able to register for all workshops, meals, and tours. If you have not already made your own reservations, you also will be able to arrange for hotel accomodations.

Fig. 4.10

The layout of a text column is determined by the settings for margins and paragraph indents.

1.25-inch right margin

1.5-inch right indent

2-inch right indent

0.5-inch left indent

0.5-inch first-line indent

0.75-inch left indent

1.25-inch left margin

block. By the same token, the *right indent* is the distance between the right margin and the right edge of the text block. The *first-line indent* is the distance between the left indent and the beginning of the first line in the paragraph.

The program sets the default ruler settings (those for the normal paragraph) at 1.25 inches for left and right margins and 0 inches for the left, right, and first-line indents. These margins leave a print area 6 inches wide on an piece of paper 8.5 inches wide.

The 0-inch mark on the ruler represents the left edge of the print area, not the left edge of the paper. Two triangular markers stacked one above the other at the 0-inch mark control the left indent (the marker on the bottom) and the first-line indent (the marker on the top); one larger triangle at the 6-inch mark controls the right indent. The positions of the three markers change to reflect the settings for a selected paragraph.

One effective method of emphasizing a paragraph is indenting its left side, or both its left and its right sides. Notes and long quotations often are set off in this style, known as the *nested paragraph* style.

Do the following to change the left and right indents for a block of text:

1. Select the paragraphs you want to change.

2. Drag the ruler's left-indent marker (the bottom triangle on the left) to the desired indent.

3. Drag the right-indent marker (the right triangle) to the desired indent.

Practice using the indent markers to nest the paragraphs below the "Payment" heading at the end of the Registration Packet: use a 0.75-inch (3/4-inch) left indent and a 0.5-inch (1/2-inch) right indent. Select the section and then drag the left-indent marker to the 0.75-inch mark, and the right-indent marker to the 5.5-inch mark. In a few seconds, the selected "Payment" section assumes a narrower shape (see fig. 4.11).

A keyboard shortcut automatically nests a paragraph by indenting its left edge a distance equal to one default tab stop. You simply select the paragraph and press Shift-Command-N. Both the paragraph's left indent and the first-line indent are affected. Every time you press Shift-Command-N, the indents move another increment to the right. To reverse the indents, just use Shift-Command-M to move the indent markers to the left by the same increment. Try this method on the paragraphs you just indented to see how easy the shortcut is.

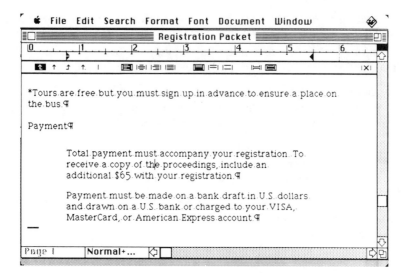

Fig. 4.11

Paragraphs indented on both the left and right sides.

In addition to the nested paragraph, you also have another option to set off your paragraphs in the text—the typical *first-line indent*, in which the first line of text is indented an amount of spaces determined by you. Indenting a paragraph's first line is a simple matter of moving the first-line marker on the ruler.

To indent the first line of one or more contiguous paragraphs, do the following:

1. Select the paragraph or paragraphs you want to change.

2. Drag the first-line-indent marker (the top triangle on the left) to the position where you want the line to begin.

In the Registration Packet document, select the paragraph below the "Advance Registration" heading. To indent the first line 0.5 inch, drag the first-line-indent marker from the ruler's 0-inch mark to the 0.5-inch mark. A paragraph indent of 0.5 inch is a common format. This format is even easier to produce with a shortcut: simply press Shift-Command-F.

Creating Hanging Indents

Whenever you move the left-indent marker, Word moves the first-line-indent marker the same distance in the same direction, thereby maintaining the relative positions of the two markers if you nest a paragraph.

To create a *hanging indent*, however, you must sever temporarily this connection between the markers. The hanging-indent procedure involves *outdenting* the first line of a paragraph—that is, extending the first line farther to the left than the rest of the paragraph.

You can create a hanging indent in one of three ways. After you select the paragraph or paragraphs to which you want to apply the hanging-indent format, you can do any of the following:

- Set both markers where you want the left indent and then move the first-line-indent marker back out to the position where you want the first line to begin.

- Set both markers where you want the first-line outdent and then hold down Shift while you move the left-indent marker to the right.

- Press Shift-Command-T.

The first time you press Shift-Command-T, you create a hanging indent equal to the distance of a default tab stop. Every time thereafter that you press Shift-Command-T, the entire hanging indent moves another increment to the right.

To practice making hanging indents, create some of them in the Registration Packet document. Before you begin, insert and format an introductory paragraph. Place the insertion point at the end of the line that contains the title and press Return to insert a new line with the same format. Then type the following text:

Your registration packet contains the following information:

Next, you need to list beneath the introductory paragraph the enclosures that come with the packet. Type the items shown in figure 4.12. Notice that each item begins with a large dot, called a *bullet*. The Macintosh supplies several symbols for use as bullets; this dot is produced by pressing Option-8.

You are ready to format the hanging indents. For practice, try two methods—one for the first two items, and another method for the rest of the items.

Use the ruler to format hanging indents in the following manner:

1. Select the paragraphs you want to format.

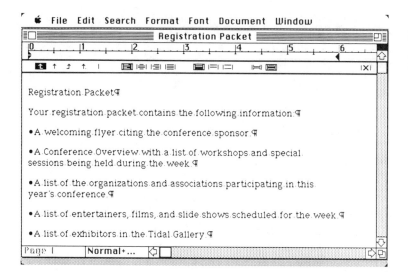

Fig. 4.12

The bulleted list of enclosures.

In this case, select the first two items.

2. Move the left-indent marker (the bottom one) to the right on the ruler and release the mouse button.

3. Now carefully point the mouse so that the tip just covers the top triangle, the first-line-indent marker. Hold down the button and drag back to the left. If you move both markers, move them back and experiment until you discover how to move just the top one.

The goal in creating a hanging indent is to have the first character after the bullet align with the left indent of the remainder of the paragraph. Sometimes the alignment process requires a little trial and error. If you don't like the effect you get, use Undo Formatting in the Edit menu. You should get what you want if you move the first-line indent 1/8 inch to the left of the left indent. At this point, your document looks like the one in figure 4.13.

Now, try another technique, the Shift-Command-T approach, to format hanging indents in the following manner:

1. Select the paragraphs you want to format.

2. Press **Shift-Command-T**.

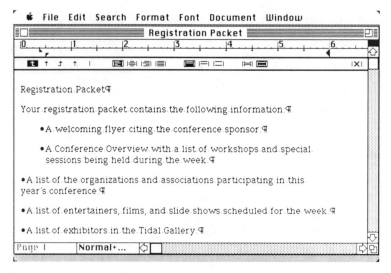

Fig. 4.13

The first two hanging indents.

The first line of each paragraph maintains its position, but Word indents the remaining lines 0.5 inch.

Use this second method to format the remaining three items in the list of enclosures. When you finish, your list should look like the one in figure 4.14. The result is a bit ragged because the two sets of items have different left indents. You now have an excellent excuse for learning how to standardize the formatting of a section of text after you have formatted parts of the text differently.

To standardize the formatting within a set of paragraphs, do the following:

1. Select all the paragraphs that you want formatted the same way.

If you select paragraphs that contain contradictory formatting, the bottom half of the ruler changes to a shaded pattern, as shown in figure 4.15. The indent markers reflect the formatting of the first paragraph. To instruct Word to change the format of the entire selection, you need to adjust one of the markers.

2. Drag the first-line-indent marker a bit; release the mouse button; and then return the marker to its previous location.

This action designates the formatting design of the first paragraph as the design for all the paragraphs. In other words, the first paragraph's formatting is applied to all the selected paragraphs.

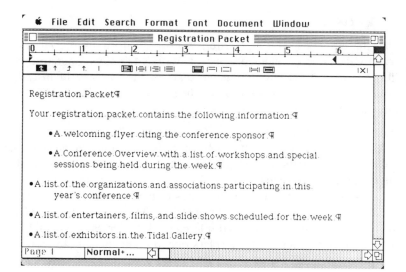

Fig. 4.14

Different levels of hanging indent.

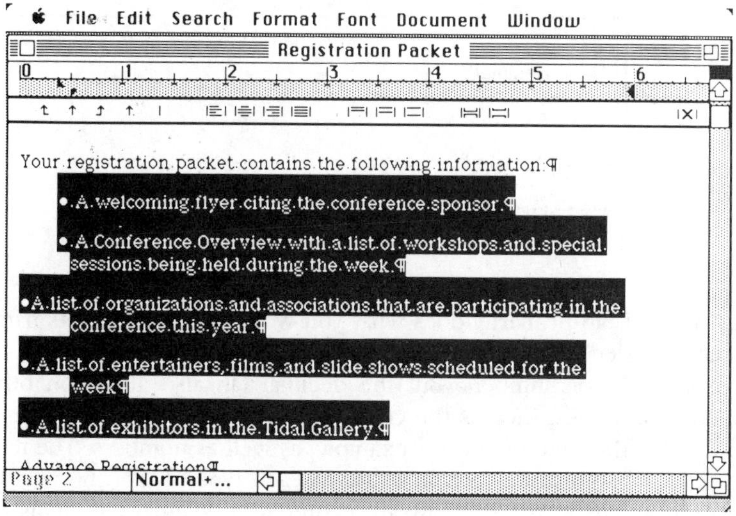

Fig. 4.15

Word shades the bottom half of the ruler when you select paragraphs that contain contradictory formatting.

For this exercise, select all the bulleted items in the enclosures list so that you can make all their left indents the same. Then move and replace the first-line-indent marker. All the items take on the format of the first item.

Setting Tabs

Like the tab stops on a typewriter, Word's tab stops are a convenient way to align certain elements of text. Word's tab stops operate much like the ones on a typewriter: when you press the Tab key, the insertion point jumps to the next tab stop. But the similarity ends here, and Word's flexibility becomes apparent.

Word provides many tab options. For every new document, Word provides default tab stops at 0.5-inch intervals, but you can change this default interval in the Page Setup dialog box. The default tab stops also align text on the left (left-aligned), but you can change that setting, too. In addition, Word has three other types of tabs to offer you: centered, right-aligned, and decimal. When you use the full menus, a separate icon representing each type of tab is displayed on the ruler, as shown in figure 4.16. (The short-menu ruler displays only the left-aligned tab icon.)

Fig. 4.16

The ruler's tab icons.

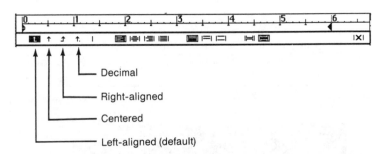

Each type of tab primarily does what you would expect from its name, except the decimal tab. The primary purpose of the decimal tab is to align columns of numbers. But the decimal tab also aligns on other punctuation marks, such as the colon, so that you can use the decimal tab to align the time of day, for example, as well as numbers. The table in figure 4.17 illustrates a typical use of each type of tab: the tabs for all the headings in the top row are centered; a decimal tab aligns the first column (a list of times); the "Workshop" column is aligned with a left tab; and the numbers in the "Attendees" column are aligned with a right tab.

To set a tab, do the following:

1. Select the paragraphs in which you want the tabs to apply.

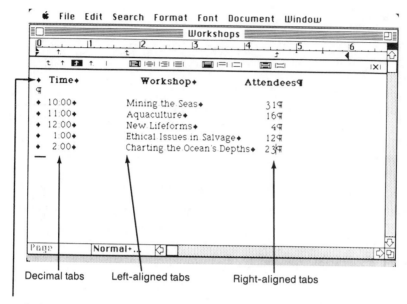

Fig. 4.17

*A table that
uses Word's
four tab
formats.*

2. Select the type of tab you want to set by clicking the appropriate icon.

3. Click the location on the ruler where you want to set a tab.

The program marks the location with a copy of the selected tab icon.

After the tab marker is on the ruler, you can adjust the position of the tab by dragging its marker to the left or right. To remove the tab, drag its marker off the ruler.

Practice setting various types of tab stops in the "Registration Fees" section of the sample document. As shown in figure 4.18, you need to replace the space between the description of the item and the associated fee with a tab character in each of the four entries. Because you have not set any custom tab stops yet, the fees are positioned at the first default tab stop following the item's description.

After you have inserted the tab characters, select the entire section and experiment with setting and removing each type of tab stop. Position the tab marker at about the 4-inch mark on the ruler. Figure 4.19 shows the effect of a decimal-aligned tab stop at 4 inches.

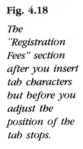

Fig. 4.18

The "Registration Fees" section after you insert tab characters but before you adjust the position of the tab stops.

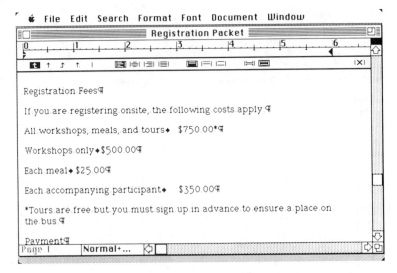

Fig. 4.19

The "Registration Fees" section after you set a decimal-aligned tab stop at 4 inches.

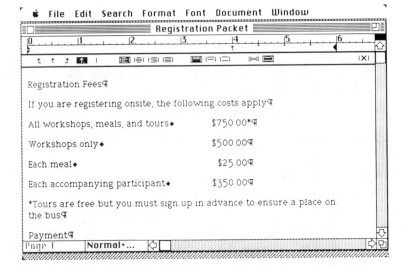

Drawing Vertical Rules

To the right of the ruler's decimal-aligned tab icon is the vertical line icon (see fig. 4.20). You use this icon to insert *vertical rules* (vertical lines) within selected paragraphs of a document. You set the positions of vertical rules in much the same way as you set the positions of tab stops: you click the vertical line icon and then click the desired position on the ruler.

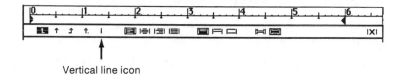

Vertical line icon

Fig. 4.20

The ruler's vertical line icon.

Typically, you use the vertical line icon to draw rules to separate the columns of tables. To draw such a rule, do the following:

1. Select the paragraph or paragraphs within which you want to draw a rule.

For this example, select the four items in the fee schedule under the "Registration Fees" heading.

2. Click the vertical line icon.

3. Click the position on the ruler at which you want to draw a rule.

In this case, click the 3.5-inch mark. Word draws a rule through the four paragraphs, as shown in figure 4.21.

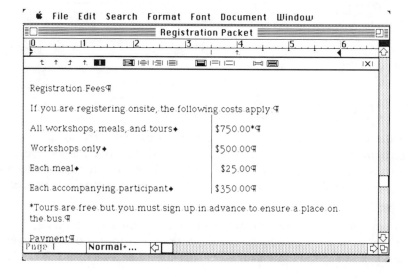

Fig. 4.21

The "Registration Fees" section after you draw a vertical rule at 3.5 inches.

Notice that the new vertical rule does not affect the functioning of the decimal tab you previously set at the 4-inch mark.

To remove a vertical rule, do the following:

1. Select the paragraph or paragraphs from which you want to remove a rule.

Again, select the four items in the registration fee schedule.

2. Drag away from the ruler the vertical rule icon you want to remove.

In this case, drag away the icon positioned at the 3.5-inch mark. Word removes the rule from the four paragraphs.

Using the Normal Paragraph Icon

When you first start to experiment with formatting, you can get hope-lessly entangled in all the options. If a paragraph begins to look more like hieroglyphics than the English language, quickly set things straight by selecting the paragraph and clicking the normal paragraph icon (the X in the ruler; see fig. 4.22). Miraculously and obediently, the program restores all the default paragraph settings: left-justified, single-spaced, and closed paragraph spacing. In this cleanup frenzy, the program also restores the tab stops to the default 0.5-inch intervals (or to the default interval specified for tabs in the Page Setup dialog box).

Fig. 4.22

The ruler's normal paragraph icon.

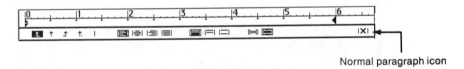

Normal paragraph icon

The Paragraph Command

The basic formatting features available from the ruler are adequate for creating almost any type of document. But Word, which is more than a *basic* word processor, gives you tools to design much more detailed formats. One of those special design tools is the Format menu's Paragraph command.

When you choose the Paragraph command, you see the dialog box shown in figure 4.23. The formatting options available in the Paragraph dialog box are the same as the ones on the ruler; others are available only through this command. However, all these options work in the same way that choices in the ruler do: they affect the selected paragraphs.

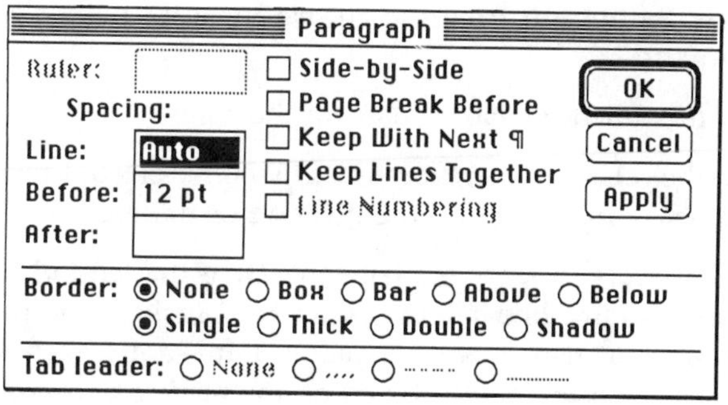

Fig. 4.23

The Paragraph dialog box.

The Paragraph dialog box has three buttons, two of which you should know by now. The OK button implements the options you have specified and closes the dialog box; Cancel closes the dialog box but doesn't change any options.

The Apply button is a useful feature, new in Word, Version 3. After selecting the options you want, you can click Apply to see what your text looks like with those formats. The dialog box remains open. If you don't like the results, you can select other options and click Apply again. The Paragraph dialog box is one of the program's largest command windows. When you use the Apply button, you usually need to drag the dialog box down or to the side in order to view the affected text. You can move the box out of your way by dragging its title bar.

When you open the Paragraph dialog box, it shows the formatting options of the paragraph containing the insertion point.

Adjusting Ruler Settings

Even if you didn't turn on the ruler, the Paragraph command displays the ruler as well as the Paragraph dialog box. Ruler, the first option in the dialog box, remains shaded until you click one of the indent or tab markers on the ruler. Then the Ruler label changes to a bold Left, Right, First, or Tab, which reflects the marker you clicked. In addition, the box to the right of the option displays the marker's current position. Take a look at how the Ruler option works.

To display the current position of a marker on the ruler, do the following:

1. Select the paragraph in which you want to check the settings.

In this case, select the second paragraph under the "Onsite Registration" heading.

2. Choose **Paragraph** from the Format menu or press **Command-M**.

3. Click the indent or tab marker on the ruler.

The Ruler label changes to reflect the currently selected marker. The box to the label's right displays the position of the marker.

Move some markers to see what happens. Drag the left-indent marker to 1 inch and the first-line-indent marker to 2 inches. The position of the first-line-indent marker is displayed as 1 in—not 2 inches—in the dialog box. The measurement is based on the marker's position relative to the left indent, not to the left margin. In this case, the first-line indent is 1 inch from the left indent.

Now drag the first-line indent back to 0 inches and watch the marker's position in the dialog box change to -1 in. The marker now is in a negative position relative to the left indent. Next, drag the first-line indent to 1.5 inches.

Drag the right-indent marker to 3.5 inches. The dialog box shows 2.5 in—not 3.5 inches—because the program measures the right-indent marker's position relative to the right margin, not to the left margin. Finally, click OK. The paragraph should look similar to the one in figure 4.24.

Changing Paragraph Spacing

The Line box in the Paragraph dialog box displays the selected paragraph's line spacing. The program's default line spacing—single-spaced—corresponds to 12 points between the bottom of the text in one line and the bottom of the text in the next line. If you change the line spacing, you always can return to automatic spacing (12 pt) by typing *0* or *auto* in the Line box.

When you designate line spacing in the ruler on your screen, you are limited to single-, one-and-one-half-, or double-spacing. But you have an almost unlimited line spacing selection in the Paragraph dialog box because you can specify your own measurements.

Two options in the Paragraph dialog box, Before and After, control how much space is inserted before and after a paragraph. You specify both of these measurements in points. Between adjacent paragraphs, the

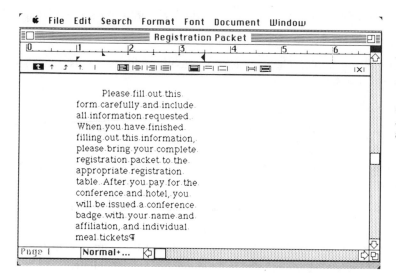

first paragraph's After measurement is added to the second paragraph's Before measurement. For example, if you add 12 points after a paragraph and then add 12 points before the following paragraph, the program inserts 24 points of space between the two paragraphs.

Arranging Paragraphs on the Page

Four options in the Paragraph dialog box help determine the relationships between paragraphs on a printed page: Side-by-Side, Page Break Before, Keep With Next ¶, and Keep Lines Together.

Think of Word, Version 3's, new Side-by-Side option as a fancy tab setting. Normal tab settings work only for single lines of text. Sometimes, however, you'll create documents (scripts or tables that have paragraphs of text, for example) that require columns of related paragraphs. In these cases, you can use the Paragraph command's Side-by-Side option to tell the program to print selected paragraphs beside each other.

Before selecting the Side-by-Side option, you need to set left and right indents that narrow the paragraphs so they do not overlap. For example, on the ruler you might set a right indent of 2.75 inches for one paragraph and a left indent of 3.25 inches for another so that they are printed side-by-side with a 0.5-inch space between them. The program takes care of the line breaks and spacing.

Specifically, to create two side-by-side paragraphs, do the following:

1. Select the first (the left) paragraph.

For this example, select the first paragraph under the "Onsite Registration" heading.

2. Choose **Show Ruler** from the Format menu.

3. Set the left and right indents for the first paragraph.

To make the paragraph 2.75 inches wide, leave the left indent set at 0 inch and set the right indent 3.25 inches from the right margin (at the ruler's 2.75-inch mark).

4. Select the second paragraph and set the left and right indents for it.

In this case, select the second paragraph under the "Onsite Registration" heading. If you want a 0.5-inch space between the two paragraphs when they are side-by-side, set the left- and first-line-indent markers of the second (the right) paragraph 2.75 inches from the right margin (at the ruler's 3.25-inch mark). Make certain that the right-indent marker is at the 6-inch mark, flush with the right margin.

5. Check the paragraphs on the screen. If they overlap, narrow one or both of them; otherwise, they will not print side by side.

6. Select both paragraphs.

7. Choose **Paragraph** from the Format menu.

8. Click the **Side-by-Side** option and then **OK** to close the dialog box.

Word usually displays side-by-side paragraphs one beneath the other on-screen. You can preview the printed layout of a document, however, by choosing the File menu's Page Preview command (see Chapter 6). Figures 4.25 and 4.26 show side-by-side paragraphs in normal document view and in page preview mode.

Normally, Word decides automatically where to break pages. However, you can tell Word to begin a new page in one of two ways: by manually entering a page break or by specifying in the Paragraph dialog box that the paragraph you have chosen in the text should begin a new page. To insert a page break manually, you simply press Shift-Enter to display a dotted line across your screen. The dotted line signals the program to start a new page with the succeeding text. If you manually entered

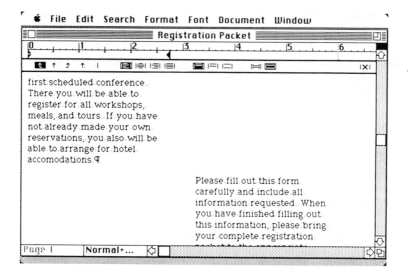

Fig. 4.25

Side-by-side paragraphs displayed in normal document view.

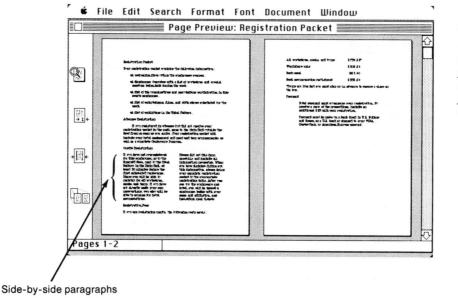

Side-by-side paragraphs

Fig. 4.26

The same side-by-side paragraphs displayed in page preview mode.

a page break and no longer want it, you can delete the page break by following this procedure: move the window pointer to the left margin and just below the page break line, make an insertion point, and press the Backspace key.

A manually inserted page break functions as a separate element, attached to neither the preceding nor subsequent paragraph. When you select a paragraph and specify Page Break Before in the Paragraph dialog box, however, you actually are formatting the paragraph to begin a new page. The program inserts a page-break marker that is not visible until you repaginate your document.

The paragraph now functions as a unit with the page break; if you move the paragraph, the page break moves with the paragraph. This step can be confusing. If you cut a paragraph formatted with Page Break Before and paste the paragraph elsewhere, Word prints the paragraph at the top of a new page unless you reformat the paragraph. For this reason, this option is best used only when you know you always want a page break to precede the paragraph.

Keep With Next ¶ is another option that controls page breaks, but this option instructs the program not to start a new page between the selected paragraph and the one that follows it. Keep With Next ¶ is the best option for preventing the program from breaking a page between a heading and the following paragraph.

Keep With Next ¶ also is convenient for formatting tables that you want to keep on one page. Select all the lines in the table except the last line and specify Keep With Next ¶ so that the program prints the entire table on one page. If the table won't fit, the program moves the entire table to the top of the next page.

The last line of the table is linked with the rest of the table by the Keep With Next ¶ setting for the preceding line. If you select the last line of the table when setting this option, Word links the paragraph following the table with the last line of the table and prints not only the table but also the paragraph on one page. If any part of the paragraph won't fit, the program moves the table and the paragraph to the top of the next page.

Of course, the Keep With Next ¶ option applies only if you press Return at the end of each line in the table and make each line a separate paragraph.

There will be times, however, when you want to keep together the lines of a paragraph—either lines that Word has wrapped to fit within your document's margins or lines you have created by pressing Shift-Return (see the discussion under "Drawing Lines and Boxes"). Unless you select the Keep Lines Together option, Word does not automatically keep your paragraph's lines on one page. The only exception to this rule occurs with a potential *widow* (a paragraph's last line appearing at the top of a page) or *orphan* (a paragraph's first line appearing at the bottom of a page) that might be separated from the rest of its paragraph by a page break. Word keeps a widow or an orphan with its respective paragraph. To keep *all* lines in a paragraph together on one page, whether the lines contain a widow, orphan, or an entire table of information, select the Keep Lines Together option.

Numbering Lines

Another new feature in Word, Version 3, is its capability to number the lines of a single paragraph, a page, or an entire document. Line numbers are printed but usually are not displayed, although you can view them in page preview mode. Line numbers are useful for measuring the lengths of sections of text and for keeping track of the location of specific information.

The Line Numbering option usually is shaded and unavailable because you don't actually use the option to add line numbers to a document. To activate the Paragraph command's Line Numbering option, first select the Section command's Line Numbering option. Word now makes the option available in the Paragraph dialog box and automatically selects (checks) Line Numbering. You then can click the option to turn off line numbers in selected paragraphs. For more information on line numbering, read the discussion of the Section command in the next chapter.

Drawing Lines and Boxes

Borders can be used to separate blocks of text, to frame text or graphics, to delineate columns of numbers, and to enhance the appearance and readability of your document. The border options available from the Paragraph command include boxes, bars (vertical lines on either side of a paragraph), and horizontal lines (above or below the paragraph, or both). The lines and boxes can be thin, thick, or double, and they also can have a shadow beneath them.

Word applies borders only to individual paragraphs. If you select a block of text that has several paragraphs and then select the Box option, each paragraph is boxed separately, with just one horizontal line inserted between the paragraphs (see fig. 4.27).

To include several paragraphs in the same box, you need to make them into a single paragraph by substituting new-line characters for the paragraph marks at the end of each paragraph. To insert a new-line character, first delete the old paragraph mark and then press Shift-Return instead of Return.

Fig. 4.27

The registration fee schedule with different borders drawn around each paragraph.

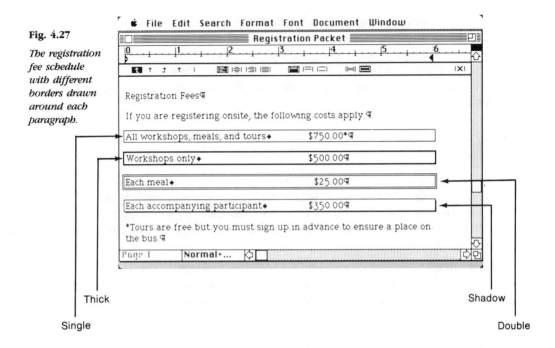

Thick

Single

Shadow

Double

In preparation for the next exercise, move the "Registration Fees" section to the top of the screen so that you can see the text when you open the Paragraph dialog box. Then go ahead and delete the paragraph marks at the end of the first three items in the fee schedule and replace the paragraph marks with new-line characters by pressing Shift-Return. The four items are now one paragraph, controlled by the formatting stored in the paragraph mark at the end of the fourth item.

To put a border around a paragraph, do the following:

1. Click an insertion point within the paragraph.

In this case, click an insertion point anywhere within the four registration fee items.

2. Choose **Paragraph** from the Format menu.

3. In the Border section, click the **Box** option.

4. Select the border style you want.

For this example, select the Shadow style.

5. Press **Return** or click **OK** to implement your choice.

As shown in figure 4.28, Word draws a box with a shadow around the entire fee schedule.

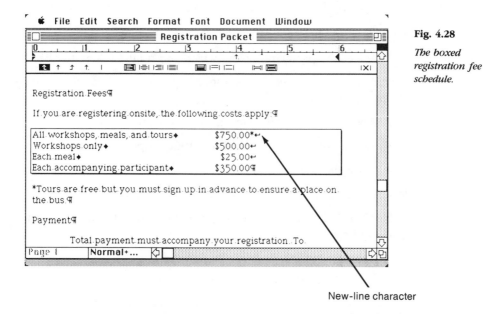

Fig. 4.28

The boxed registration fee schedule.

New-line character

The program draws the box to fit within the paragraph's left and right indents, not to fit the width of the text in the paragraph. Sometimes, the results appear a bit off-balance, as they do in the example in figure 4.28. To remedy this balance problem, you can change the paragraph's indents so that the box is in proportion with the text. Because borders are a paragraph format, changing the indents shrinks or expands the border but otherwise keeps the border intact.

To adjust the width of a box, do the following:

1. Click an insertion point in the boxed paragraph.

2. Adjust the positions of the left and right indents, as necessary.

In this case, move the right-indent marker to the 4.5-inch mark on the ruler. Word redraws the box so that the box is more in proportion to the items in the fee schedule.

If you edit the text in a boxed paragraph, Word automatically makes all the adjustments necessary to keep the border intact. If you add text, Word expands the border; if you delete text, Word shrinks the border.

In addition to boxing paragraphs, you can use the Border option to draw lines above, below, to the left, and to the right of paragraphs. You might use lines to emphasize banner headlines or to set off a note or warning in a document.

To draw a line below a paragraph, do the following:

1. Select the paragraph below which you want to draw the line.

For this example, select the "Advance Registration" heading, including the paragraph mark.

2. Choose **Paragraph** from the Format menu.

3. In the Border section, click the **Below** option.

4. Click the style of line you want.

In this case, click the Double option.

5. Click **OK** to close the dialog box and implement the selected options.

The double-line format is shown in figure 4.29.

Fig. 4.29

A heading emphasized with a double line.

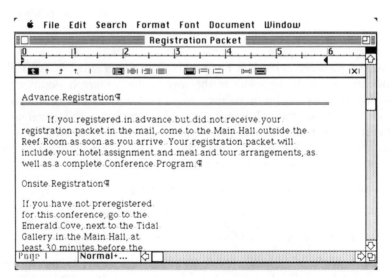

Experiment by applying the other border options to the other paragraphs. Combine borders with various levels of indentation so that you can see how lines and boxes adjust to fit the shape of the text they embellish. When you finish experimenting, you can remove any border by choosing None.

Adding Tab Leaders

The last set of options in the Paragraph dialog box is labeled Tab leader. *Tab leaders* are marks that Word inserts between the last character preceding a tab stop and the first character following the tab stop. The Tab leader options cannot be selected until you click a tab stop—either a default or a custom tab stop—in the ruler.

The default Tab leader setting is None. The other three options are dots, hyphens, or underscore lines. Dots and hyphens are used frequently in tables of contents, lists of figures, and other elements of printed documents. Underscore lines can be used with empty tab stops in forms or other documents to create lines that don't extend from margin to margin (as the lines created by the border options do). Figure 4.30 shows a table formatted with all three leader options.

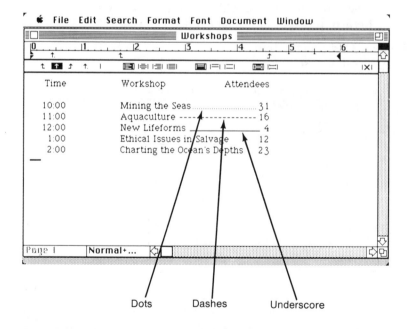

Fig. 4.30

The available tab leader styles.

To add tab leaders to tabular material, do the following:

1. Select the table.

In this case, click an insertion point anywhere in the Registration Packet fee schedule.

2. Choose **Paragraph** from the Format menu or press **Command-M.**

3. Click a tab stop in the ruler.

Click the decimal tab stop at the ruler's 4-inch mark.

The tab leaders instantly become selectable.

4. Click the tab leader option you want.

For this example, select the dash leader option.

5. Click **Apply**.

Be sure that you like the effect. If you don't, you can click another option and click Apply again. In this case, the dashes look too prominent, so change the option to dots and then click Apply again to make the document look more appealing.

6. When you are satisfied with the results, click **OK** or press **Return**, to close the Paragraph dialog box.

Figure 4.31 shows the results.

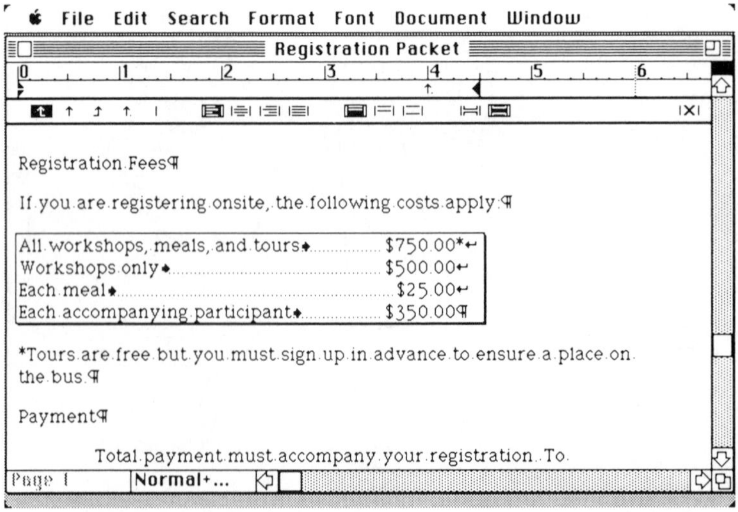

Fig. 4.31

The fee schedule with dot leaders.

Keyboard Shortcuts

After you are familiar with selecting paragraph formatting options by changing the setting on the ruler or by selecting options from the Paragraph dialog box, you can speed up the formatting process by using keyboard shortcuts. We already have discussed many of these keyboard shortcuts in this chapter; table 4.1 lists them for reference (see also the Quick Reference Guide at the end of the book).

Table 4.1
Keyboard Shortcuts for Paragraph Formatting

Format	*Shortcut*
Plain paragraph	Shift-Command-P
Double-space	Shift-Command-Y
Open-space	Shift-Command-O
Nest	Shift-Command-N
Unnest	Shift-Command-M
First-line indent	Shift-Command-F
Hanging indent	Shift-Command-T
Flush-left	Shift-Command-L
Flush-right	Shift-Command-R
Centered	Shift-Command-C
Justified	Shift-Command-J
Side-by-side	Shift-Command-G

Formatting Characters

The paragraph formatting features that you have just learned are *structural*; that is, they affect the positioning of text lines without changing the appearance or emphasis of the characters within the text lines. In this section, you learn *character formatting*—how to change the style, font, and size of characters, words, and larger units of text.

The distinction between style and font is important. Each *font* is a unique set of characters—the 26 letters in both upper- and lowercase, and a complement of numerals, punctuation marks, and symbols—designed with aesthetics in mind, to create a certain look or "feel." On the other hand, a *style*—bold, italic, underlined, and so on—is applied to a font's characters to give them a particular emphasis. Word gives you considerable range in choosing both the fonts and the styles that embellish the fonts.

Size, the other character formatting option, varies considerably from font to font. Because of the precision of points (72 points per inch), typographers use points as a unit of measure. The program adheres to this unit of measure when Word sizes the type. For some fonts, the sizes you select are limited to 8, 10, 12, and perhaps 14 points. For other fonts, the range of selectable sizes may be anywhere from 2 to 127 points. You can type any number between 2 and 127 into the Font Size field of the Character command's dialog box, however, and the program attempts to create that size type. But be warned: the results may not be completely accurate or aesthetically pleasing.

Word gives you three ways to change the look of the characters in your document: you can choose options from the Format or Font menu, select options in the Character command's dialog box, or implement options by using their keyboard shortcuts. We discuss the techniques for all three character formatting methods in the following sections.

The Format and Font Menus

The basic character formatting commands are available from both the short and full versions of the Format and Font menus. The full Format menu contains also the Character command, with which you can specify simultaneously a variety of options. For now, consider the basics of the Format and Font menus.

Changing Styles

Both the short and full Format menus offer the most common character styles: Plain Text, Bold, Italic, Underline, Outline, and Shadow (see fig. 4.32). You can apply these styles to anything from a single character to the whole document. All the styles except Plain Text are cumulative; in other words, you can specify that a piece of text be both bold and outlined, for example. If you choose Plain Text, however, Word removes any other applied styles from the selected text.

To apply a style by using the Format menu, do the following:

1. Select the text of which you want to change the look.

2. Choose the style you want from the Format menu.

As you can imagine, you can produce dramatic effects by combining character styles. Apply the Bold, Underline, and Shadow formats to the "Onsite Registration" heading in the Registration Packet document (see fig. 4.33).

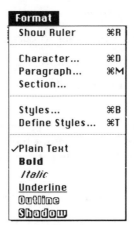

Fig. 4.32

The Format menu's character styles.

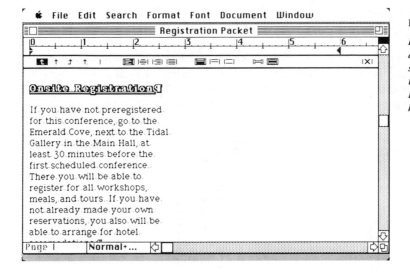

Fig. 4.33

Bold, Underline, and Shadow styles applied to the "Onsite Registration" heading.

You can use a simple method to determine the styles that you have applied to a piece of text. When you select one character in the text, a check mark appears on the menu before each style that has been applied to that character. When you select more than one character and the same styles have been applied throughout the selection, a check mark again appears on the menu before each applied style. If a style has been applied to some characters and not to others, then the style is not checked.

Do the following to remove a style:

1. Select the text of which you want to change the look.

2. Choose the style you want to remove.

Word removes the style from the selected text, and the check mark from the menu.

As you experiment with character formatting, notice that the new text you type within a formatted block assumes the style of the text surrounding it. To enter text in a style other than that of the surrounding text, do the following:

1. Click an insertion point where you want to begin typing.

2. Choose from the Format menu the style you want for the new text.

3. Start typing.

Changing Fonts and Sizes

The default font and size varies depending on which fonts are available in your System folder. On our machine, the default font is New York and default size is 12 points (described as 12-point New York). However, the Font menu provides several other choices (see fig. 4.34).

Fig. 4.34

The Font menu.

What criteria should you use when selecting fonts and sizes for different parts of a document? To a certain extent, your decisions undoubtedly will reflect your own taste. However, knowing something about typographical design conventions will help you develop a balanced, pleasing product.

As we've already mentioned, a font is a family of characters of similar design. We can use two sets of basic characteristics to describe a font: serif and sans serif, and monospaced and proportionally spaced. Each set offers mutually exclusive options—a font is either serif or sans serif, for example.

A *serif* is a crossline at the end of the main stroke of a letter. Fonts that have serifs are called, appropriately, *serif fonts*; those that don't have serifs are called *sans serif fonts* (sans means without). Many people feel that serif fonts give a document a more traditional, and perhaps more formal, look than sans serif fonts. Serif fonts also are reputed to be easier to read than sans serif fonts because the serifs lead the eye from one character to another.

Monospaced fonts produce characters that resemble typewriter characters. Each character takes up the same amount of space on a line, regardless of the actual width of the character. An i, for example, occupies the same space as an m. Proportionally spaced fonts, on the other hand, produce characters that take up only the amount of space they need. To most people, proportionally spaced fonts produce more professional-looking results than monospaced fonts, perhaps because the proportionally spaced fonts resemble the fonts used by typesetters.

Beyond these two sets of basic characteristics, each font has its own distinctions. For example, one font may be delicate in appearance while another may look heavy. Your selection of one rather than the other probably will depend on the content of your document. Figure 4.35 shows an example of each of the fonts listed in Word's Font menu.

When designing a document, you need to choose not only an appropriate font but also an appropriate size. Typographical design conventions—and common sense—decree that the size of each element should reflect that element's relative importance in the document. Using different font sizes is thus a quick and easy way of establishing the hierarchy of headings, and of setting off headings and other elements from the main body of the text.

Font sizes are measured in points, with 72 points in 1 inch. Thus, if you specify a font size of 18 points, the characters are 0.25 inch high (18 is one-fourth of 72). This height is measured from the bottom of the letters extending below the line to the top of the letters extending above the line and has nothing to do with the size of such characters as *a*, *e*, *i*, *o*, or *u*. As a result, one font may appear larger than another, even though you specify the same size for both fonts (see fig. 4.35, in which all the fonts are 12 point).

Fig. 4.35

An example of each font in the Font menu.

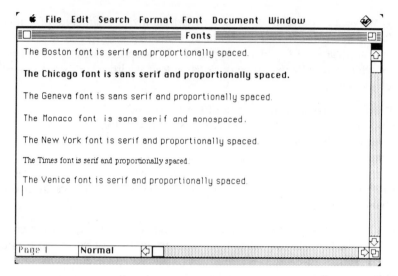

Figure 4.36 shows the New York font (which is a serif, proportionally spaced font) and the Monaco font (which is a sans serif, monospaced font) in each of the five sizes listed on the Font menu.

Fig. 4.36

The New York and Monaco fonts in five sizes.

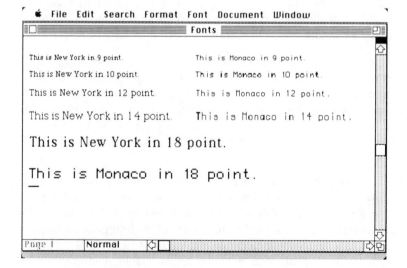

As you may have noticed in figure 4.34, when you pull down the Font menu, Word puts a check mark in front of the currently active font and size. Word also displays the sizes in outline type, which indicates the font sizes actually installed on your Macintosh. If a size is not available, Word displays the size in plain type.

Now that you know a little about fonts and sizes, try changing the font and the size of one of the sample document's elements.

To change the font and size of your text, do the following:

> 1. Select the text you want to change.

In this case, select the main heading, "Registration Packet."

> 2. Choose a font from the Font menu.

Change the font to Geneva.

> 3. Choose a size from the Font menu.

Change the size to 18 point.

The Character Command

If you have experimented with the commands discussed thus far, most of the options available in the Character dialog box should be familiar to you (see fig. 4.37). These options are in five categories: Character Formats, Font Name, Font Size, Position, and Spacing. As you did with the Paragraph command, you can choose these options, apply them to selected text, and then try other options if the results are unsatisfactory. Remember that you can drag the dialog box out of your way to view text.

If you select a piece of text before you choose the Character command, the checked Character Formats boxes reflect the styles currently in effect. Click an empty check box to apply the associated style to the selected text or click a selected check box to remove the associated style. If your selection has conflicting character formatting, the check boxes all appear shaded (and no boxes are checked). Under these circumstances, you must click a check box two times to remove the associated style. (The first click selects the option; the second click removes the style.)

Fig. 4.37

The Character dialog box.

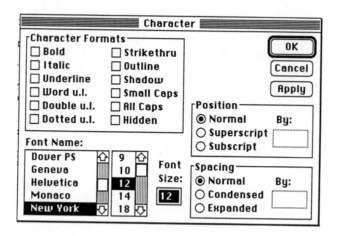

Applying Styles

Figure 4.38 illustrates the format options available in the Character Formats boxes of the Character dialog box. Checking the Character Formats boxes instead of choosing styles individually from the Format menu is a faster way to apply several styles at one time. For practice, apply some of the character formats to the various parts of the Registration Packet document.

Fig. 4.38

The character styles available in Word, Version 3.

 ⌘ File Edit Search Format Font Document Window

Bold	Shift-Command-B
Italic	Shift-Command-I
<u>Underline</u>	Shift-Command-U
Word <u>Underline</u>.	Shift-Command-]
<u>Double Underline</u>	Shift-Command-[
Dotted Underline	Shift-Command-\
~~Strikethru~~	Shift-Command-/
Outline	Shift-Command-D
Shadow	Shift-Command-W
SMALL CAPS	Shift-Command-H
ALL CAPS	Shift-Command-K
Hidden	Shift-Command-X

Page 1   Normal+...

Selecting Fonts

The Character dialog box displays a list of all the fonts installed in your Macintosh. The font list may be longer than the one on the Font menu, which includes only commonly used fonts. If the list is too long to fit in the Font Name list box, use the scroll bar on the right of the box to scroll through the list.

Do the following to select a font from the Character dialog box:

1. Select the text in which you want to change the font.

If all the selected text is in the same font, the program highlights that font's name in the Font Name list.

2. Click the desired font in the Font Name list box.

3. Click **OK** or press **Return**.

The dialog box closes; and Word applies your choices, including the new font, to the selected text.

A new feature in Word, Version 3, is the capability to control the fonts listed in the Font menu. Press Command-Option-+ (the plus key on the main keyboard) and select a font name from the Character dialog box. The selected font will now appear in the main Font menu. To delete a font from the Font menu, press Command-Option-- (the hyphen key on the main keyboard) and select from the Font menu the font you want to delete. See Chapter 11 for more about customizing menus.

Selecting Sizes

To the right of the list of font names is a list box that displays the sizes available for the highlighted font in the left side. If the list is too long to fit in the box, you can scroll through the list of sizes.

Selecting a size is similar to selecting a font; often, the two selections are made at the same time. You simply select the text of which you want to change the size and then highlight the desired size. The change is implemented when you click OK to close the Character dialog box.

As indicated earlier, you also can type the desired size—from 2 to 127 points—in the Font Size box. If you specify a size not included in the Font Name list, the program constructs characters of that size by scaling down the next larger size. Be forewarned that both the displayed and the printed text can appear jagged when you select a size in this manner.

Creating Subscript and Superscript Characters

Although most people write in one position on a line, mathematicians, scientists, and product-development specialists often need to type words and letters above and below lines. The most common usages of *superscript* (above the line) and *subscript* (below the line) characters are in mathematical equations, chemical formulas, and other technical notations (H_2CO_3, $E=MC^2$, and BagBuster[Plus], for example). Footnote reference marks also are commonly superscript. (Word automatically creates footnotes with a superscript reference when you use the Document menu's Footnote command; see Chapter 20.)

To format characters as superscript, do the following:

1. Select the characters you want to appear above the line.

2. Choose **Character** from the Format menu or press **Command-D**.

3. Click the **Superscript** position option.

Word displays the default point spacing (3 pt) in the By box.

4. Replace the 3 pt, if necessary, by entering a new superscript position.

5. Click **OK** or press **Return**.

Your selection appears, in the specified number of points, above the normal text line.

To format characters as subscript, follow the steps for superscript, but click the Subscript position option in Step 3.

For most purposes, you won't need to make fine distinctions in the amount of points that a superscript is raised or a subscript is lowered. The program provides a keyboard shortcut for creating superscript and subscript characters, for which the default spacing above or below the line is acceptable.

Format superscript characters by using the following keyboard shortcut:

1. Select the group of characters you want to affect.

2. Press **Shift-Command-+**. (Use the plus key on the main keyboard.)

Word automatically raises the selected characters 3 points (the default setting for superscripts) above the text line. The characters remain highlighted so that you easily can change the formatting again.

To format subscript characters by using a keyboard shortcut, follow the steps for superscript. In Step 2, however, press Shift-Command-- (the hyphen key on the main keyboard). The selected characters change to subscript and appear 2 points (the default setting) below the text line.

In Word, you can adjust the size as well as the position of your superscripts and subscripts (see fig. 4.39). Why go to the trouble of altering their size? Try printing a single-spaced mathematical or scientific paper that includes both subscripts and superscripts—without overlapping any of the characters. You'll never ask again!

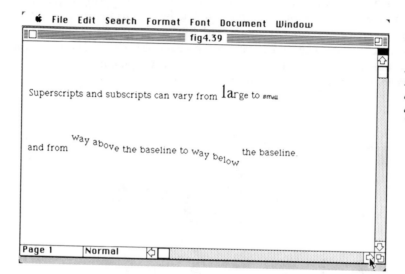

Fig. 4.39

The spectrum of superscript and subscript sizes and positions available in Word, Version 3.

You also can enlarge or reduce the size of selected superscript or subscript characters by changing the Font Size specification in the Character dialog box, or by pressing Shift-Command-> (enlarge font) or Shift-Command-< (reduce font). If you watch your screen while you use the keyboard shortcuts, you see the number of points by which the selected characters are enlarged or reduced. You can use these commands to change the size of any selected character.

Create superscript and subscript characters in the Registration Packet document by using both the Character command and the keyboard shortcuts. Vary the positions and sizes of the characters. No matter how large you make the characters, the program still positions them above or below the normal text line.

Adjusting the Spacing between Characters

The three Spacing options—Normal, Condensed, and Expanded—control
the distance between characters. Usually, you will find the default character spacing acceptable. When you work with display type, however—headlines, enlarged quotations, captions, and so on—you may
want to adjust the spacing to prevent your words from appearing too
cramped or too far apart.

Often, you may want to expand or condense the spacing between only
two characters. Suppose, for example, that you use the program to create
an advertisement for T-shirts. Your company's marketing department
considers the space between the *T* and its hyphen too great, particularly
in large type. To avoid aesthetic criticism, you select and condense the
T- combination. Figure 4.40 shows the result of such a process. Are the
results worth the effort? Evidently so: Remember, people get paid a good
salary to make this kind of design decision.

Fig. 4.40

*An example of
condensed text.*

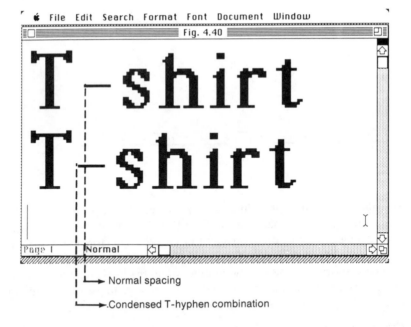

Character spacing can be expanded by as much as 14 points, or condensed by as much as 1.75 points. If you try to expand text beyond 14
points, the program displays the alert box shown in figure 4.41. A similar
alert box appears if you try to condense type below the 1.75-point limit.

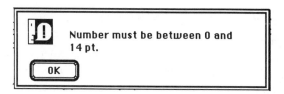

Fig. 4.41

The alert box that Word displays when you take unacceptable liberties with character spacing.

To expand character spacing, do the following:

1. Select the text in which you want to expand the spacing.

2. Choose **Character** from the Format menu or press **Command-D**.

3. Click the **Expanded** spacing option and type the number of points by which you want to expand the spacing between characters. (You don't have to type *pt.*)

4. Click **OK** or press **Return**.

Expand the spacing in the "Registration Fees" heading. Figure 4.42 shows how this heading looks if you expand the spacing to 12 points.

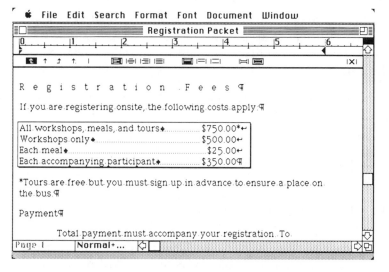

Fig. 4.42

The "Registration Fees" heading in expanded type.

Undoing Character Formatting

Having created a sample document that undoubtedly looks quite original, you may wonder whether a quick method exists for restoring your text to its normal appearance. For your example, *normal* includes all the default formats in the Character dialog box: plain, 12-point New York font, with Normal position and Normal spacing selected.

Restore the text to its default format by doing the following:

1. Select the text that you want to restore.

In this case, press Command-Option-M to select the entire document.

2. Press **Shift-Command-Space bar**.

These steps remove all custom character formatting and return the text to its default status.

Keyboard Shortcuts

The Format and Font menus and the Character dialog box offer great flexibility in character formatting. This flexibility is accompanied, however, by the necessity of dragging through long lists of menu options. To speed up basic formatting, the program has shortcuts for performing many of these formatting changes directly from the keyboard.

You often will use Word's keyboard shortcuts, listed in table 4.2, for applying character formatting to selected text. The first time you press the shortcut code, Word applies the style; if you press the code again, the program removes the style.

Word also has keyboard shortcuts for changing the font and size of a piece of selected text.

To change the font, do the following:

1. Select the text in which you want to change the font.

2. Press **Shift-Command-E**.

The label Font appears for a few seconds in the lower left corner of the active window.

3. Type the name of the desired font (or enough of the name to distinguish the font from others that are available).

Table 4.2
Keyboard Shortcuts for Character Formatting

Style	Shortcut
Bold	Shift-Command-B
Italic	Shift-Command-I
Underline	Shift-Command-U
Word underline	Shift-Command-]
Double underline	Shift-Command-[
Dotted underline	Shift-Command-\
Strikethrough	Shift-Command-/
Outline	Shift-Command-D
Shadow	Shift-Command-W
Small caps	Shift-Command-H
All caps (uppercase)	Shift-Command-K
Hidden	Shift-Command-X

To choose Geneva, you simply type *g*. You do not need to type a capital letter.

4. Press **Return**.

To change the size of your text, press Shift-Command-> to increase the size to as large as 72 points, or press Shift-Command-< to decrease the size to as small as 7 points. The same two keyboard shortcuts also increase and decrease the size of selected sub- and superscripts, as mentioned previously.

Copying and Duplicating Formatting

The task of formatting a large document would be tedious if you had to go through the entire document and continually select individual paragraphs or groups of paragraphs in order to apply a series of paragraph and character formats. Fortunately, Word provides several methods for transferring the formats of one paragraph to other paragraphs in a document.

If you want to apply a set of formats to successive paragraphs as you type, you don't have to take any special action: just format the first paragraph the way you want it; then press Return, as usual, to start each new paragraph. The program automatically applies the first paragraph's formatting to the succeeding paragraphs.

Word offers two other methods for transferring formatting. Both methods are variations on the Command-Option-V keyboard shortcut, which you can use to copy paragraph or character formats between any two locations in the same document or between two documents. The way you select the text with the format you want to copy determines whether the program copies paragraph or character formatting. If you select an entire paragraph, Word copies its paragraph format. Otherwise, Word copies the character formatting of the first character in the selection.

Try the first Command-Option-V method. To copy paragraph formatting to the paragraph that has the insertion point, do the following:

1. Position the insertion point in the paragraph into which you want to copy the formatting.

In this case, click an insertion point in the first paragraph under the "Onsite Registration" heading.

2. Press **Command-Option-V**.

The message Format from appears in the window's lower left corner and prompts you to identify the source for the format you want to copy.

3. Double-click in the selection bar adjacent to the paragraph with the format that you want to copy.

For this example, select the paragraph under the "Advanced Registration" heading.

Rather than highlight the selected text, the program underlines the text with a dotted underline (see fig. 4.43).

4. Press **Return** or press **Enter**.

Word copies the paragraph format of the underlined paragraph to the one that has the insertion point.

To copy character formatting to the paragraph that has the insertion point, follow the same steps. Instead of selecting the entire "source" paragraph in Step 3, however, select only a few characters and make sure that the first character has all the styles you want to copy. The copied formatting then is applied to any characters you type at the insertion point. Unless you type, however, no formatting is copied because you haven't selected any text in which to copy the formatting.

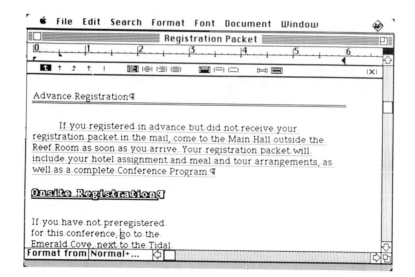

Fig. 4.43

*Word copies the
paragraph
formatting of
the underlined
paragraph to the
paragraph
containing the
insertion point.*

The weakness of the first Command-Option-V method is that you can apply the copied format to only one paragraph at a time. You can bypass this limitation by using a variation of the Command-Option-V shortcut: first select the *source* paragraph, then copy its formatting, and finally apply that formatting to another paragraph or group of paragraphs.

Using the second Command-Option-V method, copy the format of a selected paragraph to other paragraphs by doing the following:

1. Select the paragraph with the desired formatting by double-clicking in the selection bar adjacent to the paragraph.

Again, select the paragraph under the "Advanced Registration" heading.

2. Press **Command-Option-V**.

The message Format to appears in the window's lower left corner.

3. Select the paragraph you want to format (or select contiguous paragraphs by dragging through them).

In this case, select the second "Onsite Registration" paragraph. Word underlines the paragraph (see fig. 4.44).

4. Press **Return** or press **Enter**.

To give you more practice with the second method, copy the format of the paragraph under the "Advance Registration" heading to the last two paragraphs under the "Payment" heading.

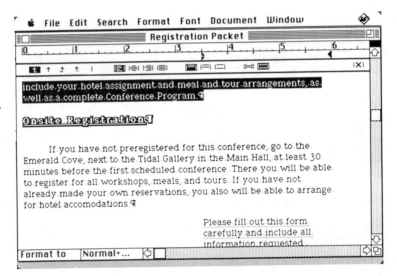

Fig. 4.44

Word copies the paragraph formatting of the highlighted paragraph to the underlined paragraph.

Preparing To Lay Out Pages and Sections

If you have followed the exercises in this chapter and perhaps experimented a bit on your own, the sample document may look a little odd. You use this document in the next chapter as you learn how to format pages and sections in preparation for printing, so practice the techniques you just learned in order to reformat the Registration Packet document (see fig. 4.45). The following are the necessary formatting specifications:

- *Title*: Geneva; 18 pt; bold; centered; 15-pt space above, 10-pt space below; double line below; 1.5-inch right indent; Keep With Next ¶

- *Headings*: Geneva; 14 pt; bold; 15-pt space above, 10-pt space below; double line below; 2-inch right indent; Keep With Next ¶

- *Bulleted list*: Times; 14 pt; 0.75-inch left indent, -0.06-inch first-line indent; 6-pt space before; 1.5-inch right indent; Keep With Next ¶ for all but final paragraph

- *Body text*: Times; 14 pt; justified; 0.5-inch left indent, 0.5-inch first-line indent; 1.5-inch right indent

- *Bold notes*: Times; 14 pt; bold; left; 1.5-inch right indent; Keep Lines Together

- *Small note*: Geneva; 9 pt; 0.75-inch left indent, -0.13-inch first-line indent; 1.5-inch right indent; Keep Lines Together

- *Boxed list*: Times; 12 pt; 0.5-inch left indent; 4-inch decimal tab; shadow box; 1.25-inch right indent; Keep Lines Together

---

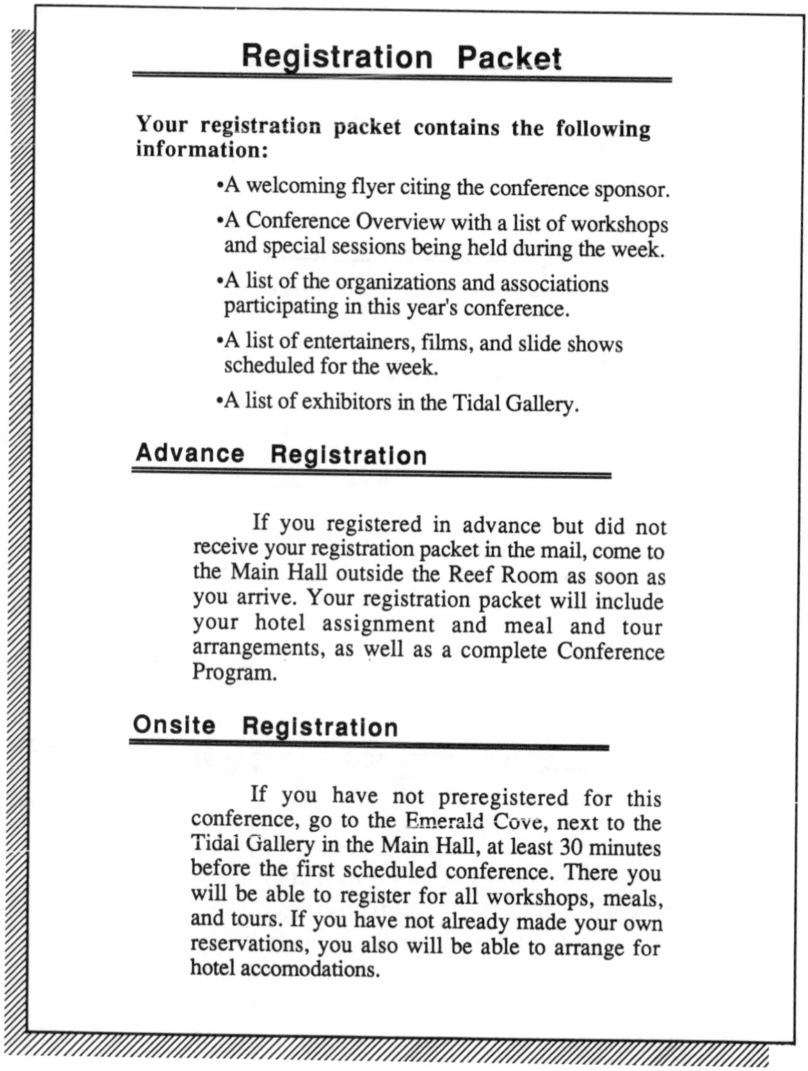

Registration Packet

Your registration packet contains the following information:

- •A welcoming flyer citing the conference sponsor.
- •A Conference Overview with a list of workshops and special sessions being held during the week.
- •A list of the organizations and associations participating in this year's conference.
- •A list of entertainers, films, and slide shows scheduled for the week.
- •A list of exhibitors in the Tidal Gallery.

Advance Registration

If you registered in advance but did not receive your registration packet in the mail, come to the Main Hall outside the Reef Room as soon as you arrive. Your registration packet will include your hotel assignment and meal and tour arrangements, as well as a complete Conference Program.

Onsite Registration

If you have not preregistered for this conference, go to the Emerald Cove, next to the Tidal Gallery in the Main Hall, at least 30 minutes before the first scheduled conference. There you will be able to register for all workshops, meals, and tours. If you have not already made your own reservations, you also will be able to arrange for hotel accomodations.

Fig. 4.45a

The Registration Packet document with full paragraph and character formatting.

Fig 4.45b

Page 2 of the Registration Packet document.

Please fill out this form carefully and include all information requested. When you have finished filling out this information, please bring your complete registration packet to the appropriate registration table. After you pay for the conference and hotel, you will be issued a conference badge with your name and affiliation, and individual meal tickets

Registration Fees

If you are registering onsite, the following costs apply:

All workshops, meals, and tours	$750.00*
Workshops only	$500.00
Each meal	$25.00
Each accompanying participant	$350.00

*Tours are free but you must sign up in advance to ensure a place on the bus.

Payment

Total payment must accompany your registration. To receive a copy of the proceedings, include an additional $65 with your registration.

Payment must be made on a bank draft in U.S. dollars and drawn on a U.S. bank or charged to your VISA, MasterCard, or American Express account.

You now know how to establish general formats for a document. But your documents will not be polished until you learn how to implement page layout. The process of achieving the proper balance of the text elements on a page often affects your choices of paragraph and character formatting. In Chapter 5, you learn how to organize a document into pages and sections and how to mold these units into a unified publication.

Laying Out Pages

If you have gone to the trouble of preparing a document for the purpose of influencing the thoughts and actions of other people, you would be foolish not to take full advantage of the power of Word and your Macintosh to make that document as effective as possible. In Chapter 4, you experimented with Word's potential when you used different fonts and styles and when you tested the program's capability to adjust spacing within and among paragraphs. You also saw how a carefully thought-out style can make a great difference in a document's effect on its intended audience. But the Word program offers even greater flexibility with its Page Setup and Section commands. These commands give you control over page layouts and enable you to produce innovative designs that complement your text and help you get your message across.

The program's basic layout tool is the Page Setup command, found on the File menu. You use this command to tell the program how you want it to handle such elements as margins (including the inner margins of documents that will be bound after printing), page depth, footnote placement, and page numbers. The Page Setup command also is the vehicle for giving special printing instructions. The program can handle odd-sized pages or a vertical printing orientation. (Of course, your printer has to be capable of handling the special instructions, too, or you won't get the results you are seeking.)

The Page Setup options generally are all you need to set up a "normal" document—a document that has only one column of text per page. To create a document that has a more complex page layout, however, you need to use Word, Version 3's, new Section command, found on the

Format menu. With this command, you can enlarge your repertoire of layout options by breaking a document into parts. You then can give each part its own distinct layout. You can designate any amount of a document as a section—from one graphic or one character to the entire file.

The section concept seems so simple that you easily can miss its full significance. One obvious use of sections is to establish separate page-numbering schemes within a large document (for different chapters of a report, for example). The program handles this task with considerable versatility. But Word's capability to establish separate page-numbering schemes within different sections is only the tip of the iceberg. Whenever you want to modify the current layout rules—to change margins or the number of columns, for example—you can establish a new section that Word integrates, without skipping a beat, into the document's main body.

In Chapter 5, you learn the parameters of a standard page as you explore the options in the Page Setup dialog box. Then you look at the additional options available with the new Section command. Finally, you practice using the two commands as you continue to prepare the Registration Packet for printing.

Working with the Page Setup Command

You use the Page Setup command, as its name implies, to define the layout of a document's printed pages. The Page Setup command is available in both the short and the full File menus. Choosing Page Setup from the full File menu produces the dialog box shown in figure 5.1.

If you choose Page Setup from the short File menu (see fig. 5.2), Word limits the options in the dialog box to those you use most frequently and reserves the more esoteric options for the full version.

Because the program's default settings are sufficient for printing a normal document, you may never need to wander from this beaten path. Don't be intimidated, therefore, by the Page Setup dialog box. Until you have learned more about the options, simply accept the program's defaults. After you understand the basic concepts of page layout, experiment with the options that appeal to your imagination. Bear in mind, though, that your printer must be capable of accommodating the options you select.

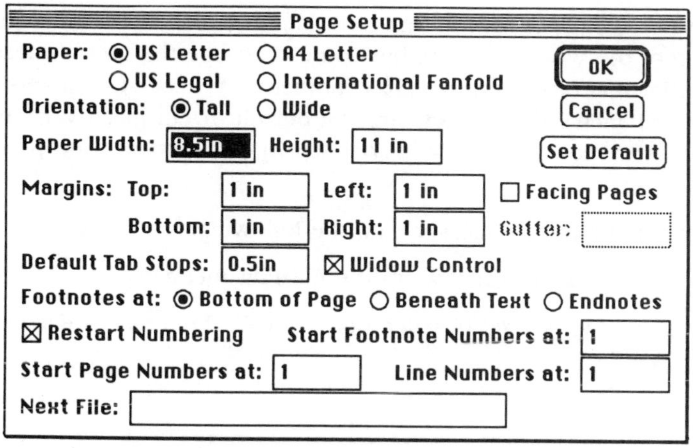

```
═══════════════════════ Page Setup ═══════════════════════
Paper:  ⦿ US Letter    ○ A4 Letter                ┌──────────┐
        ○ US Legal     ○ International Fanfold     │    OK    │
Orientation:   ⦿ Tall  ○ Wide                      └──────────┘
Paper Width: ▮8.5in▮   Height: [11 in]             ┌──────────┐
                                                   │  Cancel  │
Margins: Top:   [1 in]      Left:  [1 in]          └──────────┘
                                          ☐ Facing Pages  ┌────────────┐
         Bottom: [1 in]      Right: [1 in]               │ Set Default│
                                         Gutter: [        ]└────────────┘
Default Tab Stops: [0.5in]    ⊠ Widow Control
Footnotes at: ⦿ Bottom of Page  ○ Beneath Text  ○ Endnotes
⊠ Restart Numbering    Start Footnote Numbers at: [1]
Start Page Numbers at: [1]        Line Numbers at: [1]
Next File: [                                        ]
```

Fig. 5.1

The full-menu Page Setup dialog box.

```
═══════════════════════ Page Setup ═══════════════════════
Paper:  ⦿ US Letter    ○ A4 Letter                ┌──────────┐
        ○ US Legal     ○ International Fanfold     │    OK    │
Orientation:   ⦿ Tall  ○ Wide                      └──────────┘
Paper Width: ▮8.5in▮   Height: [11 in]             ┌──────────┐
                                                   │  Cancel  │
Margins: Top:   [0.5in]     Left:  [0.81in]        └──────────┘
                                                   ┌────────────┐
         Bottom: [0.19in]   Right: [0.75in]        │ Set Default│
                                                   └────────────┘
```

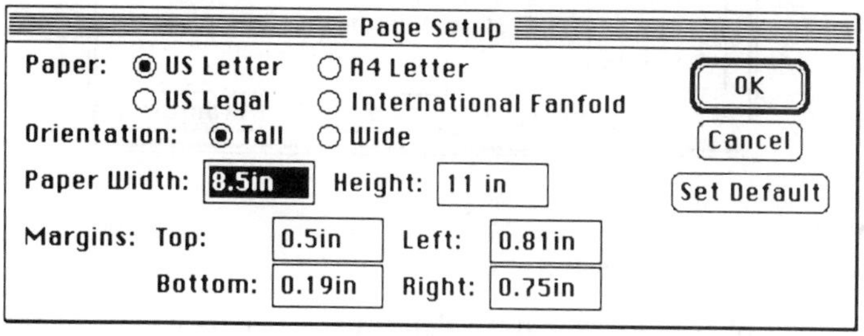

Fig. 5.2

The short-menu Page Setup dialog box.

Choosing Paper Size and Orientation

Word displays as options in the Page Setup dialog box four standard paper sizes: US Letter (8.5 by 11 inches)—the program's default size; US Legal (8.5 by 14 inches); A4 Letter (8.27 by 11.69 inches); and International Fanfold (8.25 by 12 inches). A4 Letter and International Fanfold are European paper sizes.

Unless you have changed the default paper selection in the Page Setup dialog box, the program selects the button for US Letter and displays the dimensions for US Letter paper in the Paper Width and Height boxes. If you click one of the other Paper buttons, the dimensions change to reflect the size of the new selection. For example, if you click A4 Letter, the default width and height settings change to 8.27 and 11.69, respectively.

By default, the paper sizes are given in inches in the American-language version of the Word program, but you can change the unit of measure to centimeters (rounded to 2.55 centimeters = 1 inch) or points (72 points = 1 inch). Centimeters are the default in European versions of the program; points commonly are used by typographers and printing companies.

To change the unit of measure, do the following:

1. Choose **Preferences** from the full Edit menu.

2. Select the desired Measure option in the Preferences dialog box (see fig. 5.3).

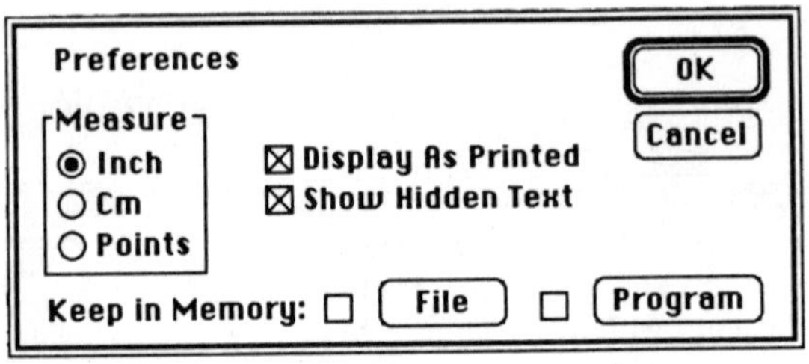

Fig. 5.3

The Preferences dialog box.

3. Click **OK** or press **Return**.

Your choice of paper orientation determines whether your document is printed vertically on the paper (Tall) or horizontally (Wide). Tall is the default setting.

Setting Paper Width and Height

The program uses the settings in the Paper Width and Height fields, along with margins and other formatting information, to determine where on the paper to print your document. As we mentioned in the preceding section, the default Paper Width and Height options (8.5 by 11 inches) correspond to US Letter, and the dimensions automatically change if you specify one of the program's other paper-size options. You don't have to stay with the four stock selections, however. If you have odd-sized paper, you can adjust the options to fit your paper size.

To print on paper that is not one of the four standard sizes, do the following:

1. Choose **Page Setup** from the short or full File menu.

2. Type the desired paper width in the `Paper Width` box.

3. Type the desired height in the `Height` box.

4. Click **OK** or press **Return**.

Setting Margins

As you learned in Chapter 4, a margin is the distance between the edge of the paper (determined by the `Paper Width` and `Height` settings) and the printed area of a document. By default, the program establishes 1-inch margins at the top and bottom, and 1.25-inch margins on the left and right of the printed area.

Do the following to change the margins in your document:

1. Choose **Page Setup** from the short or full File menu.

2. Enter the new margin dimensions in the `Top`, `Bottom`, `Left`, and `Right` margin boxes.

Unless you have changed the unit of measure in the `Preferences` dialog box, type the dimensions in inches.

3. Click **OK** or press **Return**.

Adjusting the Gutter on Facing Pages

If you print a simple letter or report—a collection of loose pages that readers leaf through—the right and left margins should be the same throughout your document. If, however, you plan to print your document on both sides of the paper and then bind the document, the margins at the center of the facing pages (the right margin of left pages, and the left margin of right pages) should be slightly wider than the outer margins. The wider margins allow for the space taken up by the binding. The center margin in a bound document is called the *gutter*.

To adjust the width of the gutter, follow these steps:

1. Choose **Page Setup** from the full File menu.

2. Select **Facing Pages**.

This option is not available in the short Page Setup dialog box.

The `Gutter` option now becomes available. (The `Gutter` option in figure 5.1 is not available because the `Facing Pages` option is not active.)

3. Enter in the Gutter box the amount of space you want to allow for the gutter.

4. Click **OK** or press **Return**.

The measurement you specify in the Gutter box is added to the right margin of your left pages and to the left margin of your right pages. For example, if you click Facing Pages and then specify a 0.5-inch gutter to facing pages with default and right margin settings of 1.25 inches, the right margin of left pages and the left margin of right pages will be 1.75 inches.

Setting Tab Stops

Word, like most conventional typewriters, automatically sets tab stops at standard intervals across a page. When you press Tab, the insertion point moves to the next tab stop to the right.

The Default Tab Stops setting in the Page Setup dialog box determines the distance between standard tab stops. By default, this setting is 0.5 inch, but you can make it any distance you want simply by typing a new measurement in the Default Tab Stops box. If you set custom tab stops, as you did in Chapter 4, they override in the ruler all default tab stops to the left of the custom tab stops.

Taking Care of Widows

A *widow* is a paragraph's last line that is cut off from the rest of the paragraph by a page break and is placed at the top of the next page. An *orphan* is a paragraph's first line that is separated from its paragraph by a page break and is left at the bottom of the page. The program selects by default the Widow Control option in the Page Setup dialog box. This option prevents the program from printing either a widow or an orphan at the top or bottom of a page, respectively. If you click Widow Control to turn it off, the program prints as many lines as possible on a page, even if a line becomes stranded.

Specifying Footnote Styles

Positioning footnotes on a page has created headaches for many writers of research reports and technical papers. The program takes away the pain of organizing footnotes on your pages and gives you three footnote formatting options at the same time. As a result, you can relax while your computer positions your footnotes. If you want, the program also automatically numbers—and renumbers—your footnotes. Both the position and the numbering of footnotes are controlled by options in the Page Setup dialog box.

The process for creating footnotes is discussed in detail in Chapter 20. For now, you need to know only that the footnote options in the Page Setup dialog box work with options pertaining to footnotes in other dialog boxes.

The conventions for footnote placement vary, but the program has enough options to satisfy any employer's or publisher's requirements. The Bottom of Page option (the default setting) prints the footnote flush with the bottom margin of the page on which its reference mark appears. The Beneath Text option prints the footnote immediately after the last paragraph on the page. With this option, you have no white space before the footnote if the text fills less than a full page. The Endnotes option tells the program to group the footnotes at the end of the document. If you divide your document into sections, however, this option places each section's footnotes at the end of that section, not at the end of the document.

The Format menu's Section dialog box gives you still more options. You can control footnote numbering in a variety of ways. If you click Restart Numbering after you click Bottom of Page or Beneath Text, Word restarts the numbering at each page break. If your document has sections and you click Endnotes, Word restarts the numbering at each section break. If you do not click Restart Numbering, Word numbers the footnotes consecutively throughout the document.

The number in the Start Footnote Numbers at box determines the starting number for footnotes. You probably will leave this setting at 1. If, however, you want to number consecutively the footnotes in a group of documents—for example, if you have separated the chapters in a thesis into their own documents—you can set the starting footnote number in each successive document to one higher than the number of the last footnote in the preceding document.

Numbering Pages and Lines

Like most word-processing programs, Word, Version 3—at your request—numbers your pages. You also can tell Word to number the lines of your document and to print, for convenient reference, the numbers along the left edge of each page. Your entries in the Start Page Numbers at and the Line Numbers at boxes determine the first number in the sequence for pages and lines, respectively.

Linking Documents

With the Next File option in the Page Setup dialog box, you can link documents for printing. This feature, new in Word, Version 3, is convenient when you work on a large project, such as a book. You can divide the project into smaller, more manageable modules and then link the modules at print time. Several people can work on different parts of a large project and combine their efforts into one printed document.

To link a document to the end of the current document during printing, do the following:

1. Choose **Page Setup** from the full File menu.

2. Type in the **Next File** box the name of the document you want to link to the current one.

3. Click **OK** or press **Return**.

4. Repeat this process for each document you want to link.

After printing the current document, the program automatically loads and prints the linked document and maintains consistent page, line, and footnote numbering, as required.

Applying the Page Setup Options

After you are satisfied with the selections and specifications you have made in the Page Setup dialog box, apply them to the current document by clicking OK in the top right corner of the dialog box. If you get cold feet and want to cancel the settings, simply click Cancel to restore the previous set of options.

You also can click the Set Default button to tell the program to apply these settings as the default for *all* new documents. When you choose the Set Default option, the program stores the settings in a file called Word Settings and then automatically applies your custom settings to your documents—even if you quit the program and then restart it. (You can restore the original default settings by deleting the Word Settings file from the Finder.)

Choosing the options in the Page Setup dialog box is all you need to do to lay out pages in a standard, single-column document. If you take full advantage of the Page Setup options and the page-break controls for formatting paragraphs (discussed in Chapter 4), a simple document virtually lays itself out with little contribution from you.

If you make a mistake, however, the program provides two commands to check and refine your page layouts: the Print Repaginate and the Page Preview commands. You probably used the Document menu's Print Repaginate command to paginate a document in Chapter 3. You also used the Page Preview command in Chapter 4 to view side-by-side paragraphs. In Chapter 6 you will learn how to use the Page Preview command to view page layouts. Before you actually lay out a document, however, make things a little more challenging by adding the Section command to your repertoire.

Working with Sections

Often, an element of your document may not fit in the universal page setup scheme. You may want to number the introductory pages of a long report in *i, ii, iii* style, for example, rather than in standard *1, 2, 3* style. Or you may want to run a heading across the top of three columns of text. At times like these, you probably will start thinking of sections.

With the Section command, you can create—in just one document—a complex business report with several distinct sections (for example, a letter of transmittal, front matter, the text, appendixes, and an index). Each section can have a distinct page format, including running heads, footnote position, column layout, and page number type and location. You also can use the Section command to control column breaks when you're printing more than one column on the page—a handy feature indeed, as you'll see.

Instead of pausing here to marvel at all the innovative touches made possible by the Section command, however, limit yourself to examining a single, dignified application of this command (see fig. 5.4). Your own imagination then can take over. Remember: The section concept may be simple and sensible, but it offers great potential.

To create a section, position the insertion point where you want the section to begin and then press Command-Enter. This step inserts a section mark—a double dotted line—across the width of your document. You can divide a document into as many sections as you want. As you will see, you have a great deal of freedom to decide where to begin

Fig. 5.4

The front page of a flyer demonstrating the use of the Section command to integrate different page formats within a single page.

Single-column section

Two-column section

Single-column section

Two-column section

Info Express Inc.

14320 NE 21st Street   Suite 18   Bellevue, WA 98007   206-641-3434

THE RTDDA SYSTEM
Real-Time Data Display and Acquisition

This is the system that has revolution-ized **real-time** acquisition and imaging of sonar survey data.

Developed by Info Express Inc., this versatile, compact, affordable, and well-tested system includes multiple **80286 and 68020 microprocessors** in its CPU (central processing unit) and uses a **super-high-resolution color monitor** to display images of the seafloor and seismic profile data.

Scanstore and **Scanzoom**, the system's user-friendly software modules for realtime and postprocessing analysis, allow random access to 120 megabytes of survey data. While the system is online, a laser disc drive records the data on **optical disc cartridges**, each storing the equivalent of **30 hours** of sonar records.

The RTDDA system is a combination of computer hardware and software that is licensed to individual users for the purpose of recording sonar data on WORM (write once, read many) cartridges and performing onboard or postsurvey data analysis. Our advanced image-processing techniques make subtle changes in bottom reflectivity, which are not evident on the graphic paper record, easily discernable on the high-resolution screen.

The zoom feature and digitizing capability are extremely useful for target analysis and for interpreting the sedimentary structure from the profile data. Cartographically accurate mosaics of the seafloor can be created using a special software module that corrects the tracks for true towfish position and selects the optimum portion of each trackline record.

An Offer You Can't Refuse

Send us a sample of your analog or digital data on magnetic media. We will create a file on optical disc and send you a hard-copy sample of what we can do to enhance the image. Compare it to the original graphic record and you to will be convinced of the advantages of the RTDDA image processing system.

each section and to coordinate page numbers, footnotes, and headers and footers among sections.

Until you break up your document by adding a section mark, Word treats your entire document as one section. When you create a new section, the program automatically gives the new section the properties of the section preceding it. You can change these properties by clicking an insertion point in the new section and choosing the Section command from the Format menu. This step displays the Section dialog box with all its options (see fig. 5.5).

After you briefly examine the Section options in the following paragraphs, you practice using the options to solve a thorny publications problem.

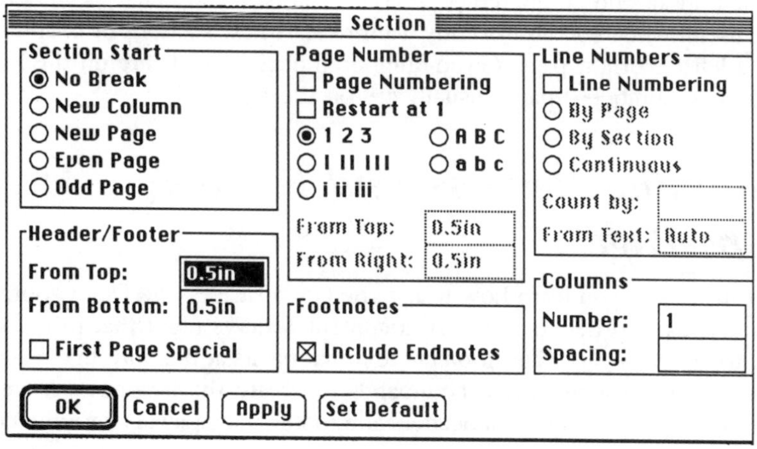

Fig. 5.5

The Section dialog box.

Controlling the Section Starting Point

With the options in the Section Start area of the Section dialog box, you can control where the new section is printed in your document. Examine each option to determine which choice is the best for each new section.

When you select the No Break option, the program prints sections continuously instead of starting each section on a new page. The most common reason for selecting No Break is to create a page that has both single- and multiple-column layouts (see fig. 5.4).

If, however, the preceding section and the new one have the same number of columns, you can apply the New Column option to start a new section while simultaneously forcing a new column that begins with the text below the insertion point. If the new section does not have the same number of columns as the preceding section, the new column is forced to the top of the next page. Any section formatting (such as line numbering) begins with the new column.

Clicking the default New Page option forces a page break at the section mark. You may want to start a section on a new page, for example, when you begin a new topic in a report.

The Even Page option not only starts the section on a new page but also makes the new page an even-numbered one by inserting a blank page if necessary. Similarly, if you select the Odd Page option, the program starts printing the new section on the next odd-numbered page and inserts a blank page before the new section if the preceding section ended on an odd-numbered page. The Even Page and Odd Page options are useful when you consistently want to start new sections or chapters on a left or a right page. (Even-numbered pages usually are on the left side; odd-numbered pages usually are on the right side.)

Positioning Headers and Footers on the Page

In Chapter 13, you learn how to use the Open Header and Open Footer commands in order to add to a document *headers* (text that prints at the top of each page) and *footers* (text that prints at the bottom of each page). You must use these commands to create the header or footer text. Only the placement of headers and footers on a page is determined in the Section dialog box.

The default placement of headers and footers is 0.5 inches from the top or bottom of the page. To change the default setting of the headers and footers in the section that has the insertion point, do the following:

1. Choose **Section** from the Format menu.

2. Type the desired position in the From Top or From Bottom box.

(You also can use the margins icon in the Page Preview command; see Chapter 6.)

3. Click **OK** or press **Return**.

If you inadvertently specify that the header or footer be printed outside the currently specified margin (within the text area), the program prints the header or footer exactly where you specify and adjusts the margins to accommodate the header or footer text.

If you select the First Page Special option, the program adds two commands—Add First Header and Add First Footer—to the Document menu. With these commands, you can create a different header and footer for the first page of a document or section. If you don't want a header or footer printed on the first page, however, just choose the Add First Header or Add First Footer command and make sure that the window that the program displays is blank.

Adding Page Numbers to Your Document

Have you ever dropped a folder filled with unbound, unnumbered pages from a document? Do you have any desire to *repeat* that experience? To prevent the resulting chaos from the preceding scenario, you can choose from several options in the Page Number area of the Section dialog box. You can add page numbers to your document, restart the numbering sequence at *1*, specify the number format, and adjust the position of the number on the page.

One of the most common reasons for dividing a document into sections is to accommodate the numbering of pages within chapters or other distinct units. Clicking the Page Numbering option turns on page numbering and all its options for the current section. An alternative to specifying page numbers in the Section dialog box is including them in a header or footer by clicking the page number icon in the Header or Footer window. (You learn how to display these windows in Chapter 13.) You also can add page numbers with the page number icon in the Page Preview window (described in Chapter 6).

Regardless of the method you use to assign page numbers, the numbering format is determined with the Page Number options in the Section dialog box. For example, if your document includes separately numbered introductory materials—such as a table of contents, a preface, and an acknowledgment page—tradition demands that you restart page numbering at the beginning of the main text. You start the main text in a new section and click the Restart at 1 option for that section. (The Restart at 1 option affects page numbering whether Page Numbering is selected in the Section dialog box or the page number icon is clicked in the Page Preview, Header, or Footer window.)

The program provides several formats for numbering pages—numeric (1, 2, 3); upper- or lowercase alphabetic (A, B, C; a, b, c); and upper- or lowercase Roman numerals (I, II, III; i, ii, iii). You can change the number format within a document by creating a new section, clicking Restart at 1, and selecting the new format.

To include a section identification with each page number (for example, *A-1*, *A-2*, *A-14*; or *1.1*, *1.2*, *1.14*), you should put the page number in a header or footer rather than set the page number from the Section dialog box.

When you choose numbering schemes for the sections in your document, bear in mind that people often associate certain types of information with certain numbering formats. For example, lowercase Roman numerals often are used for a book's front matter, and capital letters frequently designate appendix pages (*A-1*, *A-2*, and so forth). Ask the following two questions to develop a pagination sequence for your document: (1) Does the sequence help your readers know where they are? (2) Does the sequence help them find what they're looking for?

The entries in the two boxes at the bottom of the Page Number area designate where page numbers are printed on a page. The default settings are 0.5 inch from the top of the page and 0.5 inch from the right edge of the page, but you can change these settings and print the page numbers elsewhere in the margin.

The number in the From Right field is the distance that page numbers will be printed from the outside edge of each page if you select the Facing Pages option in the Page Setup dialog box. Thus, by default, page numbers are printed 0.5 inch from the left edge of the paper on even-numbered (left) pages, and 0.5 inch from the right edge of the paper on odd-numbered (right) pages.

Including Endnotes in a Section

Two options—Footnotes at in the Page Setup dialog box and Include Endnotes in the Section dialog box—work together to control whether footnotes are printed at the bottom of the page that has their footnote references, at the end of a section, or at the end of the document.

The default setting in the Page Setup dialog box causes the program to print a footnote at the bottom of the page on which its reference mark appears. To print footnotes at the end of a section, however, first click the Endnotes option in the Page Setup dialog box and then select the Include Endnotes option in the Section dialog box (the default). If you have not created any sections, the footnotes are printed at the end of the document. To group all footnotes at the end of a document that has several sections, first click the Endnotes option in the Page Setup dialog box and then deselect the Include Endnotes option for every section except the last one. You can use the same technique to print several sections' endnotes together at certain section breaks.

Adding Line Numbers

Some documents, such as legal documents, often include line numbers. You easily can add line numbers to your text and control their sequence by selecting one or more of the Line Numbers options in the Section dialog box. Turn on line numbering by clicking the Line Numbering option. Until you complete this step, the rest of the options in this area of the dialog box remain unselectable.

The program adds line numbers to blank lines created by pressing Return or Enter, but does not add them to the lines added by the line-spacing options in the Paragraph dialog box. Footnotes are not numbered, but graphics are; the number appears in the margin next to the bottom left corner of the graphic. If you add or delete lines of text or graphics, the program automatically renumbers all lines for that page or section.

The default sequence for numbering lines is By Page, starting with the number *1* at the top of each page. Two other options are available: By Section and Continuous. Clicking the By Section option causes the program to restart the numbering sequence at the beginning of each selected section. If, however, you want the line numbers to run continuously throughout a document, choose the Continuous option.

In the Count by box, you instruct the program to number lines at regular intervals. The default setting—1—numbers every line, but you can change this number to any one you want. You might, for example, number every 5th or every 10th line.

The entry in the From Text box determines the distance between the line numbers and the text. With a single column of text, the default setting (Auto) places the line numbers 0.25 inch to the left of the text. With multiple columns, the default setting places the numbers 0.13 inch to the left of each column. You can, as usual, change the setting to suit your taste and the requirements of your document.

Creating Multiple Columns

The last two options in the Section dialog box control how many columns are printed on each page and the amount of space between the columns. Even if you specify multiple columns, your document is always displayed as a single column in the normal document window. You must choose the Page Preview command (explained in the next chapter) to see how multiple columns look when they are printed.

The entry in the Number box determines the number of columns printed across a page. Taste and readability are the primary limits on the number of columns you can create. The default is a single 6-inch-wide column, based on the default settings of 1.25 inches for right and left margins on standard 8.5-by-11-inch paper.

If you create a two-column text by typing *2* in the Number box, the program automatically inserts a 0.5-inch space between the columns. This number is displayed in the Spacing box. You can make the space narrower or wider by typing another measurement in this box.

Putting the Section Command To Work

How do you put to creative use the options provided by the Page Setup and Section commands? Set up a test case with the Registration Packet document you created in Chapter 4.

Suppose that, at your boss's request, you have compiled a Registration Packet document for the International Pacific Oceanographic Conference (see fig. 4.45). You feel pretty smug after having produced an attractive two-page piece that presents the conference information in clean, readable form. You even managed to find a decent page break and to include both double-underlines and a shadow box without sinking to the "cute" level. Quietly pleased, you deposit the printed conference flyer on your boss's desk as you leave your office.

The next day, however, the president emeritus of your company arrives, with flyer in hand. He congratulates you on your fine work and says the flyer is just perfect, but he also wants to see—on the first page—a list of the 32 companies exhibiting at the conference. He's reluctant to ask, but he would appreciate your boxing the list—perhaps with a "doodad" or two—similar to the one in a mailer he received recently from the International Society for the Preservation of Amoeba Rights.

Flustered, you try hard not to panic, as you see your state-of-the-art document tottering on the brink of disaster. You stare at the list of companies. How in the world do you discreetly advertise a multitude of exhibitors and not wreak havoc with page 1 of your flyer?

The program comes to the rescue: this job is for the Section command. You mentally run through your options. The insert does not need to be flashy if it is spacious and well presented. What if you make the list in 6-point type? Can you squeeze in three—perhaps four—columns? Can you shoehorn the list, box and all, into the bottom 2 inches of the page?

Because multiple columns are required, you must create a new section. Follow the steps in the next exercise to learn how to add the list to the document.

First, add the list of company names (see fig. 5.6) to the bottom of the Registration Packet document. In Chapter 6, the list of names eventually is moved to the bottom of the first page of the document; but, for now, just type and format the names at the end of the Registration Packet. After you type all the names, provide a known starting point for formatting by selecting the list and clicking the X at the right end of the ruler in order to apply the program's default paragraph styles.

ABC Oil and Gas Exploration	Naval Ocean Systems, Inc.
Big Business Mining Operators	Neptune Diving Association
Celestial Navigation Equipment	Ocean Engineering Association
Deep-Sea Submersible, Inc.	Oceanographic Society
Environmental Watch Council	Offshore Systems, Inc.
Faulty Seismographic Institute	Oil and Gas Equipment Co.
Geotechnics, Inc.	Petroleum Council of America
Hydrological Instruments Co.	Quality Navigation Systems
Info Express Inc.	Rope Masters, Ltd.
Institute for Ocean Sciences	Seaman Brothers Nautical Supply
Jurassic Marine Institute	Tectonics, Inc.
Kelp Processors Incorporated	Underwater Technology
Lighthouse Boat Builders	Vortex Deep Sea Gear
Marine Surveyors, Ltd	Water Express River Rafting
Maritime Society	Xcellent Mapping and Surveying
National Oceanographic Institute	Zytex Computers, Inc.

Fig. 5.6

The list of exhibitors.

The entire document currently is a single section. Before you apply section formatting to the list, you must separate the list from the rest of the document with a section break.

To create a new section, do the following:

1. Place the insertion point where you want the new section to start.

In this case, place the insertion point immediately before the first name in the list.

2. Press **Command-Enter**.

Word forces a section break and marks it with a double dotted line. Everything above the line is in the first section; everything below the line is in the second section.

Your next task is to decide how many columns to use and what size to make the characters. This step usually requires experimenting. We decided to push our Apple LaserWriter to the limit by designing four columns of 6-point type.

To break the list into columns, do the following:

1. Choose **Section** from the Format menu. (The insertion point still should be in the second section.)

2. Click **New Column** in the Section Start area.

3. Type in the Columns area the number of columns you want in the Number box.

In this case, type *4*.

4. Specify the amount of space between columns in the Spacing box.

In this case, type *0.4*.

5. Press **Return**.

Word formats the entire list as a four-column section. The immediate effect is to squeeze the list into a much narrower space and to force the long company names to wrap to several lines. To solve this problem, change the font and size to 6-point Times.

Because the 32 names in the list fit easily into one column, your next task involves forcing the program to start new columns at the 9th, 17th, and 25th names by creating short sections of the desired depth.

Do the following to force column breaks:

1. Click an insertion point in front of the name with which you want to start a new column.

In this case, click the insertion point in front of the 9th name.

2. Press **Command-Enter**.

The double dotted line that appears above the selected line is a section mark.

Repeat Steps 1 and 2 two times with the insertion point in front of the 17th and 25th names. The exhibitors list now is formatted as four columns of 6-point Times type. Figure 5.7 shows how your screen should look. (In the next chapter, you will see how the columns look in the finished document.)

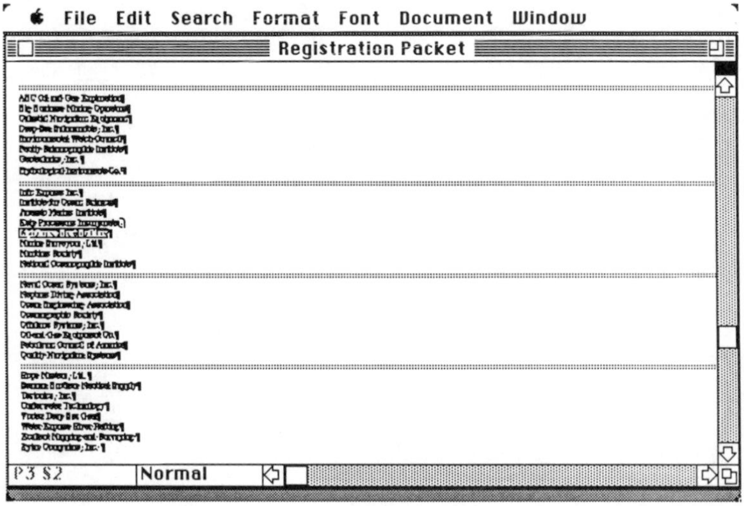

Fig. 5.7

The list of exhibitors formatted as four sections (columns) of equal depth.

But what about other problems? Can 32 company names eventually coexist on the same page as a list of 5 enclosures? Is 6-point type perceptible to the human eye? For answers to these and other questions, read Chapter 6, in which you learn how to preview and change your page layouts by using Word, Version 3's, new Page Preview command. As you broaden your repertoire of formatting options, you begin to understand that being able to modify your pages to make them "look right" before you print them is important, and timesaving, too.

Previewing Pages

The Macintosh is better than most computers at displaying text on-screen the way it is printed on paper. But Word still is limited in what it can display in the normal document window. For example, the document window does not show headers, footers, footnotes, and page numbers the way they are printed. Nor does it show side-by-side paragraphs or more than one column of text.

You don't have to resort to guessing how your document will look, however. With the program's Page Preview command, new in Version 3, you have not only a bird's-eye view of your pages before you print them but also the chance to make changes to the pages and to see quickly the results on-screen.

In subsequent chapters in this book, you occasionally will see graphics we created by using the Page Preview command. We designed these graphics to show you how your document should look after you complete the steps in the examples. The powerful Page Preview command is equally useful to you, however, when you want to see the results of your own formatting.

In this chapter, you learn how to activate the Page Preview window and to scroll through its bird's-eye view of your document. You also magnify an area of a page to see the text more clearly. You study the Page Preview window's special features—page number icons and the markers for margins, pages, sections, headers, and footers. And you learn how to manipulate these markers to make formatting changes that otherwise would require setting Paragraph, Page Setup, and Section options. You apply these techniques to the exhibitors list that you created in Chapter 5.

Before you experiment with the Page Preview features, become familiar with the Page Preview window and how to move around it. Start by opening the Registration Packet document. Then choose Page Preview from the File menu to preview the pages of your open document.

The window displayed when you choose Page Preview looks similar to the standard document window, but the function of the Page Preview window is quite different. Against the Page Preview window's shaded background, the program displays one or two pages of a document just as the pages will look when you print them (see fig. 6.1).

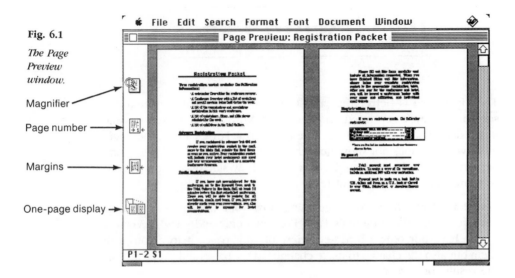

Fig. 6.1

The Page Preview window.

Magnifier

Page number

Margins

One-page display

Both the number of pages displayed in the Page Preview window and the window's display format depend on two things: whether you have formatted your document for facing pages (by choosing the Facing Pages option in the Page Setup dialog box) and where you have positioned the insertion point when you choose Page Preview. When you do not format your document for facing pages, the Page Preview window displays two pages separated by a space (see fig. 6.1). If, however, you do format your document for facing pages, the Page Preview window typically resembles the one in figure 6.2, with an even-numbered page on the left and an odd-numbered page on the right.

The pages in the Page Preview window obviously are clear enough for you to distinguish the parts of your document. Unless you have used

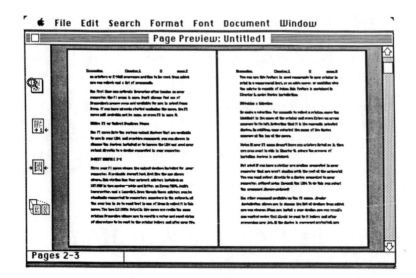

Fig. 6.2

*Previewing
facing pages.*

large type (18 points or larger), however, the pages generally are not readable. But don't worry: you can zoom the screen, as you will see, to make even the smallest type legible. Page Preview, in short, is a useful, powerful feature of Word 3.0.

With Facing Pages not selected, position the insertion point in the first page of the document and choose Page Preview; this procedure displays page 1 of the document in the left page and page 2 in the right page. Position the insertion point in the first half of page 2 and choose Page Preview to produce an identical display. However, positioning the insertion point in the second half of page 2 and choosing Page Preview displays page 2 in the left page and page 3 in the right page. This display pattern operates throughout the document. If you want to display a particular page as well as the text on the preceding page, position the insertion point in the first half of the page; if you want to display a particular page and the text on the following page, position the insertion point in the second half of the page.

With Facing Pages selected, position the insertion point in the first page of the document and choose Page Preview; this procedure displays page 1 of the document in the right page (the left page is blank). Positioning the insertion point in page 2 produces the same display. Position the insertion point in page 3 to display page 2 on the left page and page 3 on the right page. From this point, the program considers each even page and its facing odd page a set (called a *spread*). The program displays the spread no matter where within the even or odd page you position the insertion point.

Page Preview should display pages as just described. Sometimes, however, Word may display page 1 regardless of where you position the insertion point; in this case, you may need to choose Repaginate from the Document menu before choosing Page Preview, in order to get Word to display the spread you want. At other times, if you select Page Preview while working on an odd-numbered page, the program may display that page in the right page and nothing in the left page. You may find these idiosyncrasies annoying but not annoying enough to dissuade you from using the powerful page preview feature.

Scrolling in Page Preview Mode

When you work in the Page Preview window, you can use the vertical scroll bar, the scroll arrows, or the 2 and the 8 keys on your numeric keypad to scroll forward and backward through your document. If you work with facing pages, you press the 2 key to scroll to the next pair of pages, or you press the 8 key to scroll to the previous pair. Clicking the scroll bar's down- or up- arrow or clicking just below or above the scroll box moves you by the same increments forward or backward, respectively, through the document. You can move quickly through a multipage document by dragging the scroll box.

If you are not working on facing pages, the same actions move you one page at a time through the document. The following sequence occurs, for example, if pages 3 and 4 are displayed and you click the down-scroll arrow: page 3 disappears; page 4 moves to the left side of the window; and page 5 appears on the right side of the window.

To get a feel for page preview mode, move the cursor around the document on your screen. Use the scroll bar or the 2 and 8 keys on the numeric keypad to advance and backtrack through your document.

As you scroll through the document, notice how the page and section numbers (in the *P1S1* format) change in the window's lower left corner. If you have not paginated your document (by printing it or choosing Repaginate from the Document menu), Word automatically paginates the document when the program opens the Page Preview window. If the pages displayed in the Page Preview window have more than one section, the program shows the range of pages and sections, such as *P1S1-P2S4*. This message tells you that Word is displaying all the text from page 1 and section 1 through section 4 on page 2.

Note that Word does not display page numbers consecutively if you click
Restart at 1 in the Section dialog box. Clicking this box restarts page
numbering at *1* at the section break. If you click this box, Word may
display P1 even though you're not at the beginning of your document.
In such cases, the scroll box's position in the scroll bar is a good guide
to the approximate location in your document.

The Page Preview command would be useful even if its previewing function were all you could do with the command; Page Preview offers much
more, however. Now that you know your way around, tour the icons
along the left side of the Page Preview window.

Using the Page Preview Icons

Four icons lie along the left edge of the Page Preview window. The
magnifier icon, at the top, magnifies an area of the page to the text's
full printed size. Beneath the magnifier icon, the page number icon adds
and positions page numbers. The margins icon displays markers for headers, footers, page numbers, and page and section breaks. You can manipulate these markers to move the corresponding elements around on
the page. The one-page display icon, at the bottom, controls whether
you preview one or two pages at one time.

The Magnifier Icon

The program displays the pages at a reduced size so that you can preview
a full page (or two pages) of text on the Macintosh screen. Seeing the
full page allows you to examine the overall page balance. You then can
use the magnifier icon, superimposed on a page icon in the upper left
corner of the Page Preview window, to preview an area of the page in
its actual printed size.

When you magnify an area of a document, the program adds a horizontal
scroll bar to the bottom of the Page Preview window (see fig. 6.3). You
can use either this scroll bar or the 4 or 6 keys on the numeric keypad
to scroll left or right across the magnified page. You also can use either
the vertical scroll bar or the 2 or 8 keys on the numeric keypad to view
up or down the magnified page. While Word magnifies the page, you
cannot select the other icons in the Page Preview window.

To magnify an area of the page, do the following:

1. Click the magnifier icon.

Fig. 6.3

A magnified page.

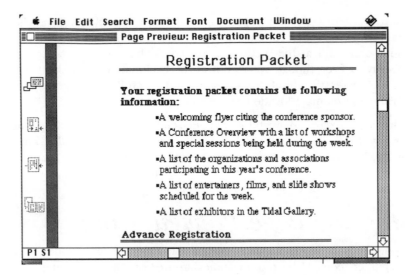

The pointer assumes the shape of the magnifying glass superimposed on the miniature page.

2. Drag the magnifying glass to the text you want to examine more closely.

3. Click the mouse button to display the text in its actual printed size.

Word displays a screenful of text; the area beneath the magnifying glass is at midscreen. The magnifying glass changes back to a pointer, and the page icon from which you dragged the magnifying glass changes to a reduced page icon.

4. Now use the horizontal and vertical scroll bars or the appropriate numeric keypad keys, to display different parts of the magnified page.

Although you can view the different parts of your document while you use the magnifying mode, you cannot change a magnified area. If you decide to make changes after you examine the pages, you must return to the Page Preview window or to the document window. To return to the Page Preview window, click the reduced page icon in the upper left corner of the window. The screen then displays the normal Page Preview window and its two miniature pages.

An alternative to selecting the magnifier icon is double-clicking the area you want to enlarge. The program zooms in on the text, and the magnifier icon changes to the reduced page icon, just as the magnifier icon does when you use the magnifying glass.

The Page Number Icon

Using the page number icon in the Page Preview window is one of several methods for adding page numbers to your printed document. Like the other methods (using the Section dialog box or including a page number in a header or footer), using the page number icon has its advantages and disadvantages. Using the page number icon while you view the entire document page—including the header, footer, footnotes, and graphics—may help you determine the page number's most effective or attractive position. But you cannot position page numbers as accurately with the icon as you can by specifying their position in the Section dialog box.

How much precision is necessary in the placement of page numbers dictates which page-numbering method you use. In the Page Preview command, the page number icon moves in increments the size of a Macintosh screen pixel—.06 inch. (Sometimes the increment of movement is .07 inch.) In the Section dialog box, however, you can specify the position in hundredths of an inch or in hundredths of a point. Fortunately, for most documents you create, such precision is not necessary, and its lack is more than offset by the ease of using the Page Preview window to position the page number.

You can use the page number icon in two ways. If you have no preference for where on the page your document's page numbers appear, you can just double-click the page number icon. The program automatically inserts a page number 0.5 inch from the top and right edges of the paper.

If you have selected Facing Pages in the Page Setup dialog box under the File menu, Word places a number at the corresponding location on the opposite page. For example, if you double-click the page number icon to place a page number 0.5 inch from the top and right edges of a right, odd-numbered page, a page number appears 0.5 inch from the top and left edges of the facing page as well.

If you want a page number in a different location, you can use the mouse effectively. Do the following to set manually the location of page numbers:

1. Click the page number icon.

The pointer changes to a large number *1* with inward-facing arrows on either side.

2. Move the pointer to the desired location on the page in the Page Preview window.

In this case, drag the pointer until it is centered in the bottom margin of your document's first page (see fig. 6.4).

Fig. 6.4

Positioning a page number with the page preview mode's page number pointer.

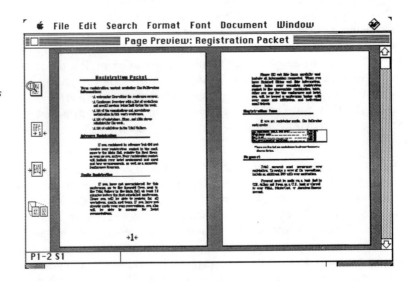

3. Click the mouse button.

The screen is redrawn, and a page number appears where you just clicked the mouse (and in the corresponding location on the opposite page if you have selected Facing Pages).

If you change your mind and want to move the page number to another location, simply repeat the preceding steps. After the screen is redrawn, the page number appears in its new place.

If numbers are on facing pages, you can relocate a page number on either page. Word automatically adjusts the page number location on the opposite page.

Although you cannot use the mouse to position page numbers with the same precision you get when you use the From Top and From Right boxes in the Page Number area of the Section dialog box, you can use Page Preview to locate numbers manually with acceptable accuracy.

For example, if for the preceding Step 3 you press and hold down the mouse button to drag the pointer (rather than just click the mouse), the page number box in the bottom left corner of the Page Preview window displays coordinates for the pointer's distance from the upper right corner of the paper. The first number is the distance from the right edge of the page, and the second number is the distance from the top edge. You could use that procedure to type the numbers in the From Right and From Top boxes in the Section dialog box.

When the page number box displays the set of coordinates you want, release the mouse button. Word redraws the page and displays it with a smaller page number instead of the pointer surrounded by arrows. The page number box returns to its normal display and shows the page and section numbers for the current page.

If you want to verify the distances of the page number from the top and right edges of the page, look at the From Top and From Right boxes in the Section dialog box. The coordinates you have selected manually are displayed there. Remember that the page number's position is a section format. If your document is divided into sections, the change you make applies only to the section or sections displayed on that page. To place page numbers in the same position throughout an entire multisection document, use the Section command. Select the whole document by pressing Command-Option-M. Then choose the Section command, click the Page Numbering box, and type the page number locations in the From Top and From Right boxes.

If you decide to position page numbers with the mouse, Word provides several ways to magnify the page so that you easily can find the best coordinates. You can drag the magnifier icon to an area of the page that will contain the page number and then click on that area, or you can double-click on that area to enlarge it. After the area is magnified, you can view the pointer's changing coordinates in the lower left corner of the screen while you drag the pointer to its correct position. The coordinates displayed on-screen when you release the mouse button reflect the new position of the page number.

This new set of coordinates is different in that the first number is the distance of the pointer from the *left* edge of the page. Like the preceding set of coordinates, the second number is the distance from the top of the page. If you subtract the first number of this new set from the width of the page, the result is a number you can use as the first coordinate for positioning the page number with the page number icon. For example, if the page is 8.50 inches wide, and if for a particular document 7.31 inches from the left side of the page is the best horizontal location for a page number, you will want to position the page number 1.19 inches from the right edge of the page when you use the page number icon to do so. If you need to fine-tune the location with even greater precision, however, use the From Top and From Right boxes of the Section dialog box.

If you want to magnify quickly the upper left corner of a page (or of a two-page spread if two pages are visible), simply double-click the magnifier icon. Word conveniently redraws the screen and enlarges the upper left corner.

Notice that when the screen is magnified, the increments of movement are the same numerically as those without magnification, but you can drag the pointer a perceptible distance before a number changes. Magnification thus lets you pinpoint a page number location with fewer changes of the coordinates as you drag the mouse slowly to pick the exact set of numbers.

In the next section, you learn how to delete page numbers from the Page Preview window.

The Margins Icon

When you create a simple document, you can use the program's default settings for the placement of headers, footers, footnotes, and page numbers. The default settings, which accommodate these elements in most standard documents, print the page so that each element is clearly distinguishable from the others.

After you start to design more complex pages that have banner headings, multiple columns, graphics, and other features, however, you undoubtedly will have to adjust the margins. You can alter them by entering measurements in the Page Setup dialog box (described in the previous chapter), or you can use the margins icon in the Page Preview window to change not only the margins but also the placement of headers, footers, and page breaks.

When you click the margins icon, the program adds a variety of lines and boxes to a page in the Page Preview window (see fig. 6.5). The vertical lines represent the left and right margins, and the horizontal lines that extend across the width of the page control the top and bottom margins. All four lines have a black square, or *handle*, at one end. Dragging this handle allows you to adjust the location of the corresponding margin. A single dotted horizontal line between the left and right margins indicates a page break; a double dotted line indicates a section break.

The header, footer, and page number are enclosed in dotted boxes. To make the lines and boxes appear on the other page, simply click that page.

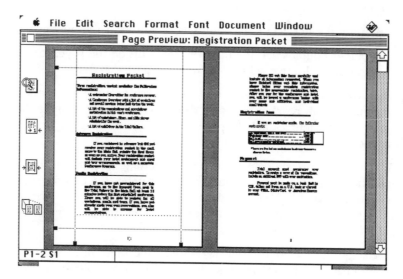

Fig. 6.5

The lines and boxes that appear when you click the margins icon in the Page Preview window.

When you use the margins icon, the mouse pointer becomes a plus sign, and you can move all the boxes and lines by dragging them around the page. As you move the elements, the program displays their position in the page number area. And as we mentioned in the previous section, you even can remove page numbers from the page.

To delete a page number from the Page Preview window, do the following:

1. Click the margins icon.

2. Drag the page number box off the page.

When you change the margins or page breaks in the Page Preview window, the program reformats all the affected pages. For example, if you increase the right or left margin and thereby decrease the available text area on a page, Word moves the text that has been squeezed from one page to the next and repaginates the entire document. Experiment a little to see how the repagination process works.

Use the margins icon to change the left or right margin in the following manner:

1. Click the margins icon in the Page Preview window.

2. Click the black box at the end of the vertical line that marks the left or right margin.

The pointer changes to a plus sign.

3. Drag the line to the location where you want the new margin.

4. Either double-click the page or click outside the page, to reformat the text within the new margins.

When you change the location of a page break or a section break, the program instantly redraws the page. When you change the margins, however, you must double-click the page or click outside the page, to redraw the page.

To change the margin back to its original setting, drag the margin line until the number in the page number box matches the original setting. Remember that the program's default margin settings are 1 inch from the top and bottom edges of the page and 1.25 inches from the right and left edges.

To change the top or bottom margin, use the same process that you use for changing the left and right margins. When you adjust the top or bottom margins, however, you need to consider the placement of headers and footers in relation to the main text. If the header or footer placement looks awkward after you change the top or bottom margin, you easily can move the header or footer.

To change the position of a header or footer, do the following:

1. Click the margins icon in the Page Preview window.

2. Drag the header or footer box up or down to the desired location.

3. Click outside the page to reposition the header or footer inside its box.

Because headers and footers fill the entire space between the left and right margins, you can't move them right or left in the Page Preview window. To reposition the header or footer text in relation to the left and right margins, you need to return to the Header or Footer window and make the adjustments there (see Chapter 13).

The One-Page Display Icon

The bottom icon in the Page Preview window is the one-page display icon, which you can use to toggle back and forth between a one- and two-page display. Use this handy icon when you have a one-page document and you don't want to be distracted by a blank page next to the one on which you're working. Or, use the icon when you don't want to be distracted by a second page in a multiple-page document while you reformat the first one. Regardless of your reasons, you can change the default Page Preview window by clicking the one-page display icon.

The program usually displays the single page in the middle of the screen. If you would rather display the page on the left side of your screen, hold down the Shift key while you click the icon.

Putting Page Preview To Work

When you finish creating and formatting a document into the appropriate number of sections and columns, you quickly can reformat a page, parts of a page, or the entire document by using the Page Preview icons. Page Preview gives you a chance to see the reformatting results before you go to the trouble of printing them.

To practice using the Page Preview window and icons, put on your harried-conference-coordinator's hat and tackle the Registration Packet. Recall that at the end of the previous chapter, you were saddled with a bulky list of 32 exhibitors that you must squeeze onto the first page of the document.

As conference coordinator, you find yourself in an unfortunate and all-too-common predicament: believing that your document's design and production are finished when someone else insists on the addition of a few lines. The solutions seldom are simple, but Page Preview helps you to move quickly through potential solutions and to test and eliminate options as you go.

Developing a migraine is one way to react to the conference coordinator's task. Another way is to approach the task as though it were a sophisticated video game. After you get the hang of it, dodging in and out of Page Preview as you click buttons, open windows, and drag icons in an effort to defy the formatting limits can be rather exhilarating.

Reformatting a Sample Document

If you are ready for the challenge, glance again at figure 5.7, which shows the list of exhibitors tacked onto the end of the Registration Packet document and formatted as a separate section. The first problem is positioning the list at the bottom of the first page of the document. The second problem—not a small one—is adjusting the surrounding text so that all the material fits neatly and coherently on the original two pages.

As a first step in formatting the list, peek at it in the Page Preview window. Figure 6.6 shows what you see on-screen if you choose Page Preview while you are looking at the list. If your display shows the first and second pages of the document instead of the second and third pages, click the down arrow in the vertical scroll bar to display the second and third pages.

Fig. 6.6

Page Preview shows the list in four columns.

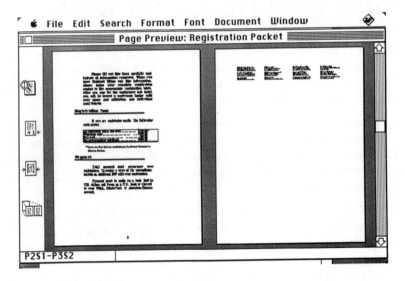

When you are ready to continue, click the close box in the upper left corner of the Page Preview window to return to the document window.

So far, so good. Next, you decide to tell attendees the purpose of the list by adding a short, explanatory note above the list (see fig. 6.7). Because you want this note to span all four columns of names, simply add it as another paragraph below the normal text (but above the section break). Place the insertion point at the end of the paragraph preceding the list and press Return two times to provide a little "air." Then type the note.

After typing the note, select it and choose Show Ruler from the Format menu. Click the centered icon, set the left and first-line indents at the 0-inch mark, and set the right indent at the 6-inch mark. Choose Hide Ruler from the Format menu and then format the note in 10-point type (by choosing 10 Point from the Font menu). All the required text is now present and formatted.

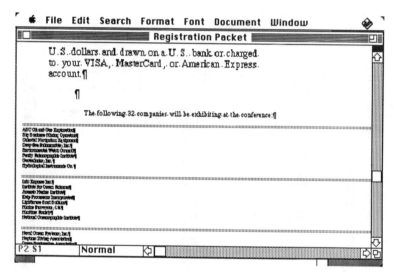

Fig. 6.7

The introductory note inserted above the list.

The next change is to set off the list and its introductory note by inserting one line above the note and another below the list. Putting a line above the unit is easy: just select the paragraph mark on the line above the introductory note; choose Paragraph from the Format menu; and pick the type of border desired (Above and Single). Inserting the line below the list is only slightly more difficult because the line requires a new section, formatted for a single column.

To place a line below a multicolumn list, do the following:

1. Insert a paragraph mark after the list.

2. With the insertion point placed just in front of the new paragraph mark, press **Command-Enter** to insert a section break.

3. Choose the **Section** command from the Format menu.

4. Double-click the **Number** box and type **1**. Press **Return**.

5. Choose **Paragraph** from the Format menu.

6. Select the **Line** and **Below** options from the Border area.

7. Press **Return**.

Look again at the document in the Page Preview window. The first line and the introductory note are on page 2, but the four-column list still is on page 3 (see fig. 6.8).

Fig. 6.8

The list section breaks between the second and third pages.

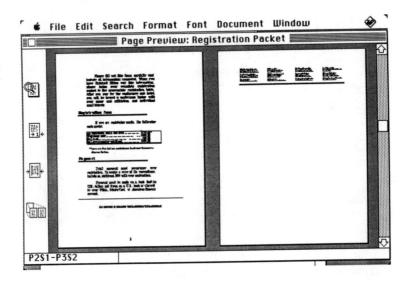

Your next task is to move the list section to the first page. First, you must make one formatting change. You specified in Chapter 5 that each section of the list should start a new column. Remember that if successive sections are formatted for different numbers of columns, then the program, in addition to starting a new column, begins a new page at the section break. To prevent the list of exhibitors from being printed on page 2 of the Registration Packet instead of on page 1, you need to position the insertion point anywhere within the list, choose the Section command, and specify No Break in the Section Start area.

Positioning the List Section

The list has taken shape. Now, you are ready to move the list to the first page and guess at the initial placement. You can cut and paste entire sections as easily as you can a few lines of text. Remember, however, that section-formatting information is stored in the double dotted line at the bottom of the section. You must move the section mark with the text above it to retain section formatting.

To move a section or sections, do the following:

1. Select the sections you want to move.

In this case, select everything from the line above the list to the line below the list. This selection crosses section boundaries, but because the main body of the document has the same section formatting as the top line and the introductory note in the list unit, no formatting is lost in the move.

2. Choose **Cut** from the Edit menu.

3. Click an insertion point at the location in which you want to paste the selection.

In this case, click at the beginning of the second paragraph under the "Onsite Registration" heading.

4. Choose **Paste** from the Edit menu.

Look again at this document in the Page Preview window (see fig. 6.9). Moving the list has made the page-break problem worse.

Squeezing Your Text

How can you whittle the document back to two pages? You have many options for "squeezing" the format; we list several methods in the following bulleted items. To reformat the main body of the Registration Packet, however, you'll need to use a combination of methods to accommodate the list of exhibitors.

Experiment a little to see what kinds of solutions you can create. Sometimes these trial-and-error exercises can twist things around so much that you can't find your way back to where you started. To recover your original formatting, your only option (unless, of course, you had the forethought to work on a copy of the document) is to return to the document window and quit the program without saving any changes. Because you can get bogged down in formatting experimentation, you

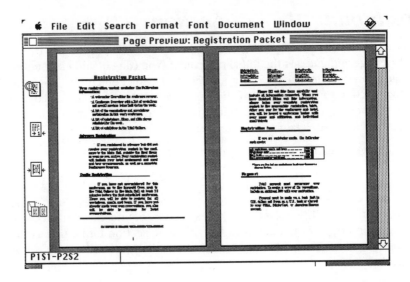

should *always* save editing changes before you begin any bold formatting experiments. If you find that you need to preserve both the original and the new formatting, you can save the newly formatted document with a new name (choose Save As from the File menu). When you finish, the first page will look something like figure 6.10.

To print more text per page, you can use any of the following methods:

- Remove or reduce space between paragraphs

The Spacing area of the Paragraph dialog box contains boxes labeled Before and After. You can type a number to specify how many points of space the program inserts before or after selected paragraphs. We removed the spacing before the lines in the bulleted list.

- Vary line spacing

The spacing between lines of text is controlled by your entry in the Line box of the Paragraph dialog box's Spacing area. You can specify points of spacing to open or close the distance between lines in the selected paragraph.

- Vary the margins

The sizes of the top, bottom, left, and right margins can be controlled by Page Setup options or by manipulating markers in Page Preview.

- Vary the right and left indents

Registration Packet

Your registration packet contains the following information:

- A welcoming flyer citing the conference sponsor.
- A Conference Overview with a list of workshops and special sessions being held during the week.
- A list of the organizations and associations participating in this year's conference.
- A list of entertainers, films, and slide shows scheduled for the week.
- A list of exhibitors in the Tidal Gallery.

Advance Registration

If you registered in advance but did not receive your registration packet in the mail, come to the Main Hall outside the Reef Room as soon as you arrive. Your registration packet will include your hotel assignment and meal and tour arrangements, as well as a complete Conference Program.

Onsite Registration

If you have not preregistered for this conference, go to the Emerald Cove, next to the Tidal Gallery in the Main Hall, at least 30 minutes before the first scheduled conference. There you will be able to register for all workshops, meals, and tours. If you have not already made your own reservations, you also will be able to arrange for hotel accommodations.

The following 32 companies will be exhibiting at the conference:

ABC Oil and Gas Exploration	Info Express Inc.	Naval Ocean Systems, Inc.	Rope Masters, Ltd.
Big Business Mining Operators	Institute for Ocean Sciences	Neptune Diving Association	Seamen Brothers Nautical Supply
Celestial Navigation Equipment	Jurassic Marine Institute	Ocean Engineering Association	Tectonics, Inc.
Deep-Sea Submersible, Inc.	Kelp Processors Incorporated	Oceanographic Society	Underwater Technology
Environmental Watch Council	Lighthouse Boat Builders	Offshore Systems, Inc.	Vortex Deep Sea Gear
Faulty Seismographic Institute	Marine Surveyors, Ltd	Oil and Gas Equipment Co.	Water Express River Rafting
Geotechnica, Inc.	Maritime Society	Petroleum Council of America	Xcellent Mapping and Surveying
Hydrological Instruments Co.	National Oceanographic Institute	Quality Navigational Systems	Zytex Computers, Inc.

Fig. 6.10

The completed first and second pages of the Registration Packet, including the list of exhibitors.

> Please fill out this form carefully and include all information requested. When you have finished filling out this information, please bring your complete registration packet to the appropriate registration table. After you pay for the conference and hotel, you will be issued a conference badge with your name and affiliation, and individual meal tickets
>
> ### Registration   Fees
>
> If you are registering onsite, the following costs apply:
>
> | | |
> |---|---|
> | All workshops, meals, and tours .... | $750.00* |
> | Workshops only .... | $500.00 |
> | Each meal .... | .$25.00 |
> | Each accompanying participant................... | $350.00 |
>
> *Tours are free but you must sign up in advance to ensure a place on the bus.
>
> ### Payment
>
> Total payment must accompany your registration. To receive a copy of the proceedings, include an additional $65 with your registration.
>
> Payment must be made on a bank draft in U.S. dollars and drawn on a U.S. bank or charged to your VISA, MasterCard, or American Express account.

The indents work in conjunction with the margins to determine the amount of space available for text. Because indent settings are applied to individual paragraphs, the indent settings offer more flexibility than margin settings. We changed the right indent from 1.5 inches to 0.5 inch, adjusting the lines below the headings for balance.

* Change the size of some of or all the text

You easily can make room for a few more lines of text simply by reducing the text size from 12 points to 10 points. If smaller text looks cramped, consider changing fonts. If your document contains many headings, more subtle heading formatting often saves space.

* Condense text

The Spacing area in the Character dialog box has buttons for Normal, Condensed, and Expanded text, and a box in which you can specify the points of space to be inserted between characters. (Using the points of space between characters generally is not as effective as simply using smaller type.)

- Edit the copy

You always can cut text from your document—and often not call attention to the change. While you are working in Page Preview, look for short lines that can be eliminated by cutting a word or two from a paragraph. Combine paragraphs and cut excess verbiage. These types of changes can improve the look of your document and save much formatting time.

Saving Your Formatting Changes

If you've followed the rather circuitous route to corralling the list of exhibitors at the bottom of page 1 in the Registration Packet document, you should have some idea of how challenging a seemingly simple change to a document can be. You also should have gained an appreciation for the program's Page Preview command—your best ally when the formatting gets tough.

By now, your sample document should be as "ready" as you want it to be. Even if the president emeritus doesn't approve the Registration Packet, we do. So, proceed to Chapter 7 and start printing.

No-Fuss Printing

Few people write for the sheer pleasure of writing. Even fewer are content to imprison words of wisdom within the confines of computers. With your Macintosh computer and the Word program, you can perform all your writing tasks, from simple correspondence to The Great American Novel. This combined power would be useless, however, if it were not complemented by superior printing capabilities.

One of the benefits of owning a Macintosh is its capability to reproduce beautifully your work on the printed page. When the Mac's printing capability is combined with the versatility of Word's programs, you can enhance your work to an unprecedented level. Moreover, you can get superior printing results on a variety of printers: Apple's ImageWriter, ImageWriter™ 2, the new and improved ImageWriter™ LQ, LaserWriter, LaserWriter Plus, and Apple daisywheel printers; the Diablo 630, NEC 7710, and Brother letter-quality printers; and plain serial printers. Because the program supports the PostScript page-description language for the LaserWriter, you can print Word documents directly on any high-resolution typesetting machine that also supports the PostScript language. PostScript language is a programming language designed exclusively for printer control; PostScript permits personal computers (including the Macintosh) to communicate with even the most sophisticated typesetting machinery.

Regardless of which printer you use, you should read the owner's manual that comes with your printer. Knowing your printer's capabilities and fully understanding its peculiarities help you get the most from your particular Macintosh-Word-printer combination.

Although the program offers many options that affect the way your document appears in printed form, the default settings for these options probably can handle most of your printing needs. If the default settings do not meet your printing needs, however, this chapter details other options that will. You also learn how to prepare your Macintosh to print your Word documents and how to print a document from within Word. In addition, you learn how to print a document by using the Macintosh Finder.

Setting Up Your System To Print

When you first start Word on the Macintosh, you automatically are set up to print on the Apple ImageWriter. If you want to print some material on an ImageWriter, just connect the cables, load some paper, and choose the Print command from the program's File menu. To use any other printer supported by Word, you need to install the printer resource file for that printer.

Installing Printer Resource Files

The Word Utilities disk holds the resource files for all the printers supported by the program. A printer resource file translates to the proper format the program's formatting codes and other printer-related information for a particular printer. Installing any printer resource file is a simple matter of copying the file to your working copy of Word's Program disk (or the disk you use to start your Macintosh).

If you plan to use different printers for different types of documents, you should move the resource files for all the printers to your working Program disk (if you have room) and then use the Apple menu's Chooser command to switch among printers. Figure 7.1 shows the dialog box displayed when you select the Chooser command.

With the Chooser command, you tell the program which of the available printers currently is connected to the Macintosh. The program then modifies the options in the Print command's dialog box to reflect that printer's capabilities. For example, if you print with the LaserWriter, the Print dialog box can scale (either up or down) the size of the printed output. The program doesn't have this option when you select the ImageWriter, which can't scale a document.

WARNING: As you create the combination of printer resource files that you need on the Program disk, make sure you use a working copy—not

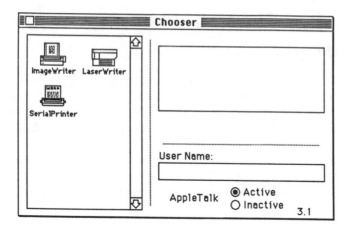

Fig. 7.1

*The Chooser
dialog box.*

the original—of the disk. You always should preserve, in its original state, the Program disk that came in the Word box, in case you damage your working disk.

Installing Fonts

One of the Macintosh's strong points is that it can use many varieties of fonts. Besides those that come with the program, hundreds of fonts are available. Apple supplies a basic set with the Macintosh and a few more with the LaserWriter and the LaserWriter Plus. To flex your design muscles, however, other software manufacturers (called *third-party* manufacturers) supply whole libraries of fonts.

To use a third-party font from within the program, you must copy that font onto your working copy of the Program disk (or the disk you use to start your Macintosh), using a program called Apple® Font/DA Mover Utility. This program, with directions for its use, usually is included with the Macintosh, the LaserWriter, and most third-party fonts.

After you copy a font to your working Program disk, you can select the font either from the Font menu or from a list available when you choose the Format menu's Character command.

Choosing Printing Options with the Print Command

The contents of the Print dialog box vary significantly, depending on the capabilities of the printer selected in the Chooser dialog box and the version of the printer driver installed on your Program disk. Figures 7.2 and 7.3 show the dialog boxes for an ImageWriter and a LaserWriter Plus. The ImageWriter is the basic dot-matrix printer available for the Macintosh, and the LaserWriter is one of the more sophisticated laser printers on the market. Choose the Print command from the File menu to see how the options for your printer compare with the ones described in the following sections.

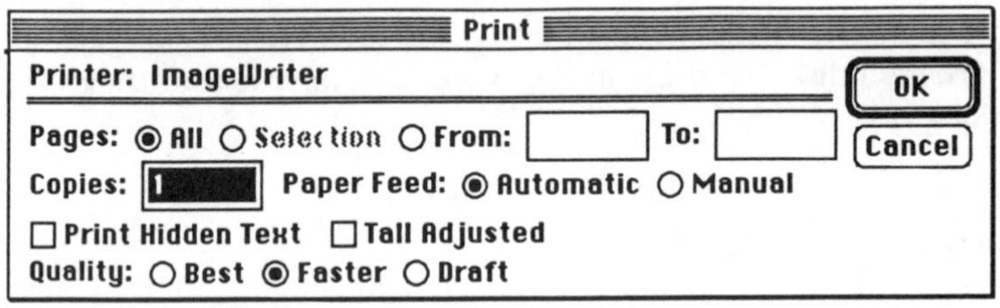

Fig. 7.2

The Print dialog box for the ImageWriter.

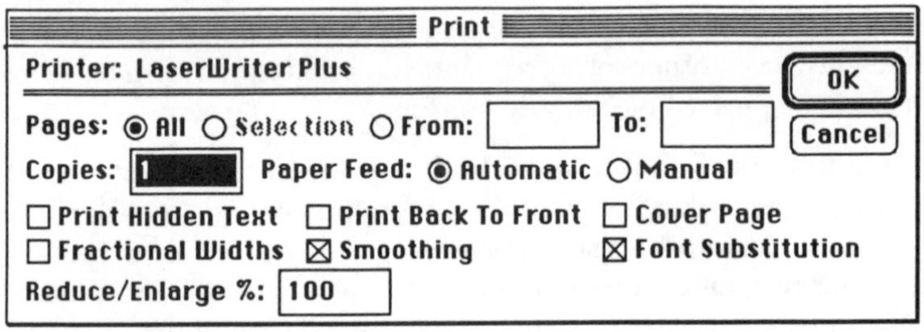

Print
Printer: ImageWriter   [**OK**]
Pages: ◉ All ○ Selection ○ From: [   ]   To: [   ]   [**Cancel**]
Copies: [**1**]   **Paper Feed:** ◉ Automatic ○ Manual
☐ Print Hidden Text ☐ Tall Adjusted
Quality: ○ Best ◉ Faster ○ Draft

Fig. 7.3

The Print dialog box for the Laserwriter Plus.

Print
Printer: LaserWriter Plus   [**OK**]
Pages: ◉ All ○ Selection ○ From: [   ]   To: [   ]   [**Cancel**]
Copies: [**1**]   **Paper Feed:** ◉ Automatic ○ Manual
☐ Print Hidden Text ☐ Print Back To Front ☐ Cover Page
☐ Fractional Widths ☒ Smoothing ☒ Font Substitution
Reduce/Enlarge %: [100]

The default settings in the Print dialog box meet the needs of many types of documents. But you should be familiar with the other printing options available so that you know how to handle documents that require special printing techniques. Therefore, rather than reviewing the options in the dialog box of just one Macintosh printer, we explain all the options available with the two printers most commonly used with the Macintosh. We include some of the more sophisticated options in this review to show you what Word and the Macintosh may be able to do for your documents.

Options Available with All Printers

The four basic printing options—specifying pages, choosing the number of copies, specifying a paper-feed method, and printing hidden text—are available on all printers.

The Pages option offers three choices: You can accept the All default setting, which tells the program to print the entire document; you can print just the text you have selected; or you can specify a range of pages to print.

Printing just a block of text (a paragraph, for example) is easy. Follow these steps:

1. Select the text you want to print.

2. Choose the **Print** command.

3. Click the Pages option's **Selection** button.

The Selection button is not available unless you first select a piece of text.

4. Click **OK** or press **Return**.

In this method of printing, note that *only* the selected text is printed. The program does not include page numbers, running heads, or any footnotes referenced within the selection.

With the page-range option, you can print anything from a single page to the entire document. To print a single page, for example, do the following:

1. Choose the **Print** command.

2. Click the Pages option's **From** button.

3. In both the From and To boxes, type the number of the page you want to print.

4. Click **OK** or press **Return**.

To print from one specified page through another specified page, do the following:

1. Choose the **Print** command.

2. Click the Page option's **From** button.

3. In the From box, type the beginning page number; and in the To box, type the ending page number.

4. Click **OK** or press **Return**.

Do the following to print from one specified page through the end of the document:

1. Choose the **Print** command.

2. Click the Page option's **From** button.

3. In the From box, type the beginning page number; leave the To box blank.

4. Click **OK** or press **Return**.

Use Arabic page numbers (*1, 2, 3*, and so forth) in the Print dialog box's From and To boxes, even if you have specified page numbers in a different style (such as Roman numerals) in the Section dialog box. Word uses the page numbers specified in the Print dialog box for its own navigational purposes, but the program prints the page numbers in the specified style.

If the document includes several sections, you must include the section number in the page range. Type the page number, the letter *S*, and then the section number. For example, to print from page 24 of the second section through page 13 of the fourth section, type *24S2* in the From box and *13S4* in the To box.

The Copies option is a Macintosh version of a copying machine. To instruct the program to print more than one copy of the portion of a document specified with the Pages option, type the desired number of copies in the Copies box.

Your selection of a paper-feed method determines whether the program continuously sends one page after another to the printer or pauses between pages. Click the Paper Feed option's Automatic button for both form-feed and individual sheets of paper that are fed into the printer by an automatic sheet feeder. To print on envelopes, acetate sheets (to use with overhead projectors), or other such nonstandard items, click the Manual button and manually feed each sheet into the printer.

To print any hidden text included in a document, select the Print Hidden Text option in the Print dialog box. You need to select the Print Hidden Text option even if you already have selected the Show Hidden Text option in the dialog box for the Preferences command (available on the Edit menu).

Options Available with the ImageWriter

Some handy printing options—such as controlling the proportion of graphics and specifying print quality—are available only with the ImageWriter printer.

Use the Tall Adjusted option when you print graphics (such as charts) formatted for the Page Setup command's Tall orientation. (*Orientation* refers to the orientation of the paper: Tall prints text and graphics across the narrow dimension of the paper; Wide prints across the long dimension of the paper.) Clicking Tall Adjusted ensures that the program prints these graphics in the correct proportion. You should be aware, however, that using this option can distort text slightly and affect line, paragraph, and page breaks.

The ImageWriter is the only printer used by the Macintosh that currently offers a choice of print qualities. (Some earlier versions of Word also offered two print qualities for the LaserWriter.) The ImageWriter offers three qualities: Best, Faster, and Draft. The low-quality Draft mode eliminates character formatting to speed up printing; the Faster option offers standard quality and speed; and the Best option provides the highest-quality printing. Remember—the higher the quality of the print, the more time is spent in printing; therefore, your choice of a Quality option depends on whether speed or appearance is more critical to the work at hand.

Options Available with the LaserWriter

Although the LaserWriter may not offer a choice of printing options for graphics or quality, the LaserWriter does provide the following options that other printers do not have: specifying the order of printing, printing cover pages, using fractional widths, specifying "smoothing," substituting fonts, and reducing or enlarging images.

You can specify the order of printing by using the Print Back to Front option. The LaserWriter normally ejects its printed pages face up, with the first printed page on the bottom of the stack and the last page on the top. To compensate for this printing foible, use the Print Back To Front option. When you select this option, the program prints documents from the last page to the first page. This printing sequence takes a little longer, but it stacks the pages in the proper sequence.

Selecting the Cover Page option produces an extra page at the beginning of the document that lists the user's name, the application, the document title, and the date and time of printing. Where does the information for the cover page come from? Bits of information are available from the Macintosh, from Word, and from the document on which you are working. The only item you might not recognize is the user's name. The first person to load Word is given the opportunity to assign a user name to the program. Word remembers that name and displays it in the Chooser dialog box (see fig. 7.1). To change the name, you can edit it in this dialog box.

The Fractional Widths option, available in newer versions of the LaserWriter driver, improves the alignment of text in columns, but the overall effect is uncertain. If you experiment with this option, notice that selecting it makes the Font Substitution option unselectable. Also, text justified on the screen returns to a ragged edge when the text is printed.

To understand the Smoothing option, you must first understand how the Macintosh printers create their characters. The ImageWriter and the LaserWriter both create characters and graphics by printing small, rectangular "dots." The size of these dots determines the quality of print produced by each printer model. The difference between the print quality of the ImageWriter and the LaserWriter is apparent in figures 7.4 and 7.5. Figure 7.4 was printed on the LaserWriter Plus, which prints 300 dots per inch; figure 7.5 was printed on the ImageWriter, which prints 72 dots per inch. As you can see, the smaller the dots, the more refined the image.

Fig. 7.4

Text printed on the LaserWriter Plus.

Dear Salley,
    I received your letter of August 20th a week or so back, and a similar message from Howard, so I've spent the time since then knocking these chapters into shape.
    I trust that you received the signed contract not long after you wrote because I sent it a week earlier. It was good to hear that someone is interested in the manuscript. I hope that situation hasn't changed since you wrote me.

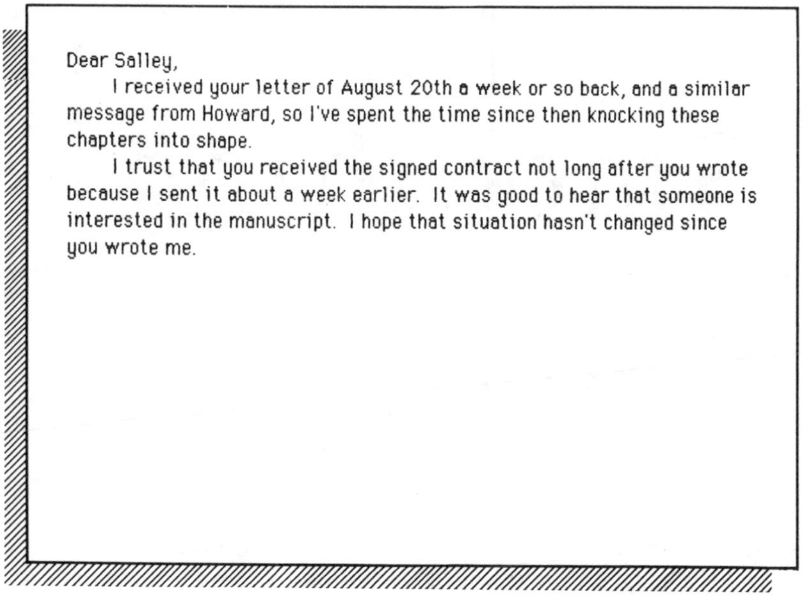

Fig. 7.5

Text printed on the ImageWriter.

If you look closely at the documents in figures 7.4 and 7.5, you can see that both printers create their diagonal and curved lines with jagged edges, caused by the "building block" method of constructing the image from rectangular dots. The LaserWriter offers a Smoothing option, which reduces the jagged-edge effect in graphics and in fonts not designed for use with the LaserWriter.

Figure 7.6 shows an enlarged view of some text before and after the smoothing process. Smoothing also helps cure the "jaggies" caused by printing a font in a nonstandard size. (The standard sizes for each font appear in outline type on the Font menu.) You pay for this more attractive output with a slight loss of printing speed.

The LaserWriter has its own set of fonts. If you format a document to include a font that the LaserWriter doesn't have, the LaserWriter output can look somewhat "rustic." Selecting the Font Substitution option in the Print dialog box tells the program to substitute a comparable LaserWriter font for the one that you specified. For example, the program substitutes the Times font for New York, and the Helvetica font for Geneva.

With the Reduce/Enlarge % option, you can tell the program to reduce or enlarge the image of each page as the program prints your document.

Fig. 7.6

*Text printed
before and after
smoothing.*

Before smoothing

After smoothing

Just type a percentage from 25 through 400 in the Reduce/Enlarge %
box, and the program prints your graphics or text anywhere from 1/4
to 4 times its original size.

Placing Your Printing Order

After defining a page layout with the Page Setup options and selecting
among the printing options just described, you are ready to proceed
with printing. You can print your document from Word or from the
Finder. Print from within Word if you want to print just one document.
If you want to print several documents, however, print from the Finder;
it automates the tasks of opening and printing, thus saving you time and
effort. In the rest of this chapter, you learn how to use both methods,
and then you try your hand at printing a document.

Printing from Word

Be sure that you know what your printing options are. If you have not
chosen the Print command in order to compare your computer's options
with the ones just described, do so now. Then you are set to begin
printing from Word.

To print a document from Word, do the following:

1. Make sure that the document you want to print is displayed in
   the document window.

Use a document that you created in an earlier session. To open a document, use the Open command and choose from the list. If you haven't created a document, type a few lines and use your new document for this exercise.

2. Choose the **Print** command from the File menu or press **Command-P**.

3. Adjust the settings in the Print dialog box, if necessary.

4. Click **OK** or press **Return**.

The program begins printing the document that is in the document window. Depending on the printer and paper-feed method you use, Word may prompt you to press Return each time the printer is ready to print another page.

To cancel the printing of a document, press Command-. (period). Don't worry about remembering this Command combination during printing because you see on-screen an alert box similar to the one in figure 7.7.

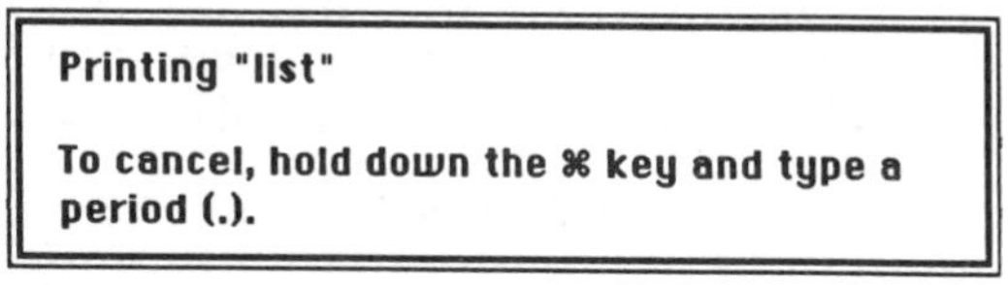

> **Printing "list"**
>
> **To cancel, hold down the ⌘ key and type a period (.).**

Fig. 7.7

The alert box that Word displays while it prints a document with a LaserWriter.

Depending on the version of the Finder you are using, the alert box displayed during printing may have a Cancel button you can click instead of pressing Command-. (period) to stop the printing process. Or, because the Printing alert box is displayed by the Finder and not by Word, you may see a third version of this alert box, which has a Pause button. By clicking the Pause button, you interrupt the printing—while you make an adjustment to the printer or answer the phone, for example—without actually canceling the printing. Click the button a second time to continue printing.

Printing from the Finder

You probably will do most of your printing from within Word, but you also can use the Print command from the Finder's File menu to print Word documents. Be aware, however, that the Finder's Page Setup command, also on the File menu, has no effect on the page layouts of Word documents. Remember to make sure that the settings (such as margin width) in Word's Page Setup dialog box are correct before you use the Finder's Print command.

The system-level Print command is useful because you can select several documents for consecutive printing. After you choose Print, no further intervention on your part is required.

To print several documents in succession, do the following:

1. If you still are experimenting with Word's Print command, quit Word and look at the directory window of your document disk.

2. Select two or more documents for printing by either dragging a dotted rectangle around the icons of the documents you want to print or holding down Shift while you click their icons.

If you don't have two documents, create and save two short Word documents to use for this experiment.

If you use the first method in Step 2, the program prints the documents in the order in which they appear, from left to right and from top to bottom, in the selection rectangle. If you use the second method, the program prints the documents in the order in which you select them.

3. Choose **Print** from the Finder's File menu.

This step automatically loads the program, which in turn loads the first document and starts printing it. If you need to cancel a print order, your program displays the Finder's Printing alert box during printing.

In Part I of this book, you have learned the basics of creating, formatting, and printing a Word document. Part II adds to these basic concepts some specialized techniques that expand your word-processing capabilities and automate some of the more complicated formatting tasks discussed in Part I.

Part II

ADDING TO
YOUR REPERTOIRE

Includes:

Using Glossaries

Working with Style Sheets

Working with Windows

Customizing Menus

Working with Graphics

Adding Headers and Footers

Checking Spelling

Hyphenating To Adjust Line Breaks

Merging Documents

8

Using Glossaries

Computers should be time-savers. Why, then, do many of us spend so much time in front of a computer screen? If you are equipped with a Macintosh and Microsoft Word, the answer is probably that you have learned the basics of operating the program and know enough to produce perfectly adequate documents, but you have had no time or opportunity to enhance your word-processing skills beyond the basics.

In Part II of *Using Microsoft Word: Macintosh Version*, you start picking up speed. You learn about the sophisticated features that make this program a real time-saver. And in terms of cutting down on keystrokes, none of these features is more powerful than the glossary.

Because you can store text in a glossary and then insert the text into a document with only a few keystrokes, you might be tempted to approach the glossary merely as compensation for less than perfect typing skills. But with just a touch of imagination, you can use the glossary as much more than a poor typist's crutch. Word's glossaries are adaptable, and they are so simple to master and to use that the glossaries can resuscitate a novice's flagging enthusiasm for computers and restore the sense of being in control.

This chapter begins by explaining the basic concept of glossaries and briefly touring the Glossary command's dialog box. Then you are introduced to the Standard Glossary, which is provided by the program for use with all documents, and you learn two methods for inserting a glossary entry into a document. Next, you create a simple glossary entry so that you know how to name, add, change, delete, and print your own entries. Finally, you learn how to create specialized glossaries and how to merge, switch between, and delete these glossaries while you work with a document.

Defining a Glossary

A *glossary* is a storage place for text and graphics. For example, after typing and formatting a piece of text, you can store the text in a glossary and later retrieve the text as many times as you want—without ever typing it again. When you use a glossary, you can concentrate on what you are trying to say rather than on the mechanics of getting words on the page.

To store text in a glossary, you need to select the text, choose Glossary from the Edit menu, assign the entry a name, and click Define. You retrieve the text with the Edit menu's Glossary command or a keyboard shortcut. You have a chance to practice both of these operations in the following sections.

Standard versus Specialized Glossaries

The program supplies a Standard Glossary, which is loaded automatically when you start the program. This glossary initially contains only two entries: date and time—the default entries in all glossaries. If the clock in your Macintosh is set properly, the date and time entries are handy because you can use them to insert automatically the current date or time into a document without consulting a calendar or clock. In addition, you can add your own entries to the Standard Glossary; so if you expect to use the same glossary entries for most of your work, the Standard Glossary may be the only one you need.

If your work is somewhat specialized (or varied), however, and you want to separate glossary entries for different kinds of documents, you can create your own special-purpose glossaries. They operate the same way as the Standard Glossary except that they must be opened from the Glossary dialog box before you can use them. You learn how to create and manipulate these glossaries later in the chapter. But first, take a look at the Glossary command's dialog box and get a feel for how glossaries work.

The Glossary Dialog Box

You can view the contents of a glossary by choosing the full Edit menu's Glossary command. The Glossary dialog box, shown in figure 8.1, is used both to save a glossary entry and to insert the glossary entry into a document.

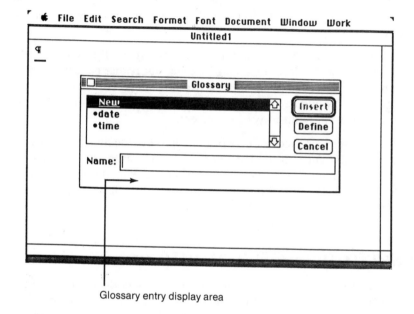

Fig. 8.1

The Glossary dialog box.

Glossary entry display area

In the top left corner of the Glossary dialog box is a list box. The first item in this box is an entry called New, which Word selects by default. You use this entry when you create your own glossary entries.

Below the New entry is an alphabetical list of the names of the entries in a particular glossary. Until you add entries of your own, the list contains only date and time, the two permanent entries. The program marks these entries with a bullet to indicate that they are supplied by the program. The list box displays only four lines at once. To view the names in large glossaries, use the scroll bar along the list box's right edge.

Three buttons—Insert, Define, and Cancel—are on the Glossary dialog box's right side. These buttons are used for both inserting and creating glossary entries.

The Name box displays the name of the glossary entry currently selected in the list box. When New is selected, the Name box is empty because the program expects you to assign a name to a new glossary entry. If you select a piece of text, choose the Glossary command, type a name for the selection, and then click the Define button, the program displays as much of the selected text as can fit in the area immediately below the Name box. This area is known as the *glossary entry display area*. An ellipsis following the text indicates that not all the text is displayed. If you select a graphic before choosing Glossary, the program represents your selection with a small, empty box the size of a large uppercase character.

After you select the name of a glossary entry in the list box, click the Insert button to close the dialog box and insert that glossary entry in front of the insertion point in the active document. For example, if you click Insert while date is selected, the current date is inserted in front of the insertion point in your document.

After you select a piece of text or a graphic in a document and type a name for the entry in the Name box, click the Define button to store the selection in the glossary with that name. Clicking the Cancel button closes the dialog box and discards any name you have typed but not assigned to an entry with the Define button.

Inserting Glossary Entries

Now that you know your way around the Glossary dialog box, use the Standard Glossary's date and time entries to learn the two methods for inserting a glossary entry into a document. The same methods insert any entry from any glossary.

Load the program and open a document, if you have not done so already. The Standard Glossary is loaded automatically and ready for you to use.

Inserting with the Glossary Command

You already know that you can insert a glossary entry into a document by selecting the entry's name in the Glossary list box and then clicking the Insert button. Try this technique with the date entry.

Do the following to insert a glossary entry into a document by using the Glossary dialog box:

1. Click an insertion point where you want the date to appear in the document.

2. Choose **Glossary** from the full Edit menu or press **Command-K** to open the Glossary dialog box.

Notice that the program selects New in the list of glossary names and that the Name box is empty.

3. In the list box, click the name of the entry you want to insert.

In this case, click date. Word displays date in the Name box, and then the program displays the current date (the current contents of the entry as supplied by your machine's built-in clock) immediately below, as shown in figure 8.2.

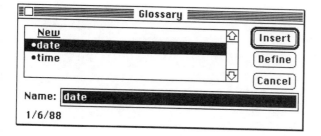

Fig. 8.2

The Glossary dialog box after you select the date *glossary entry.*

4. Click the **Insert** button.

Word closes the Glossary dialog box and inserts the current date into the document at the insertion point. If you carry out this same procedure tomorrow, the program inserts tomorrow's date.

Inserting with the Keyboard Shortcut

Finding the desired entry among the two in the Glossary dialog box was not difficult, but this may be the only time you can view all the glossary names without scrolling the list. Once you have created a few entries of your own, scrolling through them in search of the one you want may become tedious.

If you remember the name that you assigned to an entry, however, you can bypass opening the Glossary dialog box by using a keyboard shortcut to name and insert the entry (see the Quick Reference Guide at the end of the book). Try inserting the current time into a document by using the following keyboard shortcut technique:

1. Click an insertion point where you want the glossary entry to be inserted.

2. Press **Command-Backspace**.

The word *Name* replaces the page number usually displayed in the document window's bottom left corner, as shown in figure 8.3.

Fig. 8.3

The word Name *appears in the bottom left corner of the screen when you use the Glossary keyboard shortcut.*

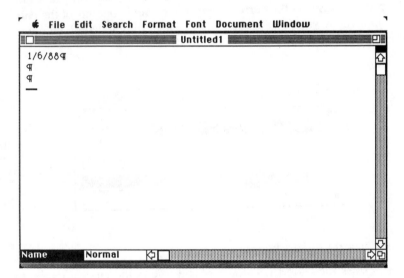

3. Type the name of the glossary entry you want to insert.

In this case, type *time*.

4. Press **Return**.

The current time is added at the insertion point, with the same character formatting as the surrounding text.

If for some reason you want to cancel the procedure before pressing Return, you can press Command-. (period). Or if you wait approximately 20 seconds, Word cancels the procedure for you.

The `date` and `time` entries are useful, but they barely tap the real potential of the glossary feature. The program gives you great freedom to store entries with names you assign in order to serve your own purposes. In the next section, you develop some idea of what you can accomplish by using a glossary entry.

Creating Your Own Glossary Entries

In regular practice, you probably should consider creating a glossary entry about the third time you type and format a complex sequence of characters. Once you create the entry, you can press Command-Backspace, type the entry's name, and press Return—as you did in the prior exercise—to insert the entry into a document.

Identifying Glossary-Entry Candidates

Your first glossary entries probably will be simple—a word with a difficult-to-remember spelling or a block of commonly used text, such as your own address. But as you become more confident with using glossaries, you may find your glossary entries becoming larger and more complex.

Glossary entries can include graphics, any amount of text, and just about any type of character or paragraph formatting. An inserted entry retains all the characteristics of the selection from which you created the entry, except for margin settings and any styles you have applied using style sheet codes. The exclusion of margin settings from the retained formatting is a convenience, making an entry adaptable to most page formats. If you format with style sheets (see Chapter 9), however, you will have to reapply the style after Word inserts the text. As you become more comfortable with the glossary feature, you probably will include more and more formatting in your glossary entries so that you do not need to format each time you insert the entries into a document.

By paying attention to spaces, tabs, and paragraph marks, you can make sure that your glossary entry puts the insertion point at the place where you want to resume typing in your text. For example, you can create a return-address glossary entry that starts with your address in a *multiline paragraph* (one with a Shift-Return at the end of each line), formatted with a 4.5-inch left indent. You can follow the address with the `date` entry and then a few blank lines for spacing. Finally, you can conclude this glossary entry with a normal paragraph beginning with the word *Dear* followed by a space.

When you insert this return-address entry into a document, Word positions the insertion point at line's end. In this case, the program positions the insertion point right after the last space in the entry. Now you are ready to type the name of the person to whom you are writing.

Figure 8.4 shows a typical return address inserted from the glossary. Go ahead and type this or a similar return address at the beginning of a new document. You then have a jump start on creating a sample document for the next exercises.

Fig. 8.4

A typical return address, which would make a useful glossary entry.

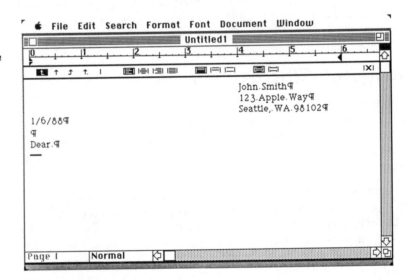

Choosing Names for Entries

When naming glossary entries, be aware of a few restrictions. Your glossary names can be no more than 31 characters, including spaces, and you cannot distinguish between entries with uppercase/lowercase style. Typing *date*, *Date*, or *DATE* inserts the permanent date entry; typing *address*, *Address*, or *ADDRESS* inserts a custom address entry. You also should develop your own style for naming entries and make your glossary names memorable, distinctive, and typeable.

A one- or two-letter code name is sufficient for a glossary name but may be hard to remember, especially if you already are trying to remember a host of keyboard formatting shortcuts. Also, once you start using style sheets, your style sheet codes add to the tangle of abbreviations. If your typing is better than your memory, you may prefer to use complete words that help you to recall, even weeks after you add the entry to the glossary, the entry's content. Or you may find a system of whimsical names easier to catalog in your mental filing system. Convenience is the governing principle here; use whatever system works best for you.

Now that you have a feel for the basic concepts, tackle the techniques. To see how to add and revise glossary entries, work through some exercises.

Creating Glossary Entries from Current Document Text

Imagine that you are writing to a friend about several research reports you have read on the subject of self-hypnosis. The first part of the letter is shown in figure 8.5. The reports were published recently in two journals with lengthy titles: *The American Journal of Clinical Hypnosis* and *Acta Neurologica et Psychiatrica Scandinavica*. Even a good typist may stumble over these lengthy titles—but not you, once you have entered them into a glossary.

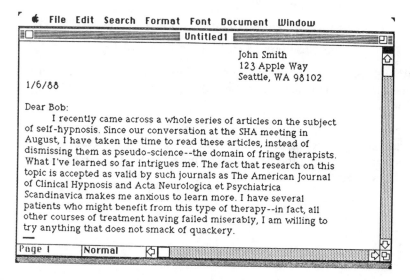

Fig. 8.5

The document from which you will create glossary entries.

In actual practice, you probably would type the names of these journals a time or two before tiring of the tedious task and deciding to transfer the titles to the glossary. For this exercise and the next one, type the first paragraph of the letter in figure 8.5, which includes the journal titles.

To create a glossary entry, do the following:

1. Select the text you want to store in the glossary.

In this case, select the second journal title.

If the text is followed by a paragraph mark and you want to include the paragraph formatting with the glossary entry, include the paragraph mark in your selection. With many entries, you will not want to include the paragraph mark because, in all likelihood, you will insert the entries in the middle of a paragraph.

2. Format the text as you want it to appear in the glossary entry.

In this case, choose Italic from the Format menu.

3. Choose **Glossary** from the full Edit menu or press **Command-K.**

4. In the Name box, type a short but representative name for the glossary entry.

You might use the name *Acta* for this entry.

5. Click the **Define** button.

The name of the new glossary entry takes its place in the list box.

6. Click the close box to close the Glossary dialog box.

The glossary entry is available now for insertion into a document with the Glossary command's Insert button or with the Command-Backspace shortcut.

Before you go any farther, create another glossary entry—the return address—by selecting everything from the top of the document through the space following the word *Dear*. Choose Glossary, type *ra* for *return address*, and click Define.

Creating Glossary Entries from the Clipboard Contents

You can create a glossary entry by pasting the contents of the Clipboard into the Glossary dialog box. This procedure is especially handy when you want to store a graphic in the glossary. For purposes of demonstration, click an insertion point at the end of the sample letter and type the name of a third journal: *The International Journal of Neurology and Psychiatry*.

To create a glossary entry with the Clipboard contents, do the following:

1. Select the item you want to store in the glossary.

In this case, select the third journal title.

2. Cut or copy the selection to the Clipboard by choosing the Cut or Copy commands in the Edit menu.

Choose the Cut command to delete the title from its current position in the letter.

3. Choose **Glossary** or press **Command-K** to open the Glossary dialog box.

4. Choose **Paste** from the Edit menu.

The name Unnamed1 appears in the list and Name boxes. (If you already have used this method to create a glossary entry and have not renamed the previous entry, the name of the latest glossary entry is Unnamed2 instead of Unnamed1.) At least a part of the pasted entry appears in the display area below the Name box (see fig. 8.6).

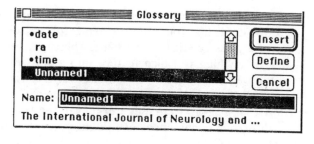

Fig. 8.6

The Glossary dialog box after you paste an entry from the Clipboard.

5. Type another name for the glossary entry.

In this case, type *ijnp*.

6. Click the **Define** button.

7. Click the close box to close the Glossary dialog box.

To see whether the glossary entry has been created successfully from the Clipboard, click an insertion point after the word *Hypnosis* in *The American Journal of Clinical Hypnosis*. Next, type a comma and a space and then press Command-Backspace. Finally, type *ijnp* and press Return. Word inserts the new title between the two existing ones (see fig. 8.7).

Fig. 8.7

The sample letter after you insert a third journal title from the glossary.

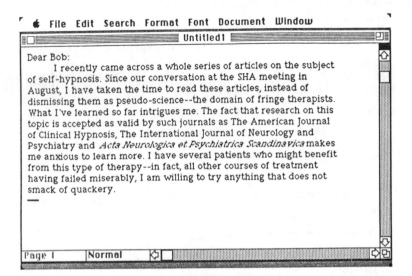

Editing Glossary Entries

One advantage of using the glossary is that you don't have to worry about making a typing error each time you enter a complex phrase, because every occurrence of a glossary entry is the same. Therefore, carefully check the spelling of anything you plan to turn into a glossary entry before you store the item in a glossary. If you discover that you have created an incorrect glossary entry or if the style or spelling of an entry simply changes for some reason, you easily can update the entry. You also can change all earlier occurrences of the entry in other documents—an easy job for the Change command in the program's Search menu (see Chapter 3).

To update a glossary entry, do the following:

1. Edit any occurrence of the glossary entry within a document, as desired; then select the edited entry.

To experiment, change *Acta Neurologica et Psychiatrica Scandinavica* into *Acta Psychiatrica et Neurologica Scandinavica*.

2. Choose **Glossary** from the full Edit menu or press **Command-K**.

3. In the list box, select the name of the entry you want to change.

In this case, select the *Acta* entry.

4. Click the **Define** button.

5. Click the close box to close the Glossary dialog box.

If you want to verify the change, click an insertion point at the end of the letter, press Command-Backspace, type *Acta*, and press Return. Word inserts the new *Acta* entry to the left of the insertion point.

Renaming Glossary Entries

Once you discover their timesaving potential, glossary entries tend to proliferate. A name may seem perfectly adequate when you first start working with glossaries, but it may lose its distinctiveness if you create whole categories of glossary entries that differ only slightly.

Suppose, for example, that you decide you need a fancy return-address entry as well as the usual, understated one; also, suppose that you want variations on the plain and fancy entries for both business and personal use. Now you need four return-address entries. Suddenly, the name for your original glossary entry—*ra*—is no longer sweet and simple. In fact, the name actually is confusing because it is no longer specific enough for your expanded needs.

In situations like this one, you need to rename the original entry so that it fits within a scheme of related but distinct names. Renaming a glossary entry is easy.

Do the following to change the name of a glossary entry:

1. Choose **Glossary** from the full Edit menu or press **Command-K**.

2. In the list box, select the name you want to change.

In this case, select the *ra* entry. The name is reproduced in the Name box.

3. Edit or replace the name.

Change the name to *sra* for *simple return address*.

4. Click the **Define** button.

5. Click the close box to close the Glossary dialog box.

Deleting Glossary Entries

Until you need to start creating specialized glossaries, you probably will store all the entries you create in the Standard Glossary. Over a period of time, the Standard Glossary can become choked with entries, necessitating long bouts of scrolling through the list box to find the entry you want to insert. If your list box becomes too crowded, you may want to scrutinize the list of entries to see whether it contains entries you are no longer using. You then can purge these entries by readily deleting them.

To delete a glossary entry, do the following:

1. Choose **Glossary** from the Edit menu or press **Command-K**.

2. Select the name of the glossary entry you want to delete.

For example, select *ijnp*.

3. Choose **Cut** from the Edit menu or press **Command-X**.

The alert box shown in figure 8.8 appears.

Fig. 8.8

The alert box that appears when you attempt to delete a glossary entry.

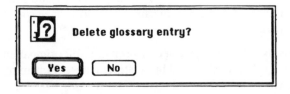

4. Click **Yes**.

The glossary entry's name disappears from the list box.

The Undo command does not restore a deleted glossary entry; however, as long as you have not copied or cut anything else, you can restore the entry by using the Paste command.

Do the following to restore a deleted glossary entry:

1. Choose **Paste** from the Edit menu.

The program pastes the entry back into the glossary with the name Unnamed1 (or Unnamed2, Unnamed3, and so on). The new entry still is selected at this point.

2. Type the entry's old name (or a new one) in the Name box.

In this case, type *ijnp*.

3. Click the **Define** button.

4. Click the Glossary dialog box's close box.

Saving Glossaries

The additions, deletions, and other changes you make to a glossary are not permanent until you save them. In the middle of a program session, you can save the glossary by using the Edit menu's Save or Save As command. If you don't deliberately save the changes, the program asks whether you want to save them when you choose Quit to exit from the program.

During a program session, if you find yourself creating numerous glossary entries (or a few complex ones) that you know you want to use again, make a point of occasionally saving the glossary. Otherwise, you can lose the glossary entries along with your unsaved editing if a power failure or other serious problem occurs.

To save the current glossary, do the following:

1. Choose **Glossary** from the Edit menu or press **Command-K**.

2. Choose **Save** or **Save As** from the File menu.

Choosing either command produces the dialog box shown in figure 8.9.

3. Type the name you want to assign to the glossary.

In this case, type *Hypnosis*.

Fig. 8.9

*The dialog box
displayed when
you choose Save
As to save a
glossary.*

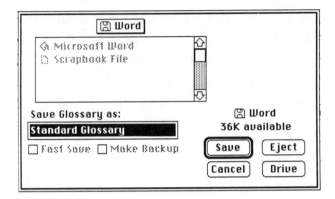

4. Click the **Drive** and **Eject** buttons if you want to save the glossary on a disk other than the one in the active drive.

The Standard Glossary is stored on the Program disk. To keep all your glossaries conveniently available, you might want to store them on the Program disk (if room is available).

5. Click the **Save** button to save the glossary.

If you typed the name of an existing glossary in Step 3, the program asks whether you want to replace the existing glossary with the current one. Click Yes to overwrite an existing glossary or click No and type a different name to create a new glossary. Once the glossary is saved, Word returns to the current document.

When you quit the program, you are prompted to save any unsaved glossary changes through the alert box shown in figure 8.10. Clicking Yes produces the Save As dialog box, just as if you had chosen Save As.

Fig. 8.10

*The alert box
displayed if you
do not save the
glossary before
choosing the
Quit command.*

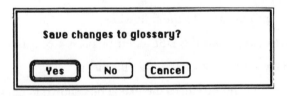

Printing Glossaries

Once you have created and saved your glossaries, you can print a copy of a glossary by opening the Glossary dialog box and then choosing the Print command from the File menu. On the left side of the paper, the program prints, in bold type, the glossary names. Word also indents the glossary entries 0.5 inch, as shown in figure 8.11. The formatting of each glossary entry is retained when you print the glossary.

Acta
    Acta Psychiatrica et Neurologica Scandinavica

date
    2/17/88

ijnp
    The International Journal of Neurology and Psychiatry

sra

                                        John Smith
                                        123 Apple Way
                                        Seattle, WA 98102
    date

    Dear

time
    12:49 PM

Fig. 8.11

A printout of the Hypnosis glossary.

Using Specialized Glossaries

If you don't want to clutter the Standard Glossary with entries used only with certain types of documents, you can store those special entries in another glossary. You can create a new glossary file at any time simply by saving the current glossary with a new name.

Unfortunately, the name of the current glossary is not displayed in the Glossary dialog box. The only way to tell which glossary is current is to examine the list of entries that identifies the glossary. If you work with several glossaries, you should include an identifying dummy entry in each one. If you begin the entry's name with a punctuation mark, the program displays the identifying entry at the top of the alphabetic listing. A typical name might be -*accounting* or -*technical*.

The Standard Glossary is the only glossary that Word automatically loads when you start the program. To use any other glossary, either merge that special glossary with the Standard Glossary or temporarily replace the Standard Glossary with the special one.

program always produces these permanent entries when you choose the Glossary command.

Three ways exist to delete a glossary. One way is to use the New command from the File menu, as explained in the previous exercise, to remove all but the standard date and time entries. Another way is to delete the glossary file from the disk by using the File menu's Delete command. A third way is to quit the program in order to return to the Macintosh Finder, drag the glossary files into the trash can, and choose Empty Trash from the Special menu.

To delete a glossary with the Delete command, do the following:

1. Choose **Glossary** from the Edit menu.

2. Choose **Delete** from the File menu.

Word now opens the Delete dialog box.

3. Select the glossary you want to delete.

4. Click the **Delete** button.

If you tell Word to delete the active glossary, the program asks you to confirm the instruction by displaying an alert box. Click Yes if you want to proceed with the deletion. Once the deletion is complete, you return to the document window.

As you become comfortable with the glossary feature, you discover many ways in which the feature can streamline day-to-day word processing.

Another program feature that can increase your speed and efficiency and help you create dazzling documents is the style sheet (discussed in the next chapter). Style sheets store formatting instructions, much as glossaries store text, and enable you to apply these instructions instantly to selected paragraphs in a document.

Working with Style Sheets

We all have opinions about "style" that usually imply a judgment about how something or someone looks. The word *stylish* usually conjures up images of someone bedecked and bejeweled in the latest fashion; the word *unstylish* evokes visions of someone less well adorned. The concept of style is complicated because it is a matter not only of personal opinion but also of context—the stylish look at corporate headquarters may be unstylish at a popular nightspot.

Publications and presentations are subject to style judgments similar to those we make about clothing. Magazines, advertisements, and display pieces—frequently eye-catching and flashy—are designed to make bold statements. Professional journals, however, which tend to be sedate and understated, convey a tone of formality. As you produce more documents with the Word program, you develop a feel for "dressing" them in styles appropriate for their tasks and messages.

After you master the more advanced levels of formatting, you will probably need a place where you can store repeatedly used formatting instructions. Storing these instructions for future use eliminates the tedious work of having to give a complex set of formatting commands again after you return to a previously used style. In Word, you can store formatting instructions as *styles*, in much the same manner that you might store outfits in a closet. And you can organize related styles into *style sheets* that you then attach to your document. Once you store several styles in a style sheet, you can enter even a complex style with one quick command.

In this chapter, you learn about the Format menu's Define Styles and Styles commands, used for creating and applying styles. After you see the basic styles in Word's default style sheet, you learn how to add, change, and delete styles of your own. Finally, you see how to merge style sheets from two documents and how to print the contents of a style sheet for reference. By the end of this chapter, you should be able to produce documents "bedecked and bejeweled" in the styles that befit their purposes.

Introducing Style Sheets

If you have followed the exercises in this book and have developed a taste for producing stylish documents, you probably have become keenly aware of the time and thought necessary for organizing a well-turned-out document. Beyond basic paragraph and character formatting, you can use all-important accessories to polish your document's appearance. For example, you may want to put precisely the same amount of space above and below all headings throughout a document, or you may want to set off border lines in a similar fashion. You may want to use both single and double borders, along with paragraphs formatted with a mixture of indents, right- and left-aligned tab stops, and a font other than the one you use for the rest of your document. The more formatting techniques in your repertoire, the more numbers and options you must remember and the more keystrokes you need for certain results.

With style sheets, however, you don't have to remember all the settings or manually re-enter them every time you want to use a style. After you define a style, which can combine any number of paragraph and character formatting options, you can save that style in a style sheet. Every new document you create comes with a default style sheet. You can add to and modify these sheets whenever you want (see fig. 9.1). By using just a few keystrokes, you then can apply to any paragraph in your document any style listed in the style sheet.

NOTE: Because all styles are applied to entire paragraphs, any character formats, such as bold or italic, that are included in the style are applied to the entire paragraph. You can change the formats of specific words within the paragraph anytime by selecting the text you want to change and using either keyboard shortcuts or the Format menu's Character command.

A style sheet can be a great help in a long document in which certain text elements require complex formatting. By creating styles, you can

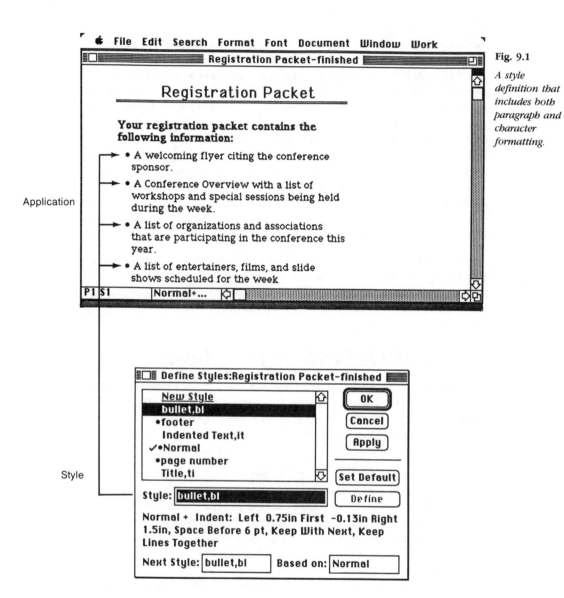

Fig. 9.1

A style definition that includes both paragraph and character formatting.

ensure formatting consistency throughout a document and save time that would be spent in dragging down menus and selecting options from dialog boxes. If your work regularly requires that you create certain types of documents—business letters, for example, or annual reports—then style sheets are even more useful. After you've created a style sheet, you can attach it to different documents so that they are all formatted in the same way.

Besides offering consistency, style sheets also have flexibility. By coordinating in two or more style sheets the code names of related styles, you can switch between style sheets to change instantly a document's appearance. For example, you might assign the code *H1* to first-level headings, *H2* to second-level headings, and *IP* to standard indented paragraphs. In a style sheet for drafts of documents, the IP code might produce a wide, double-spaced text column in 12-point Chicago—a format that's easy to read and correct. When you finish editing the draft and are ready to produce the final version of your document, you might attach a new style sheet in which the IP code produces, for example, a narrow, single-spaced text column in 10-point Times. Figure 9.2 shows a document printed first with the draft style sheet and then with the final-version style sheet.

Are you sold yet on style sheets? They are the gateway to advanced word processing. Time is money, and you can't afford to spend hours un necessarily laboring over menus, especially when you have the option of the program's power to automate formatting.

Using the Default Style Sheet

What if you like the idea of style sheets, but you are intimidated by what you may have heard about them? Aren't style sheets much more complicated than the manual formatting they replace? This book doesn't claim that styles are the easiest word-processing concept to master, but the program makes the process as painless as possible.

Word supplies a basic style sheet that has as many as 33 default styles for such standard text elements as paragraphs, footnotes, headers, and footers. When you create a document, the program attaches the basic style sheet to the document. At the outset, the style sheet has only the style represented by the ruler's normal paragraph icon—12-point New York type in a single-spaced, left-aligned paragraph format. If you add any of the other 32 basic text elements to a document, Word automatically formats that element in the program's default style and adds the style to the style sheet. Thus, you work with styles regardless of whether you realize that you are doing so.

A look at the basic styles supplied in Word's default style sheet gives you an idea about how the style descriptions and codes work. Open any document—preferably one that does not contain much manual formatting, which overrides Word's automatic formatting and obscures the default style. If you don't have such a document handy, type a line or two of text.

The RTDDA system that has revolutionized **real-time** acquisition and imaging of sonar survey data.

Developed by Info Express Inc., this versatile, compact, affordable, and well-tested system includes multiple **80286 and 68020 microprocessors** in its CPU (central processing unit) and uses a **super-high-resolution color monitor** to display images of the seafloor and seismic profile data.

Scanstore and **Scanzoom**, the system's user-friendly software modules for realtime and postprocessing analysis, allow random access to 120 megabytes of survey data. While the system is online, a laser disc drive records the data on **optical disc cartridges**, each storing the equivalent of **30 hours** of sonar records.

The RTDDA system is a combination of computer hardware and software that is licensed to individual users for the purpose of recording sonar data on WORM (write once, read many) cartridges and

Fig. 9.2

Two versions of the same document, printed with different style sheets attached.

The RTDDA system that has revolutionized **real-time** acquisition and imaging of sonar survey data.

Developed by Info Express Inc., this versatile, compact, affordable, and well-tested system includes multiple **80286 and 68020 microprocessors** in its CPU (central processing unit) and uses a **super-high-resolution color monitor** to display images of the seafloor and seismic profile data.

Scanstore and **Scanzoom**, the system's user-friendly software modules for realtime and postprocessing analysis, allow random access to 120 megabytes of survey data. While the system is online, a laser disc drive records the data on **optical disc cartridges**, each storing the equivalent of **30 hours** of sonar records.

The RTDDA system is a combination of computer hardware and software that is licensed to individual users for the purpose of recording sonar data on WORM (write

Choose Styles from the Format menu to look at the styles that the program automatically has applied to your document. If you choose Styles now, probably the only style definition you see is the one for normal paragraphs. But you also can look at an alphabetic list of the names and definitions of all of the program's automatic styles if you hold down Shift while choosing Styles from the Format menu.

To view a list of Word's automatic styles, do the following:

1. Hold down **Shift** and choose **Styles** from the Format menu to open the Styles dialog box (see fig. 9.3).

Fig. 9.3

The Styles dialog box.

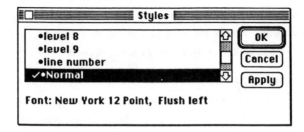

2. Scroll through the list of styles.

The list shows styles for footers, footnote references, footnote text, headers, index entries, outline headings, line numbers, page numbers, PostScript commands, tables of contents, and normal paragraphs.

3. Select different styles in order to view their formatting definitions.

When you select a style, Word displays, in the area below the list, the character, paragraph, and section settings necessary for producing that style.

All automatic styles (identified by a black dot) are based on New York—the font used for normal paragraphs. Every other style has its own characteristics. Footnotes, for example, use 10-point New York rather than 12-point. Footnote reference marks are elevated (superscripted) 3 points above the text line. Level-1 outline headings (bold, 12-point New York) have 12 points of spacing above them.

Some of the styles fall into categories and vary little from each other. For example, the only differences between index levels 3 through 9 and the corresponding outline levels are the sizes of the left indent.

To create a custom style sheet, just build on these basic styles. The process isn't difficult. You can add, change, and rearrange styles. Then, every time you instruct Word to save the current version of your document, the program automatically saves any default styles you have used along with any new styles you have defined.

You can save the style sheet in two ways: attached only to the document you're working on or part of the default style sheet that you use not only for the current document but also for any new documents you create. If you prefer to use 10-point Times rather than 12-point New York as the default font for normal paragraphs, for example, you can change the style for normal paragraphs and then specify that the style sheet containing the new normal style be used as the new default style sheet.

Understanding the Define Styles Command

The Word program's default styles will satisfy many of your basic formatting requirements for a while, but eventually you will supplement them with your own styles. You can create a new style by altering an existing one—usually the style for normal paragraphs—by using the Format menu's Define Styles command.

Before you practice creating styles, however, you should know more about the Define Styles command. With this command, you can create, revise, add, delete, and combine styles. You also can use the Define Styles ommand to apply styles to selected paragraphs.

Choosing Define Styles produces the dialog box shown in figure 9.4. Like the Styles dialog box, the Define Styles dialog box alphabetically lists the styles in use in the active document. To see those styles plus all of Word's automatic styles, press Shift while you choose the Define Styles command.

Understanding Style Definitions

When you open the Define Styles dialog box, the New Style entry at the top of the alphabetic list is highlighted. Below New Style, the styles preceded by a bullet (black dot) are automatic styles. The styles preceded by a check mark have been applied to the currently selected paragraph. At this point, probably the only style you see is Normal, for

Fig. 9.4

*The Define
Styles dialog
box.*

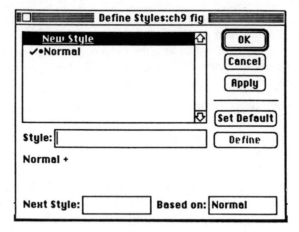

normal paragraphs; if your text contains no other styles, Normal probably
has both a bullet and a check mark in front of it. The program assumes
that any style you create is based on this style.

Below the list box is the Style box, where you type the name you want
to assign to a new style. When New Style is highlighted in the list, the
Style box is empty because the program assumes that your next action
will be to type the name of a new style you are defining.

You can assign any unique name (or names) to a style, but you will find
the name easier to remember if it reflects the style's purpose. A common
technique is to assign both a descriptive name and a two- or three-letter
code to often-used styles. The descriptive name makes the style's purpose
obvious as you scroll through the list in the Styles dialog box, and the
code is more convenient for applying styles directly from the keyboard.
To assign more than one name to a style, separate the names by commas.

When an existing style is selected in the list box, the name of the style
also is displayed in the Style box so that you can edit the name or
modify the style's formatting instructions to create a new style.

Below the Style box is an area in which the program displays the formatting instructions associated with the style selected in the list box.
You don't type directly in this area. Word provides the information automatically, showing the choices you make in the Format menu. Notice
how this style definition is organized. Because all paragraph styles except
normal are based on another style, the program first lists the base style,
followed by a plus sign and the additional formatting instructions that
make up this style.

The style for a level-1 outline heading, for example, is the same as for a normal paragraph except that the style is bold and preceded by 12 additional points of space. If you select the level-1 style in the Define Styles dialog box, the description area reads Normal+Bold,SpaceBefore 12 pt. The Normal style formatting definition reads Font: New York 12 Point, Flush left. The full definition for a level-1 outline heading, therefore, is the combination of these two descriptions. Figure 9.5 shows how the Define Styles dialog box looks with level 1 selected.

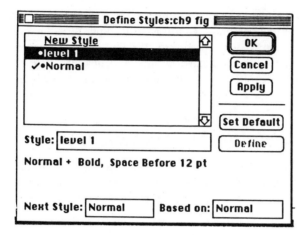

Fig. 9.5

The style definition for level-1 outline headings.

If you are creating a style, you don't have to base it on the normal style. If you hold down the Shift key when you choose Define Styles from the Format menu, the display box shows all the basic styles. You can use any existing style, even new ones you create, as a building block. Just enter in the Based on box the name of the style you want to modify. You also can change the base style later if you want. Merely replace the contents of the Based on box with another style name, and the program substitutes the definition of the new base style for the old one in the selected style's definition.

Formatting instructions for a complicated style may exceed the space available in the description area. In this case, to review all the formatting instructions, you must either open the Character and Paragraph dialog boxes to see the options selected or print the style sheet (see the last section in the chapter).

Applying the Style to the Next Paragraph

You can use the Next Style box at the bottom of the dialog box to specify the style that you want Word to apply to the paragraph following each paragraph formatted with the current style. The program automatically enters the current style in this field. This automatic application of a style to the next paragraph occurs only when you type, not when you apply styles to existing paragraphs. The application is triggered when you press Return to end a paragraph and start a new one.

The Next Style feature can be quite useful. For example, you always may want a normal paragraph to follow a heading. When you create the heading style, simply type *Normal* in the Next Style box to link these two styles. Then, after you have applied the heading style, typed the heading, and pressed Return, the program automatically switches to normal style for the paragraph that follows.

Implementing Style Definitions

The Define Styles dialog box has the usual button collection, plus two more. The OK, Cancel, and Apply buttons function much as they do with other commands, as illustrated in the following list:

- OK records any changes made to the style sheet, applies the highlighted style to selected paragraphs, and closes the Define Styles dialog box.

- Cancel closes the dialog box but does not apply any style to the text. Cancel records changes to the style sheet only if you have confirmed the changes by clicking the Define button (discussed at the end of this section).

- Apply applies the highlighted style to the selected paragraph but leaves the dialog box open so that you can make additional changes.

The dialog box also contains a Set Default button. With Set Default, you add the selected style to Word's default style sheet. If the selected style is one you have created, Word adds the new style to the default style sheet that the program loads automatically when you open a new document. If you have changed an automatic style, the program records the changes and applies them to the current document and to all documents you create. (Existing documents remain formatted according to the earlier style definition.) If you change the normal style from 12-point New York to 10-point Times and click Set Default, for example, Word automatically formats normal paragraphs in the current document and in all subsequent documents in 10-point Times type.

The bottom button, Define, becomes available when you change the name or the definition of a style. Clicking Define adds a specified style to the style sheet or modifies an existing style. When you click the Define button to record the style name(s) and formatting, the name of the new style appears, highlighted and checked, in the styles list. The program also highlights the style's name in the Styles box and displays the first word of the name in the Next Style box. The dialog box remains open so that you can make other changes.

Creating Your Own Styles

The most important consideration you make as you create a style is its effect on your document's message. Do you want to draw immediate attention to a particular passage of text? Do you want to distinguish one part of a document from another part? Do you want to create a formal, highly decorative invitation that lends an air of importance to a special event?

Whatever the purpose of your document, remember that too much variation can detract from the contents and that too little can leave your document flat and characterless. Because creating and changing styles in the program is easy, try several styles before you decide which one achieves the effect you want. When you finally decide on the appropriate style for your document, specify the style in a style sheet and attach it to your document.

To define a style in a style sheet, you can use one of the following methods: you can format a paragraph manually and then record the formatting as a style; you can open the Define Styles dialog box, select the desired formatting options, and tell the program to record your choices as formatting instructions for the new style; or you can base a new style on one that already exists.

At first, you probably will feel most comfortable using the first method. As you gain experience, however, you will find that specifying styles but not viewing their effects is faster than relying on the first method. In this section, you learn how to use all three methods.

Defining Styles by First Formatting a Paragraph

Using the program's style-record feature is the easiest way to define a style. You simply select the text with the desired formatting, choose Define Styles from the Format menu, type a name for the new style, and click the `Define` button.

To become comfortable with the process of defining a style from previous paragraph formatting, either select the title of the document now on-screen or type a new title. Use the title's formatting to practice recording styles.

To record the formatting of a paragraph as a style, do the following:

1. Format the paragraph the way you want it.

In this case, format your title in the following manner: in the Character dialog box, click `Bold`, `Venice`, `14` (points), and `Condensed`; on the ruler, click the center-alignment icon; in the Paragraph dialog box, click `Keep With Next ¶` and `Keep Lines Together`, and type *12* (points) in the `Spacing After` field. This formatting produces a title similar to the one in figure 9.6.

Fig. 9.6

A title formatted in preparation for recording a style.

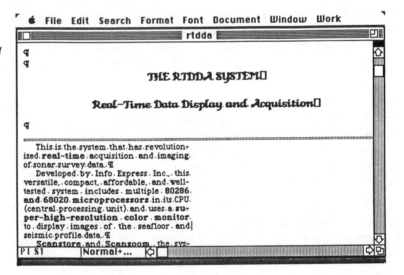

2. After the insertion point is in the fully formatted title, choose **Define Styles** from the Format menu or press **Command-T**.

In the Define Styles dialog box, Word highlights the New Style entry, selects the Style box, and displays, in the style description area, a definition of the formats applied to the title (see fig. 9.7). Notice that Normal is checked and that the Normal style also is listed in the Based on box. To record this definition as a style and add it to your document's style sheet, you must name the new style.

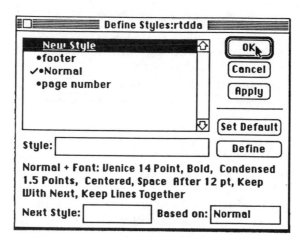

Fig. 9.7

The definition for the formats applied to the title.

3. Type a name for the new style, followed by a comma and a two- or three-character code that you choose.

In this case, name your style *Title* and assign it the code *ti*.

4. Click the **Apply** button.

Word adds the style to the style sheet and applies the style to the selected paragraph.

Applying the new style to the paragraph may seem redundant because you already have formatted the paragraph directly. But this procedure attaches a hidden code to the paragraph; the code links the paragraph's format to the instructions stored under the style's name. If you later change the style definition, the changes affect every paragraph in the document to which you attached the style. Using style sheets, therefore, lets you rapidly make formatting changes throughout a document.

The program displays the new style name and abbreviation in the list box, Style box, and Next Style box (see fig. 9.8).

Fig. 9.8

The Define Styles dialog box after you have created the new style.

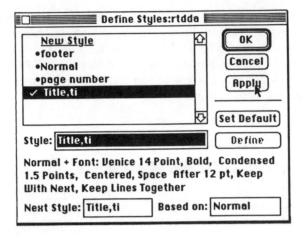

Defining Styles with the Define Styles Command

If you know which styles you want to use for the various elements of a document, you can skip the manual-formatting stage and create the styles directly in the Define Styles dialog box. If you create several styles one after the other, this method is particularly handy because you don't have to keep switching between the Define Styles dialog box and the text in order to format paragraphs.

Now, create a style for a text paragraph by using the Define Styles dialog box. Use any document to follow along.

To define a style by using the Define Styles command, do the following:

1. Choose **Define Styles** from the Format menu or press **Command-T**.

If you have not applied another style to the text containing the insertion point, Word places a check mark in front of Normal. If some other style is checked, select Normal and click Apply to return the paragraph to the normal style because the program bases the style you are ready to define on the format of the selected paragraph.

2. Specify the desired formatting by using either the Character and Paragraph commands or the keyboard shortcuts.

In this case, specify the following formats: in the Character dialog box, click Dover, 12 (points), and Condensed and then click OK to incorporate these character formats into the new style and to close the dialog box; on the ruler, set a left indent at 0.5 inch, a first-line indent at 0.75 inch, and a right indent at 5.5 inches; in the Paragraph dialog box, click Keep With Next ¶ and then click OK to incorporate this paragraph format into the new style and close the dialog box.

3. In the Style box (which is highlighted), type a descriptive name, a comma, and a two- or three-character code.

Name this style *Indented Text* and give it the code *it*.

4. Click the **Define** button.

The program adds the new style to the list and enters the style's name in the Next Style box.

If you want to define as many styles as you anticipate are necessary for the current document, repeat this process until all styles are defined. For efficiency, do not close the Define Styles dialog box or apply any of the styles until you have defined all of them.

Basing a New Style on an Existing Style

As your style collection increases, you often find that a style you need for your current document is similar to one you already have created for another document. At some point, you will feel comfortable enough with the style-creating process to start basing new styles on existing ones. When you design documents, this technique can save significant amounts of time.

Remember that if you change a style you have used as the base for other styles, the change affects each spin-off style—but only in the current document. For example, if you base a new style on one that uses bold type and then change the original style to italic instead of bold, both styles use italic rather than bold.

If you delete a base style (see the section in this chapter titled "Deleting Styles"), the deletion does not affect spin-off styles. Any styles based on the deleted style retain all the deleted style's formatting instructions as well as their own. Because all styles must be based on some other style, however, the definitions of the spin-offs step back one generation to include the complete definition of the former base style, including reference to the style on which the deleted style was based (probably normal).

You can approach the modification of existing styles in two ways. You can change the existing style and assign it a new name *before* you apply the style, or you can apply the existing style, modify it, and then assign the new name. The second method of compiling a style definition is helpful in two ways. You instantly can see the differences between the current style and the one on which you based it, and you can use this information to coordinate the current style more closely with the base style. The next exercise helps you practice the second method.

Try basing a new style on an existing one by doing the following:

1. Open a new document and type a few lines of text. Then select the paragraph.

2. Choose **Define Styles** from the Format menu or press **Command-T**.

3. In the list box, select the **Normal** style. Because Normal is checked, it is applied to the selected paragraph.

Word enters the style's name in the Next Style and Based on boxes and applies the selected style's formatting instructions to the paragraph. The instructions themselves are displayed in the description area.

4. From the formatting instructions in the style-description area, assess what you want to change to create the new style.

5. Click **New Style**.

Word removes the base style's name from the Next Style box and then replaces the base style's formatting instructions in the description area with the base style's name and a plus sign.

6. Type in the Style box the name that you want to assign to the new style.

For example, to create a double-spaced paragraph style, begin by typing *double-spaced paragraph*.

7. If you want to modify the base style's character formatting, choose **Character** from the Format menu, specify the new options, and click **OK** to integrate these options into the new style and to close the Character dialog box.

8. To modify the base style's paragraph formatting, choose **Paragraph** from the Format menu, specify the new options, and click **OK** to integrate these options into the new style and to close the Paragraph dialog box.

Try defining the style with double line spacing, a 0.5-inch first-line indent, and a justified right margin.

9. Click the **Define** button.

When you click Define, the program adds the new style to the list and displays its formatting instructions in the description area.

The on-screen definition for a style you have built from an existing style is different from the display of a style you have recorded or created from scratch. For instance, the formatting instructions trace the development of the new style. First, the name of the base style is given, and then any deleted formatting is mentioned. If you delete a base style's condensed option when you create a new style, for example, the formatting instructions for the new style show Not Condensed. Finally, the formatting instructions list the additional options incorporated into the new style.

Applying Styles

As you created styles using the Define Styles command, you gained some experience in applying them. But how do you quickly apply a style to existing text or to text you are typing?

The Word program provides several methods for applying any style to a selected paragraph or block of selected paragraphs. You can select the style in either the Define Styles or the Styles dialog boxes and click Apply; you can use a keyboard shortcut; or—if you have added the style to the Work menu (see Chapter 11)—you can choose the style just as you choose any other command.

All these methods apply the selected style to the paragraph containing the insertion point or to all selected paragraphs. Once you apply a style, it remains in effect—even if you press Return to start a new paragraph—unless you specify a different style in the Next Style text box of the Define Styles dialog box.

Styles are applied to whole paragraphs; you can't apply styles to just a word or two within a paragraph. After applying a style, however, you can manually apply character formatting to parts of paragraphs. This manual formatting has no effect on the definition of the applied style.

Applying Styles with the Define Styles and Styles Commands

With both the Define Styles and Styles commands, you can open the style sheet associated with the current document and apply a style to selected paragraphs. Applying styles from the Define Styles dialog box is a convenient step when you create and edit styles, but if you do not plan to alter a style, you can use the abbreviated Styles dialog box, which has fewer distractions. The process for applying a style is the same with either command.

Apply a style by using either Styles or Define Styles on the format menu by doing the following:

1. Select the paragraph to which you want to apply a style.

2. Choose **Styles** or **Define Styles** from the Format menu or press **Command-B** or **Command-T**, respectively.

3. Select the style you want to apply.

4. If you want to apply the style and close the dialog box, click **OK**. To apply the style and leave the dialog box open, click **Apply**.

The new style is applied to all selected paragraphs.

If you do not like the style of the new paragraph, you can choose Undo Formatting from the Edit menu to restore the original style or you simply can apply another style.

Applying Styles with the Keyboard

As with most actions in Word, you can use a keyboard shortcut to choose and apply a style (see the Quick Reference Guide in the back of the book).

To apply a style by using the keyboard, do the following:

1. Click an insertion point in the paragraph where you want to apply the style.

2. Press **Shift-Command-S**.

The program displays the word Style in the page number box in the screen's bottom left corner.

3. Type the style's two- or three-letter code, its full name, or as much of the name as necessary to distinguish it clearly from the other styles listed in your document's style sheet.

4. Press **Return**.

Applying Styles from the Work Menu

The final method of applying styles is selecting them from the Work menu, a customized menu that you can add to the program's normal menu bar. You learn how to add styles and other items to the Work menu in Chapter 11. After a style is represented on the menu, you apply the style by choosing it just as you choose any other command from a menu.

Editing Styles

As your tastes or the formatting requirements for certain types of documents change, you can edit the styles in any style sheet, including the program's default style sheet. In fact, you already have seen how to edit styles. When you create a new style based on an existing one, you actually are copying the style, saving it under a new name, and editing it to suit your purpose.

Editing a style is as easy as creating one, and you follow virtually the same steps. You can edit anything and everything that pertains to a certain style: its name and formatting instructions, the style it is based on, and the next style to which you want to link it. When you edit a style, however, any styles based on that style also change.

Changing Style Names

For several reasons, you may want to change a style's name. Like glossary entries, when you begin accumulating styles, you see that they fall into categories, and you may want to change the names of the styles to reflect both the relationship between the styles and the fine distinctions that make one style different from another. Or perhaps you want to merge two style sheets (see the "Merging Style Sheets" section in this chapter), and you must change some style names to preserve important style definitions. (If you merge two style sheets, the formatting instructions for styles in the incoming style sheet override the instructions for styles with the same name in the current style sheet.)

To rename a style, you can either replace or edit the existing name. For example, to store opening styles for several purposes—perhaps for use in letters, reports, and memos—you might rename a style called *Opening* as *Openlet* and then create two new styles based on *Openlet* that you name *Openrep* and *Openmem*.

Follow these steps to change a style name:

1. Choose **Define Styles** from the Format menu or press **Command-T**.

2. Select from the list the style you want to rename.

3. In the Style box, select the entire style name or just the part you want to change.

4. Type the new style name or partial style name and add an abbreviation, separated from the name by a comma.

If you type the name of an existing style, the program displays an alert box (see fig. 9.9). Unless you want to merge the new style with the old one, click Cancel and type a new name in the Style box.

Fig. 9.9

The alert box displayed when you try to assign an existing style name to a new style.

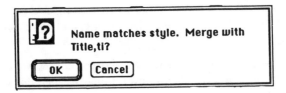

Name matches style. Merge with Title,ti?

OK   Cancel

5. Click **Define** to make the change in the style sheet or click **OK** to make the change in the style sheet, apply the style to the selected paragraph, and close the dialog box.

Changing Formatting Instructions

One of the hallmarks of a well-designed document is *harmony*—the compatibility of its elements. When you revise the formatting instructions associated with a style, the program changes the formatting of all paragraphs to which the style has been applied in the current document. Before you modify a style, therefore, you should consider how the newly formatted text blends with adjacent styles. You want to make sure that harmony is maintained before you proceed with drastic changes.

Do the following steps to edit a style's formatting instructions:

1. Choose **Define Styles** from the Format menu or press **Command-T**.

2. Select from the style list the style you want to edit.

3. Use Character, Paragraph, Show Ruler, or other formatting commands from the Format or Font menus (or use their keyboard shortcuts) to add to or modify the selected style's formatting instructions.

4. Click **Define**, **Apply**, or **OK** in the Define Styles dialog box to integrate the changes into the style.

Changing Styles on Which Other Styles Are Based

You can edit all of a style's formatting instructions except the ones associated with its base style. To change the instructions inherited from the base style, you either must edit the base style or choose another base style.

To change or eliminate the style on which another style is based, do the following:

1. Choose **Define Styles** from the Format menu or press **Command-T**.

2. Select the style for which you want to change the base style.

3. Select the name displayed in the Based on box.

4. Type the name of the new base style or press **Backspace** to delete the displayed style name.

5. Click **Define** to make the change.

If you choose a new base style, Word incorporates the base style's formatting instructions in the instructions for the current style, unless they have been overridden by your own formatting choices.

Changing the Style Applied to Following Paragraphs

You can change the style designated in the Next Style box, but you cannot delete entirely the contents of this box. Recall that the Next Style feature is solely for use when you type. When you press Return at the end of a paragraph to which you have applied the current style, the formatting of the style named in this box is applied to the following paragraph. To change the following style, simply select the style name in the Next Style box and then type the new style name.

Copying and Pasting Formatting Instructions

Occasionally, you may find that creating several styles varying only slightly from an existing style is a convenient procedure. For example, you could create one set of styles that uses single spacing; this set cuts down paper waste as you crank out draft after draft. The second set, using double spacing, could be applied when you're ready for the final printout. You can complete this step quickly by copying the original style and pasting its formatting instructions into a new or existing style on the same style sheet. (If you paste formatting instructions into an existing style, the pasted instructions replace rather than supplement all old instructions.) After pasting, you can edit the instructions, if necessary.

Copy and paste formatting instructions by doing the following:

1. Choose **Define Styles** from the Format menu or press **Command-T**.

2. Select from the list the style that has the formatting instructions you want to copy.

3. Choose **Copy** from the Edit menu.

4. Select **New Style** or the style where you want to paste the copied formatting instructions.

5. Choose **Paste** from the Edit menu.

6. Modify the new style by selecting options in the Character and Paragraph dialog boxes or by choosing commands from the Format and Font menus.

7. Supply a new name if you want to create a new style.

8. Click **Define**, **Apply**, or **OK** in the Define Styles dialog box.

Deleting Styles

You undoubtedly have a purpose for each custom style when you devise it, but dormant styles eventually do accumulate. You can delete a style by selecting its name in the Define Styles dialog box and choosing Cut from the Edit menu.

Do the following to delete a style:

1. Choose **Define Styles** from the Format menu or press **Command-T**.

2. Select the style you want to delete from the list.

3. Choose **Cut** from the Edit menu.

After Word displays the alert box (see fig. 9.10), you have the opportunity to delete the style or cancel the action.

Fig. 9.10

The alert box displayed when you try to delete a style.

4. Click **OK**.

5. Click **OK** in the dialog box to close it.

You cannot use the Undo command to restore a deleted style. If you haven't cut or copied anything else, however, and if you haven't closed the Define Styles dialog box, you can choose the Paste command to restore the formatting instructions. The old style name is not restored, but you can type that name or any other one in the Style box and then click Define to return the style to the style sheet.

Merging Style Sheets

The styles you create when you work on a document are stored in a style sheet attached to your document. When you create another document of the same kind, you can use the styles created for the related document by merging the earlier document's style sheet with the one attached to the current document.

When you merge style sheets, the incoming styles take precedence. If a style in the merged style sheet has the same name as a style in the current style sheet, Word replaces the current formatting instructions with the incoming instructions.

To merge two style sheets, do the following:

1. Open the document to which you want to attach the style sheet created for another document.

2. Choose **Define Styles** from the Format menu.

3. Choose **Open** from the File menu.

Word displays a dialog box that lists all the Word documents which have custom style sheets on the disk (see fig. 9.11).

Fig. 9.11

The dialog box displayed when you choose Open *after you choose* Define Styles.

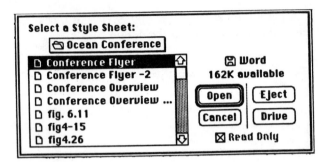

4. Double-click the name of the document whose style sheet you want to merge with the current style sheet.

This step closes the dialog box and merges the selected style sheet with the current one.

 NOTE: You can copy a single style from one style sheet to another by using multiple windows. Read how to do this in Chapter 10 in the section called "Copying Formatting between Windows."

Printing Style Sheets

To compare style sheets or to keep a list of styles for reference when you create new documents, you can print your style sheets, complete with style names and formatting instructions.

Print the style sheet associated with the current document by doing the following:

1. Choose **Styles** or **Define Styles** from the Format menu.

2. Choose **Print** from the File menu.

3. Select any desired print options and click OK.

Your printout looks similar to the one in figure 9.12.

To include the program's default styles in printed style sheets, hold down Shift while you choose Styles or Define Styles.

Becoming proficient in defining and using styles and style sheets may take you a while. Learning to use the keyboard shortcuts for defining,

```
4c
        Normal + Font: Times 6 Point, Indent:  Left  0.13in

footnote   reference
        Normal + Font: 9 Point,  Superscript 3 Point

footnote   text
        Normal + Font: 10 Point

header
        Normal +     Tab stops: 3 in Centered;  6 in Right Flush

level  1
        Normal +  Bold,  Space Before 12 pt

level  2
        Normal +  Bold,  Space Before 6 pt

level  3
        Normal +  Bold

level  4
        Normal +  Bold

Normal
        Font: New York 12 Point,  Flush left

page   number
        Normal +
```

Fig. 9.12

A printout of a style sheet.

revising, and applying styles to parts of your document also may require some practice. But the time is well spent. If you are thoughtful and thorough when you develop styles in the Word program, they can place at your fingertips a degree of power unprecedented in earlier word-processing programs.

In the next chapter, you learn how to use multiple windows in order to work with several copies of the same document or with several different documents at one time. You learn how to open and resize windows and how to copy text and formatting between windows.

Working with Windows

Windows are one of the hallmarks of the Macintosh. The first time you turned on your Mac and inserted a system disk, a window called the Finder appeared on-screen. The Finder displayed icons for all the files on the system disk. When you inserted a different disk, another window containing icons for the files on that disk appeared. You rapidly learned that you change the size of a window by dragging the size box in the window's lower right corner and that you move a window around the screen by dragging the window's title bar. When you have more text than the window can display at one time, you learned to use the horizontal and vertical scroll bars to view text from outside the window's frame.

Windows are common to almost all Macintosh programs, and in almost all programs, you use the same basic techniques to manipulate windows and the text in them. However, some programs—and Word is one of them—go beyond the basics and use windows in ways that make the job of creating polished documents easier than ever.

Throughout this book, you have been introduced one by one to some of the components of Word windows—the page number box in the lower left corner and the style name to the right of the page number, for example. The components of a Word window, some of which may not be familiar to you, are identified in figure 10.1. An overview of these components follows:

- The *close box* closes a window. If you have not saved your work, you are asked whether you would like your work saved.

237

- The *title bar* shows the name you have given your document. (If you have not named the document, the title bar displays Untitled1.)

- The *zoom box* enlarges a half-size window so that it fills the document display area or reduces a window to half size if the window already is enlarged.

- The *split bar* divides a window. Drag down the split bar to accomplish the task.

- The *vertical scroll bar* scrolls up or down, and the *horizontal scroll bar* scrolls left or right.

- The *size box* (instead of the zoom box) sizes the window the way *you* want.

- The message area at the lower left shows the current *style name* and *page number*.

Fig. 10.1

The components of a Word window.

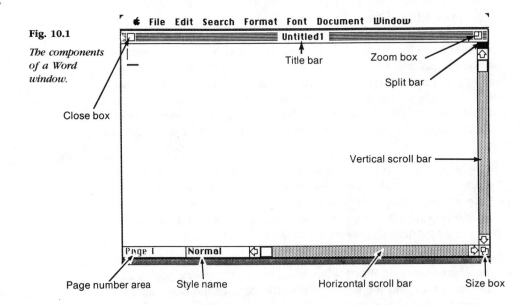

When you use Word, you can have several windows open at once on your screen. With multiple windows open, you can view text simultaneously in different parts of the same document or in different documents, and you can transfer information quickly between different documents or different parts of the same document. You also can open several different kinds of windows, including a footnote window that shows the footnote text matching the footnote reference mark in the active window. Once Word displays the windows, the techniques you use to manipulate the information in the windows are essentially the same as those you use when working in only one window.

In this chapter, you learn how to split a single window into two sections in order to view two portions of the same document. You also learn how to view the same document in several windows and how to open documents in different windows. You see how to transfer format information and text between two documents displayed simultaneously in different windows and how to access documents through the Window menu. Finally, we give you some tips for using multiple windows as you write.

Splitting a Window

You can split a single window into two sections by dragging down the split bar from its normal position at the top of the vertical scroll bar. Splitting a window with this technique is quick and easy. Although you can view and manipulate only two parts of the same document by dragging down the split bar, you can make changes in either window. Often, this simple procedure meets your editing needs.

The keyboard shortcut for splitting the window is Command-Option-S. If you press this combination when the window is not split, the split bar moves to the center of the screen, creating two sections of identical size. Pressing Command-Option-S a second time changes the two sections back to a single window.

When you split a window, Word also splits the vertical scroll bar, giving each section its own arrows and scroll box (see figure 10.2). As a result, the text in either section can be scrolled up and down independently. The single horizontal scroll bar at the bottom of the split window moves both sections left and right together.

Notice that only one section of the split window can be active at a time. To move from one section to the other, simply click the section to which you want to move. You also can use a keyboard shortcut, Command-Option-W, which moves the insertion point to the "next" window without disturbing the state of the "preceding" window. If you press Command-Option-W while working with a split window, the inactive section becomes active. If you use this keyboard shortcut while working

Fig. 10.2

A split window.

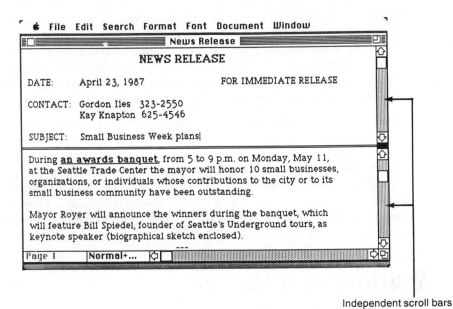

Independent scroll bars

with multiple windows, each window becomes active in turn, in the order in which you opened them.

Splitting the window can be useful when you are editing one area of a document and realize that you need to paste in a section of text from elsewhere in the document. You could, of course, scroll to the text you want to move, select and cut it, and then try to find your way back to your previous location. A quicker method, however, is to split the window so that you can display, in one section of the window, the text you want to move and, in the other section of the window, the place where you want to insert the text. Then you can cut the passage, click the insertion point, choose Paste from the Edit menu, and drag the split bar back to the top of the window to restore the full window—all in a matter of seconds.

NOTE: You also can accomplish this type of cut and paste procedure with a keyboard shortcut—without splitting the window. Click an insertion point where you want to insert the text; find and cut the text you want to move; and then press Command-Option-Z. The part of the document containing the insertion point you clicked at the beginning of this maneuver jumps into view, ready for you to paste the cut text from the Clipboard. Word records the locations of three consecutive insertion points; and each time you press Command-Option-Z, the program moves back to the preceding insertion point. When the program reaches the second previous insertion point, Word returns to the current insertion point and begins cycling through the same locations again.

Working with Multiple Windows

You can have as many as 16 windows open at the same time. You can use these windows to display copies of the same document or several different documents.

You can practice opening windows in the following exercises. Follow along as we show you how to open several copies of the same document and then how to open several documents.

Opening the Same Document in Several Windows

You can open a second copy of an open document by choosing Open from the File menu and double-clicking the document's name. The following procedure shows an alternative way to view two versions of the same document:

1. Open a document (if none is open).

2. Choose **New Window** from the Window menu.

With a number added to its name, a copy of the open document fills the screen and hides the original window.

3. Click the zoom box in the new window's upper right corner.

The window shrinks to half size and moves to the bottom of the screen.

4. Click the original document window (behind the new window) to make it active.

5. Click the original window's zoom box.

You now have two half-size windows, as shown in figure 10.3. You can use all the editing techniques you learned in previous chapters to copy or move text, graphics, and formatting between these two windows (as explained later in this chapter). Remember, though, that only one window at a time is active. The active window is the one with the highlighted title bar. Make the other window active by clicking it or by pressing Command-Option-W.

Fig. 10.3

The same document displayed in two half-size windows.

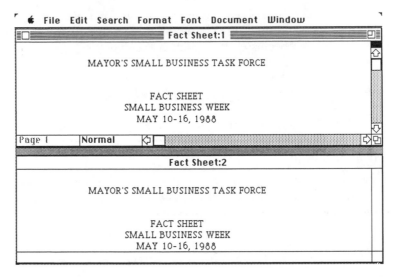

When you open the same document in more than one window, Word numbers each version and adds the names of the versions to the list of documents in the Window menu. For example, if you open a window containing a copy of a document called Entertainment, the original version is renamed Entertainment:1, and the copy is named Entertainment:2.

Bear in mind that although these documents were opened separately and have slightly different names, the two actually are the same document. The document in one window immediately reflects any change you make in the other window. The two windows exist as a single file on the disk, so saving either window with a new name simply applies that name to the single file. In the next section, however, you learn how to view two or more separate documents on the screen.

Opening Several Documents in Many Windows

One of the most common reasons for opening several documents at the same time is to transfer information or formatting between them.

To display two different documents at the same time, do the following:

1. Choose **Open** from the File menu.

2. Double-click the name of the first document you want to open.

The document opens in a full-size window.

3. Again choose **Open** from the File menu.

4. Double-click the name of the second document you want to open.

The second document opens in another full-size window, which obscures the first window.

5. Click the zoom box of the active window.

Word reduces the active window to half size and moves it to the bottom of the screen.

6. Click anywhere in the full-size window in the background to make that window active.

7. Click the full-size window's zoom box.

This action reduces the second window to half size and moves it to the top of the screen. Your screen now resembles the one in figure 10.4.

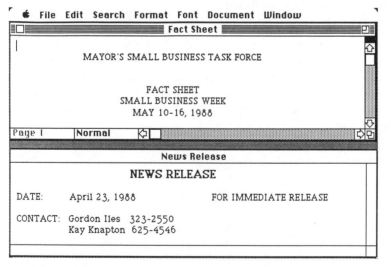

Fig. 10.4

Two documents in half-size windows.

NOTE: If you want to work on several documents at once but don't need to see the contents of more than one document at a time, you easily can keep track of and access each open document through the Window menu. If you pull down the Window menu, you see the names of all the windows you have opened. The check mark tells you which window is active. By pulling down the menu and choosing a window name, you can make any window active—even if you cannot see it behind all the other windows on the screen.

Manipulating the Windows

To benefit from the flexibility of using Word's windows, you need to know how to manipulate the windows once you have them on-screen.

As you have seen in the previous exercise, Word automatically displays, in a full-size window, the document that you open. The newly opened document occupies the entire screen and covers any windows you may have opened previously. To view the document in the hidden window, you reduce the size of the active (top) window and click the window underneath to make it active.

To reduce the size of the active window, you can click its zoom box, drag its size box, or double-click the window's title bar. Reducing the size of the window means that you can see less of the document the window displays; therefore, you may have to make greater use of the scroll bars to view the text.

If you have several windows open at the same time, a quicker way to bring the window of a document to the front is to choose that document from the Window menu (see fig. 10.5). The Window menu contains the following items: the Show Clipboard command, which displays the Clipboard's contents; the New Window command, which opens another window containing a copy of the current document; and a list of all open documents.

Fig. 10.5

The Window menu.

If only two windows are open, clicking both their zoom boxes positions them one above the other so that you can see the contents of both windows at once. If more than two windows are open, clicking their zoom boxes distributes them about the screen in a combination of half- and quarter-size windows, depending on how many windows are on-screen. The result is a configuration something like the one shown in figure 10.6.

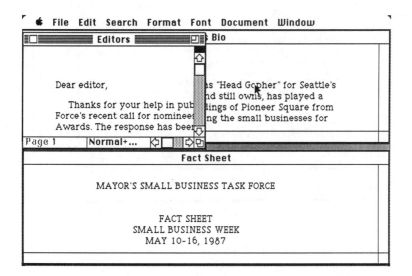

Fig. 10.6

Word's automatic distribution of three windows.

Sometimes, automatic sizing may be too much of a good thing, however. A quarter-size window is not a particularly convenient area in which to work because the small window gives you only a hint of a document's contents.

If you want to edit one of the documents in a small window, you first must enlarge that window. Word offers two ways to enlarge a window. A quick and simple method is to click the document window's zoom box to return the window to full size. Sometimes, however, zooming is not the answer because you want to continue to see all the windows. In this case, drag the size box of any window you want to shrink or enlarge. By dragging the size box, you can arrange and rearrange the windows until you find the configuration most convenient for your work. Figure 10.7 shows an arrangement that allows you to work in one window but click either of two others to make them active as the need arises.

Fig. 10.7

Resizing windows to create efficient configurations.

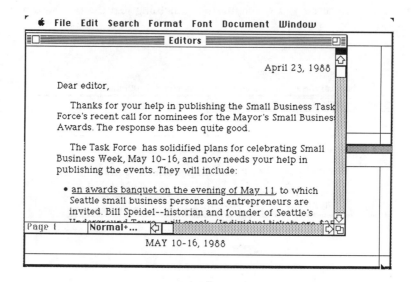

Using Keyboard Shortcuts with Windows

Transferring text or format information between documents in windows is no different from transferring the information within a single document. To move or copy text between windows, use the standard Cut, Copy, and Paste commands, plus the keyboard shortcuts discussed in Chapter 3 (see also the Quick Reference Guide in the back of the book).

In the following exercises, try practicing the keyboard shortcuts. The more you use them, the sooner you will memorize them. Then when you're typing, you can give the commands from the keyboard rather than interrupt the flow of your work by reaching for the mouse.

With each keyboard shortcut method that you learn in the following sections, you will have two options: selecting the text or the formatting you want to move or copy *before* pressing the shortcut keys (method 1), or making your selection *after* pressing them (method 2). With method 1, you work from a source document *to* a target document. With method 2, you work in a target document and bring information to it *from* a source document.

Copying Text between Windows

You can use either of the two shortcut methods to copy text between two windows or between different documents visible in these windows. Both options involve the same keyboard shortcut: Command-Option-C. The main difference between the options is whether you select the text you want to copy before pressing the shortcut keys (method 1) or after (method 2).

To use method 1 to copy text between windows, do the following steps:

1. Make certain that at least two windows are open on-screen.

2. With the pointer in one window, drag through a block of text to select it.

3. Press **Command-Option-C**.

The words Copy to appear in the page number box.

4. Moving the pointer to another window, click an insertion point where you want the selected text to appear. The insertion point will be displayed as a dotted vertical line.

If you want the selected text from the first window to *replace* text in the second window, for Step 3 drag through the text you want to replace instead of clicking an insertion point. The text you select to be replaced becomes marked by dotted underlining.

5. Press **Return**.

At the insertion point in the second window, Word inserts a copy of the text selected in the first window or substitutes that copy for text selected to be replaced.

To use method 2 to copy text between windows, do the following steps:

1. Make certain that at least two windows are open on-screen.

2. With the pointer in one of the two windows, click an insertion point where you want text to be copied from the other windows.

3. Press **Command-Option-C**.

The words Copy from appear in the page number box.

4. Move the pointer to the second window and drag through the text you want to copy to the first window. The selected material will be marked by dotted underlining.

5. Press **Return**.

At the insertion point in the first window, Word inserts a copy of the text selected in the second window.

NOTE: With method 2, you click an insertion point in the first step of the procedure; therefore, you cannot select text to be *replaced* by the copy operation of method 2. (If you select text as your first step, you start method 1 instead of method 2.) If copying between windows involves replacement, choose method 1.

Moving Text between Windows

The process for moving text between two locations is similar to that for copying text, except that you use Command-Option-X instead of Command-Option-C. Command-Option-X also has two variations, depending on whether you select the text you want to move before (method 1) or after (method 2) pressing the keyboard shortcut.

To use Command-Option-X to move text between windows (method 2), do the following:

1. Click an insertion point in one of the two windows.

Word will insert here the text you plan to move.

2. Press **Command-Option-X**.

The words Move from appear in the upper window's page number box.

3. Click anywhere in the other window to make the window active.

4. Select the text you want to move.

Word places a dotted underline beneath the selected text.

5. Press **Return**.

The selected text is cut from the second window and inserted at the insertion point in the first window.

Copying Formatting between Windows

In Chapter 4, you learned how to use the Command-Option-V keyboard shortcut to copy character and paragraph formatting from one piece of text to another. You can use the same shortcut to copy formatting between two different documents, each in its own window. Here, however, the Command-Option-V technique has an additional twist. If you copy formatting that has been applied to a document with a style sheet code, Word adds the copied style to the style sheet of the document to which you are copying.

Using Multiple Windows As You Write

The advantages of using multiple windows extend beyond word-processing convenience because windowing also can be a useful writer's tool. For instance, you can name and save a document as you begin writing it and then open a related document, for reference, in a second window. A press release, for example, may require dates, times, and conference titles from a schedule created earlier. By opening the schedule document in a second window, you easily can copy or transfer the information into the press release.

You also can set up a work document and then create supplementary documents in separate windows for categorizing information as you sort through it. In transcribing notes for a research paper, for instance, you may store information in three files called Literature Search, Procedures, and Results. These files can be transformed later into chapters in a thesis.

Or as you edit a document, you may want to transfer to an outtakes (or trash) file all the snippets you don't need in the current document but are reluctant to discard altogether. An outtakes file is a far better storage area for this type of information than the Scrapbook or a glossary, especially if you are the kind of literary pack rat who can amass incredible amounts of "I know I'll use this somewhere" information that might otherwise bog down system operations.

As you can see, using multiple windows can speed your writing and word-processing tasks, particularly when you are working with long documents. In the next chapter, we show you another organizational aid: customized menus. You learn how to gather the commands, styles, glossary entries, and documents you use most often into Word's Format, Font, and Work menus for easy access.

Customizing Menus

We've gone to some lengths to demonstrate how you can take advantage of Word's amazing power while you create and edit documents. Dozens of commands are available from the menus, and Word offers several hundred options through dialog boxes. At this point, however, you may feel burdened by all your word-processing knowledge. "Life was simpler when all I had to worry about was typing letters and reports," you say. Now, you have to "create documents" and wander through a maze of formatting options requiring decisions that formerly were made by designers and marketing experts.

Take heart: all those options can be made more manageable. As you grow accustomed to working with Word, you will find that you use certain options more often than others. Using the full Font and Format menus to access only a few well-used options may become needlessly time-consuming. You can take advantage of two ways of customizing menus, however, that help you store particularly useful options and commands at your fingertips and eliminate the options you don't need.

One way to customize menus is to change the full Font and Format menus in order to give yourself direct access to the options you choose most often. (You cannot change the short versions of these menus.) In addition to providing direct access to customized Font and Format menus, Version 3 also allows you direct access to a Work menu on which you can collect related documents, glossary entries, and styles. The customized Font and Format menus and the Work menu are organizational tools that can speed up your word-processing chores considerably. Simply determine what commands and options you need on the menus, and you always will have the options handy.

Give your own word-processing needs some thought as you read this chapter. First, you learn about the options for customizing the full Format and Font menus and the general procedures for adding items to those menus. Then you learn the procedure for creating a Work menu and the specifics of adding documents, glossary entries, and styles to the Work menu. Finally, you see how to delete the items from the customized menus, and you learn some tips about large menus.

Exploring Format and Font Menu Options

Generally, you will want to approach customization from two directions. First, you probably will want to adjust the full Format and Font menus to meet your general formatting needs. Then you will want to create a Work menu that includes the text and styles you use regularly.

Each of these menus can contain as many as 31 items. The program automatically groups related items and separates the groups by inserting dotted lines between them. Each dotted line counts as an item even though it cannot be selected. Therefore, the full Format menu, which contains four groups of commands separated by three dotted lines, can hold up to 28 commands. The Font menu has room for 30 commands, and the Work menu can hold 29. You choose custom commands, styles, document names, and other items from these menus just as you choose noncustom commands from any other menu.

Now, take a look at the items you can put on the Format and Font menus.

Options for the Format Menu

The full Format menu, shown in figure 11.1, initially contains 15 items (including dotted lines), leaving 16 slots open for items of your choosing. You cannot subtract the first ten items from the menu because Word needs these items. However, you can free up some room on the menu by removing the Outline and Shadow styles, which should be used sparingly if used at all. Remember that you still can obtain these styles by using the Format menu's Character command. Therefore, remove any commands you seldom use and replace them with ones you often use (see the section titled "Deleting Menu Items").

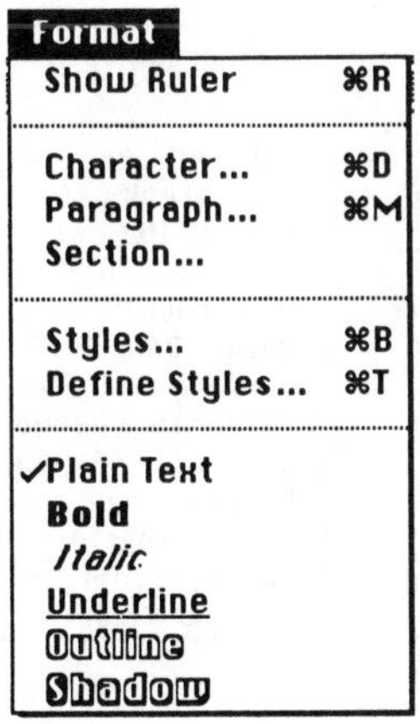

```
┌─────────────────────┐
│ Format              │
│ Show Ruler      ⌘R  │
│·····················│
│ Character...    ⌘D  │
│ Paragraph...    ⌘M  │
│ Section...          │
│·····················│
│ Styles...       ⌘B  │
│ Define Styles...⌘T  │
│·····················│
│✓Plain Text          │
│ Bold                │
│ Italic              │
│ Underline           │
│ Outline             │
│ Shadow              │
└─────────────────────┘
```

Fig. 11.1

The full Format menu.

You can include any of the following character, paragraph, and ruler options on a custom Format menu:

- From the ruler: any alignment, line spacing, or paragraph spacing option

- From the Character dialog box: any character format, position, or spacing option

- From the Paragraph dialog box: any paragraph formatting option (including border options) except line numbering, tab leaders, and ruler options

- From the Section dialog box: the First Page Special (under Header/Footer) and Number (under Column) options

The printout of partial menus in figure 11.2 shows possible formatting options, grouped according to their origin. (Some of these options have additional variations, such as the number of columns.) Obviously, you cannot include all these options on the Format menu (43 options competing for 21 slots), but these menus provide a quick reference for what is available.

Options for the Font Menu

The options available for customizing the Font menu vary with the fonts and sizes installed on your Macintosh (see the discussion of fonts in Chapter 7). Figure 11.3 shows a full Font menu for a typical Macintosh Plus connected to a LaserWriter.

Fig. 11.2

The options available for customizing the Format menu.

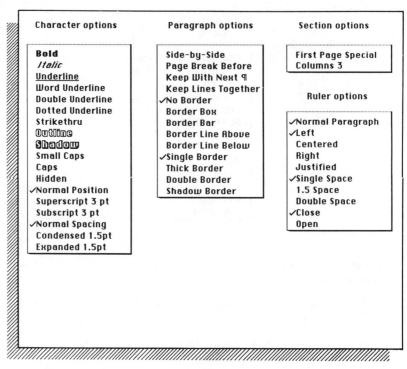

Fig. 11.3

The full Font menu for a Macintosh Plus connected to a LaserWriter.

You can eliminate all the fonts and sizes from the Font menu, thus freeing 30 slots for options you choose. However, Word allows only 25 fonts on the Font menu at one time; all other entries must be sizes.

You can include any of the following items on the Font menu:

- Any font that Word lists in the Character dialog box

- Any point size that Word already lists in the Character dialog box or that you can enter in the Font Size box

You learn how to add items to the Format and Font menus in the next section.

Adding Options to the Format and Font Menus

Now that you know the items available for customizing the Format and Font menus, you need to know how to add the different options to the appropriate menus. The procedure for adding options to the menus is no more difficult than selecting an item from a dialog box. The only difference is that you select the item with a pointer shaped like a plus symbol. You convert the pointer to this shape by holding down Command-Option while you press the + (plus) key on the main keyboard—not the numeric keypad. (Do not, however, use the Shift key with this key combination.)

When you select a Character, Paragraph, or Section option with the plus pointer, the pointer reverts to its normal shape, indicating that Word automatically has added the selected item to the appropriate menu. (The Character dialog box contains options that can be added to either the Font or Format menus, but the program knows which items belong where.) If you click an item that cannot be added to a custom menu, the pointer remains a plus sign, indicating that no action was performed. In both cases, the dialog box in which you're working remains open so that you can continue adding items to the menus.

If you try to add an item after a custom menu has reached full capacity, Word displays the alert box shown in figure 11.4. In addition, the Macintosh beeps when you try to add an item already listed on a custom menu.

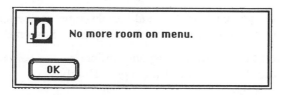

Fig. 11.4

The alert box displayed when you try to overload a custom menu.

Dialog Box Options

In the following exercise, you see how easy customizing your menus can be as you practice adding Paragraph formatting options to the full Format menu. Use the same technique to add appropriate items from any other dialog box or menu to the Format and Font menus.

To add options to the full Format menu from the Paragraph dialog box, do the following:

1. Choose **Paragraph** from the Format menu.

2. Hold down the **Command** and **Option** keys while pressing the + key on the main keyboard.

The pointer becomes a bold plus sign, as shown in figure 11.5.

Fig. 11.5

The plus pointer, used for adding items to custom menus.

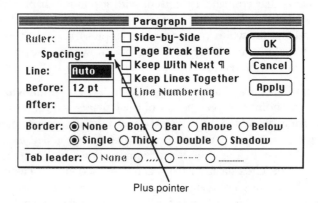

Plus pointer

3. Click the desired option with the plus pointer.

For this exercise, click Page Break Before.

The pointer resumes its arrow shape, indicating that Word has added the selected item to the Format menu.

4. Repeat Steps 2 and 3 to add any other available options.

Remember that if you click an item and the plus pointer doesn't resume its arrow shape, the item is not available for a custom menu.

5. When you finish adding paragraph options to the Format menu, click **Cancel** to close the Paragraph dialog box.

If you have pressed Command-Option-+ and then decide not to add anything, click one of the commands that cannot be altered. The normal pointer appears.

Ruler Options

To add a ruler option to the Format menu, you simply click the option's icon with the plus pointer. Available options include paragraph alignment, line and paragraph spacing, and the normal paragraph icon—in fact, all the options represented by icons except tabs, the vertical line icon, and indent settings (see fig. 11.6). To get around the restriction on tabs and indent settings, you can create a style incorporating them in the desired combination and then add that style to the Work menu.

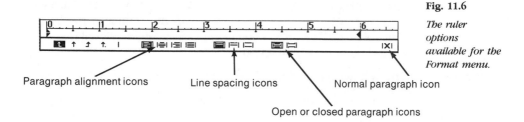

Fig. 11.6

The ruler options available for the Format menu.

Paragraph alignment icons   Line spacing icons   Normal paragraph icon

Open or closed paragraph icons

Word represents any ruler options you add to the Format menu with a descriptive word or two. For example, the program displays Left, Right, Centered, and Justified for the paragraph alignment icons; and Single Space, 1.5 Space, and Double Space for line spacing icons.

To add a formatting option from the ruler to the Format menu, do the following:

1. Press **Command-Option**-+ (main keyboard) to change the pointer to the plus sign.

2. Choose **Show Ruler** from the Format menu.

3. Click the ruler icon you want to add to the Format menu.

If the pointer resumes its arrow shape, you've chosen an available option, and the program has added the option to the Format menu.

Numeric Options

Some of the options you can add to custom menus—Superscript and Subscript positions and Condensed and Expanded spacing from the Character dialog box, and Number (of columns) from the Section dialog box—have associated numeric values. If you click the option with the plus pointer, Word adds the option and its current setting to the appropriate custom menu. Once the option is on the menu, you cannot change the option's value. With these options, therefore, you must make sure that the value is the one you want before you add the option to a menu.

You can add more than one version of numerical items to the custom menus, however. For example, suppose that you are the editor of a newsletter and you make frequent use of both double- and triple-column formats. You can store two versions of the Section command's Number option: one with a numeric value of 2 and the other with 3.

To get a feel for how this procedure works, you will add the Character menu's Superscript option in the Position box to the Format menu. The Superscript option is associated with the setting in the By box, which tells Word how many points to raise the superscripted text above the baseline of the normal text.

Do the following to add the Superscript option to the full Format menu:

1. Choose **Character** from the Format menu.

2. Click **Superscript**.

The default setting in the By box is 3 points (see fig. 11.7).

Fig. 11.7

The Superscript *field with its default setting.*

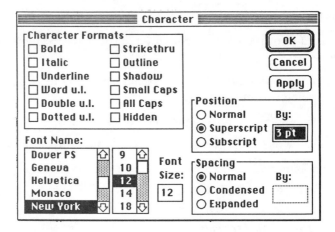

3. If the default value is not the one you want, change the value.

In this case, type 5 in the By box.

4. Move the pointer beyond the box and press **Command-Option-+** (main keyboard) to convert the pointer to a plus sign.

5. Click the **Superscript** option.

Word adds the Superscript option to the full Format menu with the number of points you specified, as shown in figure 11.8. You can now apply this custom option to selected text simply by choosing Superscript from the Format menu.

Format	
Show Ruler	⌘R
Character...	⌘D
Paragraph...	⌘M
Section...	
Styles...	⌘B
Define Styles...	⌘T
✓Plain Text	
Bold	
Italic	
<u>Underline</u>	
Outline	
Shadow	
Superscript 5 pt	

Fig. 11.8

The Format menu showing a custom Superscript option.

Building a Work Menu

The techniques for adding documents, glossary entries, and styles to a Work menu are essentially the same as those for adding options to the full Font and Format menus. All items on the Work menu must be drawn from one of three other menus. You take documents from the File menu, glossary entries from the Edit menu, and styles from the Format menu. The program automatically groups document names at the top of the Work menu, glossary entries in the middle, and styles at the bottom, as shown in figure 11.9. The program lists the items in each group alphabetically and separates the groups by dotted lines. The Work menu can hold up to 29 commands of your choosing.

Word's Work menu, new to Version 3, is useful if you consistently call on certain style or glossary items or if you often work with a particular set of documents. If you never have used a Work menu and cannot find one listed anywhere on your screen, don't panic: no Work menu exists until you add the first document, glossary entry, or style to the Work menu. When you click one of these items after pressing Command-

Fig. 11.9

*A typical Work
menu.*

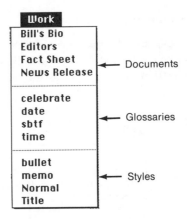

Option-+ (on the main keyboard), the program automatically adds the Work menu to the pull-down menus listed in the menu bar across the top of the screen.

You can add the following items to a Work menu:

- Any document Word can open, whether stored on any disk or on the hard drive (If you choose a Work menu document from a disk not currently inserted in one of the drives, Word prompts you to insert the proper disk.)

- Any glossary entry from the Standard Glossary or from any other glossary

- Any style from the default style sheet or from a custom style sheet

To add a document to the Work menu, press Command-Option-+ to convert the pointer to a plus sign and then choose Open from the File menu so that you can select the desired document from the alphabetized list. If you want to add an open document to the Work menu, simply click the document's title bar with the plus pointer.

To add an entry from the Standard Glossary to the Work menu, you choose Glossary from the Edit menu (or press Command-K) and then press Command-Option-+. In the Glossary dialog box, you then click the name of the desired entry. To add an entry from another glossary, first merge or switch glossaries (see Chapter 8 for techniques). You then can use the plus pointer to select the name of the desired entry in the Glossary dialog box's alphabetized list.

To add a style to the Work menu, you need to open the style sheet that contains the style. Because style sheets are attached to documents, you first have to open the relevant document. You then can choose either Styles or Define Styles from the Format menu to display an alphabetical list of all the styles in that style sheet. After this, adding the desired style to the Work menu is just a matter of clicking the style code with the plus pointer.

NOTE: When you choose an item from a menu and transfer your choice to a customized menu, the item gets copied, not moved, to the customized version. The item, therefore, remains also on the original menu.

After creating a Work menu, you still use the documents, glossaries, and style sheets in the usual ways. The advantage of the Work menu, however, is that all three types of items are conveniently available on a single pull-down menu. Another advantage is that you can open documents quickly without having to search through the documents and directories listed in the Open dialog box available from the File menu.

Deleting Menu Items

All additions to a custom menu are reversible. You also can delete all the items from the full Font menu and any item listed below Plain Text in the full Format menu. You delete items from a custom menu by using a minus pointer, created by pressing Command-Option-- (minus, the hyphen on the main keyboard).

For practice, you're going to remove the Page Break Before option that you just added to the Format menu.

To remove an item from a custom menu, do the following:

1. Hold down the **Command** and **Option** keys while pressing the – key (the main keyboard's hyphen).

The pointer becomes a bold minus sign, as shown in figure 11.10.

2. Open the custom menu you want to alter.

3. Drag down to the item you want to delete and release the mouse button.

Now that you're fully versed in adding and deleting items from custom menus, you probably will be tempted toward excess. If you find that you've created a monster, the following reminders about how to maneuver within a large menu may help.

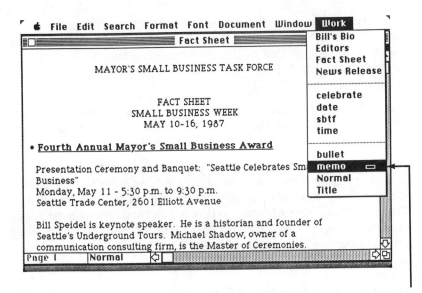

Fig. 11.10

The minus pointer, used to delete items from custom menus.

Minus pointer

Working with Large Menus

Custom menus stretch both horizontally and vertically in order to accommodate added items. For example, adding *Miss Lila Dewey's Membership Report* to a Work menu widens the menu considerably. The maximum menu width is 30 characters (about 3 inches). Document names that do not fit within this space are *truncated*, or shortened by cutting off the characters for which no room exists.

Not surprisingly, adding items also lengthens a menu. An entire menu containing the maximum 31 items cannot be displayed at one time. A triangle at the bottom or the top of the menu tells you that more options are available. To view items at the bottom of a long menu, hold down the mouse button and drag past the bottom of the menu so that the list scrolls up.

If you do have a long menu, the program provides a keyboard shortcut that helps you quickly choose a command (see Chapter 2). You can open a menu by pressing the period key on the numeric keypad and then the number of the menu. (The pull-down menus across the top of the screen are numbered from left to right; the Apple menu is 0, and the Work menu is 8.) Once you have opened the menu you want, press the first letter of the desired command to highlight that command. If several commands begin with the same letter, repeatedly press the letter to cycle through the set. For example, if you have added Superscript, Subscript, and Single Space to the Format menu, pressing *S* cycles through all the commands starting with *S*: *Section, Styles, Shadow, Superscript, Subscript,* and *Single Space.*

Remember, though, that gaining direct access to an unmanageable group of items on a custom menu defeats the purpose of tailoring the menu in the first place. Half the game is eliminating what you don't need, so be judicious in your choices.

Word's glossaries, style sheets, multiple document windows, and custom menus place an impressive array of formatting options within easy reach. These organizational features will be helpful as you tackle the advanced formatting features discussed in the remainder of this section of the book.

Working with Graphics

Microsoft Word for the Macintosh has many features that distinguish it from other word-processing programs, but no feature sets Word apart as much as its capability to integrate text and graphics in the same document. In fact, you can produce the same high-quality and attractive publications with the Word program that you can with much more complex (and typically more expensive) desktop-publishing programs. The combination of Word's graphics, page layout, and formatting capabilities actually blurs the distinctions between this word-processing program and current desktop-publishing programs.

In this chapter, you learn how to insert into a Word document a graphic created in another application. Because you may not have a graphic readily available with which to experiment, you learn also how to insert into a Word document empty frames that can be manipulated in the same manner as actual graphics. (Empty frames are useful in projects for which you must design your pages ahead of time and then leave space for graphics you paste in later.) The rest of this chapter describes how to position graphics, change their size and shape, and combine text and graphics so they function as single elements.

Inserting Graphics into a Word Document

Many Macintosh programs, such as MacDraw, MacPaint, SuperPaint, Microsoft Chart, or Microsoft Excel, are available to help you develop the types of graphics you need for your documents, ranging from free-form illustrations to business charts and graphs. These programs do not necessarily store documents in the same format, so few of them can directly open a document created in another program. Fortunately, the Macintosh Clipboard and Scrapbook solve this incompatibility problem. Any text or graphics you can cut or copy from another program can be pasted into a Word document.

NOTE: Different programs provide different amounts of information in the graphics files that the programs store on the Clipboard. Word uses only the information required to display a graphic but stores the rest of the information with the graphic; therefore, if you copy a graphic from the Word program back to the program that created the graphic, the creating program can manipulate the graphic as though it had never left. For example, if you copy a chart from Microsoft Excel to Word and then back to Excel, all the information necessary for the chart to be maintained and updated by Excel is retained in the transfer.

All graphics enter the Word program through the Clipboard and eventually are pasted into a Word document. After you have taken the initial step of cutting or copying a graphic in the originating program to the Clipboard, you can choose one of the following three routes for pasting the graphic into a Word document:

- You can transfer directly a single graphic by way of the Clipboard.

- You can transfer several graphics by a more indirect route: through the Scrapbook.

- You can use a program called Switcher™ to load both the originating graphics program and the Word program; then you can switch between the two by cutting or copying graphics from the graphics program and pasting the graphics into Word.

When you paste a graphic from the Clipboard into a Word document, Word surrounds the graphic with a frame visible only when you select the graphic or choose the Show ¶ command from the Edit menu (see fig. 12.1). Later in this chapter, you read about changing the location and size of the graphic by manipulating this frame. For now, look more closely at the steps involved in each method of transfer.

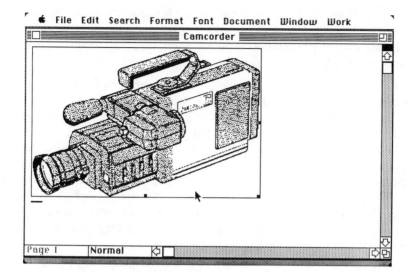

Fig. 12.1

A frame surrounds a graphic pasted into a word document.

Transferring Graphics Directly

You can transfer a graphic directly from a graphics program to a Word document and not use the Switcher.

To complete a direct transfer of a graphic into a Word document, do the following:

1. Copy to the Clipboard the graphic from the originating graphics program.

2. Quit the graphics program and load the Word document.

3. Click the insertion point in the place where you want the graphic.

4. Choose **Paste** from the Edit menu to insert into the document the graphic from the Clipboard.

Transferring Graphics through the Scrapbook

The Scrapbook is similar to the Clipboard in that you can paste into the Scrapbook the text and graphics you create with almost any program. Unlike the Clipboard, however, the Scrapbook can store more than one item. The Finder saves the contents of the Scrapbook on disk in a file called, appropriately, Scrapbook. You can rename this file; then when you again choose the Scrapbook option from the Apple menu, the program creates a new, empty Scrapbook file.

A disk can have more than one file created by the Scrapbook program, but only one file on each disk can have the name Scrapbook. Only one file called Scrapbook can be open at a time—the one on the disk from which you opened the currently loaded program. If Word and the program you use to create your graphics are stored on the same disk, the two programs share the same Scrapbook. If the programs are stored on different disks, you must copy the Scrapbook from the graphics disk to the Word disk before you can transfer into Word any graphics stored in that Scrapbook. If you don't want to lose the contents of an existing Scrapbook on the Word disk, you must rename the existing Word Scrapbook before you copy the graphics Scrapbook.

To transfer several graphics by using the Scrapbook, do the following:

1. From the graphics program, select a graphic and cut or copy it to the Clipboard.

2. Choose **Scrapbook** from the Apple menu.

The Scrapbook window opens.

Fig. 12.2

The Scrapbook window.

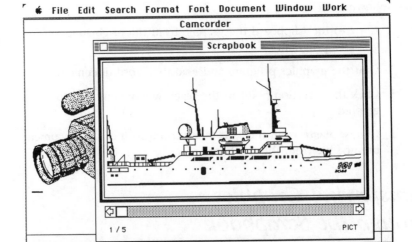

3. Choose **Paste** from the Edit menu.

A copy of the graphic appears in the Scrapbook window (see fig. 12.2).

4. Close the Scrapbook window by clicking the close box in the upper left corner.

5. Repeat Steps 1 through 4 for the remaining graphics you want to transfer.

6. Quit the graphics program and open the Word document into which you want to paste the graphics.

7. Choose **Scrapbook** from the Apple menu.

8. Use the scroll bar at the bottom of the Scrapbook to locate the graphic you want.

9. Choose **Copy** or **Cut** from the Edit menu to store the graphic on the Clipboard.

10. Close the **Scrapbook**.

11. Click an insertion point in the place in the document where you want the graphic to appear.

12. Choose **Paste** from the Edit menu.

13. Repeat Steps 7 through 12 for each graphic you want to insert.

Transferring Graphics by Using the Switcher

By far the fastest method of transferring text or graphics between another program and Word is by using the Switcher, an Apple utility distributed with Word, Version 3. To use Switcher, load the disk containing the System Folder and Switcher program and double-click the Switcher icon. Follow the menu instructions to load both Word and a graphics program, such as MacPaint. Then you instantly can switch between applications just by clicking the Switcher arrow (see fig. 12.3).

Do the following to transfer a graphic by using the Switcher:

1. From the graphics program, select the graphic you want to transfer into Word.

2. Choose **Copy** from the Edit menu to copy the graphic to the Clipboard.

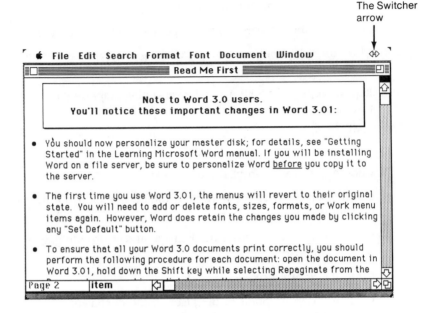

Fig. 12.3

*The Switcher
arrow.*

3. Click either end of the Switcher arrow in the upper right corner of the document window to switch to the Word program.

Clicking the Switcher arrow causes the Switcher to copy the contents of the Clipboard in the graphics program to the Clipboard in Word.

4. Click an insertion point where you want to paste the graphic in the Word document.

5. Choose **Paste** from the Edit menu.

Inserting Graphics Placeholders

Inserting graphics into Word at the same time you are developing a document is not always a convenient step. There may be times, for example, when you want to reserve space for a graphic you later paste in by hand. In the Word program, you can create space for graphics as you plan your document's layout, by inserting an empty space at each point where you want a graphic and then later supplying and positioning the graphic by hand.

To insert an empty graphics space in a Word document, do the following:

1. Click an insertion point where you want to insert the graphic.

2. Choose **Insert Graphics** from the Edit menu or press **Command-I**.

Word displays an empty 1-inch-square frame at the insertion point. If you have chosen Show ¶ from the Edit menu, the frame is displayed as a dotted line (see fig. 12.4). If you have not chosen Show ¶, the frame is invisible and the insertion point is displayed as tall as the frame.

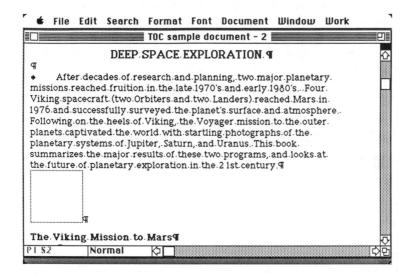

Fig. 12.4

An empty graphic frame used as a placeholder.

The frame you insert with the Insert Graphics command looks the same way and works in the same manner as the frame that surrounds any graphic pasted from the Clipboard. Use the techniques discussed in the rest of this chapter to resize and reposition the frame to see how several different page layouts look.

Selecting, Adjusting, and Sizing Graphics

After you've added a graphic to a Word document, you can select the graphic by clicking it or dragging through it. In this program, you can

select and manipulate only the whole graphic—not parts of it. To select
more than one graphic or a graphic and its adjacent text, drag through
the graphics or the graphic and text you want to select.

To select a graphic, do the following:

1. Position the pointer over the graphic.

The I-beam changes to an arrow when you move the pointer inside the
graphic's frame.

2. Click the mouse button once.

The program indicates that the graphic is selected by displaying the
graphic's frame (if it were not already visible) and by adding black boxes,
called *handles*, along the frame's right and bottom edges and in its lower
right corner (see fig. 12.5). These handles are used to change the size
of the graphic.

Fig. 12.5

*A selected
graphic.*

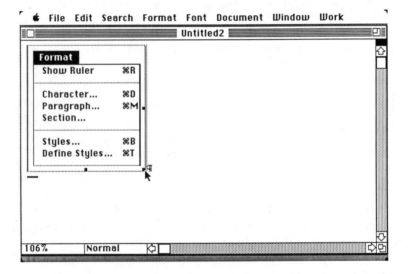

Adjusting the Size of Graphics

After you insert a graphic into a document, you can resize the graphic
by resizing its frame in one of two ways. One type of adjustment changes
the size of the frame but leaves the graphic itself the same size. If you
make the frame smaller, therefore, you see less of the graphic. In other
words, the graphic is *cropped*.

The other type of adjustment changes the size of the frame and, at the same time, proportionally adjusts the size of the graphic image within the frame. Thus, if you make the frame smaller, you make the graphic smaller. The graphic then is *scaled*. Figure 12.6 shows the effects of cropping a graphic and then scaling it.

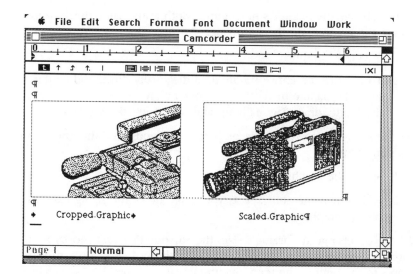

Fig. 12.6

Cropped and scaled graphics.

To resize a graphic's frame for both cropping and scaling, you drag the graphic's handles. You can vary the size of the frame from about 1/4-inch square to an area 22 inches wide and as tall as you want. When you resize the frame, Word automatically centers the graphic within the frame area. If the frame is too small to hold the entire graphic, the program crops the graphic and displays only the portion of the graphic that fits. To display the full graphic, you must enlarge the frame.

To scale a graphic as you resize its frame, hold down the Shift key while you drag a handle. If you resize a graphic's frame after you scale the graphic, the graphic reverts to its original size.

To change the width of the graphic frame without scaling the graphic, follow these steps:

1. Select the graphic.

2. To reduce the frame's width, drag to the left the handle on the right edge of the graphic frame; to widen the frame, drag to the right the same handle.

To change the height of the graphic frame without scaling the graphic, do the following:

1. Select the graphic.

2. To shorten or lengthen the frame, drag up or down the handle on the bottom of the frame.

And to change the graphic's height and width at the same time without scaling the graphic, do the following:

1. Select the graphic.

2. To enlarge the entire frame, drag diagonally down and to the right the handle in the frame's lower right corner; to reduce the frame, drag diagonally up and to the left the entire frame.

Do the following to resize the graphic frame and scale the graphic at the same time:

1. Select the graphic.

2. Hold down the Shift key as you drag one of the sizing handles on the graphic frame.

When you change the frame's size, the surrounding text moves to accommodate the graphic. If the frame is within a line of text, the text moves to the right as the frame width increases. Figure 12.7 shows how the Word program adjusts the text to accommodate an enlarged graphic.

Fig. 12.7

When you enlarge or reduce a graphic, Word rewraps the surrounding text.

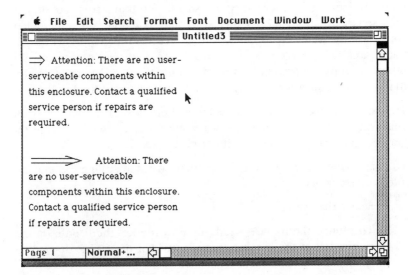

As the height or width of the graphic frame changes, the program displays that dimension in the page number box in the screen's bottom left corner. When you change the overall size of the frame by dragging the corner handle, Word displays the percentage of change. For example, *150%* means that you have changed both the horizontal and vertical dimensions to 1 1/2 times their original size.

To enlarge a graphic's frame beyond the size of the Macintosh window, you first use the appropriate handle to drag the frame out to the window border. Then you scroll vertically or horizontally in the document to expose more window area and resume dragging the graphic's frame until the frame is the size you want.

After enlarging or reducing the size of a graphic's frame, you can quickly return it to its original size by double-clicking within it. If the frame is empty, it shrinks to a 1-inch square, which is the default size. If the frame contains a graphic, then double-clicking inside the frame reduces (or enlarges) the frame to the smallest size that holds the full-size graphic.

Repositioning Graphics

Unlike MacPaint, MacDraw, and other graphics programs, Word does not include a frame handle for moving graphics. The program treats each graphic as a single character that you can select and move, just as you would do with any text character, by using the Edit menu's Cut and Paste commands or the Return, Backspace, or Tab keys. If the graphic is in a paragraph by itself, you also can use the ruler or the options in the Paragraph dialog box to set up separate indents or tab stops to position the frame.

Do the following to move a graphic elsewhere on a page:

1. Select the graphic by clicking inside its frame.

2. Choose **Cut** from the Edit menu to move the graphic to the Clipboard.

3. Click an insertion point in the location where you want to reinsert the graphic.

4. Choose **Paste** from the Edit menu.

To move the graphic up or down on the page, do the following:

1. Click an insertion point to the left of the graphic.

2. Press **Return** to move the frame down the page one text line at a time or press **Backspace** to move the frame up one line at a time.

You can move the graphic horizontally across the page by doing the following:

1. Click an insertion point to the left of the frame.

2. Press **Tab** to move the frame in 0.5-inch increments to the right (or to the next tab stop); if the frame is not already at the left margin, press **Backspace** to move the frame to the left.

Now that you know how to select, size, and adjust graphics, you learn in the next section how to position them attractively, relative to the text.

Combining Text and Graphics

If a graphic is the only "character" in a paragraph, you can use various paragraph formatting techniques to control its position relative to the adjacent text. For example, with the Paragraph command's Side-by-Side option, you can instruct the program to print text beside a graphic. Or you can ensure that a block of text appears immediately above or below a graphic by formatting the text or the graphic with the Keep With Next ¶ option. You also can combine text and a graphic as a single graphic unit.

Printing Text and Graphics Side by Side

If you have enough room on your page, you can position a caption or other associated text beside a graphic. You can make the graphic any size you want, of course, but when you choose the side-by-side layout, consider whether reducing the size of the graphic to accommodate the text undermines the graphic's purpose.

Printing paragraphs side by side, as you learned in Chapter 4, requires setting the indents for the two paragraphs so that they occupy different areas of the text column (see fig. 12.8). You use the same technique to print text and graphics side by side.

To print a block of text beside a graphic, do the following:

1. Make sure the graphic is a separate paragraph: a paragraph mark must precede and follow the graphic.

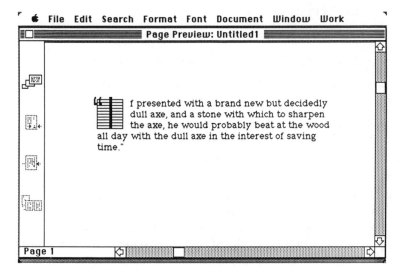

Fig. 12.8

A text paragraph and a graphic "paragraph" are positioned to print side by side.

2. If the ruler is not displayed, choose **Show Ruler** from the Format menu.

3. Use the ruler to note the width of the graphic.

4. If you want the text printed to the left of the graphic, make sure the text is the paragraph immediately before the graphic. If you want the text printed to the right of the graphic, make sure the text immediately follows the graphic.

The instructions in the following steps are for printing the text to the right of the graphic (so that the graphic precedes the text).

5. Select the graphic.

6. Move the **right-indent marker** to the right edge of the graphic frame.

7. Select the text.

8. Move the **left-indent marker** to the right of the graphic's right indent.

For example, if the right edge of the graphic's frame is at the ruler's 3-inch mark, move the text paragraph's left-indent marker to at least 3 1/8 inches.

9. Select both paragraphs.

10. Choose **Paragraph** from the Format menu.

11. In the Paragraph dialog box, click the **Side-by-Side** option.

12. Click **OK** to apply the formatting and close the Paragraph dialog box.

Consider the balance of the two paragraphs now. You can adjust the size of the graphic, the indents, the space above and below each paragraph, the font size, and the wording of the text paragraph to achieve a satisfactory balance.

Page Preview is an excellent tool for helping you achieve balance between the graphic and your text (see Chapter 6). Use the Page Preview command to look at how the text and graphic will appear when they are printed. Sometimes the printed results are quite different from what you expect because the graphic's frame is not printed unless you add a border or a box via the Paragraph dialog box. Without this visual "anchor," graphics can appear lopsided, or they can appear to take up a lot less room on the page, thus destroying the balance you may have struggled to achieve by making adjustments to the text paragraph, the graphic, or both. Previewing your layout to make sure you have no surprises always is worth the time you spend.

You are not limited to two side-by-side paragraphs: you can have as many as space allows. Arrange the paragraphs on-screen from top to bottom as you want them to print from left to right. Then set the indents for each one so that the paragraphs don't overlap and format them to print side by side. Figure 12.9 shows three "paragraphs" arranged across the page.

Attaching Text to Graphics

You sometimes may need to make sure that the program doesn't casually throw a page break between a block of text and a graphic. Perhaps you have created in your documents graphic frames ready for the manual insertion of photographs that need credit captions. Separating the photographs from their credit lines not only would be a blemish on your layout but also might cause embarrassment or hard feelings. You can make sure that Word always prints a paragraph of text on the same page as a graphic by formatting the top unit in the pair with the Paragraph command's Keep With Next ¶ option.

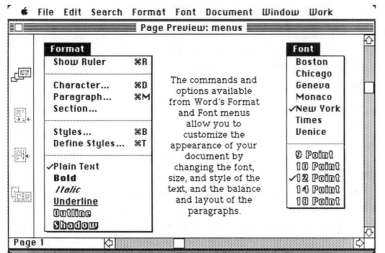

Fig. 12.9

A more complex mixture of text and graphics.

To specify that a block of text and a graphic print on the same page, do the following:

1. Select the text, or the graphic, that comes first in the document.

2. Choose **Paragraph** from the Format menu or press **Command-M**.

3. Select the **Keep With Next ¶** option.

4. Click **OK** to close the Paragraph dialog box.

This technique prevents Word from inserting a page break between the two elements. If the text is a caption, you also need to prevent a normal page break within the text paragraph by formatting the paragraph with the Keep Lines Together option.

These paragraph options usually are sufficient for controlling your page layout, especially if you have ultimate control of the document. Neither option, however, can prevent someone else from breaking up the unit by inserting a paragraph break manually within the text paragraph or between the text and the graphic. If you want to make your page-break controls tamperproof, you need to instruct the program to treat the text as part of the graphic. The next section describes this process.

Converting Text to Graphics

Word's versatility is hard to beat. Not only can you work with graphics created by other programs, but you also can convert text into graphics and then stretch, shrink, or frame the text as you would any other graphic.

You might want to convert text to a graphic for the following reasons:

- To change the text's size or shape to achieve a special effect

- To bind text blocks together so that they are printed on the same page

- To transfer a block of text to another Macintosh program (For example, the only way you can move a complex formula from one program to another and keep all formatting intact is by moving the formula as a graphic, as shown in fig. 12.10.)

Fig. 12.10

A complex formula converted from text to a graphic to retain all formatting.

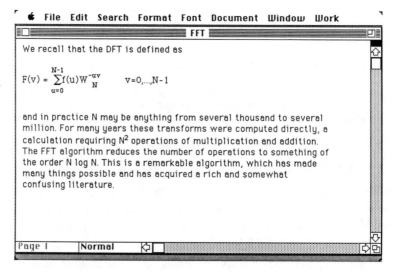

After you convert a block of text to a graphic, however, you cannot edit the characters within the text or convert the graphic back to text. To make changes, you must start over again with the text version. Experience says that making a copy of a block of text before converting it to a graphic is a good idea.

WARNING: Before you select the text to convert to a graphic, make sure that formatting symbols—paragraph marks, end-of-line marks, and so forth—are not displayed. (Choose Hide ¶ from the Edit menu to turn them off, if necessary.) Otherwise, the symbols become part of the graphic, and you no longer can remove them by choosing Hide ¶.

Do the following to convert a block of text to a graphic:

1. Select the text you want to change into a graphic.

If you want to combine text with an existing graphic, drag through both of them to select them as a unit.

2. Press **Command-Option-D** to copy the text to the Clipboard as a graphic.

3. Choose **Paste** from the Edit menu or press **Command-V** to paste the Clipboard contents back into the document, in place of the still-selected text.

You now can rescale and move the text within the graphic frame just as you would do with any other graphic.

Formatting Graphics

Because Word treats a graphic just like any other text character, you can apply normal character and paragraph formatting to the graphic. The situations in which you would use character formatting are somewhat limited, however. For example, how often are you going to apply superscript formatting to a graphic in order to raise it slightly above the text line? Instead, you are more likely to use paragraph formatting options. You may find the border option especially useful.

Remember that the frames used for scaling or cropping graphics in Word documents are not printed. To put a printable frame around a graphic, you need to select one of the border options from the Paragraph dialog box.

To add a shadow box to a graphic, do the following:

1. Make sure the graphic is a separate paragraph.

2. Select the graphic.

3. Choose **Paragraph** from the Format menu or press **Command-M**.

4. Select **Box** and **Shadow**.

5. Click **OK** to apply the options to the selected graphic and close the Paragraph dialog box.

Figure 12.11 shows a graphic framed with a shadow box.

Fig. 12.11

*A graphic
formatted with
a shadow box.*

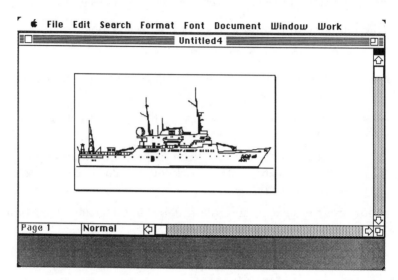

The graphic's built-in frame and the lines and boxes produced by the border options may not be the same size. Remember from Chapter 4 that the lines and boxes produced by the border options are governed by the paragraph's left and right indents. You might have to adjust these indents to produce lines and boxes that have pleasing proportions for a graphic.

If a page layout requires a graphic to span a specific space, remember that you also have the option of creating a border and then rescaling the graphic to fit within the border. You control the amount of white space above and below the graphic with the Paragraph dialog box's Before and After fields.

The versatility of Word's graphics capability not only provides benefits to the user but also invites abuse. If you're not careful, you can get carried away easily and use gratuitous graphics that actually detract from a document's message. We certainly don't advocate the use of Word and the Macintosh to produce pages overrun by curlicues and doodads. However, we strongly encourage you to work with some simple graphics until you feel comfortable with incorporating them into your documents and designing different page layouts. Used with taste and moderation, a well-developed graphic, such as a masthead, can give otherwise routine documents the polished, professional look that makes people stop and read them.

Adding Headers
and Footers

A *header* is any text printed at the top of all or selected pages of a document; a *footer* is any text printed at the bottom of all or selected pages. Most publications provide headers or footers—sometimes both—as signposts to let readers know where they are or to help them locate specific sections of the publication. These signposts usually consist of such information as the publication's name, the topic, or the title of each section, as well as the page number.

Earlier versions of Word offered very limited header and footer capabilities. You could print both a header and a footer on every page, but each header or footer was limited to a single line containing a page number, the date and time, and some text. With Version 3, Word's header and footer capability has been greatly expanded. You now can do the following:

- Print and control the position of headers or footers on selected pages

- Create headers and footers that include more than one line of text

- Include graphics as well as text in the header or footer

- Exclude the header or footer from a document's first page or create a special header or footer for the first page

- Make complementary header or footer pairs for facing pages in a document printed on both sides of the page

- Create distinct header and footer sets for individual document sections, using Word, Version 3's, new Section command

Of course, you don't have to use all these capabilities—header designs can be as simple or as complex as you want. Unless your work requires the use of fancy headers or you have a burning desire to use headers to dress up your documents, you probably can ignore most of the more advanced header options.

This chapter begins with a discussion of uses and designs for headers and footers and then introduces the full set of header and footer options available for various parts of a document. Next, you learn how to create headers and footers and how to view them and adjust their position in the Page Preview window.

Finally, you practice designing headers. First you create a pair of headers for facing pages of a document that will be printed on both sides of the page. Next you create a first-page header that emulates a letterhead. By the end of the chapter, you will know the basics of working with headers and footers and will have some idea of what you can do with them in your text.

Making Creative Use of Headers and Footers

You follow almost identical procedures to create both headers and footers: choose either the Open Header or Open Footer command from the Document menu and then type and format the header or footer in a special window. Headers and footers do have different uses, however, and their designs can vary greatly from one another. After learning the simple steps for creating these text elements, you may want to browse through books and magazines to glean ideas of how best to design your own headers and footers.

A carefully planned header can transform a plain document into a professional-looking publication. For example, Word easily accommodates folio-style headers, which you see in newspapers and magazines. These headers convey basic information, such as the date and publication name (see fig. 13.1).

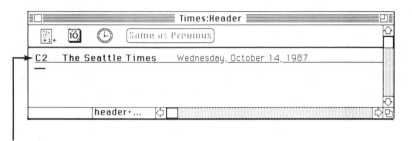

Fig. 13.1

A folio-style header.

Newspaper header, reproduced in header window

As well as making a document look impressive, a header, when used with Section-command settings, can perform complex ordering tasks. For example, figure 13.2 shows the header for a multipage printout of a survey's results. This header performs two functions: its first paragraph (beginning with the words *Academic Computing Center*) conveys standard header information, and its second paragraph (beginning with *Name*) repeats the questionnaire headings at the top of each page.

Header ⎯⎯⎯

Academic Computing Center				User Survey		page 1
Name	ID #	Age	Sex	Own a Computer?	Brand	Primary Use
Joan Lambert	L152	18	F	yes	Delta	school
Greg Child	C324	30	M	yes	IBM PC XT	work
Caitlin Donovan	D115	19	F	no		
Keith Wagner	W092	19	M	yes	AT Clone	school
Catherine Ruiz	R267	29	F	no		
Jack Daniel	D231	41	M	yes	Compaq	
Paul McKenzie	M123	3	M	yes	XT Clone	work
John Doe	D000	?	M	yes	IBM PC XT	work

Fig. 13.2

A two-paragraph header that incorporates both page number and questionnaire headings.

When designing footers, keep in mind they are humble in nature. Unlike headers, which as the first element on a page tend to attract the reader's eye and can therefore support a dramatic design, footers generally should be more subdued. They should never distract the reader from the text above. Do not ignore Word's footer options entirely, however. Any and all formatting and design options for headers can be put to good use in crafting understated yet stylish footers.

If you give the matter a little thought, you may be surprised at how many special uses you can find for footers. You might, for example, create a footer that prints a "sign-off" list so that coworkers can indicate their review of a report (see fig. 13.3). You also can use a footer to provide a framework within which to tally subtotals when scoring the pages of a standardized test. Or if you are preparing a document for publication, you can create a footer that includes a copyright statement.

Fig. 13.3

A footer with "sign-off" lines.

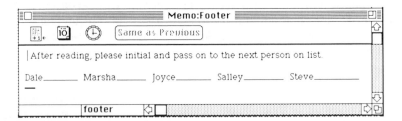

Working with Headers and Footers

Creating headers and footers is a simple matter of choosing one of a series of Open Header or Open Footer commands from the Document menu and then typing and formatting text in the header or footer window. For a simple document, Word provides two basic commands: the Document menu's Open Header and Open Footer commands. With these commands, you can format a header or footer for all pages of the document. You also can use settings in the Page Setup and Section dialog boxes to produce additional header and footer commands. You need to understand all these commands before you try creating your first header or footer.

The Header and Footer Commands

When you begin a new document, Word includes the two basic header and footer commands—Open Header and Open Footer—on the Document menu (see figure 13.4). Choosing either command opens a window in which you can create and format a block of text that Word will print on every page of the document.

```
┌──────────────────────────────┐
│ Document  Window             │
├──────────────────────────────┤
│ Open Header...               │
│ Open Footer...               │
│ ┄┄┄┄┄┄┄┄┄┄┄┄┄┄┄┄┄┄┄┄┄┄┄┄┄┄┄  │
│ Footnote...          ⌘E      │
│ Repaginate           ⌘J      │
│ ┄┄┄┄┄┄┄┄┄┄┄┄┄┄┄┄┄┄┄┄┄┄┄┄┄┄┄  │
│ Outlining            ⌘U      │
│ Spelling...          ⌘L      │
│ Hyphenate...                 │
│ Index...                     │
│ Table of Contents...         │
│ ┄┄┄┄┄┄┄┄┄┄┄┄┄┄┄┄┄┄┄┄┄┄┄┄┄┄┄  │
│ Calculate            ⌘=      │
│ Renumber...                  │
│ Sort                         │
└──────────────────────────────┘
```

Fig. 13.4

The Open Header and Open Footer commands on the Document menu.

If, however, you want to create a different header or footer for the first page of a document, first choose the Section command from the Format menu and select First Page Special. Word then adds two more commands to the Document menu: Open First Header and Open First Footer. These two commands actually give you four options. As well as letting you create a different header or footer for the document's first page, the commands allow you to exclude the header and footer from the first page. For example, the first page of a report commonly is given special treatment, and the header and footer are excluded so as not to detract from the report's design.

When you choose Open First Header or Open First Footer, Word automatically displays in the window the text of any header or footer you have created for the other pages of the document. You can edit this text to create a new header, or you can specify no header or footer by deleting the text entirely.

If you have formatted a document to print on both sides of the page (by selecting Facing Pages in the Page Setup dialog box), Word substitutes four commands for the Open Header and Open Footer commands on the Document Menu: Open Odd Header, Open Even Header, Open Odd Footer, and Open Even Footer. With these commands, you can create pairs of headers or footers for printing on facing pages. In books, for example, the book or section title often is printed on left (even) pages, balanced by a chapter title on right (odd) pages. You also can use these commands to print page numbers on the outer edges of facing pages by positioning the page number flush-left on even-numbered pages and flush-right on odd-numbered pages.

If you exercise both the First Page Special (Section command) and Facing Pages (Page Setup command) options, the Document menu grows to include six header- or footer-related commands, as shown in figure 13.5. Impressive as this array is, your options go even further. If you divide your document into sections, you can make an entire set of headers and footers for each section of the document. For example, you can create a different header for each chapter of a book or each division of a proposal.

Fig. 13.5

The Document menu after Facing Pages *and* First Page Special *have been selected.*

Document	Window
Open First Header...	
Open First Footer...	
Open Even Header...	
Open Even Footer...	
Open Odd Header...	
Open Odd Footer...	
Footnote...	⌘E
Repaginate	⌘J
Outlining	⌘U
Spelling...	⌘L
Hyphenate...	
Index...	
Table of Contents...	
Calculate	⌘=
Renumber...	
Sort	

If your sole purpose in creating headers is to number the first page and the odd and even pages of a three-section document, the prospect of creating nine headers may not be particularly appealing. But don't worry. Word automatically carries the header or footer text from one section to the next, as it does with any other Section formatting. If the only element you want to change from section to section is the page number, you need to create only one set of headers or footers. If, on the other hand, you want to change the header for each section—for example, to include a different title in each section's header—you can open each section's header window and edit the contents. If you make a change in the header or footer of one section that you want to be reflected in the headers or footers of subsequent sections, instead of making the same change over and over in each window, you simply click each successive window's Same as Previous button. (We discuss this button and other elements of the window in the next section.)

NOTE: When creating special first-page or facing-pages headers or footers, you can save time by creating a basic header or footer with the Open Header or Open Footer command before selecting the Facing Pages or First Page Special option. Word then displays that header or footer in the window for any other header or footer you create, and you can edit the basic header or footer as required.

The Header and Footer Windows

The windows for all the header and footer options are essentially the same, and you can format and position them all in the same way. For convenience, we focus the following discussion on headers, the more common of the two features, and draw your attention to any process or procedure different for footers.

You can choose the header commands from the Document menu and type and format text and graphics in the header window before, during, or after creating the main text of the document. Regardless of which header command you choose, Word displays the basic header window shown in figure 13.6.

Header windows look and function much like normal document windows. You can drag a header window around the screen, change the window's size, and scroll horizontally and vertically through the window's contents. The only normal window element missing is the split bar. When you open a blank header window, the insertion point is po-

Title bar

Fig. 13.6

The header window.

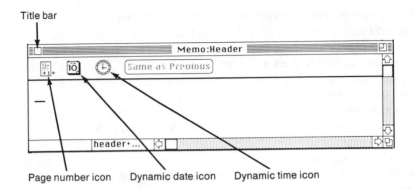

Page number icon   Dynamic date icon   Dynamic time icon

sitioned below the icons in the header window's upper left corner. To create a header, you type text or paste in text or graphics by using the same techniques you would use in a document window. You then can format the header in any way you choose.

The only difference among the various header windows is in the title bar, which reflects the document's name and the header type. All header windows have three icons for inserting the dynamic date, the dynamic time, and page numbers in a header, as well as a `Same as Previous` button (located below the title bar). Clicking an icon inserts the current page number, date, or time in the header at the insertion point. Word boxes an entry, as shown in figure 13.7, to indicate that its content is *dynamic*, meaning that Word inserts the current page number, date, or time in the header at the time of printing.

Fig. 13.7

A dynamic time entry in a header window.

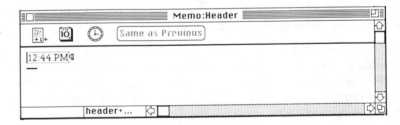

Word treats the page number, date, and time entries in the header and footer as single characters. To select an entry, just double-click it. You then can apply character formatting to the entry, just as you would to any other character.

You cannot select the Same as Previous button, however, unless the currently open header window contains a header different from the corresponding header in the previous section. The headers will be different only if you have edited or replaced the header in the previous section. Clicking the Same as Previous button replaces the current header with the previous header.

Now, see how well you can put these features to work.

Creating a Sample Header

In this section, you practice creating a header that displays the page number, date, and time. After using Page Preview to examine the header, you explore various options for positioning and formatting the header to achieve the look you want.

Creating Headers

You can add a header to any document that includes at least a few pages of text. For this exercise, the document you choose should not be formatted for facing pages or include sections.

To add to all the pages in a document a header that includes page number, date, and time entries, do the following:

1. Choose **Open Header** from the Document menu.

2. Use the Space bar or the Tab key to position the insertion point where you want the first entry to appear in the header.

3. Click the icon for the first entry.

4. Repeat Steps 2 and 3 to add the two other entries.

To duplicate the header shown in figure 13.8, click the date icon, press Tab, click the time icon, press Tab, and then click the page number icon.

5. Close the header window by clicking its close box.

The document window doesn't show any evidence of the new header. To see the results of your work, you need to use the Page Preview command. (For a full discussion of Page Preview options, see Chapter 6.)

Fig. 13.8

A simple header containing dynamic date, time, and page number entries.

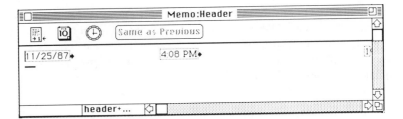

Previewing Headers

The Page Preview window is an excellent tool for correcting any header design errors. A sense of balance is important with headers. What may seem eye-catching and interesting in the isolation of the header window can overpower the text and be irritating or distracting on page after page of a printed document.

You can choose Page Preview—and most other commands—with the header window open. You then can alternate quickly between the reduced image of a two-page spread in the Page Preview window and the full-size header in the header window and make adjustments as necessary. Because the header you have created appears on every page of the document, you don't have to worry about the position of the insertion point within the document when you choose Page Preview. Almost any location in the document produces a two-page spread sufficient for viewing odd- and even-page headers. If you want to view a special first-page header or a section header, however, you need to position the insertion point before choosing Page Preview.

To preview a header in the Page Preview window, do the following:

1. Choose **Page Preview** from the File menu.

The display should look similar to the one shown in figure 13.9.

2. Click the magnifier icon to change the pointer's shape to a magnifying glass.

3. Click any of the three entries in the header.

In the magnified image, notice that choosing Page Preview removes the boxes from around the date, time, and page number entries and inserts the current settings (see fig. 13.10).

Header →

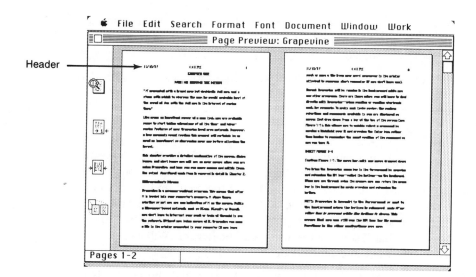

Fig. 13.9

*The Page
Preview window
showing a
header with
date, time, and
page numbers.*

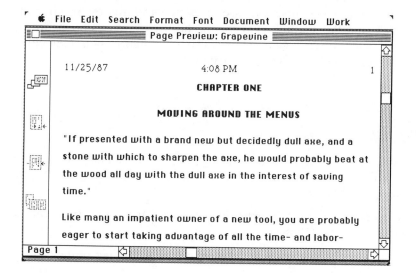

Fig. 13.10

*The magnified
page preview of
a header.*

4. Click the page icon that replaced the magnifier icon to the left of the window in order to return the display to the original two-page spread.

In the next section, you learn basic techniques for positioning headers.

Positioning Headers

Unless you give other instructions, Word uses default values to position headers and footers on the page. The program normally positions headers in the top margin, 0.5 inch from the top of the page, and footers in the bottom margin, 0.5 inch from the bottom of the page. The default placement is generally acceptable for page numbers and one-line headers and footers. But what if you want to use a six-line header? Will a cataclysmic collision of header and text occur?

Don't worry—the relationship between the text and the header is dynamic, and the header always has the right of way. When you fill the margin to overflowing with a header, Word simply pushes the text down to make room. If you prefer not to leave such decisions up to the program, you can, of course, exercise precise control over the width of the margin and the starting point for the header by using options in the Page Setup and Section dialog boxes. (For more information about either of these dialog boxes, refer to Chapter 5.)

Positioning Headers in Page Preview Mode

If you are not concerned about being precise, you can move the header up and down within the confines of the top margin while working in page preview mode.

To reposition the header while you are working in the Page Preview window, do the following:

1. Click the margins icon (the third icon to the left of the window).

Word draws a box around the header, as shown in figure 13.11, marking the margins and page breaks with various types of dotted lines.

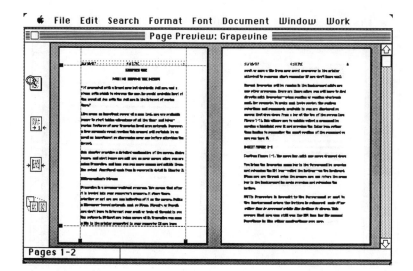

Fig. 13.11

*A boxed header
after you have
clicked the Page
Preview
window's
margins icon.*

2. Reposition the header by dragging its box.

Any change made to the displayed page affects all pages to which that type of formatting applies.

If you want to see how Word coordinates the header text with the margins, return to the document window and add several lines to the header. Then choose Page Preview again and click the margins icon. Notice that the top margin has moved down to accommodate the deeper header, as shown in figure 13.12. Notice also that Word has adjusted the page break. Enlarging the header causes Word to repaginate all the pages in the document.

Using the margins icon works well for rough positioning, but you probably will want to use Word's Section-command options, discussed in the next section, for fine-tuning. As you use both techniques, notice that the movement of the header in the Page Preview window is reflected in changes in the position displayed in the Section dialog box.

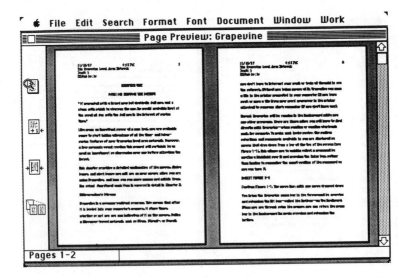

Fig. 13.12

The top margin, adjusted to accommodate a multiline header.

Positioning Headers with the Section Command

You can control the vertical position of a header by manipulating the setting in the From Top box in the Header/Footer area of the Format menu's Section dialog box. If the document contains several sections, however, before choosing the Section command, be sure that the insertion point is in the section containing the header you want to position. If you are still in the Page Preview window, you need to return to the document window.

Do the following to change the vertical position of a header:

1. Choose **Section** from the Format menu.

2. Type the desired measurement in the From Top box in the Header/Footer area.

3. Click **OK** to record the settings and close the dialog box.

Positioning Headers Outside the Margins

Controlling the horizontal positioning of a header can be a little more complex. The relationship of the header's left and right boundaries to the page's left and right margins is not dynamic: in other words, Word does not give the header the right of way. If the header text is too wide to fit within the left and right margins, Word wraps the lines, just as it would any other text.

To keep long header lines intact by extending a header into the margins of the page, you can instruct Word to outdent the header by setting negative left and right indents. As with any other paragraph formatting, you can control the formatting of the header with either the ruler or the Paragraph command. For practice, use the ruler to stretch the simple header you created earlier so that it extends beyond the page margins.

To extend a header beyond the left- and right-page margins, do the following:

1. Choose **Open Header** from the Document menu.

2. Choose **Show Ruler** from the Format menu.

Word moves the header text down and displays the ruler at the top of the header window.

3. Hold down the Shift key and click the left arrow on the horizontal scroll bar to move the ruler to the right (see fig. 13.13).

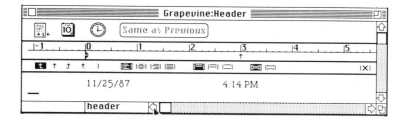

Fig. 13.13

The ruler, outdented into the left margin.

4. Drag the ruler's left-indent marker to the left of the left-margin marker. (The left-indent marker is the top one of the two.)

In this case, set the left-indent marker at -0.75 inch.

5. Click the horizontal scroll bar's right arrow to move the ruler to the left.

6. Drag the right-indent marker to the right of the right-margin marker.

For this example, set the right-indent marker at 6.75 inches.

The space available for the header now extends to 0.5 inch from the left edge of the page to 0.5 inch from the right edge of the page. However, the header currently occupies only part of this space. You can spread the header across the available space by adjusting the tabs that separate the entries.

7. Set tabs at about 2.5 inches and 6 inches.

Setting new tabs removes the default tabs, repositioning the time and page number. Figure 13.14 shows a page preview of the reformatted header. The header extends well beyond the margins of the text, and the text elements in the header are evenly distributed.

Fig. 13.14

The outdented header with the date, time, and page number spaced out for balance.

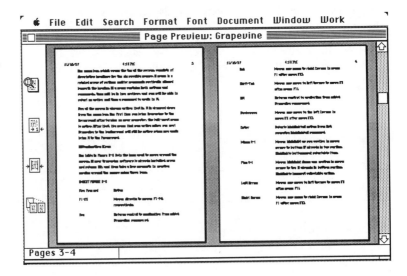

You also can outdent a header by using the Paragraph command's Ruler settings, but you have to click the indent markers on the ruler before you can specify new settings in the Paragraph dialog box. By the time you display and click the markers, you might as well move them.

Formatting Headers

As you saw in the preceding exercise, you can use indents, as well as other paragraph formatting, to create pleasing spacing within headers. With thoughtful use of tabs and paragraph alignment, you can distribute text and graphic elements within the indents to create the desired effect. You also can use the full range of character formatting to customize headers.

In the following exercises, you are going to create a pair of headers for the odd and even pages of a bound document and then a special first-page header that prints a letterhead. Following along with these exercises will give you a feel for some of the decisions and procedures involved in creating attractive headers and footers.

Customizing Headers for Odd and Even Pages

To explore what you can do with headers, you are going to develop facing-pages headers for a book (see fig. 13.15). For this exercise, you can use any document at least two pages long.

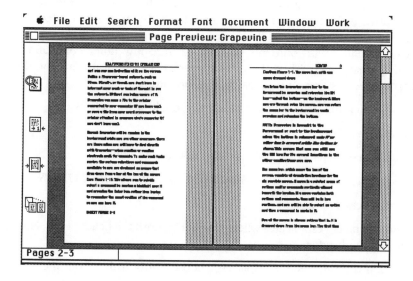

Fig. 13.15

A page preview of coordinated facing-pages headers.

Notice the balance between the two headers in figure 13.15. The page numbers are aligned with the outer edge of the text. The titles (the book title on the left page and the chapter title on the right page) are positioned an equal distance from their respective page numbers. And the line beneath the header extends well into the inner margins—almost to the binding. You could exactly duplicate these headers by measuring the page size, margins, gutter, and so on. But for this demonstration, simply duplicate the general appearance of the headers.

To establish the general page setup for facing-pages headers, do the following:

1. Load the document for which you want to create headers.

2. Choose **Page Setup** from the File menu.

3. Select **Facing Pages**.

4. Click the **Gutter** box and type **1.5 in** (or just **1.5**).

5. Click **OK**.

To create the even-page header, do the following:

1. Choose **Open Even Header** from the Document menu.

The only difference between the Open Even Header window and the Open Header window you saw earlier is the title. If the document you loaded already has a header, Word displays the header in the header window. Before you can create a new header, you need to select the old header text and press Backspace to clear the header window. If you experimented with outdents earlier, use the Show Ruler command in the Format menu. When the ruler appears, click the X at the right; this procedure restores normal paragraph formatting.

2. Click the page number icon to insert it at the left margin.

3. Press **Tab**.

4. Press **Caps Lock** and type the title of the book.

For this example, we typed *GRAPEVINE GUIDE TO OPERATIONS*.

5. Press **Tab** again.

The second tab establishes where the line beneath the header ends. Now, format the header.

6. If the ruler is not displayed, choose **Show Ruler** from the Format menu.

7. Insert a left-aligned tab stop at the 1-inch mark.

This tab stop positions the title.

8. Click the right arrow on the horizontal scroll bar to scroll the ruler to the left. Now insert a right-aligned tab stop at the 6.5-inch mark.

As mentioned before, this second tab stop anchors the line you are going to have Word draw beneath the entire header. Notice that you have set this tab beyond the ruler's right-indent marker. The capability of tabbing past the right-indent marker seems to be a "bug" in Word. If this "problem" goes away (if Microsoft fixes the bug), you will have to drag the right-indent marker to the 6.5-inch mark.

9. Select the entire header and press **Shift-Command-U** to underline it (or choose **Underline** from the Format menu).

The header for even pages is now complete. The header window should look something like the one in figure 13.16.

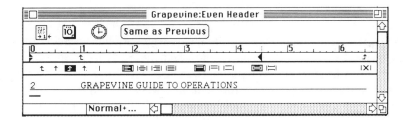

Fig. 13.16

An example of an even-page header.

Do the following to create the complementary odd-page header:

1. Choose **Open Odd Header** from the Document menu. Delete any header text that is left from your previous experiments.

2. Press **Tab** twice and type a one-word chapter title. (Caps Lock should still be toggled on.)

3. Press **Tab** again and click the page number icon.

4. Set a left-aligned tab stop at 3 inches and a right-aligned tab stop at 4.5 inches. (The ruler should still be visible.)

5. Hold down the Shift key and click the left arrow in the horizontal scroll bar several times to display several inches of the ruler to the left of the 0-inch mark.

6. Drag the left-indent marker for the header to -2 inches.

7. Select the entire header and press **Shift-Command-U** to underline it.

You have now finished the header for odd pages. The header window should look something like the one in figure 13.17.

Fig. 13.17

An example of an odd-page header.

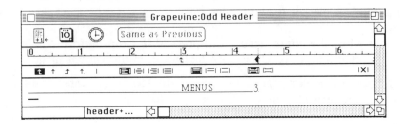

When you print the document, the facing pages should resemble those in figure 13.18. The program applies each header to the appropriate page: even headers on even-numbered pages and odd headers on odd-numbered pages. (To follow the style of a book exactly, however, you probably would want to exclude the header from the first page of each chapter or section of the document.)

Creating Special First-Page Headers

Often, you may find that the header you create for the pages of a document is not appropriate for the first page. Sometimes, you may want to omit altogether the header and footer from the first page. At other times, you may want to create a special first-page header. For example, for documents such as letters, you may want to create a header that acts as a letterhead.

To create a special first-page header that prints a letterhead, do the following:

1. Open a new document.

2. Choose **Section** from the Format menu.

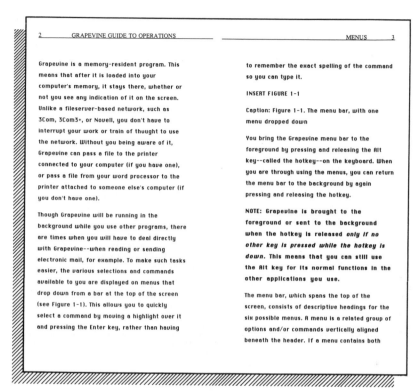

Fig. 13.18

Odd- and even-page headers like those that might be used in a book.

3. Click **First Page Special** and then click **OK** to close the Section dialog box.

4. Choose **Open First Header** from the Document menu.

5. Type and format the text of the header you want to appear on the first page.

For practice, you might want to duplicate the header, shown in figure 13.19, that consists of two lines of text set off with a double line. You also can dramatize the letterhead by pasting a graphic into the header.

If you decide to use a special first-page header as your letterhead, you probably will want to create another header, as shown in figure 13.20, for subsequent pages. To preserve your letterheads, you can save as a *template* (a sample) a document that is blank except for these headers. Then you can open the document and save a copy with a new name each time you want to create a letter. Alternatively, you might want to store both headers in the glossary so that they are available for use whenever you need them.

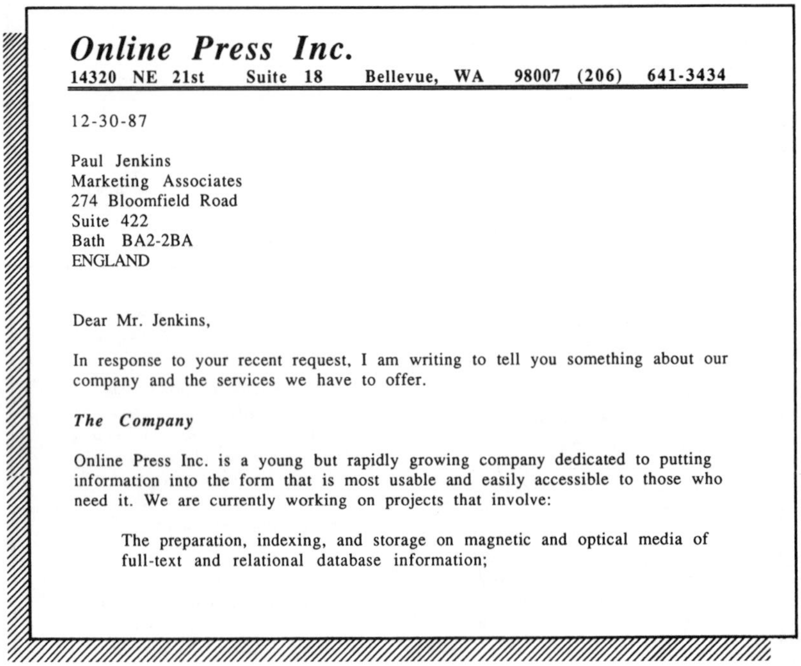

Fig. 13.19

*A sample
letterhead.*

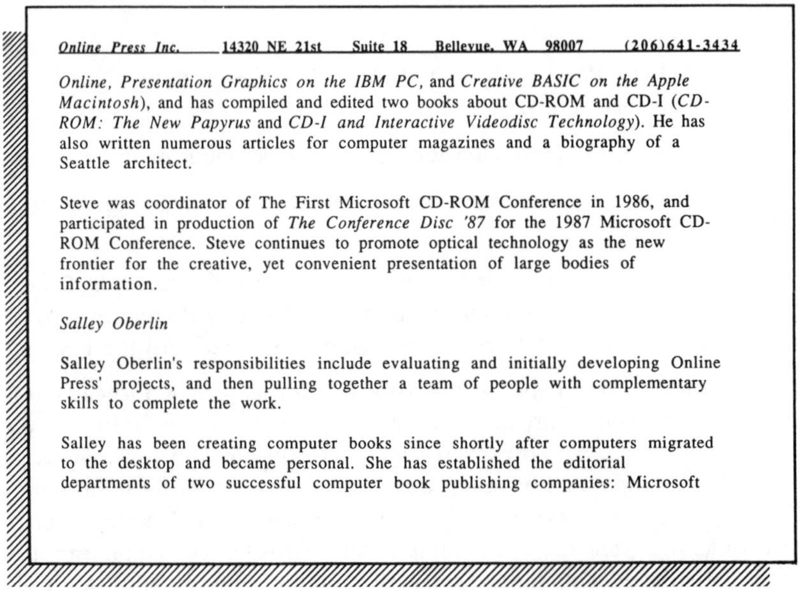

Online Press Inc.

14320 NE 21st   Suite 18   Bellevue, WA   98007   (206)   641-3434

12-30-87

Paul Jenkins
Marketing Associates
274 Bloomfield Road
Suite 422
Bath BA2-2BA
ENGLAND

Dear Mr. Jenkins,

In response to your recent request, I am writing to tell you something about our
company and the services we have to offer.

The Company

Online Press Inc. is a young but rapidly growing company dedicated to putting
information into the form that is most usable and easily accessible to those who
need it. We are currently working on projects that involve:

> The preparation, indexing, and storage on magnetic and optical media of
> full-text and relational database information;

Fig. 13.20

*A companion
header for
letters longer
than one page.*

Online Press Inc.   14320 NE 21st   Suite 18   Bellevue, WA   98007   (206)641-3434

Online, Presentation Graphics on the IBM PC, and *Creative BASIC on the Apple
Macintosh*), and has compiled and edited two books about CD-ROM and CD-I (*CD-
ROM: The New Papyrus* and *CD-I and Interactive Videodisc Technology*). He has
also written numerous articles for computer magazines and a biography of a
Seattle architect.

Steve was coordinator of The First Microsoft CD-ROM Conference in 1986, and
participated in production of *The Conference Disc '87* for the 1987 Microsoft CD-
ROM Conference. Steve continues to promote optical technology as the new
frontier for the creative, yet convenient presentation of large bodies of
information.

Salley Oberlin

Salley Oberlin's responsibilities include evaluating and initially developing Online
Press' projects, and then pulling together a team of people with complementary
skills to complete the work.

Salley has been creating computer books since shortly after computers migrated
to the desktop and became personal. She has established the editorial
departments of two successful computer book publishing companies: Microsoft

Storing Headers in the Glossary

You can use the Cut, Copy, and Paste commands to move text and graphics in and out of the header windows just as you do in other windows. As a result, you also can make a glossary entry of an intricately formatted header or footer. Storing headers in the glossary not only saves formatting time but also helps you maintain consistency among headers.

Storing in the glossary the dynamic date and time entries from the header window may be particularly useful. Unlike the Standard Glossary's permanent date and time entries, the entries pasted from the header window remain dynamic in a document: the program always inserts the current time and date when you print the document. You can use this new glossary entry anywhere in your document, not just in the header or footer.

To make a glossary entry of a dynamic date or time entry from a header, do the following:

1. Choose a header command from the Document menu to open a header window.

If a current header contains the dynamic entry you want to transfer to the glossary, you can copy the entry from that header and skip Step 2.

2. Click the appropriate icon to insert a dynamic entry in the header.

3. Select the entry by dragging through it or double-clicking it.

4. Choose **Cut** or **Copy** from the Edit menu to cut or copy the selected entry to the Clipboard.

If you opened the header window solely to create a dynamic glossary entry, choose Cut to transfer the entry to the Clipboard and then close the window.

5. Choose **Glossary** from the Edit menu to open the Glossary dialog box.

6. Choose **Paste** from the Edit menu to insert the dynamic entry in the Glossary dialog box.

Word considers the entry a graphic and represents the entry with a box in the glossary entry description area, as shown in figure 13.21. The program gives the entry the name Unnamed1. You can change this name to something more appropriate, such as *Dynadate* or *Dynatime*.

Fig. 13.21

A box representing the dynamic date entry, pasted from the Clipboard as a graphic.

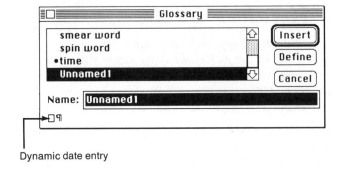

Dynamic date entry

7. Type a name for the new entry in the active Name box.

8. Click **Define** to record the entry.

This procedure conveniently puts the entry in the Standard Glossary. To add the entry to any other glossary, open the appropriate glossary before pasting the entry from the Clipboard (see Chapter 8 for more information).

When you insert the glossary entry into a document, the entry assumes the form it has in the header: a boxed date. The date in the box has no bearing on the date inserted when the document is printed. The program updates all dynamic entries throughout a document each time you repaginate by choosing Page Preview or by printing the document.

As you become comfortable using headers and footers, you will find that they provide a great deal of flexibility for creating signposts to guide your readers through documents. Because the formatting and positioning of headers and footers are flexible, you also will start to think of many creative uses for them—as banner headlines across multiple columns, for example, or fancy titles for newsletters.

Checking Spelling

We all have idiosyncrasies—in the way we walk, talk, dance, sleep, eat, and think. And those of us who spend time tapping away at a computer keyboard (or playing the piano) soon discover that our fingers have their own idiosyncrasies. Fingers often move in patterns we can't seem to change, no matter how hard we try. The fact that our fingers can "learn" patterns of movement has its positive side, however: 15 years after mastering a piano piece, we still can sit down at the keyboard and "feel" our way through the music, albeit a little haltingly. The negative side is that we probably will repeat the same mistakes we made 15 years before.

When it comes to word processing, you may have noticed that you tend to make the same mistakes again and again. Perhaps you habitually type *grphics* instead of *graphics*, or *teh* instead of *the*. Fortunately, when you use Word, you can ignore such imperfections while trying to put words on the page. You can go for speed, knowing that you can correct the typos later with Word's Spelling command.

When you choose the Spelling command from the Document menu, Word checks each word in your document or in a selected part of your document against the 80,000 permanent entries in the program's Main Dictionary. If your vocabulary includes unusual words, such as proper nouns or words pertaining to your particular line of work, you can create your own user dictionaries, which Word uses to verify the spellings of any words that the program can't find in its Main Dictionary. If Word comes across a word not found in either the Main Dictionary or the open user dictionaries, the program pauses. You then can type the correct spelling, ignore the word (leaving the spelling the same), or add the word to a dictionary.

In this chapter, you first learn the basic procedure for checking your spelling and take a tour of the Spelling dialog box. You then find out more about Word's dictionaries, including when and how to create, open, and close user dictionaries. Finally, you work through a spelling check with a sample document.

As you work your way through this chapter, remember that Word's spelling checker is incapable of correcting improper syntax, moving misplaced modifiers, or identifying words spelled correctly but used incorrectly, such as *feet* instead of *foot*. Using the Spelling command should not take the place of a thorough scrutiny of your work. Word takes the drudgery out of spelling checks, but the burden still is on you to make sure that your documents do not contain errors.

Performing Spelling Checks

The purpose of a spelling check is to save proofreading time—and eye-strain—as well as to correct errors efficiently. When you're working on a document, you probably will find the check only as useful as it is fast. Word speeds up the process of checking your spelling by anticipating what you probably will want to do with a word not included in a dictionary. If the program's guess is correct, simply press Return to confirm the action and resume the search for the next "unknown" word. Thus, you usually can keep your hands on the keyboard while performing a spelling check.

To check the spelling of an entire document, do the following:

1. Click an insertion point in front of the first character in the document.

You can initiate a spelling check from any point in a document. However, because Word performs the check from the insertion point to the end of the document, you normally will want to move the insertion point to the top of the document before choosing the command. If you forget to move the insertion point, Word displays the alert box shown in figure 14.1 when the check reaches the end of the document. To resume the spelling check at the top of the document, click OK.

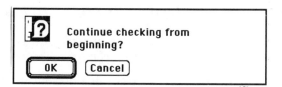

Fig. 14.1

The alert box displayed when a spelling check reaches the end of a document.

2. Choose **Spelling** from the Document menu.

Word loads the Main Dictionary and an empty user dictionary and displays the Spelling dialog box shown in figure 14.2. If Word cannot find the Main Dictionary on the disk in your Macintosh, an alert box appears. Simply insert the disk that contains the dictionary.

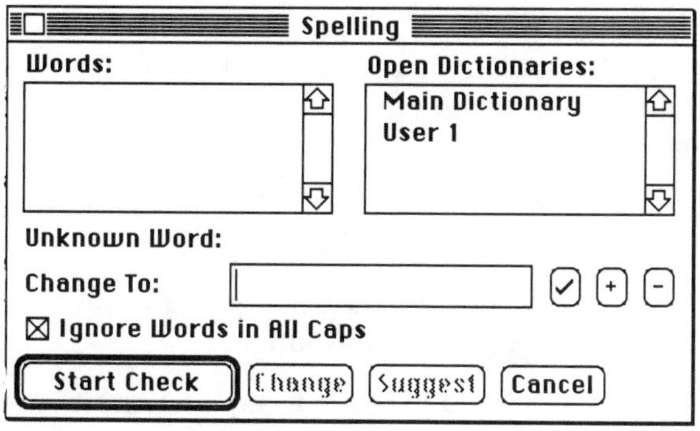

Fig. 14.2

The Spelling dialog box.

3. If you have used acronyms, such as AFL-CIO, in your document and you don't want Word to waste time stumbling over them, leave the Ignore Words in All Caps box checked. If you want Word to check the spelling of uppercase words, click the box to deselect this option.

4. Press **Return** or click **Start Check** to start the spelling check.

Word moves through the document, checking each word against those in the Main Dictionary and stopping when the program finds an unknown word.

The fastest way to handle unknown words that are typos is simply to type the correct spelling in the Change To box. If Word locates an unknown word that is a misspelling, you can type the word again or let Word suggest a replacement. If the unknown word is spelled correctly but is simply too specialized to be in the Main Dictionary, you can tell the program to ignore the word or to add it to a user dictionary. The Spelling command is most useful if you understand all these options.

Exploring the Spelling Check Options

The Spelling dialog box looks deceptively simple, but it is packed with options that control the following basic types of operation:

- Correcting misspellings and typos in a document

- Making, deleting, opening, and closing the user dictionaries that supplement the permanent Main Dictionary

During a spelling check, Word displays unknown words in the Unknown Word area. Beneath this area is the Change To box, which displays the word that will be substituted for the unknown word. To the right of the Change To box are three buttons that enable you to interact with a user dictionary in the following ways:

- To verify the spelling of a word typed in the Change To box, click the Check button (positioned just to the right of the Change To box).

- To add the word in the Change To box to the selected user dictionary, click the Plus button.

- To delete a word from a dictionary, select the word in the Words list and click the Minus button.

User dictionaries are discussed in detail in the section titled "Working with Dictionaries."

The Open Dictionaries list box in the top right corner of the dialog box displays the names of all open dictionaries. When you choose the Spelling command, Word automatically opens the Main Dictionary and the default user dictionary, called User 1. (You learn how to open other dictionaries in the section titled "Closing and Opening User Dictionaries.")

The empty Words list box in the top left corner of the dialog box is used if you click the Suggest button at the bottom of the Spelling dialog box. Word uses the list box to display words similar to the unknown word.

The other buttons along the bottom of the Spelling dialog box constitute a sort of control panel. The leftmost button initially is labeled Start Check. When Word displays an unknown word, the button becomes No Change. You use the next button, Change, to tell Word to replace the unknown word with the word displayed in the Change To box. To the right of the Change button is the Suggest button, which is available whenever a word is displayed in either the Unknown Word area or the

Change To box. When you click Suggest, Word searches the dictionaries for words similar to the one displayed and lists the results of its search in the Words box. The rightmost button is the Cancel button, which closes the Spelling dialog box so that you can continue working with the document.

As a spelling check progresses, the control buttons alternate between being selectable and unselectable, and Word highlights the button (by placing a border around the button) you are most likely to use at any particular point in the process.

Correcting Typos

If Word spots a typo and you know the correct spelling, the simplest and fastest way to fix the spelling is to retype the word without consulting a dictionary. To make this correction easy, Word places the insertion point in the Change To box.

To replace a typo with the correct spelling, do the following:

1. Type the correct word in the Change To box.

When you start typing, Word highlights the Change button, making this button the default choice (see fig. 14.3).

```
╔═══════════════ Spelling ═══════════════╗
║ Words:              Open Dictionaries:    ║
║ ┌──────────────┐△   ┌──────────────────┐△║
║ │              │    │ Main Dictionary  │ ║
║ │              │    │ User 1           │ ║
║ │              │    │                  │ ║
║ │              │▽   │                  │▽║
║ └──────────────┘    └──────────────────┘ ║
║ Unknown Word: publihser                   ║
║ Change To:  ┌───────────────┐ ✓  +  −    ║
║             │ publisher      │            ║
║             └───────────────┘            ║
║ ⊠ Ignore Words in All Caps                ║
║ ( No Change )  [[Change]] (Suggest) (Cancel) ║
╚═══════════════════════════════════════════╝
```

Fig. 14.3

The highlighted Change *button, activated when you type a word in the* Change To *box.*

2. Press **Return** or click the **Change** button.

When Word comes across the next occurrence of the same typo, the program automatically enters your previous correction in the Change To box and highlights the Change button. All you need to do is click the Change button or press Return to make the correction.

Verifying Your Spelling

If you want to verify that the word you typed in the Change To box is spelled correctly before substituting the word throughout the document, click the Check button to the right of the Change To box. If Word can't find the word in an open dictionary, the program displays the word in the Unknown Word area, as shown in figure 14.4. You then can treat the new spelling as you would any other unknown word—type another version, consult any open dictionary, ignore the word, or add the word to a user dictionary.

Fig. 14.4

Word's response after you click the Check button to verify the word you have mistyped in the Change To *box.*

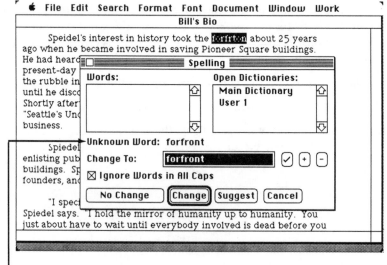

Word in Change To box displayed here if misspelled

NOTE: If you misspell a word in the Change To box and don't take the time to have Word verify the spelling, you may introduce an error throughout your document under the guise of a correction. When you make a correction, Word assumes that you want the same correction made in subsequent encounters of the mistake; therefore, Word displays your correction in the Change To box each time it encounters the initial mistake. Adding a typo or misspelling to a user dictionary (by clicking the Plus button) has far-reaching negative effects for all your future documents, too. The moral: Type carefully and verify often.

Looking Up Words

If the unknown word identified by Word is misspelled and you don't know the correct spelling, the spelling-check process gets somewhat slower. In this situation, your hand must leave the keyboard to click the Suggest button. The program then displays in the Words box a list of words similar to the unknown spelling. If Word cannot find any similar words, an alert box appears, displaying the message Unable to suggest alternative. If similar words are found, the program guesses which word you will choose by displaying it at the top of the list, highlighted, as shown in figure 14.5.

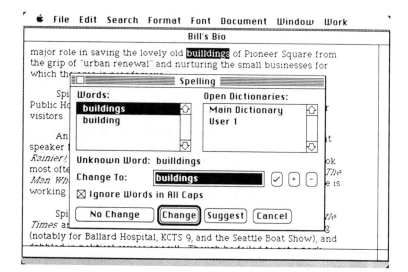

Fig. 14.5

The Spelling dialog box after you click the Suggest *button.*

Word also displays the selected word in the Change To box and highlights the Change button. If you concur with Word's correction, simply press Return to accept the alternate spelling. If you recognize another word in the list as the correct spelling, click the word and then click Change (or press Return).

If you don't see anything that looks right, you're on your own. Consult a printed dictionary or technical reference—or a librarian—and then type the correct spelling. (Sometimes, changing the word to one you do know how to spell is quicker.)

Marking Words in the Text

If you cannot take the time during the current spelling session to track down the correct spelling for an unknown word, you can mark the unknown word by typing something unique in the Change To box and pressing Return. Later, you can use the Find or Change command to locate the word and deal with it at your leisure.

You might, for example, type *XXXbioaccumulation* to mark all occurrences of *bioaccumulation*. You can later supply the correct spelling through a document-wide change procedure. Or you can search nimbly on the *XXX* to locate all marked words. The marker is simply a reminder—something to catch your eye so that you do not forget to resolve the problem.

Handling Unusual Spellings

Documents often contain perfectly sensible spellings that would never make Webster's Dictionary. These spellings include proper names and specialized technical terms. If the word displayed in the Unknown Word area falls into this category, you have two choices: simply press Return (or click No Change) to speed past the correct but unusual spelling or click the Plus button to add the word to the selected user dictionary. If you press Return or select No Change, the No Change button changes to Continue Check, and Word continues the search. If you click Plus, Word assumes that the spelling is correct and automatically searches for the next unknown word.

Deleting Words from User Dictionaries

Using the Minus button to delete a word from the selected user dictionary probably will not be an option you exercise often during a spelling check—unless you happen to notice a misspelled word in the dictionary. To remove such a word, simply select the word in the Words list box (the dictionary still should be selected) and click Minus. (For more details on deleting entries, see the section titled "Eliminating Words in User Dictionaries.")

Limiting a Spelling Check

The time required to check a document's spelling is determined by the length of the document and the number of misspelled words. You can save time when working on a long document by limiting the text you subject to a spelling check.

If you select a block of text before choosing the Spelling command, Word checks only the words in the selection. Limiting a spelling check in this way is convenient when you want to check the spelling of a passage you have added to a previously checked document. You also can select a single word and have Word quickly check its spelling without your having to refer to a printed dictionary.

What if the document contains text you don't want verified, such as notes to yourself or to a colleague? Instead of selecting in turn the passages you do want checked, you can use one of two methods to make sure Word ignores the text you don't want the program to check.

In the first place, Word excludes, by default, words in all capitals from a spelling check. The logic is that these words (usually acronyms) somehow are immune to typos and normally need not be checked. The option also offers a handy way to exclude certain passages from a spelling check. You can type notes within the text in all capitals, making them easy to spot. The Ignore Words in All Caps option makes sure the program doesn't get bogged down in needlessly checking notes you don't intend to print anyway.

Second, an even better way to exclude such passages as notes from a spelling check is to format the notes as hidden text: the Spelling command checks only displayed text. Before the spelling check, toggle off the Show Hidden Text option in the Preferences dialog box; by following this procedure, you ensure that Word skips over the notes. This method also eliminates the need for deleting notes before printing a document—you simply can hide them.

Suspending and Extending Spelling Checks

Word is flexible enough to allow you to suspend a spelling check in order to edit a passage. Suppose that something adjacent to an unknown word catches your eye. Rather than relying on your memory to return to that passage after you complete the spelling check, you can suspend temporarily the spelling procedure while you edit the passage.

To suspend and resume a spelling check, do the following:

1. Click the **Cancel** button or the Spelling dialog box's close box.

2. Edit the document as necessary.

3. Choose **Spelling** to resume the spelling check.

The Continue Check button is highlighted in the dialog box.

4. Press **Return** or click **Continue Check**.

The spelling check continues from the insertion point.

Actually, you don't have to close the Spelling dialog box to work on a document. You can resize the document window so that both the Spelling dialog box and the document are displayed, as shown in figure 14.6. Then you simply can click the area you want to make active.

Fig. 14.6

A document window reduced so that both the window and the Spelling dialog box are visible.

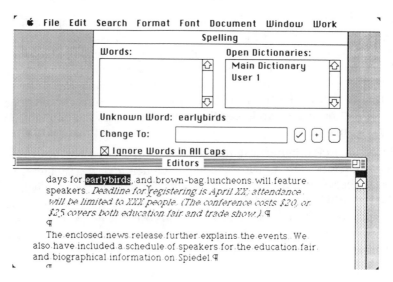

You also can open several documents before choosing the Spelling command and then activate each document; this procedure enables you to continue a spelling check through the entire set. Word continues the spelling check at the insertion point in the most recently activated document. You may want to use this method to check the spelling of a series of linked documents because the program does not automatically go from one to another.

Working with Dictionaries

As you've seen, Word supplies two dictionaries for use with the Spelling command: the Main Dictionary, which contains about 80,000 permanent entries, and a default user dictionary, called User 1, to which you can add words you don't want the program to identify as unknown. Because Word automatically opens User 1, this user dictionary is convenient for general use. If you store all dictionary additions in User 1, you need never worry about opening and closing dictionaries, supplying a name when you save dictionary changes, or selecting a dictionary as you add or delete words.

User 1 is handy for storing any text you use frequently, such as names and addresses. Doubtless, you know how to spell the names of the people with whom you regularly correspond. But unless all your friends have names like White, Green, Mason, or Gates, Word probably will not find them in the Main Dictionary during a spelling check, and you constantly will be clicking No Change to tell the program to skip these "unknown words."

If you need to, you can create other user dictionaries by using the File menu's New command (see the next section). You can rename, close, and open these dictionaries at any time by choosing Spelling and then using the normal File menu commands.

Creating Specialized Dictionaries

You can create a new user dictionary any time the Spelling dialog box is open. For some types of work, specialized user dictionaries can be helpful. For example, if you work with technical documents in several disparate, jargon-laden fields, opening a specialized user dictionary can prevent Word from grinding to a halt every time the program encounters a technical term specific to one particular field. By storing words in specialized dictionaries, you also minimize the number of entries Word has to check in User 1, thereby saving time during spelling checks.

To create a new user dictionary, do the following:

1. Choose **Spelling** from the Document menu.

2. Choose **New** from the File menu.

Because the Spelling dialog box is open, rather than open a new document, Word opens a new dictionary and supplies the name User 2 (or 3, 4, or 5, depending on how many dictionaries you have created during the session). The program adds the name of the dictionary to the Open Dictionaries list, as shown in figure 14.7. You can use the dictionary under the name that automatically appears in the list box, or you can rename the dictionary.

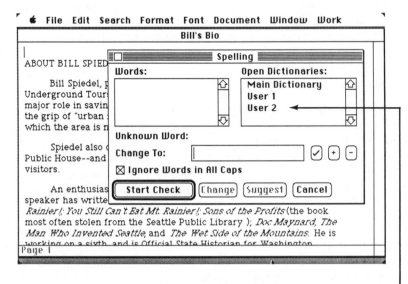

Fig. 14.7

A newly created dictionary.

New dictionary

Do the following to rename a user dictionary:

1. Choose **Spelling** from the Document menu.

2. Click the name you want to change in the Open Dictionaries list box.

3. Choose **Save As** from the File menu.

Word displays the dialog box shown in figure 14.8. The selected dictionary name is displayed in the Save Current Dictionary as box. Anything you type will replace this name.

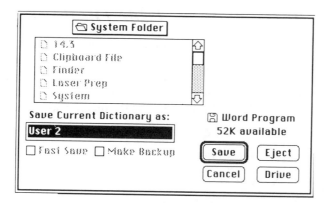

Fig. 14.8

*The Save As
dialog box used
to save a user
dictionary.*

4. Type the name you want to give the user dictionary.

5. Press **Return**.

The Save As dialog box closes, and the open Spelling dialog box, in which
the new name has replaced the old in the Open Dictionaries list,
appears.

NOTE: This process does not actually rename the dictionary; a copy of
the dictionary is saved with the new name. If you have previously saved
the dictionary under the old name, that dictionary remains on the disk.
To remove the old dictionary from within Word, use the File menu's
Delete command or drag the dictionary to the trash from the Finder.

When you quit Word, the program notifies you of any unsaved changes
to a user dictionary through the alert box shown in figure 14.9. If you
choose to save the changes, Word displays the standard Save As dialog
box. You can save the dictionary with its current name or supply a new
name. If you have made changes to several user dictionaries, individual
alert boxes ask whether you want to save the changes to each one.

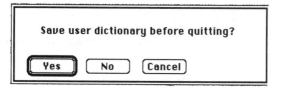

Fig. 14.9

*The Save User
Dictionary alert
box.*

Closing and Opening Use

During an editing session, you can open a
any time. Because Word searches all open
word in the Main Dictionary, keeping ope
needed during a spelling check is a good
tionaries does not change if you close one

To open a user dictionary, do the followin

1. Choose **Spelling** from the Documen

2. Choose **Open** from the File menu.

Word displays the dialog box shown in figure 14.10.

Fig. 14.10

*The Open dialog
box used to
open a
dictionary.*

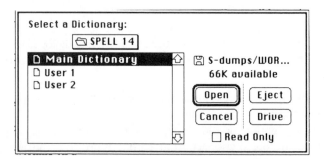

3. Double-click the name of the desired user dictionary.

If the dictionary you want to open isn't listed, locate and load the disk
on which the dictionary is stored. Then double-click the name in the
new list. The dialog box closes, and Word adds the dictionary to the
Open Dictionaries list in the Spelling dialog box.

To close an open user dictionary, do the following:

1. Choose **Spelling** from the Document menu.

2. Click the dictionary's name in the Spelling dialog box's Open
   Dictionaries list.

3. Choose **Close** from the File menu.

Word alerts you to any unsaved changes in the dictionary you are trying
to close. Then the dictionary name disappears from the list. The dictionary remains closed until you reopen it.

Selecting User Dictionaries

When Word checks the spelling in a document, the program first compares each word with the entries in the Main Dictionary. If no match is located, the program continues the comparison with the words in any open user dictionaries. If none of the open dictionaries contains a match, the program gives you the option of changing or ignoring the word. You also can add the word to a user dictionary so that the program will not stumble over the word during future spelling checks.

When you open the Spelling dialog box, User 1 is the active user dictionary. To add a word to a dictionary other than User 1, click the name of that dictionary in the list (to select the dictionary) and then click the Plus button. Throughout the spelling check, or until you select another user dictionary, that dictionary remains active. If you interrupt the spelling check by closing the Spelling dialog box, User 1 again becomes the default recipient of new words.

Word lists user dictionaries in the Open Dictionaries box in the order in which they were opened and, by default, makes the dictionary at the top of the list the default recipient of the words you add. You can make a dictionary other than User 1 the default user dictionary by reordering the dictionaries in the list box.

To change the default user dictionary, do the following:

1. Close all user dictionaries listed above the one you want to be the default dictionary.

2. Reopen the user dictionaries.

The program still searches each dictionary for word matches, but now you can add entries to the top dictionary without the other dictionaries getting in the way.

Eliminating Words in User Dictionaries

If you frequently use specialized user dictionaries, you probably will want to do occasional housecleaning—removing unnecessary entries and maybe even unneeded dictionaries.

To delete a word from a user dictionary, do the following:

1. Choose **Spelling** from the Document menu.

2. In the Open Dictionaries list, click the name of the user dictionary containing the word you want to eliminate.

The Words list box displays the words in the selected user dictionary.

3. Scroll through the Words list and click the entry you want to delete.

Word displays the entry in the Change To box, as shown in figure 14.11.

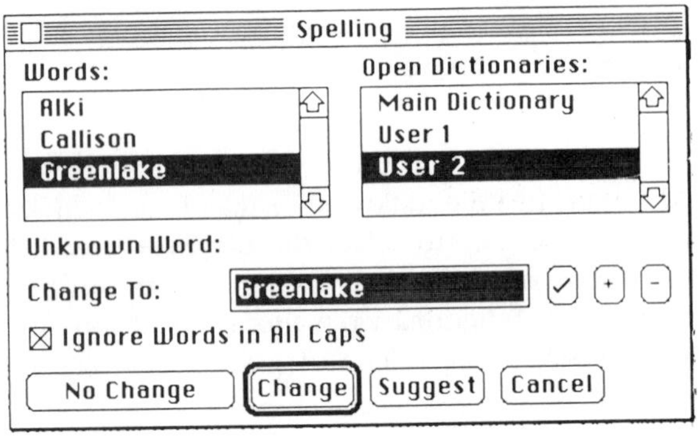

4. Click the **Minus** button.

The program deletes the entry from the Words list and from the loaded version of the dictionary. You must save the changes to this dictionary when you quit Word in order to update the disk file.

Do the following to delete a user dictionary:

1. Choose **Spelling** from the Document menu.

2. Choose **Delete** from the File menu.

3. In the dialog box that appears, double-click the name of the dictionary you want to delete.

You also can delete a user dictionary from the Finder by dragging the dictionary's icon into the trash.

Now that you've learned the nuts and bolts of conducting spelling checks, take a look at the Spelling command in action.

Performing a Spelling Check on a Sample Document

To demonstrate Word's ability to check spelling, we decided to give the Spelling command a real workout. Figure 14.12 shows the document we used: a love letter written by a Mr. Smythe, who has, shall we say, a way with words. You may want to run a spelling check on one of your own documents, but you'll have more fun if you follow along with Mr. Smythe as he checks his document. (You even might want to store the love letter as a glossary entry—this type of effusion is hard to come by, and you never know when an example like this one might come in handy.)

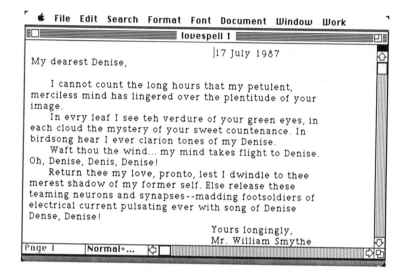

Fig. 14.12

A sample document, ready for a spelling check.

To check the spelling of an entire document, do the following:

1. Click an insertion point at the beginning of the document.

2. Choose **Spelling** from the Document menu.

3. Press **Return** or click the **Start Check** button.

As the spelling check begins, Word pauses at the first unknown word—*Denise*. The word is displayed in the Unknown Word box and is highlighted in the text, as shown in figure 14.13. Knowing that *Denise* is a word he uses often, Mr. Smythe decides to add the name to the User 1 dictionary.

Fig. 14.13

Denise—*the first
unknown word
in the spelling
check.*

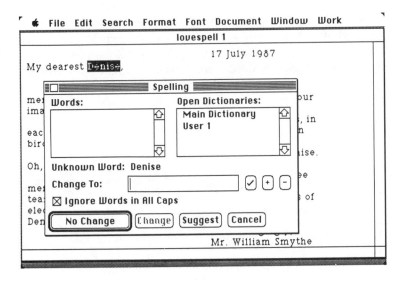

4. Click the **Plus** button.

Word selects User 1 and displays the added word in the Words box (see
fig. 14.14). From now on, *Denise* will be ignored by the program.

Fig. 14.14

*The new User 1
dictionary entry.*

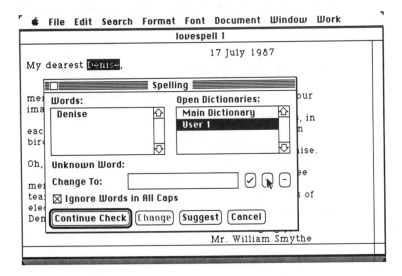

5. Press **Return** or click **Continue Check** to resume the spelling check.

The next unknown word is *petulent*. Mr. Smythe can't recall the correct spelling of this word, so he decides to look it up.

6. Click the **Suggest** button.

The dialog box now looks like the one in figure 14.15. The program displays the correct spelling in the Words box and highlights the correctly spelled word in the Change To box.

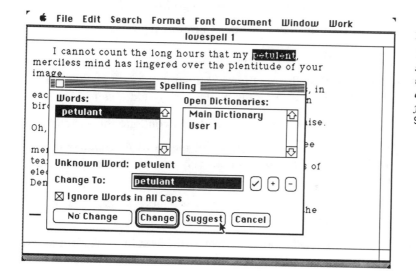

Fig. 14.15.

The correct spelling of the word petulant, *displayed when you click the* Suggest *button.*

7. Press **Return** or click **Change** to accept the new spelling.

Word resumes the spelling check, stopping next at *plentitude*. Mr. Smythe could have sworn that spelling was correct, but again he decides to check the program's dictionary.

8. Click **Suggest**.

This time, Word suggests two words—*plenitude* and *platitude*—with a preference for the former. *Plenitude* also edges out *platitude* in Mr. Smythe's mind.

9. Press **Return** or click **Change**, to accept the suggested spelling and resume the search.

Word next stumbles over *evry*. Mr. Smythe has no trouble discerning that this word should be *every*.

> 10. Type **every** in the Change To box and then press **Return**.

The spelling check continues. At the next unknown word—*teh*—Mr. Smythe again types the correct spelling.

> 11. Type **the** and press **Return**.

Word highlights *birdsong* and selects the No Change button. This spelling looks fine to Mr. Smythe.

> 12. Press **Return** to accept the spelling of *birdsong*.

Denis is the next unknown word, an obvious typo.

> 13. Type **Denise** and press **Return**.

Word pauses at *thee*, the next unknown word. Because his favorite pastime is writing sonnets, Mr. Smythe decides to add *thee* to User 1.

> 14. Click **Plus** to add *thee* to User 1 and continue the search.

Mr. Smythe feels strongly enough about the word *footsoldiers* to keep this spelling in the letter but not strongly enough to add the word to a dictionary.

> 15. The No Change button is selected, so ignore *footsoldiers* by pressing **Return**.

Wisely, Mr. Smythe adds both of his names, the next two unknown words, to User 1.

> 16. Click the **Plus** button to add *William* to User 1.

> 17. Click the **Plus** button to add *Smythe* to User 1.

Arriving at the end of the document, Word now displays the Continue Checking alert box.

> 18. Click **OK**.

The alert dialog box closes, revealing a corrected document.

Now that the spelling check is over, review Word's performance:

- The program identified *verdure*, *countenance*, *clarion*, and even *madding* as correct spellings. This performance was downright heroic!

- Word did not trip over the scientific term *synapses*, a plural form.

- The program acknowledged the slang word *pronto*.

- The dictionary even picked up on the archaic *waft* spelling.

- Word also identified as unknown words *birdsong* and *footsoldiers*, both words for which Mr. Smythe should have requested suggestions or checked a dictionary. *Birdsong* is correct as spelled, but *footsoldiers* should be two words—*foot soldiers*. Mr. Smythe's laziness led to a spelling error.

However, the spelling check missed three misspellings:

- The program considered *teaming* acceptable because the word seemingly is based on the correct spelling of the word *team*. The spelling should be *teeming* (meaning filled to overflowing), which Word's Main Dictionary does not include.

- Word accepted *Dense*. Sometimes a mistyped word simply makes sense to the program if a correct spelling of a similar word is found in Word's Main Dictionary.

- The final mistake was brought on by Mr. Smythe himself. By adding *thee* to User 1, he prevented Word from locating the misspelling of the word *the* later in the same line. The word *thee* probably should be deleted from the dictionary.

As for the phrase *Waft thou the wind*—no computer program can guard against appallingly incorrect use of perfectly spelled words.

Though the Spelling command cannot identify all misspellings, you can see that the program is a big help—even if the language of your documents is out of the ordinary. Don't be tempted to rely totally on the command for proofing your work, but do use the Spelling command to save time—and your eyes—for work other than checking for typos.

Another habit you want to develop is calling on Word's Hyphenation command to improve the appearance of a document. In the next chapter, we discuss the Hyphenation command and other options for formatting hyphens within text.

Hyphenating To Adjust
Line Breaks

You probably have never sat down at your typewriter or computer with the purpose of learning the rules for hyphenation. But after looking up words in the dictionary over and over again, you may have caught on to the intricacies of the process. Unless you actually are inserting hyphens into your text, however, hyphenation probably never crosses your mind—until the hyphens show up where they shouldn't or when they are conspicuously absent.

In the typewriter era, people would hyphenate words at the ends of lines in order to squeeze as much text as possible onto each line. Then the users of early word-processing programs stopped using hyphens at the ends of lines because most word-processing programs automatically "wrapped" the text down to the next line by moving words that would not fit on the line.

The current word-processing phase brings with it desktop-publishing capabilities that allow you to mold text into whatever shape best suits your purpose: for example, you can display text in three skinny columns or wrapped around a graphic. Although word processors like Word, Version 3, make innovative layouts easier to achieve, pleasing results often depend on the judicious use of hyphens.

Two primary reasons exist for using hyphens. The first reason is to conform to spelling and language-usage conventions for hyphenating compound nouns, compound adjectives (such as side-by-side), and certain proper names (including surnames). The second reason is to improve the appearance of a document by breaking lines to eliminate unnecessary or distracting white space (see fig. 15.1).

Fig. 15.1

*Uneven spacing
caused by
narrow
columns.*

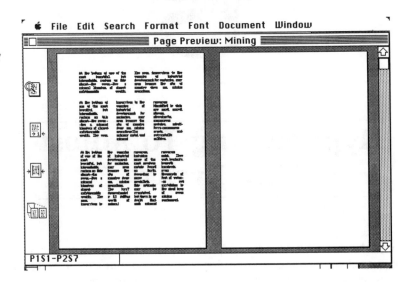

Figure 15.1 shows a page preview of unhyphenated text in standard two-, three-, and four-column formats. Notice how distracting the white space is as the columns become narrower. If you work with narrow columns, develop the habit of using hyphenation as a polishing touch. The spacing adjustments resulting from new line breaks cannot hurt, and you may be surprised at how much the adjustments improve a document's appearance.

This chapter's focus is on the second use of hyphens—improving the appearance of a document. To that end, the Document menu's Hyphenate command offers you the following flexibility in hyphenating a document:

- You automatically can hyphenate a whole document or only a selected area of text.

- You can tell the program to pause so that you may approve each suggested word break.

- You can select a single word and choose Hyphenate to verify possible places to insert a hyphen.

Faced with the need to adjust a line break by hyphenating a word, you may find that your hyphenation skills are rusty. Is it *an-other* or *a-nother*, *pro-bable* or *prob-able*? The Word program offers an alternative to interrupting your work and resorting to the dictionary for answers to hyphenation questions. You can hyphenate simple documents automatically in seconds by choosing the Hyphenate command from the Document menu. For more complex documents, the process is less automatic but still faster than manual hyphenation with a dictionary close at hand.

In this chapter, we discuss the features of the Hyphenate command and the Hyphenate dialog box. Then we provide you with two exercises that help you become familiar with the automatic and interactive hyphenation processes. The chapter concludes with information about other types of hyphens that assist the program in adjusting difficult line-break problems.

Reviewing the Hyphenate Dialog Box

If most of your typing consists of letters, memos, and other single-column documents, you probably haven't used the Document menu's Hyphenate command. In a standard, 65-character line, you may not notice the extra space remaining at a line's end after a long word is moved down—especially if the text is left-aligned rather than justified. For these types of documents, using the Document menu's Hyphenate command is optional. But any time you do not like the spacing in a document, you should give the Hyphenate command a try.

When you choose the Document menu's Hyphenate command, the program displays the dialog box shown in figure 15.2. The top line contains the Hyphenate box, in which the program displays the word suggested for hyphenation. Possible hyphen breaks are marked, and the program highlights its preference. A dotted line represents the document's right margin.

Below the Hyphenate box is the Hyphenate Capitalized Words button, which Word selects by default. Select this button to treat capitalized words, such as proper names, just like any other word for hyphenation purposes. If a document includes a proper name, such as the *National Institute of Neurological and Communicative Diseases and Strokes*, you quickly learn to appreciate that an initial capital letter does not exclude a word from the hyphenation process. On the other hand, you may not

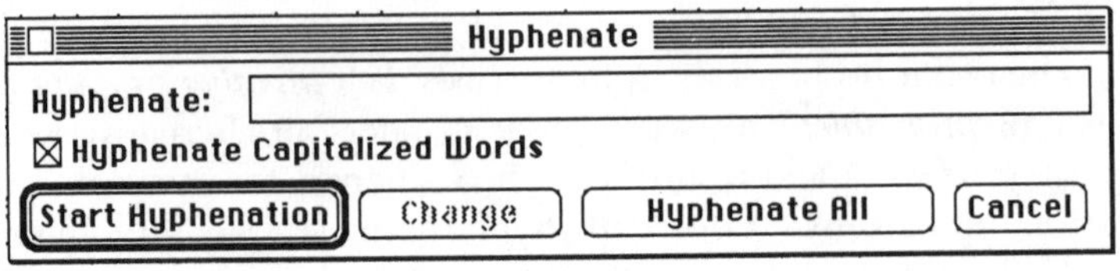

Fig. 15.2

The Hyphenate dialog box.

want to hyphenate proper names such as Rachmaninoff or Washington. To avoid splitting across lines the names of people and places, click the Hyphenate Capitalized Words option to deselect it.

At the bottom of the Hyphenate dialog box is a group of control buttons. The buttons in this area are dynamic and become selectable or unselectable depending on your previous action.

The leftmost button, Start Hyphenation, begins an interactive hyphenation process; during this process, you confirm or reject each suggested hyphen. Once the process begins, this button becomes No Change, offering an alternative to the Change button to its right. If you click Change, the No Change button becomes Continue Hyphenation.

You may select the Change button, immediately to the right of Start Hyphenation, only after the hyphenation process begins. The Change button inserts a hyphen in the word currently displayed in the Hyphenate box. Simply click Change to accept the program's preferred location for hyphenation. To insert a hyphen in a different place, click an alternate location in the displayed word before clicking Change.

The third button, Hyphenate All, instructs the program to hyphenate automatically the text. If you select a block of text before choosing the Hyphenate command, the button becomes Hyphenate Selection.

The rightmost button, Cancel, suspends the hyphenation process and closes the dialog box.

Receiving hands-on experience by using the Hyphenate command and the Hyphenate dialog box will help you better understand Word's hyphenation capabilities. In the next section, you receive this experience by working through two exercises that explain the automatic and interactive hyphenation processes.

Using the Hyphenate Command

During an *automatic* hyphenation process, the words are displayed briefly before the program adds a hyphen and moves on to the next word. During an *interactive* hyphenation process, the program displays a word and then pauses and waits for you to accept the recommended hyphen break or to click an alternate place where you want a hyphen inserted.

Hyphenating Text Automatically

You may have specific ideas about how you want your lines to break. (Maybe you have a particular page layout in mind, or you want to emphasize particular words or lines.) If you have no preferences, however, automatic hyphenation saves you time and trouble.

Automatic hyphenation does not solve all a document's line-break problems. For example, automatic hyphenation cannot fine-tune individual line breaks during the hyphenation process—a particular disadvantage when you are working with narrow columns. But the hyphenation routine still is a good starting point. After the program takes its best automatic shot, you then can improve the appearance of your document even more by manually inserting hyphens into selected words or by editing the text to fill in the gaps.

When you instruct the program to hyphenate automatically a block of text, the program examines each line in each successive paragraph; then Word determines whether hyphenation can improve the way the line breaks. When hyphenation will improve a line's appearance, the program then determines whether the word beginning the next line is a candidate for hyphenation. If the word is a candidate, the program adds a hyphen, adjusts the line ending, and reformats the remaining lines in the paragraph. The program then repeats the process with the next line.

To practice using the Hyphenate command, open any document containing at least one full screen of text. In order to follow along with the next exercise, use the document shown in figure 15.3. The language of this document is pretentious, and the document has syntactical errors and other mistakes. However, for purposes of this hyphenation exercise, type the document exactly as you see it—errors included. Set the font and size to 14-point Geneva. Also set a first-line indent of 0.5 inch and a right indent of 0.5 inch, to duplicate the line breaks in figure 15.3. Make sure a clean version of the practice document is stored on disk; if you make a mistake during the exercise, return to that document and try again.

During the hyphenation process, the program uses information in a file called Word Hyphenation to determine the suggested placement of hy-

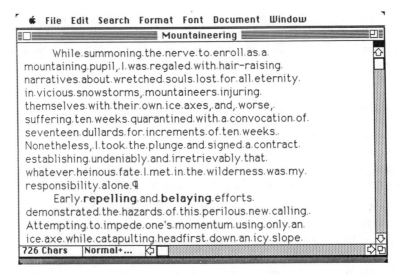

Fig. 15.3

*A sample
document for
demonstrating
the program's
hyphenation
feature.*

phens. This file is supplied on the program's Utilities disk. Before be-ginning your first hyphenation procedure, make sure Word Hyphenation is copied to your hard disk or is on a disk in one of your drives.

To adjust line breaks by automatically inserting hyphens in a document, do the following:

1. Position the insertion point at the beginning of the document.

2. Choose **Hyphenate** from the Document menu.

The program displays the Hyphenate dialog box. By default, Word high-lights the Start Hyphenation button and selects Hyphenate Capitalized Words.

3. To begin an automatic search, click **Hyphenate All**.

Each word hyphenated is flashed briefly in the Hyphenate box. For the sample document, the program hyphenates six words: *mountaining*, *narratives*, *vicious*, *undeniably*, *demonstrated*, and *Attempting*. At the end of the routine, the program displays the alert box shown in figure 15.4.

Figure 15.5 shows the results of the automatic hyphenation process on the sample document.

Now that you have worked through an exercise using automatic hy-phenation, try the interactive hyphenation exercise in the next section.

Fig. 15.4

The alert box that signals a hyphenation routine has reached the end of a document.

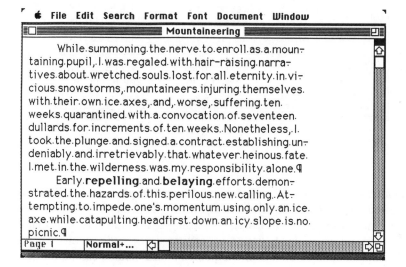

Fig. 15.5

The results of an automatic hyphenation process.

Confirming Placement of Hyphens

Working with the Hyphenate command helps you develop a feel for situations in which the automatic process does not work well. The following situations are examples of the problems that may occur with automatic hyphenation:

- Line-spacing problems often occur in justified text.

- Line-spacing problems almost always increase as the column width narrows (see fig. 15.6).

- The program may want to insert a hyphen in already hyphenated, compound adjectives (such as *hearing-impaired* or *hand-finished*). Style manuals usually frown on using more than one hyphen in such adjectives and consider the typed hyphen to be the only acceptable place to break them.

Fig. 15.6

Line-spacing problems created by narrow column width.

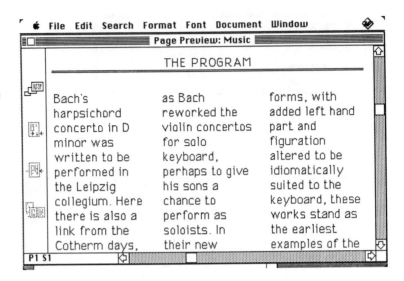

Before you try using the interactive hyphenation process on the sample document, choose Undo Hyphenate from the Edit menu to reinstate the document's original line breaks. Choosing this command immediately after an automatic hyphenation procedure cancels the results. (If you performed another action in the program and cannot cancel the new line breaks, close the document window without saving the changes to the document. You then can reload the original version of the document from disk.)

To confirm the hyphens suggested during a hyphenation process, do the following:

1. Position the cursor at the beginning of the document.

2. Choose **Hyphenate** from the Document menu.

3. Click **Start Hyphenation** or press **Return** to begin the routine.

As shown in figure 15.7, the program suggests hyphenating the word *mountaining* to improve the break of the line above. Word displays two hyphen breaks and highlights the one the program considers best; Word also indicates the position of the right margin with a dotted, vertical line. (Notice that the program does not judge the correctness of the word.) Word, assuming that you will reject the suggested break, highlights the No Change button.

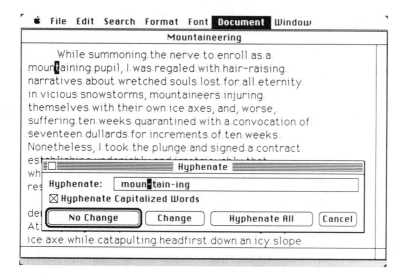

Fig. 15.7

*The first
suggested
hyphen break.*

4. Accept the proposed break by clicking **Change**.

The program moves on to suggest hyphenating the word *narratives* after its second syllable. Do not accept Word's hyphen choice.

5. To order a different hyphen break, click at another location in the word displayed in the **Hyphenate** box.

In this case, click after the first syllable to change the proposed line break (see fig. 15.8). Only two hyphen breaks are possible with the word *narratives*. In a word that offers several hyphen-break possibilities, selecting a break to the right of the dotted-line margin marker is useless because the first part of the word would not fit on the line. At the break you selected, the program inserts an optional hyphen that won't print because it doesn't end a line. (Optional hyphens are discussed in more detail in the section titled "The Optional Hyphen.")

6. Click **Change** to order the new hyphen break.

The program inserts the hyphen, rebreaks the paragraph, and proceeds to the next suggested hyphen break in the word *themselves* (see fig. 15.9).

7. Click **Change** to accept this break.

8. Click **Change** again to accept the next proposed line break (in the word *seventeen*) and to move to the next suggested break.

Fig. 15.8

*An alternate
hyphen break
selected for
adjustment.*

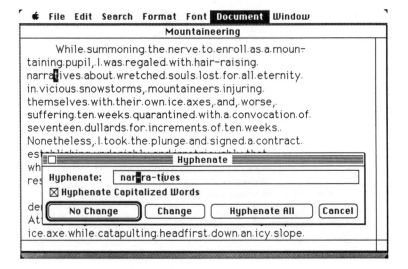

Fig. 15.9

*The third stop in
the automatic
Hyphenate
routine.*

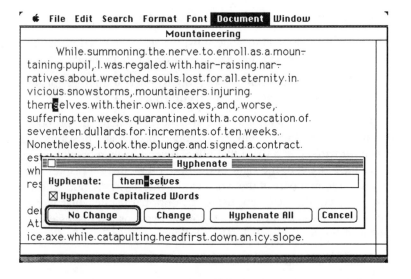

In the sample document, the program displays the word *nonetheless*, which presents an interesting situation. The program suggests only one hyphen break, but two are equally appropriate—after either *none* or *the*. You can order a hyphen break whether or not the program suggests the break.

9. Click a new location to the left of the margin marker in order to change the proposed line break.

Click after the first *e* in *nonetheless* to see how the program adjusts the line without arguing about the choice (see fig. 15.10).

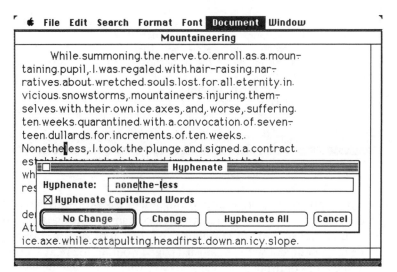

Fig. 15.10

A selected break that the program did not suggest.

10. Continue clicking the **Change** or **No Change** button until you see the alert box shown earlier in figure 15.4.

In the sample document, accept the proposed breaks in the words *demonstrated* and *Attempting*.

11. Click **OK** to end the search.

Figure 15.11 shows the new line breaks. As you can see, the difference is not dramatic between this document and the one in figure 15.5. When you work with wide, single-column documents, the results of automatic and interactive hyphenation processes usually are similar. Use the faster option routinely; save the interactive process for documents containing trouble spots.

You can take two approaches to hyphenation. The first approach is to type the document, format the text as necessary, and then use the Hyphenate command to correct any glaring line-break problems. The mechanics of this approach already have been explained.

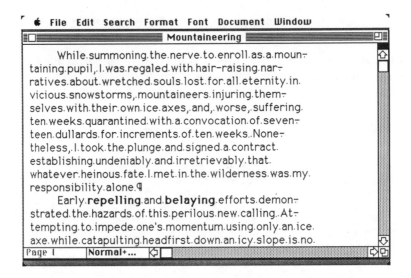

Fig. 15.11

*The results of
an interactive
hyphenation
process.*

The second approach involves anticipating line-break problems and adding different types of hyphens to assist the program in solving the problems. You are most likely to consider using this approach in a display piece or in a document with an unusual page layout. In the next section, you see the types of hyphens available to you when you take the second approach.

Influencing Line Breaks

In addition to the normal hyphen (-), the program provides two other types of hyphens that enable you to control the shape of your text: nonbreaking hyphens and optional hyphens. All three hyphens look the same when printed, but the program treats them differently.

The Normal Hyphen

The *normal hyphen*, available on the top row of the main keyboard, does exactly what you expect. Usually, you use normal hyphens in compound words, such as *state-of-the-art* and *short-term*. This type of hyphen is always visible on-screen and is always printed.

A word containing a normal hyphen sometimes occurs at the beginning of a line; in this case, the program may break the word at the hyphen to adjust the previous line break.

The Nonbreaking Hyphen

The *nonbreaking hyphen* prevents the program from splitting a hyphenated word across lines; essentially, this type of hyphen forces the program to break the line in front of the word. For example, breaking such words as *T-cell*, *2-foot*, and *x-ray* generally is not acceptable. In these cases, use a nonbreaking hyphen instead of a normal hyphen to preserve the word intact.

After you insert nonbreaking hyphens where you want to prohibit hyphenation, the program then can hyphenate automatically. You no longer need to be concerned about whether the resulting line breaks affect the meaning or readability of your document. Insert nonbreaking hyphens by pressing Command-~ (tilde). The program always displays and prints these hyphens.

The Optional Hyphen

Unlike the normal hyphen, the *optional hyphen* has nothing to do with the meaning of a word. The only use for the optional hyphen is for adjusting line breaks to improve a document's appearance. Word displays and prints optional hyphens only if the program uses them. (The program also displays the hyphens on-screen if you choose Show ¶ from the Format menu.)

The program uses optional hyphens to adjust line breaks when you choose the Document menu's Hyphenate command. Suppose that after telling the program to hyphenate a document, you change the document's margins or indents; the effects of the hyphenation procedure are lost. You do not have to remove the optional hyphens that the program inserted.

You can insert optional hyphens within your text to suggest syllable breaks for the program to use when adjusting line breaks. To insert an optional hyphen, press Command-- (hyphen). As with normal hyphens, the program takes advantage of optional hyphens to break lines when appropriate, even if you do not use the Hyphenate command.

If you type an optional hyphen in a word, the program ignores all other possible hyphen breaks (those that would be identified during a hyphenation process). Thus, you can add an optional hyphen to limit the hyphen breaks (to those *you* prefer) that the program might use in an automatic hyphenation process.

If you want to check where the program might break a word, select the word and choose Hyphenate from the Document menu. In the dialog box that appears, the program displays the word with all optional hyphens that might be added during a hyphenation process.

For example, if you select the word *endocrinological*, the Hyphenate dialog box appears, as shown in figure 15.12. Notice that the program supplies four optional hyphens. Instead of allowing the program to break a line on one of these hyphens, you may prefer that the line be broken after the first *o*. If you add an optional hyphen at that point, the program then ignores the original four hyphen breaks identified in the Hyphenate dialog box.

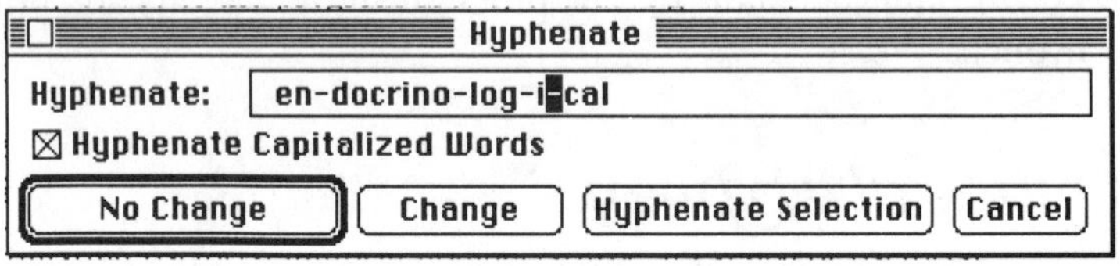

Fig. 15.12

Checking where the program might hyphenate the word endocrinological.

Previously, you used the Undo Hyphenate command to remove the optional hyphens that the program inserted during the automatic hyphenation exercise. Use Undo Hyphenate only if no other editing or formatting action was carried out after choosing the Hyphenate command. You also can use another command to remove these optional hyphens—the Change command.

To remove optional hyphens with the Change command, do the following:

1. Click an insertion point at the beginning of the document or select the text from which you want to remove optional hyphens.

2. Choose **Change** from the Search menu or press **Command-H**.

3. Type ^- (a caret followed by a hyphen) in the **Find What** box.

4. Leave the **Change To** box blank.

5. Click **Change All** or press **Return**.

An Editing Tip

The Hyphenate command works fine if the hyphenation challenge is not too great. However, line-break problems caused by narrow columns of text are difficult for the command to handle.

For example, because of the narrow column in the document shown in figure 15.13, the Hyphenate command leaves some rather wide gaps within lines. With this narrow-column format, Word occasionally may break a line short of the justified right margin. In such cases, you need to adjust line breaks by editing the text. Shuffle around phrases, "pad" the text (with words such as *that*), or choose different words.

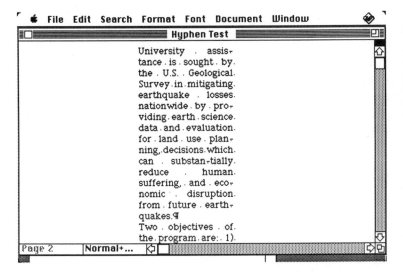

Fig. 15.13

A document's appearance, not greatly improved by the Hyphenate command.

Hyphenation may never become part of your daily routine—your work may never require you to use hyphenation. But an understanding of Word's hyphenation options clears the way for layouts more interesting than the conventional, single-column document.

16

Merging Documents

Until a few years ago, we easily could distinguish personal mail from promotional materials—or junk mail. The former was addressed to us personally, and the latter was addressed to "Occupant." With rare exceptions, those days are gone. Now, direct mail advertising not only is addressed specifically to us but also contains personalized statements which give the impression that the letter writers actually are acquainted with us.

Direct mail advertising obviously is not created by some kind of magic. Companies just purchase mailing lists with information about us and use print merge techniques to insert the information into form letters.

You don't have to be a big company with a mailing list to take advantage of these techniques. You can use Word's Print Merge command to address Christmas cards, solicit subscriptions to a new magazine, or create forms for repeatedly printing the same type of information.

In this chapter, you first learn the basic techniques for using the program's print merge feature. You then see how to use conditional instructions to vary the contents of a form letter. Finally, you apply these techniques to the task of printing mailing labels.

Creating Documents
for Print Merging

The concept behind print merge is simple. The following description of a form letter example makes the concept even easier to understand.

To use the print merge feature to tailor a form letter for several recipients, you first need to create two documents, called the *main document* and the *data document* (see fig. 16.1). The tricky part in this process is to use correctly a few simple instructions in the main document and to organize properly the data document.

The main document includes the following three elements:

- The text of the letter, which usually doesn't vary from copy to copy

- *Placeholders*, enclosed in chevron symbols ($\ll\gg$) and replaced at merge time by information, such as the recipients' names and addresses, that varies from copy to copy

- Chevron-enclosed print merge instructions that guide the program during the print merge process

Fig. 16.1a

Examples showing a main document and its corresponding data document.

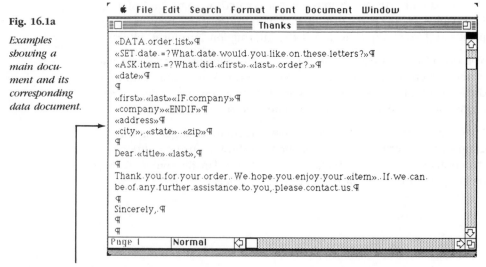

Main document

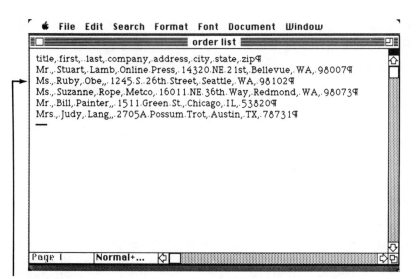

 File Edit Search Format Font Document Window

order list

title,.first,..last,.company,.address,.city,.state,.zip¶
Mr.,.Stuart,.Lamb,.Online.Press,.14320.NE.21st,.Bellevue,.WA,.98007¶
Ms.,.Ruby,.Obe,,.1245.S..26th.Street,.Seattle,.WA,.98102¶
Ms.,.Suzanne,.Rope,.Metco,.16011.NE.36th.Way,.Redmond,.WA,.98073¶
Mr.,.Bill,.Painter,,.1511.Green.St.,.Chicago,.IL,.53820¶
Mrs.,.Judy,.Lang,,.2705A.Possum.Trot,.Austin,.TX,.78731¶

Page 1   Normal+...

Data document

Fig. 16.1b

Examples showing a main document and its corresponding data document

The data document is a list of all the information that varies from recipient to recipient. The set of information for each recipient constitutes a *record*. Each record is divided into categories, called *fields*, which hold individual items of information, such as a person's first name, last name, and so on. The fields in the data document correspond to the placeholders in the main document.

When you choose the Print Merge command from the File menu, the program automatically opens the data document and substitutes the information in the document's fields for the corresponding placeholders in the main document. The program merges one copy of the main document for each record in the data document.

To practice creating each of these documents, follow along with the next exercise. Imagine that you want to sell by mail a computerized city map you have developed. You want to use the print merge feature to produce a simple form letter that cuts down on the time required to generate the personalized thank-you-for-your-order enclosures you slip into each package.

Creating the Main Document

You create the main document the same way you would create any other document—by typing, editing, and formatting text, using the appropriate

Word commands. Before following along with this exercise, load a new document by choosing New from the File menu.

To create a main document, do the following steps:

1. Insert a left chevron symbol ($<<$) by pressing **Option-** (backslash).

2. Type the word **DATA** and the name of the data document.

In this case, type the name of the data document—*order list*—that you will create in the next section.

3. Press **Shift-Option-** to insert a right chevron symbol ($>>$) and then press **Return**.

You have typed a DATA instruction, which tells the program the name of the data document that contains the information you want to merge. A DATA instruction always precedes all other print merge instructions in a main document. Normally, you type the DATA instruction on a line by itself, as you have done in Steps 1 through 3.

4. Type the text of the main document and include placeholders enclosed in chevrons where necessary.

Type the letter shown in figure 16.2 and omit the first line (the DATA instruction, which you already have typed). Be sure to put chevrons around the placeholders (see Steps 1 and 3).

5. Format the placeholders with the format you want for the variable information that will replace them.

Formatting a placeholder automatically formats the information that will replace the placeholder. For example, if you make the $<<$first$>>$ and $<<$last$>>$ placeholders in the main document bold, the program formats each recipient's first and last names in bold type. (The program actually applies the format of a placeholder's first character to the entire replacement, but formatting the entire placeholder makes the character style more obvious as you review the main document.)

6. Choose **Save As** from the File menu and save the main document with a descriptive name.

In this case, save the document with the name *Thanks*.

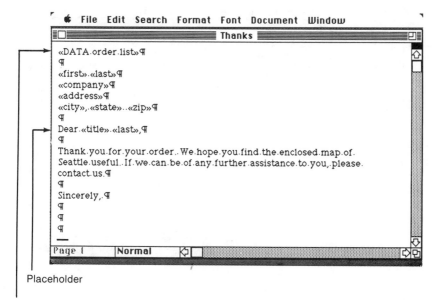

Fig. 16.2

A sample main document.

Placeholder

DATA instruction

Creating the Data Document

Suppose that you are sending out maps to five people today. You need to create a data document (see fig. 16.3) so that you can use the Print Merge command to merge five thank you letters in one operation. First load a new document by choosing New from the File menu. Then create the data document and save it as a separate file.

The first record in a data document, called the *header record*, lists the names of the fields that make up each record. These field names correspond to the placeholders used in the main document. The field names are separated by either commas or tabs, as is the information in the records that follow the header record. (Notice that spaces are allowed between the fields; the program drops any spaces between the comma and the first character of the field name.) A paragraph mark signals the end of one record and the beginning of another one.

To create a data document, do the following:

1. Type the data document's header record, separating field names with commas or tabs, and press **Return**.

Fig. 16.3

A sample data document.

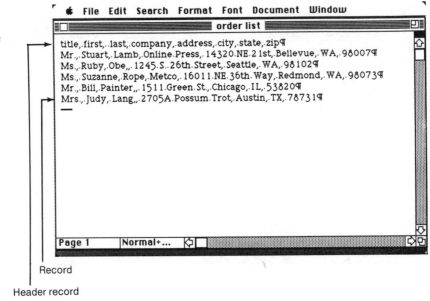

Record

Header record

For this exercise, use figure 16.3 as a guide.

2. Type the records, separating fields with the same separator used in the header record, and end each record by pressing **Return**.

For the program to associate the proper information with each place-holder in the main document, the fields in the records must appear in the same order as the field names in the header record. To leave a field blank, you mark it with the comma or tab that normally separates the field from surrounding fields. (You don't have to mark missing fields at the end of a record; omitting the fields does not disturb the order.) The blank company field in the second record illustrates this principle (see fig. 16.3).

3. Choose the **Save As** command from the File menu to save the data document.

For this example, save the data document with the name *order list*.

NOTE: The program always reads information from the disk version of the data document when print merging. If you open and change the data document, the program does not recognize the changes until you save them.

Using the Print Merge Command

After you set up main and data documents, you are ready to use the Print Merge command. For practice, print merge the five thank you letters. Before you begin, make sure that your printer is turned on and ready.

Do the following to print merge a document:

1. Open the main document and make sure its window is active.

You don't have to open the data document. The program retrieves information from the data document but doesn't display the document in a window.

2. Choose **Print Merge** from the File menu.

Choosing Print Merge displays a dialog box (see fig. 16.4). For now, accept all the program's default settings.

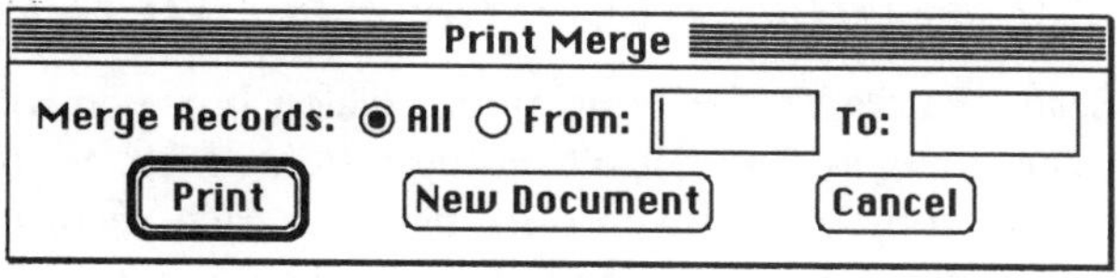

```
▓▓▓▓▓▓▓▓▓▓▓ Print Merge ▓▓▓▓▓▓▓▓▓▓▓
Merge Records: ◉ All ○ From: [        ]  To: [          ]
   ( Print )    ( New Document )    ( Cancel )
```

Fig. 16.4

The Print Merge dialog box.

3. Press **Return**.

The program prints one copy of the form letter for each record in the data document and replaces the main document's placeholders with the information in the data document's fields.

When you choose Print Merge, the program looks for the data document named in the main document's DATA instruction on the disk in the active drive or in the current hard disk directory. If Word doesn't find the data document there, the program displays a dialog box (see fig. 16.5). You can use the Drive and Eject buttons to direct the program to the correct document.

Having successfully completed your first print merge, look at the options offered by the Print Merge dialog box. Word gives you two basic choices when you merge documents. You can print merge a customized copy of the main document for every record in the data document or for only some of the records. You either can send the copies directly to the printer or store them in a new document that you can print later.

Fig. 16.5

The dialog box displayed when the program cannot locate the data document.

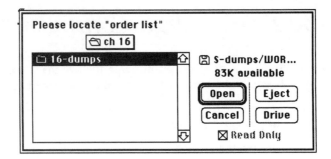

If the form letters do not print properly, check to make sure that you have placed chevrons around all placeholders and that you have spelled the placeholder names consistently. In the data file, check to make sure that each record has exactly the same number of commas that the header record contains.

Controlling Which Records Are Merged

The Merge Records area of the Print Merge dialog box controls how many records are merged. The default setting is All, which, as you have seen, merges one copy of the main document for each record in the data document. If you want to merge only a specified range of records, you can click the From button and enter a beginning record number in the From box and an ending record number in the To box. Records are numbered just as you would expect: the first record after the header record is number 1, the second is 2, and so on.

You can use the Document menu's Sort command also to group records for print merge operations (described in the section titled "Sorting Data Documents To Print Sets of Records").

Controlling Where Records Are Merged

The Print and New Document buttons control whether the program prints the merged copies of the main document or merges them in a new document on-screen. By default, the copies are printed. The New Document option is useful for testing your use of print merge instructions and for previewing the merged copies. After you proofread the results of the print merge operation on-screen, you can close the new document, choose Print Merge again, and click the Print button.

To archive the results of the print merge—if you use print merge to create customer statements, for example—you also can save the new document. Then you can print the merged document later by using the Print command. If necessary, you can edit the merged copies before printing them. Saving the document also is convenient if someone else will be printing it. Just give that person the merged document, which can be loaded and printed in Word to get the same results as merging a main and data document.

The first print merge exercise was easy because the documents were simple. The program's print merge feature actually is very powerful. In the next two sections, you learn how to set up main documents and data documents to take advantage of this power.

Using Print Merge Instructions

The Print Merge command is essentially a simple but specialized programming language embedded within the Word program. The command has seven basic instructions and a few variations. You insert these instructions into the main document to control the content and appearance of your merged copies.

These instructions are described (in alphabetical order) here. The instruction, shown in capital letters, may be followed by text, field names, or other information in italics. You type the words that are not in italics exactly as they appear, and you substitute for the italic words any text pertinent to the situation in which you use the instruction. If words are enclosed in quotation marks, you must include the quotation marks when you use the instruction. Work through the rest of the chapter and create more sample documents to see what you can do with these instructions.

ASK

The ASK instruction makes the program pause during merging. Word then prompts you to type the contents of a field included in the main document but not in the data document. The program asks for the information before Word merges each new copy of the document. The ASK instruction must precede the first occurrence in the main document of the placeholder associated with the field. The instruction, therefore, generally is included at the top of the main document, immediately after the DATA instruction. The ASK instruction has two variations.

<<*ASK field =?*>>

Before each copy of the main document is merged with a record from the data document, the first variation of the ASK instruction displays a simple dialog box that has a question mark and a box in which you type the information for the field. This variation is adequate if the document has only one ASK instruction and you know what kind of information is required. Otherwise, this variation can be confusing.

<<*ASK field =?prompt*>>

The second variation of the ASK instruction includes a prompt you use for specifying the kind of information needed. The prompt you type between the question mark and the >> is displayed in the ASK dialog box exactly as typed. The prompt can be as long as three lines, but a prompt that long usually is unnecessary.

To practice using the ASK instruction, imagine that your company has expanded and that you now offer to your customers computerized maps of six cities. You want to modify the thank you letter to reflect your more diverse product line. Insert an ASK instruction (see the second line of fig. 16.6) in the *Thanks* main document you created earlier. For the instruction to work properly, you also need to modify the body of the letter to include the <<item>> placeholder (see fig. 16.6). At merge time, the ASK instruction prompts you to type the item each customer has ordered.

DATA

As you know, the DATA instruction tells the program which data document has the information to be merged with the main document. This instruction must precede all other print merge instructions and placeholders in the main document. Usually, the DATA instruction is included on the first line. A main document can have only one DATA instruction, but it can be in one of two variations.

<<*DATA data document name*>>

The first variation of the DATA instruction—the most common form—simply specifies the name of the document that holds the required header and data records.

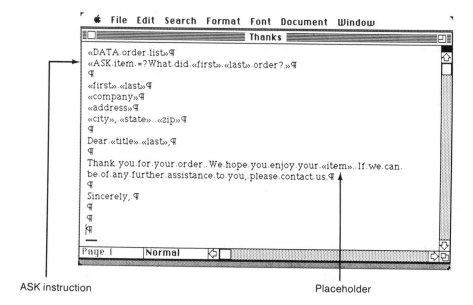

ASK instruction   Placeholder

Fig. 16.6

*An example of
the ASK
instruction.*

<<DATA *header document name, data document name*>>

The second variation of the DATA instruction lets you store the header record in a separate document from the data records. You include in the instruction both document names, separated by a comma. This variation is useful, for example, if you have several form letters that use different placeholders for the same information. By creating a separate header document for each form letter, you can avoid making multiple copies of the data document.

IF...ENDIF

IF...ENDIF is the most powerful print merge instruction in the program. IF...ENDIF also is the instruction most similar to a programming language command. If you are familiar with any programming language, the purpose of the IF...ENDIF instruction is apparent; if not, the following explanation and examples should help you understand how to unleash the command's power.

The IF...ENDIF type of instruction, known as *conditional*, tells the program under what circumstances to merge information from the data document into the main document. You can use three basic variations of the IF instruction with the Print Merge command.

<<IF field>>text to merge<<ENDIF>>

The basic IF instruction tells the program to include something in the merged copy of the main document only if a specific field contains information. The text to merge can be anything from a single word to an entire document. You can have the program print an invoice, for example, only if something is in the amount field. In this case, the entire text of the invoice would appear between the IF and ENDIF sections of the instruction.

This type of IF instruction often is used in mailing labels. For example, a company name is inserted in the mailing label if the record includes a company name; the extra blank line is deleted if no company name exists.

<<IF field ="text to match">>text to merge<<ENDIF>>

The second variation of the IF instruction tells Word to compare the contents of the named field with the text enclosed in quotation marks. If the two text strings match (including capitalization), the program inserts in the merged document the text you specify (the text not enclosed in quotation marks).

You might use this variation in an invoice to include a special comment to customers who order a certain product or who live in a certain city or state. For example, in an invoice sent to all residents of Washington state, you might include the following instruction:

<<IF state ="WA">>Please note that this invoice includes Washington state retail sales tax.<<ENDIF>>

<<IF field (=, >, or <)number>>text to merge<<ENDIF>>

The third variation of the IF instruction compares the contents of a named field with a number by using one of three comparison operators: = (equal to), > (greater than), or < (less than). If the comparison is true, the program inserts the specified text.

You could use this variation to include special information in letters sent to people who live within a certain ZIP code area. The instruction might read as follows:

<<IF zip =98007>>Since you live in the area, please drop by for a visit.<<ENDIF>>

Another example might read as follows:

<<IF total>100>>Please remit payment in full within 14 days.<<ENDIF>>

ELSE

All three variations of the IF...ENDIF instruction can be modified to include the ELSE instruction. ELSE specifies an alternate action to be taken if the condition in the IF...ENDIF instruction is not met. The ELSE instruction takes the following generic form:

<<IF *field* ="*text to match*">>*text to merge*<<ELSE>>*alternate text to merge*<<ENDIF>>

When Word encounters the ELSE instruction, the program inserts the text preceding ELSE if the named field contains the text enclosed in quotation marks. If the field doesn't include the text, the program inserts the text following the ELSE instruction at the placeholder.

INCLUDE

With the INCLUDE instruction, <<INCLUDE *document name*>>, you can insert any Word document into another document during the print merge operation. Enter the instruction where you want the second document inserted into the main document, as in the following example:

<<IF status ="repeat order">>><<INCLUDE discount schedule>>

Word inserts the included document into the main document with all formatting intact, just as though you had opened and inserted the document in the usual way.

An included document does not have to be on the same disk or in the same hard disk directory as the main document. If you include a document from another disk or directory, the program displays at merge time a dialog box similar to the one in figure 16.5.

The INCLUDE instruction often is used in conjunction with IF...ELSE...ENDIF to insert one of several documents, depending on whether a condition is met. You could include different notes in a billing, for example, depending on the contents of a field that indicated an account status. The notes could range from a thank you note to a warning that the account would be turned over to a collection agency unless payment was made, as in the following example:

<<IF account ="overdue">>><<INCLUDE Collection Agency Referral>>><<ELSE>>><<INCLUDE Preferred Customer Sale>>><<ENDIF>>

NEXT

The NEXT instruction tells Word to read the next record from the data document and not to begin a new copy of the main document. The program continues creating the same copy of the main document but uses the new field information. This instruction often is used in conjunction with an IF instruction that makes the program skip records that do not meet certain conditions. You see an example of this type of instruction in the section titled "Using the IF Instruction To Select Records."

SET

You can use three variations of the SET instruction to supply information that may change every time you merge a batch of documents. Like the ASK instruction, the SET instruction must precede the first occurrence of the placeholder associated with the field in the instruction. SET generally is placed at the top of the main document and follows the DATA instruction. Unlike the information supplied in response to an ASK prompt, however, the information supplied in response to a SET prompt is used in all copies of the main document created during that print merge operation.

<<SET field =text to merge>>

The first variation of the SET instruction is convenient if the text associated with a field rarely changes. You enter the variable text in the main document along with the SET instruction before you choose Print Merge. For example, the following instruction directs the program to replace each <<client>> placeholder with *Microsoft*:

<<SET client =Microsoft>>

If you use the second or third variation of the SET instruction, Word prompts you for the variable information before the program starts the print merge operation.

<<SET field =?>>

This instruction is the simpler of the remaining SET variations and displays a dialog box (see fig. 16.7). This instruction is adequate if a main document has only one SET instruction and you can remember easily the kind of information needed.

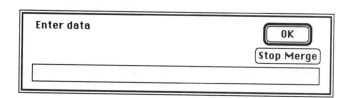

Fig. 16.7

The SET dialog box.

<<SET field =?prompt>>

If a document contains several SET instructions or if you have a poor (or overtaxed) memory, use the third variation of the SET instruction. You can include a prompt in this variation to ask for the appropriate information. The prompt typed between the question mark and the >> is displayed in the dialog box exactly as you type the prompt.

As an example of the SET instruction, insert in the *Thanks* main document the instruction shown in the second line of figure 16.8. For the instruction to work properly, you also need to insert the <<date>> placeholder shown on the fourth line.

At merge time, this SET instruction makes the program display a dialog box (see fig. 16.9). The information you type replaces the <<date>> placeholder in every copy of the main document created during the print merge operation.

Besides tailoring the print merge operation with instructions you have inserted in the main document, you can refine your data documents to make print merging more efficient.

Fig. 16.8

An example of the SET instruction.

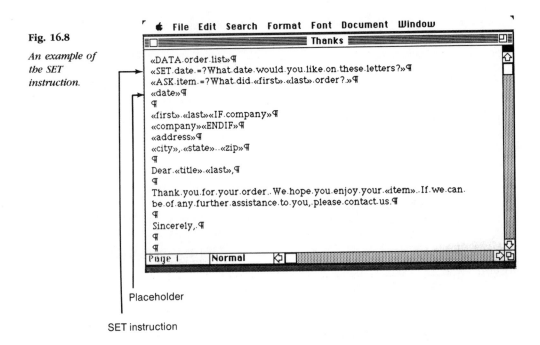

Placeholder

SET instruction

Fig. 16.9

The SET dialog box produced by the sample SET instruction.

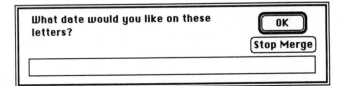

Using Data Documents

In the sample data document you are using, each record fits on a single line, although you don't have to observe this limitation in Word. A record can have as many as 256 fields that extend to several lines. You must, however, end each record with a paragraph mark and maintain the fields in the order in which they are listed in the header record.

A data document can include fields not used in the main document, and the order of the fields in the data document does not have to reflect the order of their use in the main document. As a result, you can make master data documents to use with several main documents.

Using Commas and Quotation Marks in Records

If the information in a field contains the separator character you have used to separate one field from another (a comma or a tab), you must enclose the entire field in quotation marks. The quotation marks instruct the program not to read the character within the field as the beginning of a new field. For example, commas sometimes are used within addresses, as in *300 Main Street, Suite 10*. If commas also separate the fields in the record, you need to enclose the entire address in quotation marks, as in *"300 Main Street, Suite 10"*.

NOTE: You can enclose all field entries in quotation marks, even if none of the entries includes the separator character. This technique is convenient when you copy information from database programs. If you consistently enclose fields in quotation marks, you will not have to check each field's contents for the separator character.

If you must use quotation marks within the text of a field, then simply double the quotation marks. For example, a name field entry for *Mr. Richard "Jonah" Jones* would be typed *"Mr. Richard ""Jonah"" Jones"*.

Sorting Data Documents To Print Sets of Records

Sorting records within a data document gives you flexibility in ordering print merge operations. Using the Sort command, you can sort a selected set of items in either ascending order (A through Z, or 1 through 9) or in descending order (Z through A, or 9 through 1). If you use commas to separate the fields in a data document, you can sort the records only on the first field. If you use tabs as separators, you can sort the records on any field.

To sort a data document on any field, do the following:

1. Make sure the fields are separated by tabs.

2. Select the column of field entries you want to sort.

To select a column, hold down the Option key and drag the pointer from one corner of the column to the diagonally opposite corner (see fig. 16.10).

3. Choose **Sort** from the Document menu.

Fig. 16.10

The highlighted column of field entries selected for sorting.

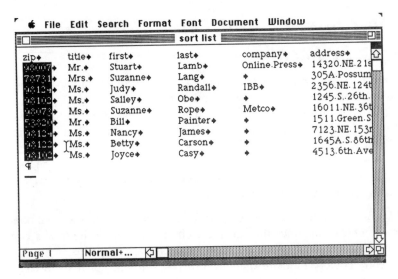

The program sorts the records. Sorting the records in figure 16.10 produces the order shown in figure 16.11.

Fig. 16.11

Records sorted by ZIP code.

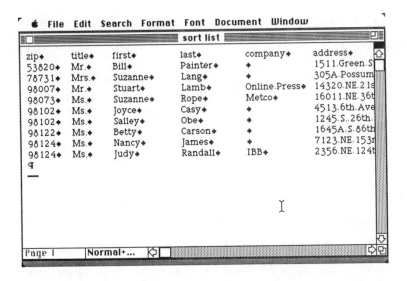

The Sort command can be put to good use in print merge operations. You might, for example, want to sort by ZIP code the records in a data document containing name and address information for bulk mailings.

Sorting by ZIP code lets you put mailing labels or envelopes in the order that meets postal service standards for grouping and bundling mailers.

By sorting into ZIP code order, you have the option of merging only a specified group of records. For example, you might want to target an advertising campaign toward residents of certain mailing districts. After you have sorted a name-and-address data document by ZIP code, you can create special data documents that hold the records for specific areas. Or you can use the Print Merge dialog box's From and To settings to have the program merge only the records for a certain area.

NOTE: You can use Word's line-numbering feature to number the lines in your data document and then specify the block of lines to be printed. The program doesn't display line numbers in the document window, but you can check them in the Page Preview window or by printing the data document.

You can carry out a series of sort operations to refine the selection of records before you choose the Print Merge command. For example, suppose that you want to let all the doctors who live in a particular region know about a new laboratory service. The doctors' names and addresses are stored in a general-purpose name-and-address data document. You first sort the entries in the courtesy (title) field to group together the records for people who use the *Dr.* title. Then you sort only this group by ZIP code to identify the doctors who live close enough to take advantage of the service.

Keep the Sort command in mind as you prepare for print merge operations. Often, sorting is useful in organizing data records for selective print merging. If you can insert tabs between all fields in a data document and not cause the records to break into two lines, you probably should use tab separators instead of comma separators to give yourself the option of sorting on any field.

Coordinating Database Files with Data Documents

Database programs provide a convenient method for entering, organizing, and retrieving information. If you already have stored in a database program information that you now need for a Word data document, you usually can instruct the database program to move selected records to a new document.

Most database programs offer the option of producing a file in print merge format, with either commas or tabs between the fields. If your database program does not offer this option, you still can copy the desired records to the Clipboard and paste them into a Word document. Then after you add a header record, you are ready to merge the records with a main document.

You already have tried the Print Merge command's simplest and most common application: form letters. But form letters can be more complex than the one you merge printed earlier. The next section describes how versatile Print Merge can be when you use conditionals and other instructions to alter the contents of a form letter while you merge it.

Using Print Merge Instructions in Form Letters

Form letters can vary in complexity from a simple note that includes only one piece of unique information to an elaborate publication that merges information from various sources to form a document tailored to its recipient. The difference in complexity primarily is a matter of how much information you make available and how you use the program's print merge instructions to include portions of that information.

A form letter that does not hold much variable information may not require a data document. You can use SET and ASK instructions to make the program prompt you for all variable information. (As you have seen, you also can make Word prompt you only for certain information while you consult a data document for other information.)

Earlier in this chapter, you incorporated into the *Thanks* main document several print merge instructions: DATA, ASK, and SET. The next sample form letter demonstrates the uses of other instructions to build more complex documents.

Nesting IF Instructions

The IF instruction is a powerful tool for printing one block of text out of several, depending on the contents of a field. For even greater flexibility in tailoring a form letter based on information about the letter's recipients, you can *nest* conditional instructions—that is, include one set of instructions within another. For example, you can add specific text only to letters sent to certain people.

The instruction and paragraph in figure 16.12 show one use of nested conditionals. Suppose that you are sending a form letter to the three groups of people—speakers, exhibitors, and attendees—participating in the fictional oceanographic conference used in the examples in Part 1 of this book. Within the exhibitors' group, you want the letter to foreign exhibitors to include an explanation of special visa and customs requirements. None of the other letters will include this information.

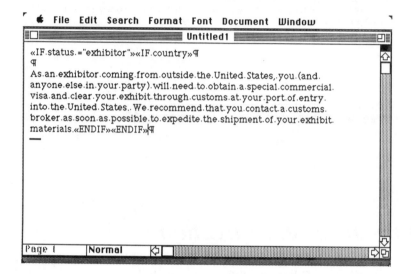

Fig. 16.12

An example of nested IF instructions.

The nested IF instructions in figure 16.12 tell the program to merge the paragraph that follows the instructions only if the letter is addressed to an exhibitor who lives in a foreign country. You need to tack onto the end of a normal paragraph the conditional portions of the two IF instructions in order to avoid creating a blank if the IF condition is not met.

You then coordinate the main document for the conference form letter with the data document shown in figure 16.13. The status and country fields narrow down the set of people who will receive information about visas and customs. The status field must identify the recipient as *exhibitor*, and the country field must contain information. When you print merge the main document, the special visa and customs information is included only in letters to foreign exhibitors. Note that for United States residents, the country field is blank, but the comma after it still is used. Remember that every record must have exactly as many commas as the header record.

Fig. 16.13

The data document used for identifying foreign exhibitors for the print merge operation.

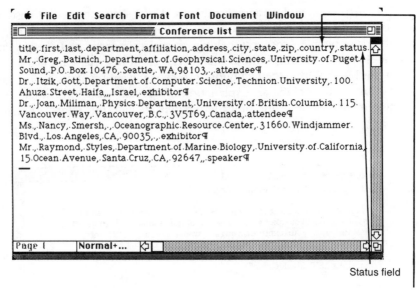

 File   Edit   Search   Format   Font   Document   Window

Conference list

title,.first,.last,.department,.affiliation,.address,.city,.state,.zip,.country,.status.
Mr.,.Greg,.Batinich,.Department.of.Geophysical.Sciences,.University.of.Puget.
Sound,.P.O..Box.10476,.Seattle,.WA,98103,.,.attendee¶
Dr.,.Itzik,.Gott,.Department.of.Computer.Science,.Technion.University,.100.
Ahuza.Street,.Haifa,,,Israel,.exhibitor¶
Dr.,.Joan,.Miliman,.Physics.Department,.University.of.British.Columbia,.115.
Vancouver.Way,.Vancouver,.B.C.,.3V5T69,.Canada,.attendee¶
Ms.,.Nancy,.Smersh,.,.Oceanographic.Resource.Center,.31660.Windjammer.
Blvd.,.Los.Angeles,.CA,.90035,.,.exhibitor¶
Mr.,.Raymond,.Styles,.Department.of.Marine.Biology,.University.of.California,
15.Ocean.Avenue,.Santa.Cruz,.CA,.92647,,.speaker¶

Page 1   Normal+...

Status field

Country field

Using the ELSE Instruction

The IF...ENDIF instruction lets you insert a block of text if a specified condition is met. Otherwise, the program includes only the main document's normal text. As mentioned earlier, you can add an ELSE instruction to an IF...ENDIF instruction in order to insert an alternate block of text if the specified condition is not met. Figure 16.14 shows an IF...ELSE...ENDIF instruction that would merge one of two sentences into the conference form letter, depending on whether the recipient is a speaker. Speakers are invited to a special reception, while exhibitors and attendees are given the opportunity to be greeted by Ms. Eisenbrand in the lounge.

Using the INCLUDE Instruction

If the special paragraphs for speakers, exhibitors, and attendees are lengthy, you may want to store each paragraph or set of paragraphs in a separate document and use an INCLUDE instruction to merge the appropriate document into the form letter. Figure 16.15 shows instructions you could insert into the conference form letter to include ad-

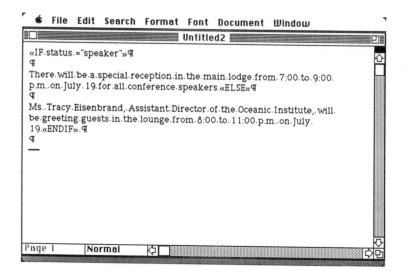

Fig. 16.14

*An example of
the ELSE
instruction.*

ditional documents. This modification would insert the document named *Attendee* if the status of the recipient was *attendee*, and so on.

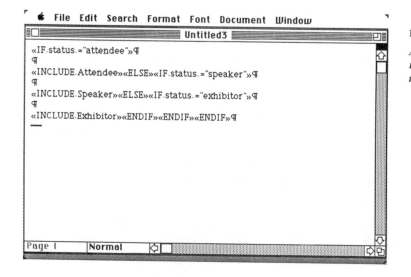

Fig. 16.15

*An example of
the INCLUDE
instruction.*

Using the IF Instruction
To Select Records

You can include the entire text of the main document as the *text to merge* element of an IF...ENDIF instruction. This is a nice feature when you want to merge the entire document with records that contain only certain information in a particular field. When an IF instruction affects the merging of an entire main document, the IF instruction must follow immediately the DATA instruction on the first line and precede all text to be printed.

For example, to merge letters only for people who live in Washington, you can include the following instruction at the top of the main document:

<<DATA maillist>><<IF state ="WA">>

text of main document

<<ENDIF>>

As the program prepares to merge each record with the main document, Word checks the contents of the state field and prints the letter only if the state is *WA*.

If a data document includes numeric data, you can use a mathematical operator in the IF instruction to determine whether Word should merge a record. The simplest case is instructing the program to skip a record if a numeric entry in a particular field is equal to, less than, or greater than a specified number. You tell Word to skip the record by using the NEXT instruction.

A manufacturer can include in a data document for an advertising mailer, for example, a field called quantity. The field contains the number of items each customer has ordered during the past year. To send a letter to only those people who have ordered 100 or more items during the past year, the manufacturer includes the following instruction:

<<IF quantity>100>><<NEXT>><<ENDIF>>

Every time Word encounters an entry less than 100 in the quantity field, the program skips to the next record instead of merging the current one. Therefore, only records with 100 or more in that field are merged.

Next, look at another Print Merge use: creating mailing labels.

Creating Mailing Labels

To experiment further with print merge techniques, you will create simple main documents that read names and addresses from a data document, and then you will print mailing labels. The format for the main document varies, depending on whether you want to print directly on envelopes or on labels and on whether the labels are in a single column or in multiple columns per page.

You begin the exercises by preparing a main document to print a single column of continuous-feed labels. Then you modify the main document to print three columns of labels. Finally, you adapt the main document to print labels on a LaserWriter.

Printing Single-Column Labels

Single-column, continuous-feed mailing labels are available in many sizes from most office supply stores. The single-column format probably is the most efficient if you print labels only occasionally or only in small quantities.

Creating the Main Document

Figure 16.16 shows a main document that prints a single column of 4-by-1-inch address labels. As you can see, the document does not have much information. The DATA instruction on the first line identifies the data document as *maillist*, but the document contains no text other than placeholders, punctuation, and spacing. The information in the data document's fields provides everything else.

Other significant elements of the main document for mailing labels are as follows:

- The first placeholder, <<name>>, is on the same line as the DATA instruction.

If this placeholder were on the second line, the paragraph mark ending the DATA instruction would make the program print a blank line at the top of every label.

- The comma after <<city>> and the spaces after <<state>> are included in the main document because they are part of every merged address, just as if you were typing the addresses individually.

Fig. 16.16

The main document for single-column mailing labels.

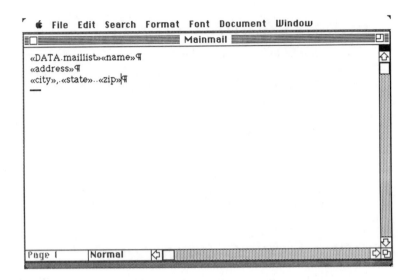

You should limit the information in the fields of the data document to text that varies.

- Upper- and lowercase distinctions are immaterial when you type the placeholders.

- Because names are assigned to the fields only so that they can be used as placeholders, you can assign any names that make sense to you.

The only requirement is that the placeholders in the main document must match the field names listed in the header record of the associated data document.

To create a main document for printing mailing labels, do the following:

1. Open a new document and type the print merge instructions for the main document (see fig. 16.16).

To enter a left chevron symbol (<<), type *Option-\\.* To enter a right chevron symbol (>>), type *Shift-Option-\\.*

2. Use the **Save As** command from the File menu to save this main document with the name *Mainmail.*

The second step is important because you will modify this document in different ways in later sections to create two other mailing-label formats.

Formatting Pages

You can apply any character and paragraph formatting to a main document; the character formatting of *Mainmail* is up to you. The margins and paper-size settings, which you control through the Page Setup command, are the critical formatting steps when you print mailing labels.

The program considers each merged mailing label an individual document and prints each document on a new page. The document's "page size," therefore, must match the size of the mailing label in use. The page height equals the distance from the top of one label to the top of the next label. The page width equals the width of the label. You set the margins to give the address as much room as possible.

A typical continuous-feed, single-column mailing label is four inches wide by one inch deep. Set up a page to accommodate a label of this size.

Do the following steps to set the page format for 4-by-1-inch, single-column mailing labels:

1. Choose **Page Setup** from the File menu.

2. Specify **4 inches** in the Paper Width box and **1 inch** in the Height box.

3. Set the top margin to **0.1 inch**, the bottom margin to **0 inch**, the left margin to **0.2 inches**, and the right margin to **0 inch**.

4. Click **OK**.

The main document now is prepared for printing mailing labels, but first create the data document.

Creating a Master Data Document

As you know, a data document is simply a storage place for information you want the program to merge into one or more main documents. For these exercises, you initially create the *maillist* data document (see fig. 16.17), which meets the requirements of the *Mainmail* main document. Later, you add to this data document so that it can be used with another main document and remain accessible from *Mainmail*. The size and format of the labels you want to print do not affect the data document's organization or content.

Do the following to create a data document for printing mailing labels:

1. Open the main document you will use for printing the labels.

Fig. 16.17

The maillist *data document.*

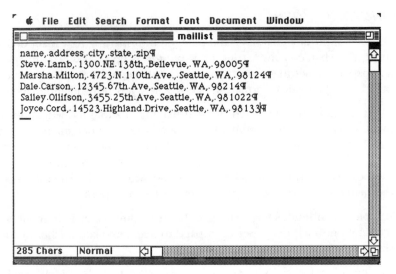

2. In a second window, open a new document, which will become the data document.

3. Click the zoom boxes for both documents to reduce both windows to half-screen size.

Step 3 lets you confirm the spellings of placeholders in the main document and make sure you include all the placeholders as you list fields in the data document's header record.

4. On the first line of the new document (the header record), type the field names used in the main document. Separate the field names with commas.

5. Press **Return** to end the header record.

6. On the line below the header record, type the first record and order the fields according to the field names in the header above.

Remember to enclose in quotation marks any field that has a comma within it.

7. Press **Return** after the last field entry.

8. Enter a few more data records so that the program can print several labels.

9. Save the document with the name *maillist*.

Merging the Mailing Labels

Printing a set of mailing labels requires two basic materials: single-column, blank mailing labels and a continuous-feed printer that can accommodate them. The *Mainmail* document should print continuous-feed mailing labels properly on any printer other than the LaserWriter. (An explanation about how to print mailing labels on the LaserWriter is in the section called "Formatting Mailing Labels for the LaserWriter.")

If you don't have the labels or the printer, don't despair. You can merge the labels in a new document on-screen in order to become comfortable with the process. Even if you have the items required to print the labels, merging the labels on-screen is good for testing your print merge documents to confirm that they work as anticipated.

To merge the mailing labels in a new document, do the following steps:

1. Make sure the main document (*Mainmail*) is open and active.

2. Choose **Print Merge** from the File menu.

Word displays the Print Merge dialog box. By default, the Print button, which causes the program to merge the documents while it prints them, is selected. The New Document button merges the documents on-screen so that you can preview and edit the results before you print them.

3. Click **New Document**.

The program opens a new, full-size window and displays the mailing labels, one after another, separated by double dotted lines that indicate section breaks (see fig. 16.18).

You can save this document in the usual way and print it later by using the Print command. You also can proofread the new document for any errors in the coding you used for merging the main and data documents. You might want to use the new document to edit individual merged documents and add truly personal notes. Other than your editing additions, the printed results are the same as those obtained when you print the documents directly with Print Merge.

Viewing the merged document in the Page Preview window gives you a more accurate idea about the appearance of the labels. Choosing Page Preview from the File menu produces the display shown in figure 16.19.

If you move the pointer over a label in the Page Preview window and press the mouse button, the pointer's distance from the upper left corner of the label is displayed in the window's page number box. For example, positioning the pointer in a label's lower right corner and pressing the

Fig. 16.18

The mailing labels displayed in a new document.

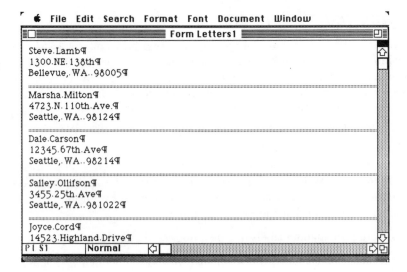

Fig. 16.19

A single-column mailing label in page preview.

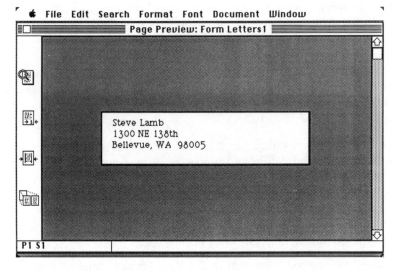

mouse button displays (4.00, 1.00) in—the dimensions of the label, as set in the Page Setup dialog box.

Page Preview is particularly useful when you create mailing labels in a three-column format because the document window can display the labels only in a single column.

Printing Three-Column Labels

If you make a few minor modifications to the main document, you can print labels in three columns on continuous-feed paper. The modified main document looks like the one in figure 16.20.

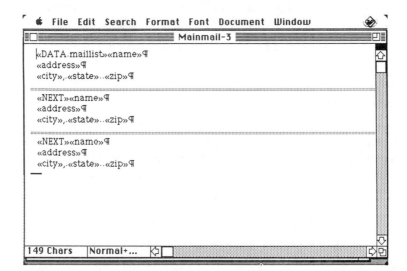

Fig. 16.20

The main document for printing labels in three columns.

Before modifying *Mainmail*, you may want to save a copy of it with a new name—perhaps *Mainmail-3*, for the three-column version. The two copies not only preserve the single-column version but also give you a new version with which to experiment.

To convert the main document for single-column mailing labels to one for three-column labels, do the following:

1. Select everything from <<name>> through the paragraph mark after <<zip>>.

2. Choose **Copy** from the Edit menu or press **Command-C**.

3. Click an insertion point after <<zip>> and press **Return** to create a blank line below the address.

4. Choose **Paste** two times from the Edit menu or press **Command-V** two times to insert two copies of the address placeholders.

5. Insert a NEXT instruction before the second and third occurrences of <<name>>.

The NEXT instruction tells the program to merge the next record from the data document into the current copy of the main document instead of moving on to the next copy.

6. Click an insertion point in front of the first NEXT instruction and press **Command-Enter** to insert a section break.

7. Press **Command-Enter** in front of the second NEXT instruction.

The document should look similar to the one in figure 16.20. The only missing element is the page formatting.

A page of three-column labels obviously is wider than a page of single-column labels. You need to change the paper-size specifications in the Page Setup dialog box to accommodate the new format. Then you need to change the number of columns in the Section dialog box.

To format for three-column labels, do the following:

1. Choose **Page Setup** from the File menu.

2. Specify **8.5 inches** in the Paper Width box.

3. Change the 1-inch setting in the Height box if the labels you are using are a different depth.

4. Set the top margin to **0.1** inch and the bottom, left, and right margins to **0** inch.

5. Click **OK** to register the settings and close the dialog box.

6. Choose **Section** from the Format menu.

7. Click **New Column** in the Section Start area.

8. Type **3** in the Number box in the Columns area.

9. Click **OK**.

10. Select the entire document and choose **Show Ruler** from the Format menu.

11. Move the left-indent marker about 1/8 inch to the right to prevent the labels from being printed at the very edge of the paper.

The main document should be ready for printing. If the data document does not contain at least six names, add a few. Then choose Print Merge from the File menu and click New Document to see how the program merges the data. The screen display does not look different from the display for single-column labels. If you choose Page Preview from the File menu, however, you see a display similar to the one shown in figure 16.21. You can magnify this image and use the pointer to check the exact placement of each label.

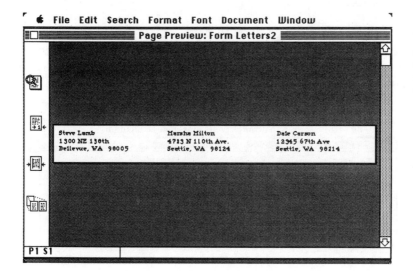

Fig. 16.21

Page preview showing three-column mailing labels.

Formatting Mailing Labels for the LaserWriter

The main documents you just developed can be modified to produce mailing labels of any standard size in several layout variations. Your only limitation is that you must print these documents on a printer that prints one line at a time. Most printers print one line at a time except for laser printers, such as the LaserWriter. Laser printers create an image of a complete page and then transfer that image to paper all at one time. This printing process requires a different merging procedure.

Various sizes of blank labels are available on sheets of paper that feed through a LaserWriter. With a little effort, you can modify the *Mainmail-3* document to print these labels. The modification involves creating as many copies of the address placeholders as you have labels on the sheet. The tricky part is calculating the correct spacing.

Following are the steps required to print labels on a standard LaserWriter sheet containing ten rows of three labels. To set up a different config- uration, measure the labels, the margins on the sheet containing the labels, and the space between the labels. Then adjust the margin and column-spacing settings accordingly.

Do the following steps to modify *Mainmail-3* to print mailing labels with the LaserWriter:

1. Insert two blank lines below each address block.

The blank lines are used for vertical positioning. The program's default font size is 12 points, which prints 5 lines per inch. As you can see in figure 16.22, each address block is now 5 lines.

Fig. 16.22

Several five-line address labels to be printed on a LaserWriter.

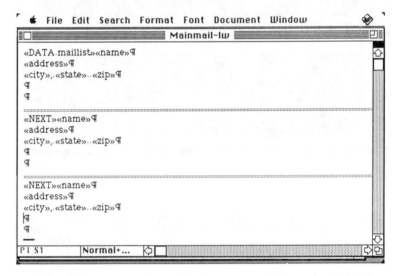

2. Select the second address block (<<NEXT>> through the paragraph marks after <<zip>>).

3. Copy the selected address placeholders.

4. Click an insertion point in front of <<name>> in the first address block.

5. Press **Command-V** nine times to paste nine copies of the address block in the first section.

6. Repeat Steps 4 and 5 to create a total of 10 sets of address placeholders in each of the other 2 sections.

The main document now contains print merge instruction sets for producing 30 address labels. A section break follows the 10th and 20th sets.

7. Choose **Page Setup** and select **US Letter**.

Selecting US Letter changes the Width setting to **8.5** and the Height setting to **11**.

8. Change the top margin to **0.5** and the left and right margins to **0.2** and then press **Return**.

9. Select the entire document.

10. Choose **Show Ruler** from the Format menu and return the left-indent marker to **0** inch.

11. Choose **Section** from the Format menu, change the column spacing to **0.13** inch, and press **Return**.

These settings should make possible your printing of mailing labels on a LaserWriter. Add about two dozen more records to the data document. Then choose Print Merge and select New Document to see whether the program correctly merges the labels. A page preview of the merged labels should look like the one in figure 16.23.

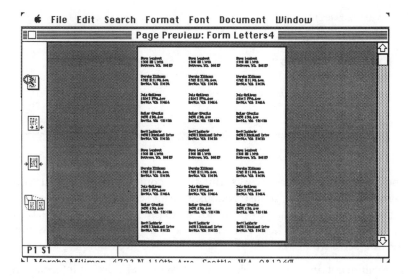

Fig. 16.23

Three-column mailing labels for the LaserWriter in page preview.

Before finishing this discussion of mailing labels, look at the solution to a common problem. What if your data document is missing a field that usually fills one of the lines in the main document? For example, an address in a small town may have no street address. In this case, the program simply prints the label with a blank line and moves on to the next field. If the blank line doesn't bother you, then no problem exists. If you don't like the blank line, the next section describes how to fix the problem.

Avoiding Blank Lines in Mailing Labels

The simplest solution is to make each record in the data document a single field. Rather than break the address into components, type the address as you want it to be printed but press Shift-Return (to insert a new-line character) instead of Return at the end of each line. Figure 16.24 shows a data document set up in this manner.

Fig. 16.24

A data document containing addresses set up as single fields.

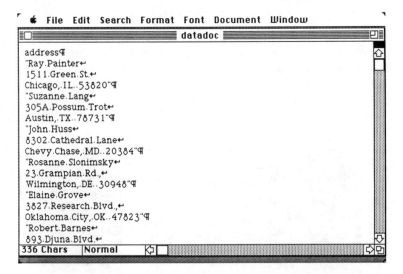

The single-field solution works, but the technique prevents you from using Word's print merge instructions to print selectively parts of a mailing list. You might want to print, for example, all records that have a ZIP code equal to 98125. You cannot sort the ZIP codes unless they are in a separate field.

You can maintain separate fields and still skip over missing information, however, by making use of the program's IF...ENDIF instructions. By inserting an IF instruction in the *Mainmail* main document (see fig. 16.25), you can make the program print the company name between the recipient's name and address only if a record in the *maillist* data document contains information in the company field.

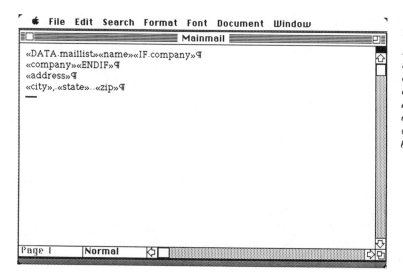

Fig. 16.25

IF...ENDIF instruction that causes the company line of an address to be omitted if the company *field is blank.*

For this instruction to work properly, you must add a company field to the *maillist* data document. You can include the company field anywhere in the data document.

To add a field to a data document, do the following:

1. Open the data document.

2. Type the name for the new field (in this case, **company**) at the beginning of the header record.

3. With the insertion point still in the header record, choose **Change** from the Search menu.

4. Type ^**p** in the Find What box; type ^**p,** in the Change To box; and click **Change All**.

Step 4 replaces all paragraph marks with paragraph marks followed by commas. The effect is to insert a comma at the beginning of every data record.

5. Scroll through the document and insert a company name in front of the new comma in the appropriate records.

Leave a few of the newly added company fields blank to test the process. The commas in the empty fields instruct the program to skip the field without leaving a blank line during the print merge operation.

This technique works with the documents for single-column and three-column mailing labels, but the program probably will have problems in merging the document for the LaserWriter. Because each row of labels in this document isn't considered a separate document, the additional lines in some labels affect the placement of other labels.

The techniques demonstrated in this chapter can save you considerable time when you must send similar information to many people. As you experiment with the program's print merge feature, you will find that it has many other useful applications.

In Part 2 of this book, you have learned organizational and formatting skills that help you produce attractive documents with a minimum of effort. Part 3 delves into the advanced word-processing techniques offered by Word. If you work with large, complex documents, these advanced features can help you organize your thoughts as well as produce sophisticated documents.

Part III

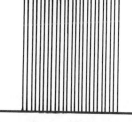

USING ADVANCED FEATURES FOR LONG DOCUMENTS

Includes:

Outlining Documents

Creating an Index

Creating a Table of Contents

Creating Footnotes

Outlining Documents

Outlining is a way to organize your thoughts and develop a carefully structured document. Although some people think outlines stifle creativity, a Word outline offers such flexibility that the outline actually can stimulate creativity. The outline provides a means for easily rearranging headings, subheadings, and body text so that you are no longer a prisoner of a structure too difficult and time-consuming to change. With Word, you can try numerous structures and choose the one that works best.

An outline is a means to an end—a foundation on which you can build a structured, well-organized document. You can use Word's Outlining command to create an outline that becomes an integral part of the document. Then you can view the document in two modes: document mode (the familiar full-text view) and outline mode, which displays only headings. As you see in this chapter, you can use the outline not only to provide an overview of a document but also to rearrange the document.

Using the Outlining command is easy enough that the process of creating an outline quickly will become second nature to you. You need to learn only a few simple techniques. In this chapter, you jump right in—creating an outline, setting and changing heading levels, and adding text. You learn how to collapse and expand subheadings and text, how to move easily through a document, and how to reorganize sections by reorganizing their headings. You learn also how to apply styles to a document by applying them to the document's outline and how to use the Document menu's Renumber command to number headings. And finally you learn how to print the outline.

Learning the Functions of the Outline View Icons

Before you create your first outline, you need to understand the functions of the icons that appear in the outline view's icon bar when you choose the Outlining command from the Document menu (see fig. 17.1). We briefly discuss the four basic functions performed by these icons.

Fig. 17.1

The icon bar displayed in outline view.

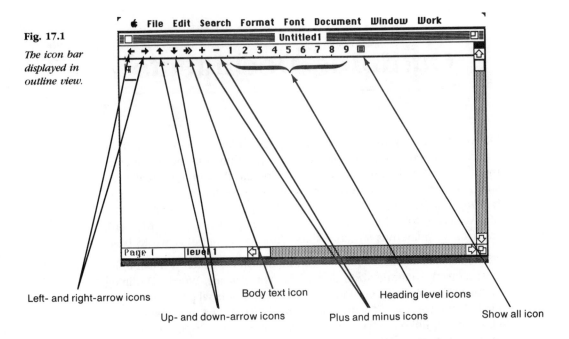

Left- and right-arrow icons

Up- and down-arrow icons

Body text icon

Plus and minus icons

Heading level icons

Show all icon

Raising and Lowering Heading Levels

The left- and right-arrow icons raise and lower the level of the selected heading. For example, selecting a first-level heading and clicking the right-arrow icon lowers the heading to second level. Clicking the left-arrow icon raises the heading back to first level.

You also can raise and lower heading levels by pressing the keyboard's Right- and Left-Arrow keys.

Moving Headings within the Outline

The up- and down-arrow icons move selected headings and text up and down within the outline (and thus within the document). For example, if you select a heading in your outline, clicking the up-arrow icon causes the heading to move up one line, effectively changing places with the heading above. Clicking the down-arrow icon moves the heading down to its original position. (Moving the headings has no effect on their assigned levels in the outline, however.)

You also can move selected headings up and down by pressing the keyboard's Up- and Down-Arrow keys.

Designating Body Text

Use the *body text* icon (the double right-pointing arrow) to designate something you have typed as body text rather than as a heading. In outline view, Word displays only the first line of each paragraph of body text.

Collapsing and Expanding the Outline

The minus and plus icons collapse and expand selected headings and text beneath higher-level headings. *Collapsing*, in this case, means removing the selected headings and text from the display. *Expanding* means restoring the collapsed headings and text to the display. For example, if you select a first-level heading and click the minus icon, the second-level headings disappear. Clicking the plus icon redisplays the lower-level headings.

The numbers to the right of the plus and minus icons control the number of heading levels displayed (or printed) in an outline. Each heading level corresponds to a number: first-level headings are 1; second-level headings are 2; and so on. Clicking a number displays all headings at and above the associated level. For example, clicking 2 displays only first- and second-level headings; clicking 1 displays only first-level headings.

The last icon, known as the *show all* icon, expands the outline to display all headings and text entries.

Now you are ready to create a sample outline. In the following discussion, bear in mind that Word's flexible outline processor does not impose a rigid outlining procedure. The next section simply illustrates the techniques for creating an outline.

Creating an Outline

The traditional approach to writing a document—especially one more than a few pages long—is to start by outlining the points you want to make. For the purposes of this discussion, assume that your work habits coincide with tradition. You are sitting with a blank document window in front of you, your fingers hovering over the keyboard, ready to construct an outline.

Outlining the Main Topics

You don't just sit down and type, off the top of your head, an outline with three or four different levels. The process is more evolutionary. You start by typing the main topics and shuffling them into a logical order. Then you develop each main topic, typing headings under each for the points you want to make. You may start with the first topic and work down the list. Or you may jump (in no particular order) from topic to topic, perhaps dealing first with the topics you know most about.

To outline the main topics (first-level headings) for a document you are going to write, do the following:

1. Choose **Outlining** from the Document menu.

Your screen switches from document view to outline view. The check mark next to the Outlining command on the Document menu means you can switch back to document view by again choosing the command. You can tell that you are in outline view because a bar containing the outlining icons is displayed across the top of the window (see fig. 17.1). As you see in the exercises, you use these icons to structure the outline.

2. Type your first main-topic heading and press **Return**.

In this case, type *The Basic Argument for Rebellion* and press Return. Word starts a new paragraph, and you can type another first-level heading.

3. Type your next first-level heading.

Type *Why the United States Must Rebel*. The outline should look like figure 17.2

At this stage in the process, don't worry about the exact wording of the headings; you can edit them later. Nor do you have to be concerned with the exact order of the headings, because you can reorder topics whenever you choose.

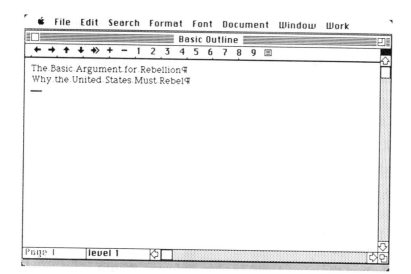

Fig. 17.2

The first two main headings.

Adding Lower-Level Headings

Adding lower-level headings to your outline is almost as easy as entering the main topics (the first-level headings). In the following exercises, you duplicate the outline in figure 17.3.

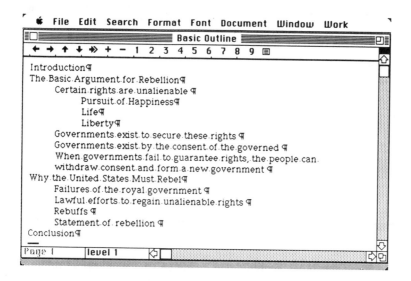

Fig. 17.3

The sample outline.

3. Click the **right-arrow icon** or press the keyboard's **Right-Arrow key** to change the heading level to level 3.

The paragraph mark moves 0.5 inch to the right, to the 1-inch indent for a third-level heading.

4. Type the third-level heading and press **Return**.

For this example, type *Pursuit of Happiness*. Pressing Return causes Word to start a new line at the same level as the preceding line. Again, the program continues the level-3 formatting until you change the heading level.

5. Now type the other third-level headings that will appear under this second-level heading and press **Return** after all but the last one.

In this case, type *Life*, press Return, and then type *Liberty*.

At this point, the outline should look like figure 17.6.

Fig. 17.6

The outline with third-level headings.

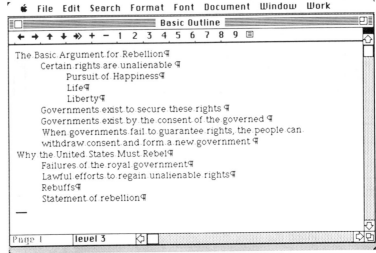

Adding Higher-Level Headings

As you look over the outline, suppose that you want to add an introduction and a conclusion to the document. You need to add first-level headings for each of these sections.

Adding the "Introduction" heading is simple. If you click an insertion point in front of the first word in the outline (*The*) and press Return, the new line created at the top of the document has the same formatting as the first-level heading beneath it. All you have to do is type *Introduction.*

To add the "Conclusion" heading at the end of the document, you need to raise the format from second level back to first level by doing the following:

1. Click an insertion point in front of the paragraph mark that ends the second-level heading under which you want to insert a first-level heading.

In this case, click an insertion point between the word *Rebellion* and the paragraph mark that ends the last subtopic.

2. Press **Return**.

You have created a blank line on which you can type a new second-level heading.

3. Click the **left-arrow icon** or press the keyboard's **Left-Arrow key** to change the heading level to level 1.

The paragraph mark moves 0.5 inch to the left, flush with the margin.

4. Type the first-level heading and press **Return**.

In this case, type *Conclusion.* Your outline should look like the one shown in figure 17.3.

Now that you have typed the basic outline, position the insertion point in one of the headings and try lowering the heading several levels by clicking the right-arrow icon. Notice that lowering a heading below level 9 causes the heading to become body text, which you normally designate by using the double-arrow icon.

Practice raising the heading by clicking the left-arrow icon and then, after you have finished experimenting, return the heading to its correct level. Now you can add numbers to the sample outline to reinforce the outline's structure.

Numbering Outline Heading Levels

You can differentiate between topics and subtopics within an outline by using the Document menu's Renumbering command to establish numbering and lettering schemes. Word provides a variety of formats for numbering headings and several options for renumbering the headings as you restructure a document.

To number an outline, do the following:

1. Click the **9 icon** to collapse any body text paragraphs under headings.

(Your sample outline does not yet contain body text.)

2. Choose **Renumber** from the Document menu.

Word displays the dialog box shown in figure 17.7.

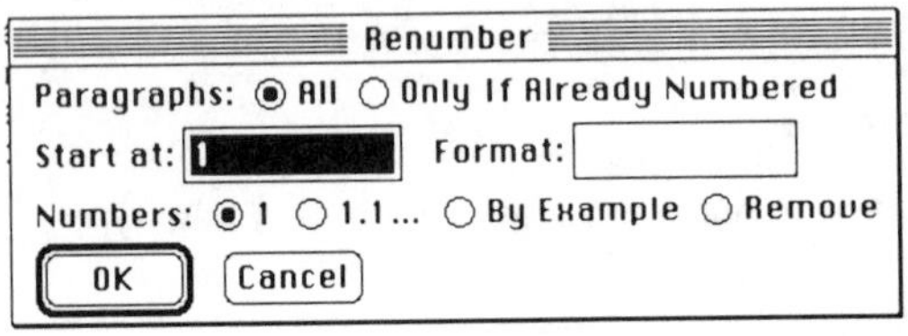

Fig. 17.7

*The Renumber
dialog box.*

```
┌─────────────────── Renumber ───────────────────┐
│ Paragraphs: ⦿ All ○ Only If Already Numbered    │
│ Start at: [1        ]  Format: [            ]   │
│ Numbers: ⦿ 1 ○ 1.1... ○ By Example ○ Remove      │
│ ( OK )  [ Cancel ]                              │
└─────────────────────────────────────────────────┘
```

3. Set the options to number the outline in the format you want.

For the sample outline, specify the standard *I.A.1.a.* format in the Format box. The periods, which serve as separators, instruct Word to format four levels of heading. (Other separator options are explained in the next section.)

To number all displayed paragraphs, accept All, the default setting in the Paragraphs area. And to tell Word to begin numbering with the Roman numeral *I* the first heading in the outline, accept the 1 in the Start at box. Finally, accept the default 1 selection in the Numbers area to tell Word that you want a whole number (or a letter) at each heading level rather than decimal numbers graduated according to the level (*1* for level 1, *1.1* for level 2, *1.1.1* for level 3, and so on).

4. Click **OK** or press **Return**.

Word adds the appropriate number or letter, followed by a tab, at the beginning of each heading (see fig. 17.8).

Now take a closer look at the numbering options and how they affect the entry in the Start at box.

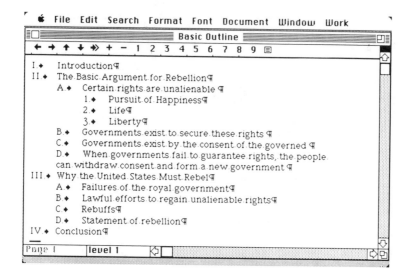

Fig. 17.8

*The sample
outline with a
number/letter
format.*

Specifying the Number or Letter Scheme

Word offers a variety of numbering and lettering schemes. By default, Word uses Arabic numerals followed by periods at all levels of heading. If you leave the Format box blank, the default scheme is applied. You can tell Word to use a decimal scheme (*1*, *1.1*, *1.1.1*, and so on) by specifying *1* in the Format box and selecting the 1.1 option in the Numbers area. Figure 17.9 shows the sample outline with decimal numbering. Also at your disposal is any combination of Arabic numerals, upper- and lowercase Roman numerals, and upper- and lowercase letters.

The default separator character is a period, but you may prefer to use commas, hyphens, slashes, semicolons, colons, left or right parentheses, left or right braces ({ }), or left or right brackets ([ ]). You can use only one separator character in the Format box.

If you want to use a special numbering scheme that Word does not recognize, you can number the first heading manually and then click the By Example button to instruct Word to follow your scheme when numbering the other headings in the outline.

Fig. 17.9

*The sample
outline with
decimal
numbers.*

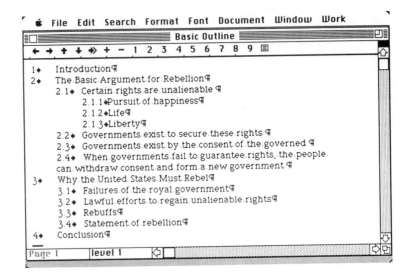

Specifying the Beginning Number or Letter

The `Start at` box tells Word with which unit to begin numbering headings. Word assumes that you want to begin at the beginning (with the equivalent of *1*) at all levels, unless you supply other numbers.

Because all `Start at` box entries must be Arabic numerals, you have to convert other numbering or lettering schemes to their Arabic equivalent. Thus, in the preceding example, *1.1.1.1* in the `Start at` box would tell Word to start at *I.*, *A.*, *1.*, and *a.* as the program encounters headings at those levels. (When you are numbering an entire outline, however, you can ignore the `Start at` box because Word assumes that you want to start with the equivalent of *1*.) If, on the other hand, you want the outline to start at *I.C.1.a.*, you should specify *1.3.1.1* in the `Start at` box.

Word's numbering options are far-ranging, and you have many options for adjusting Renumber settings. For instance, if you tell Word to start at *5.12.1*, using the format *I-1.a*, the beginning number of *V-12.a* is produced. The Renumber options are nice to have when you need them, but in reality, you will very rarely use such unusual outline settings.

The interplay of the `Start at` and `Format` boxes becomes important, however, when you want to renumber only parts of an outline. When you select an area of an outline for renumbering, you need to tell Word with which number to begin the numbering scheme. You may want to renumber in this way after reorganizing part of a large outline (see the section called "Renumbering after Reorganizing"). For small outlines, however, renumbering the whole outline by using the default Start at setting is easier.

Renumbering Outlines

Not only does Word number automatically the headings in an outline, but the program also can renumber them. To see how the renumbering process works, add a few third- and fourth-level headings under the "Failures of the royal government" second-level heading (see fig. 17.10). Use the Renumber command to integrate this new section into the outline's numbering scheme.

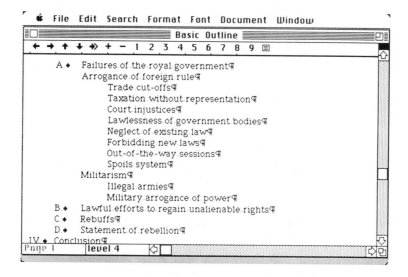

Fig. 17.10

The sample outline with added subheadings.

To renumber just part of an outline, follow these steps:

1. Select the area you want to renumber.

For this example, select the "Failures of the royal government" heading and the subheadings you just added.

2. If the selection contains any body text, click the **9 icon** to collapse the text.

3. Choose **Renumber** from the Document menu.

The settings in the Renumber dialog box reflect the format and number of the heading that begins the selection. In this case, the settings are correct. If they weren't correct (for example, if you were renumbering a section that you had rearranged), you would need to adjust the settings to maintain a consistent numbering scheme.

4. Press **Return** to renumber the selection in the established format.

Figure 17.11 shows the newly numbered section.

Fig. 17.11

Additional subheadings integrated into the numbering scheme.

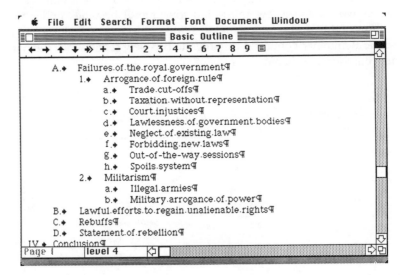

In an outline in which only some heading levels have been numbered (first- and second-level headings, for example), clicking the Only If Already Numbered button in the Renumber dialog box's Paragraphs area enables you to renumber the outline without having to collapse un-numbered headings.

To remove numbers from an outline, all you have to do is click the Remove button in the Renumber dialog box's Numbers area.

NOTE: Your outline is now more than one screen long. You can scroll through it by using the scroll arrows or the scroll bar.

Building a Document from an Outline

Once you have developed an outline for your document, you can start adding text paragraphs. You can add text in either outline or document view and move between the two as necessary by choosing the Outlining command from the Document menu.

Word displays only the first line of each paragraph of body text that you type in outline view and ends the line with an ellipsis to indicate that the paragraph includes additional, undisplayed text. The line is indented 0.25 inch farther than the preceding heading. Because everything but the first line disappears, you should type the text as though it were a heading and then, after proofreading your typing, designate the text as body text. (If you are going to type paragraph after paragraph, use document view—it's easier.)

To see how easily an outline can be expanded progressively into a complete document, add the introductory text shown in figure 17.12 to the sample outline.

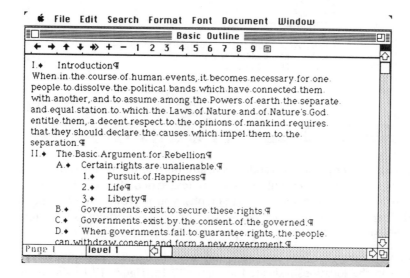

Fig. 17.12

Text typed as a heading so that all the text remains visible.

To type a paragraph of body text in an outline, do the following:

1. Click an insertion point at the end of the heading under which you want the text to appear and then press **Return**.

In this case, click an insertion point between "Introduction" and the paragraph mark that ends the line. Initially, whatever you type after you press Return has the same format as the preceding heading and therefore is displayed on-screen.

> 2. Type the paragraph.

Type the paragraph in figure 17.12.

> 3. With the insertion point still in the paragraph, click the double-arrow icon (the body text icon).

Everything but the first line of the paragraph disappears from the screen (see fig. 17.13).

Fig. 17.13

The text after you designate it as body text.

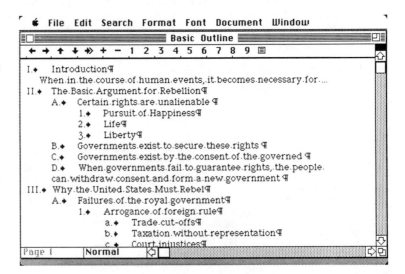

Because other paragraphs added beneath this one will be formatted automatically as text, you will not see any text typed after the first line. If you need to type a series of paragraphs, you probably should type all the paragraphs as headings before you format any of them as body text. Then simply select the paragraphs and click the body text icon.

In preparation for later exercises, add two additional paragraphs of body text in the locations indicated in figure 17.14. Figure 17.14 shows the two paragraphs after they have been designated as body text.

Type the following text paragraphs where indicated in figure 17.14:

He has kept among us, in times of peace, Standing Armies without the consent of our legislatures.

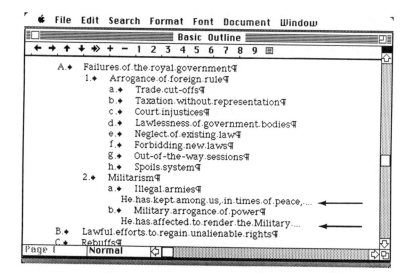

Fig. 17.14

Two more body text paragraphs.

He has affected to render the Military independent of and superior to the Civil power.

You also can add body text to an outline by pasting the text from the Clipboard, just as you would in document view. Word adds the text at the same level as the insertion point. Then, using the body text icon, you can designate the text as body text.

If you want to paste in elaborately formatted text, such as a table imported from another program, you probably should use the outline to find where you want to paste the text and then switch to document view in order to paste. If you try to paste in outline view, the outline may format the text in unexpected ways.

Controlling the Outline Display

Once you start developing a document, you tend to focus on the section you are writing. Keeping the big picture in mind can be difficult, especially when you work with long documents. The purpose of any outline is to reveal the structure of a document by making evident the relationships between the headings and subheadings.

Word's outline view enables you to remove from the display some subheadings and body text while retaining useful items for reference. You can display all the subheadings and body text under some headings, while collapsing the subheadings and text under others; or you can display only those headings above a certain level. Word retains collapsed material in the outline and represents that material in the display with a dotted line beneath the appropriate heading (see figure 17.15).

Limiting Displayed Heading Levels

To adjust the outline display, you can use the number icons (1 through 9) in the outline icon bar to display only headings at and above a certain level. The result of this technique, which can be used either on an entire outline or on only one selection, is a quick overview of a document.

To change the level of heading displayed throughout an outline, click the number icon that corresponds to the lowest heading level you want to display. Watch the display change as you try clicking several numbers. Figure 17.15 shows the sample document after the 2 icon has been clicked to display only first- and second-level headings.

Fig. 17.15

The sample outline displaying first- and second-level headings.

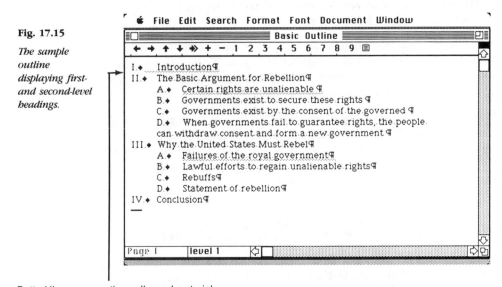

Dotted line representing collapsed material

Now restore the full display. Word makes the process easy. To display all levels of the outline, click the show all icon (to the right of the 9 icon). This step displays all heading levels and the first line of each paragraph of body text.

Collapsing Material beneath Headings

To collapse material beneath a heading, select the heading and then either click the minus icon or press the minus key on the numeric keypad. If you select the entire heading, this procedure collapses all material between the selected heading and the next heading of the same level (or higher). On the other hand, only the lowest level of subheading or the body text is collapsed if you simply click an insertion point in the heading. To collapse progressively higher levels of heading, either click the minus icon repeatedly or press the minus key.

Follow along with the next exercise to see how both of these methods work. First, collapse an entire set of subheadings; then achieve the same result by collapsing heading levels by increments.

To collapse all subheadings and text under a heading, do the following:

1. Select the entire heading (including the paragraph mark) above the material you want to collapse.

For this example, select the second first-level heading—"The Basic Argument for Rebellion."

2. Click the minus icon or press the minus key on the numeric keypad.

All subheadings and text disappear. A dotted line marks their position in the outline (see fig. 17.16).

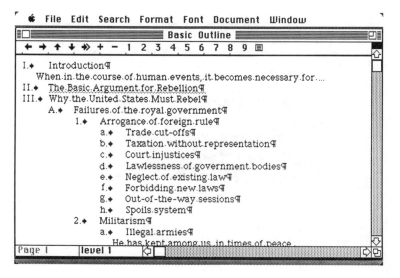

Fig. 17.16

Subheadings collapsed under a selected heading.

To expand all the material collapsed beneath a heading, follow these steps:

1. Select the underlined heading, including the paragraph mark.

2. Click the plus icon or press the numeric keypad's plus key.

The subheadings you just collapsed are expanded.

Now collapse by increments the same group of subheadings by first clicking an insertion point in "The Basic Argument for Rebellion" heading and then clicking the minus icon. Watch the level-3 headings collapse. Then click the minus icon again to collapse the second-level headings. All subheadings disappear and a dotted line marks their position in the outline. Now expand this section of the outline (with the insertion point in the first-level heading) by clicking the plus icon twice. Notice how the section expands in increments, too.

Perhaps you want to collapse one area of an outline so that you can view another area in detail. To do so, you use a variation of the technique you used to collapse all headings under a selected heading.

To collapse all subheadings and text in one area of an outline, follow these steps:

1. Select the area you want to collapse.

Try selecting the section shown in figure 17.17. Notice that the level of the last heading in this section is higher than that of the first heading.

Fig. 17.17

An area ready for collapsing.

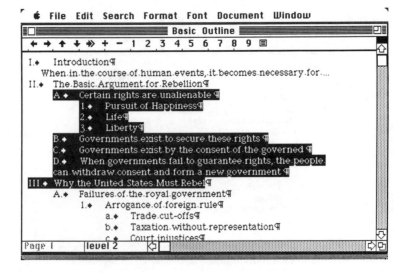

2. Click the **minus icon** or press **Command-minus** on the numeric keypad to collapse the selection.

Only the underlined second-level heading remains, even though the selection contained a first-level heading.

Again, expanding the entire underlined heading restores all the collapsed headings—those at a lower level as well as those at a higher level. Before you continue, expand the subheadings you just collapsed.

Reorganizing Documents by Reorganizing Their Outlines

The outline view provides a quick, visual way to reorganize a document. Instead of going through the process of selecting, cutting, and pasting a large area of text, you simply collapse the subheadings and body text beneath the first heading in an area in the outline and then move the heading. Word moves all the collapsed material as well.

The program provides two methods for moving headings and collapsed material. For short moves, you can use the up- and down-arrow icons or the Up- and Down-Arrow keys. To make longer moves faster, you can cut and paste. Working with the sample outline, you practice both methods so that you can see how the collapsing and moving techniques work together.

Reorganizing with Icons

Before you add body text to an outline, you may want to improve the logic of your argument by reorganizing the headings.

To move a heading with the up- and down-arrow icons, do the following:

1. Click an insertion point within the heading.

In this case, click an insertion point in the third-level heading "Pursuit of Happiness."

2. Click the up-arrow or down-arrow icon, to move the heading up or down in the outline.

You can click the icon as many times as you like. Whenever you do click the icon, the heading changes places with the heading above or below it. To move "Pursuit of Happiness" down in the outline, click the down-arrow icon twice. The outline should look like the one in figure 17.18.

Fig. 17.18

The "Pursuit of Happiness" heading after adjustment.

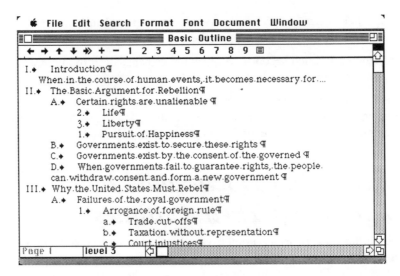

You can use the same procedure to move not only a single heading but also all the subheadings and text collapsed beneath that heading. Thus, taking the time to outline a document really can pay off by saving you time when you edit the document.

To move a section of a document with the up-arrow and down-arrow icons, do the following:

1. Click in the selection bar next to the first heading in the section you want to move. By doing so, you select the entire heading.

2. Click the minus icon to collapse the subheadings and body text beneath the selected heading.

For this example, under the third-level heading "Militarism," collapse the fourth-level headings "Illegal armies" and "Military arrogance of power" and their text paragraphs (refer to fig. 17.14).

3. Click an insertion point within the heading.

In this case, click an insertion point in "Militarism."

4. Click the up-arrow or down-arrow icon to move the heading and the collapsed material up or down in the outline.

Click the up-arrow icon repeatedly to move "Militarism" up in the outline until it is positioned beneath the "Failures of the royal government" second-level heading.

5. Click the plus icon to expand the collapsed material.

The results are shown in figure 17.19. As you can see, moving the "Militarism" heading moved all the subheadings and text beneath that heading.

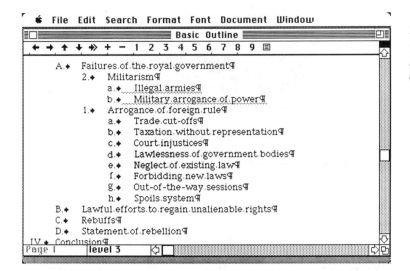

Fig. 17.19

The "Militarism" section after adjustment.

Reorganizing by Cutting and Pasting

The second method of reorganizing an outline (and the associated document) is to cut and paste sections. In long outlines, this method probably is more convenient than "walking" sections up and down the page.

Imagine that you've discovered a more logical order for the sample document's "Failures of the royal government" section. You want to move to the top of the section the block of fourth-level headings that begins with "Lawlessness of government bodies." And you want to make "Lawlessness of government bodies" a third-level heading. To do this, you need to cut and paste.

To cut and paste a section from one area of an outline to another, do the following:

1. Drag through the section to select it (see fig. 17.20).

2. Choose **Cut** from the Edit menu.

3. Click an insertion point at the beginning of the line on which you want the pasted section to appear.

Fig. 17.20

The selected section, ready for cutting and pasting.

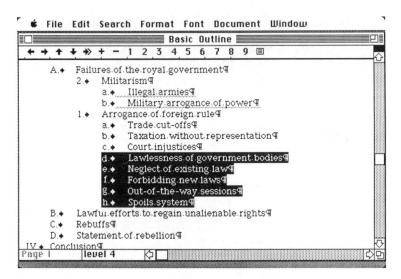

In this case, click an insertion point in front of the *2* to the left of the "Militarism" heading.

4. Choose **Paste** from the Edit menu.

The entire section is pasted in. Heading levels are maintained throughout, no matter where you reposition the section, so you still have a little tidying up to do.

5. Make any heading-level adjustments necessitated by the move.

For this exercise, simply click an insertion point in the "Lawlessness of government bodies" heading and then click the left-arrow icon to adjust the heading from fourth level to third level. The result is shown in figure 17.21.

Renumbering after Reorganizing

Having reorganized a numbered outline, you undoubtedly want to renumber the headings to reflect the new structure. In this case, you need to renumber only small portions of the outline. Because renumbering takes a great deal of computer memory and a fair amount of time, you should select only the portion that needs adjustment.

To renumber part of an outline, do the following:

1. Select the area you want to renumber.

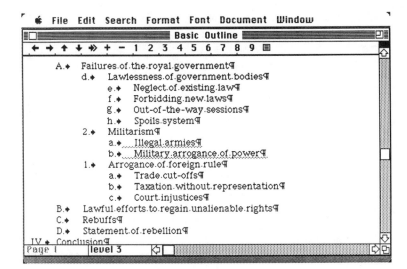

Fig. 17.21

The reorganized outline.

For this example, select the "Failures of the royal government" heading and the third- and fourth-level headings under it.

2. If the selection contains any body text, click the **9 icon** to collapse the text.

3. Choose **Renumber** from the Document menu.

4. Press **Return** to renumber the selection in the established format.

Figure 17.22 shows the dramatic results.

Now renumber also the third-level headings under "Certain rights are unalienable."

Formatting Outline Heading Levels

In outline view as in document view, Word displays the outline's page number and the section number (if applicable) in the window's bottom left corner. The box to the right of these numbers displays the automatic style associated with the selected heading. As you add a heading to an outline, Word automatically applies a default style to the heading and adds that style to the document's style sheet.

Word has nine styles for outline heading levels (level 1 through level 9) and one for body text (normal); these styles are not displayed in

Fig. 17.22

*The reorganized
and renumbered
outline.*

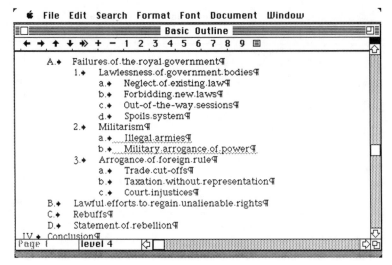

outline view. A 0.5-inch indent (one default tab stop) distinguishes one
heading level from the next. Body text is set off from the headings above
and below it by a 0.25-inch indent (half a default tab stop) and a ter-
minating ellipsis. Figure 17.23 shows the outline-view display of headings
in each of the nine automatic styles. Notice also that the figure includes
one line of body text displayed in automatic normal style.

Fig. 17.23

*The automatic
styles for nine
heading levels
and body text
in outline view.*

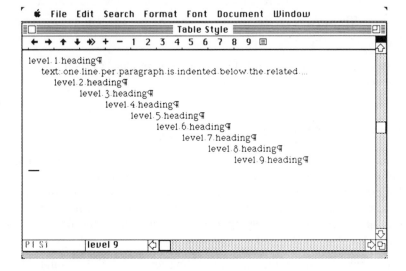

Viewing the Outline Styles in Document View

The limits you place on the display in outline view do not affect the display in document view; any collapsed headings or text appears in full. The headings, displayed with their applied styles, are bold; the first two levels have extra space above them. Figure 17.24 displays in document view the outline from figure 17.23.

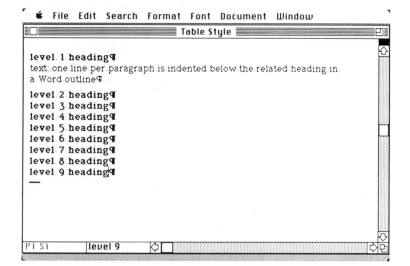

Changing the Default Styles

Because outline headings are formatted in nine automatic styles, you quickly can change the look of the headings throughout a document by changing the formats associated with those styles. The Format menu's Define Styles command gives you this capability to change heading styles. You can choose to change only the styles within the current document, or you can select the Set Default option to establish heading-level styles for all documents you subsequently create in outline view. (For details on changing style definitions, see Chapter 9.)

Changing Outline Levels
by Applying Styles

Now that the outline includes both text and headings, choose Outlining from the Document menu and take a quick look at the document in document view (see fig. 17.25).

Fig. 17.25

*The sample
outline
displayed in
document view.*

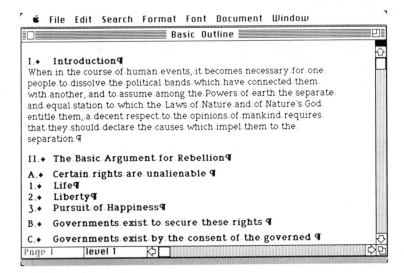

When you raise or lower a heading level in outline view, you change the style applied to the heading. The style is reflected in the style box at the bottom of the screen. You also can raise or lower a heading level in document view. Try it—just use the Format menu's Styles or Define Styles command to change the applied style.

To change the level of an outline heading from document view, do the following:

1. Select the heading you want to change.

For the purposes of this exercise, select any first-level heading.

2. Choose **Styles** from the Format menu.

The level 1 style is checked in the dialog box (see fig. 17.26).

3. Select from the styles list the style you want to apply.

Select Normal to change the heading to body text.

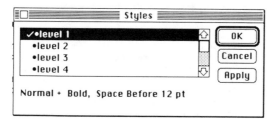

Fig. 17.26

*The level-1 style
in the Styles
dialog box.*

4. Click **OK** to apply the style and close the dialog box.

The heading changes to body text format. If you return to outline view, you'll notice that the level change also is reflected in the outline.

In preparation for the next exercise, change the heading back to first level either by clicking the 1 icon in outline view or reselecting the level 1 style in the Styles dialog box in document view.

Printing Outlines

If you want to keep the outline of a document nearby while you write, you can print the outline. Printing outlines is also a quick way to prepare presentation materials. Because Word prints only the information displayed on-screen, you could print, for example, only first-level headings for overhead projection, first- and second-level headings as handouts, and all headings as notes for a presentation you will make.

To print an outline, follow this procedure:

1. Collapse headings and text in the outline until the screen
   shows only the material you want to print.

Try collapsing all but first- and second-level headings in the sample outline.

2. Choose **Print** from the File menu or press **Command-P**.

3. Press **Return**.

The sample printed outline looks like the one in figure 17.27.

This chapter has introduced you to Word's outline processor. The more you use the Outlining command's capabilities, the more useful you will find them. In Chapter 19, we show you another advantage of outlining a document: you can convert the outline into a table of contents that easily can be updated whenever you edit or rearrange headings in a document.

Fig. 17.27

The printed outline.

    I.   Introduction
    II.   The Basic Argument for Rebellion
          A.   Certain rights are unalienable.
          B.   Governments exist to secure these rights.
          C.   Governments exist by the consent of the governed.
          D.   When governments fail to guarantee rights, the people
          can withdraw consent and form a new government.
    III. Why the United States Must Rebel
          A.   Failures of the royal government
          B.   Lawful efforts to regain unalienable rights
          C.   Rebuffs
          D.   Statement of rebellion
    IV.   Conclusion

Creating an Index

Probably one of the hardest tasks you will have to do in preparing a document for presentation or publication is to create an index. It should not be confused with a table of contents, which is a summary of the book's organization. An *index* is a concise listing of the author's material for quick access to it. An index can include a range of entries—from the topics discussed in the document to the manuscript's key words, ideas, concepts, and phrases—all compiled in a neat list of entries, sub-entries, and sub-subentries.

Creating an accurate and usable index is a challenge. Although the Word program automatically compiles the index, you must identify the words you want included. Therefore, you need to be familiar with the subjects covered in a document and know how readers are likely to search for specific information. These considerations determine which words you mark as index entries and how you classify and cross-reference them in the index.

Whether you index your own material or someone else's, keep the following points in mind:

- Know the purpose of the work to be indexed.

What kind of manuscript are you indexing? Index entries in a travel book would be different from those in a book on history, for example. Both books would have index references to places, but the travel book's emphasis would be on locality—famous sites, restaurants and hotels, and a region's famous people. The history book's emphasis would be on past events—the interpretation of the happenings at a particular place in a particular time. You must be aware of the purpose of the manuscript when you choose representative index entries.

- Be familiar with the contents and main ideas of the manuscript.

Quickly read through the entire work, even if you have written it. What are the main ideas? What concepts do you want to get across to the readers? An easy mistake for an indexer to make is to include references to subjects mentioned only in passing. For example, in an article about bald eagles, an author might mention briefly other birds commonly sighted near bald eagle habitats. Do not include the names of these birds in the index unless the author provides additional information about them in the text. Before marking an index entry, be sure that the document contains enough information on the topic to warrant including that topic in the index.

- Know the audience reading the manuscript.

Who will be reading the work? What is the typical age level, economic and social background, education level, and so on, of the readers? For example, a psychology textbook for a high school student will have an index that covers general concepts of psychology, geared to a novice exploring the field for the first time. A graduate student doing psychology research, on the other hand, needs a detailed index with terms and phrases that will provide quick access to the specific information in the book. Knowing your audience helps you predict how the reader will use the index and go about looking up a topic. With this knowledge, you can tailor your index entries to the reader.

- Be prepared to cross-reference your entries.

The difference between a good index and a bad one often centers on how you cross-reference your entries. Some ideas are discussed over several pages in a document, under several different headings. How you cover this range of pages and ideas—all centering on a related concept—is crucial to establishing a good index. Again, knowing the purpose of the manuscript, its main ideas, and the audience will help you determine what concepts to cross-reference.

In addition to the problems inherent in devising an index, creating one by hand can be extremely time-consuming and tedious, often requiring the shuffling of numerous index cards or small pieces of paper. Word's Index command eliminates most of the drudgery from the process and enables you to compile an index in a fraction of the time needed to compile one manually.

In this chapter you learn how to mark the index entries with special beginning and ending codes and format them as hidden text. You learn also that you can make an index entry a variation of the actual text of the document. You see how to cross-reference index entries and how to format the entries to suit a particular style you have in mind. As you see in the chapter, you can create a full range of index entries, from a simple, one-level entry to a whole index category with subentries and even sub-subentries.

Marking Index Entries

The first step in creating an index is to mark the index entries in the text. Then you can tell Word to compile an index from the marked entries by choosing Index from the Document menu. Word automatically puts the entries in alphabetic order and appends the index to the end of the document, separating the index from the text with a section break. You then can apply section formatting options to the index. In the process of compiling the index, Word paginates the document and adds the page number to each index entry. Duplicate entries are merged, and duplicate page numbers are deleted. Once you compile the index, you can edit and reformat the entries as you would any other text. Later, if you decide to add or delete text, use the Index command again and automatically update the page references.

Because you must use hidden text repeatedly when you mark index entries, you may want to add the Hidden option from the Character dialog box to the Format menu.

To add the Hidden option to the Format menu, do the following:

1. Press **Command-Option-+**.

Use the + key from the top of the main keyboard rather than the one from the numeric keypad (but do not press Shift).

2. Choose **Character** from the Format menu.

3. Click **Hidden** in the Character dialog box.

4. Click **OK** to close the Character dialog box.

The Hidden style appears at the bottom of the Format menu. Note that the Hidden option is selected. If you don't want to use Hidden right now, choose the option again to restore normal character formatting.

You now can choose Hidden directly from the Format menu whenever you want to create hidden text.

Marking Main Entries

To make a word an index entry, you must mark the word with a beginning and ending code. The beginning code for main entries is *.i.* and the ending code is either a semicolon, an end-of-line mark (produced by pressing Shift-Return), or a paragraph mark. Use the semicolon if the entry does not end the line or paragraph. You must always format the beginning code as hidden text. Hide an ending semicolon only if you don't want Word to print it. (End-of-line and paragraph marks never are printed, so you don't have to hide them.)

Before you start marking index entries, make sure that the Show Hidden Text option is turned on in the Preferences dialog box so that you can see the formatted index codes. (The Preferences command is on the Edit menu.) Before you compile the index, turn off the option again; otherwise, Word includes the hidden text when the program calculates page breaks.

To mark the beginning and end of a main index entry, do the following:

1. Click an insertion point in front of the first letter of the word or words you want to index.

2. Choose **Hidden** from the Format menu or press **Shift-Command-X**.

3. Type **.i.** (Don't insert a space after the second period.)

4. If an end-of-line or paragraph mark is not already after the word to be indexed, click an insertion point after the word and insert a semicolon.

5. If you inserted a semicolon, select it and choose **Hidden** from the Format menu.

Using the Glossary To Mark Index Entries

To save time when marking index entries, you can create glossary entries for the beginning and ending index codes. Then, rather than typing *.i.* and *;* each time and having to format each code as hidden text, you quickly can insert the codes, wherever needed, from the glossary.

To make an index code glossary entry and save it in the Standard Glossary, do the following:

1. Choose **Hidden** from the Format menu or press **Shift-Command-X**.

2. Type **.i.** anywhere in the current document and then select the code.

3. Choose **Glossary** from the Edit menu.

4. Type **i** as the name for this glossary entry.

5. Click **Define**.

6. Choose **Save** from the File menu. When the Save dialog box appears, click **Save** to save the new entry to the Standard Glossary. When the alert box appears, click **Yes**.

Now, whenever you want to insert the beginning index code, you simply can use the *i* glossary entry.

To mark the beginning of an index entry with a code stored in the glossary, do the following:

1. Click an insertion point in front of the first letter of the word or words you want to index.

2. Press **Command-Backspace**.

The word Name appears in the page number area at the lower left corner of the window.

3. Type **i**, the glossary name of the beginning code.

4. Press **Return**.

Word automatically inserts the beginning code *.i.* formatted as hidden text.

Because you probably will use a semicolon formatted as hidden text to indicate the end of most index entries, you can create a glossary entry for this character as well. Name the glossary entry *e* (for end) or something equally appropriate. Then each time you need to insert an ending code, just press Command-Backspace and type *e*; Word then inserts the semicolon formatted as hidden text.

Now that you have an idea of the basic procedure for marking entries, use the sample paragraph in figure 18.1 to see how Word compiles an index. The topics in the sample paragraph are discussed too superficially to represent valid index entries; however, the paragraph still is useful for demonstrating the indexing process, so go ahead and type the paragraph.

Fig. 18.1

A sample paragraph, ready for indexing.

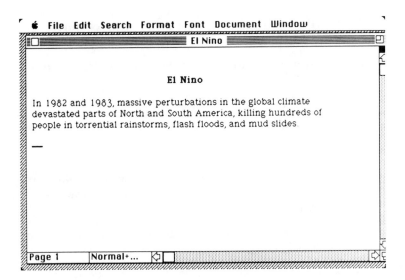

The sample paragraph is about El Niño, a rather unique weather pattern, and its side effects. The side effects should be indexed as subentries under the main entry, *El Niño*. An index of the paragraph might be arranged as follows:

El Niño
    climatic effects
        flash floods
        global
        mud slides
        North America
        rainstorms
        South America

Here, two levels of subentry are listed under the main *El Niño* entry. The first subentry, *climatic effects*, doesn't appear in the actual text of the paragraph.

Marking Subentries

Word allows up to seven entry levels in an index: the main entry and six subentry levels. However, most good indexes rarely exceed two or three levels.

When marking a word or group of words as a subentry in an index, you must type the beginning code as well as the main entry in front of the subentry and separate the two with a colon. You then format the main entry and the code as hidden text.

To mark a subentry, do the following:

1. Click an insertion point in front of the first letter of the subentry you want to index.

2. Choose **Hidden** from the Format menu or press **Shift-Command-X**.

3. Type **.i.** and then the main entry for this subentry followed by a colon. (Don't insert any spaces between the beginning code and the main entry or between the colon and the subentry.)

4. If an end-of-line or paragraph mark is not at the end of the subentry, click an insertion point after the subentry and insert a semicolon.

5. If you inserted a semicolon, select it and choose **Hidden** from the Format menu.

For example, to make *flash floods* a subentry under the *El Niño* main entry, mark *flash floods* with the standard hidden *.i.* beginning code, followed by the hidden main entry, *El Niño*. Because the subentry does not end the line, you follow the subentry with a hidden *;* ending code (see fig. 18.2).

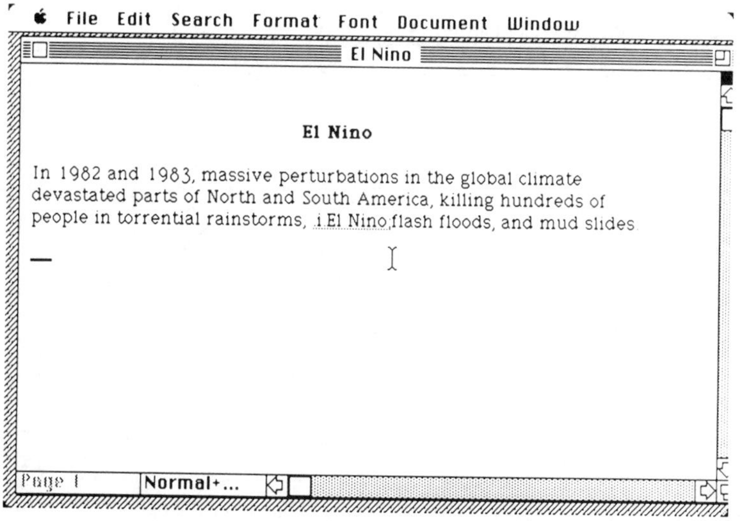

Fig. 18.2

The subentry flash floods *after coding.*

You decide that your readers will be better able to locate information if you group a number of entries under a general classification that actually does not appear in the document. The *climatic effects* subentry is an example of such a general classification. To include this classification in the sample paragraph's index, simply choose the appropriate location and insert the subentry *.i.El Niño:climatic effects;* in the text. The main entry, *El Niño*, is separated from the subentry, *climatic effects*, by a colon. Both entries are formatted as hidden text, because you don't want *climatic effects* to appear in the text.

Whenever you create an index entry that is not part of the text, such as *climatic effects*, be sure to insert the entry on the page with the related text so that the index shows the correct page number.

To duplicate the index arrangement shown previously, go ahead and mark the main entry and subentries as shown in figure 18.3. The coding may look quite complex, but once you understand the basic principles behind marking index entries, you will develop systems to help you quickly carry out the marking process. For example, you can mark all beginning codes for subentries by inserting *.i.El Niño* in front of the first subentry and pressing Command-A (Word's repeat key) at the beginning of each subsequent subentry. When you've added all the beginning entry codes, you can use the Search command to find each *.i.El Niño* so that you can insert all ending codes in the same manner. Another shortcut is to create a glossary entry for the *.i.El Niño* beginning code.

Fig. 18.3

The sample paragraph with index coding.

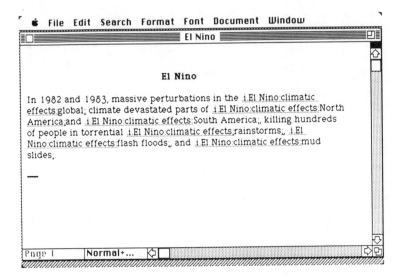

Marking Extended Entries

Sometimes, you may want to show the beginning and the end of a topic discussed on two or more pages. Rather than mark the topic as a separate index entry on each page, just mark the first- and last-page entries; Word then lists the beginning and ending pages of the entry (for example, *El Niño 7-11*). This type of index entry is called an *extended entry*.

To mark an extended index entry, do the following steps:

1. Click an insertion point in front of the first letter of the first occurrence of the entry you want to index.

2. Choose **Hidden** from the Format menu or press **Shift-Command-X**.

3. Type **.i(**. (Don't insert a space after the second period.)

4. Insert a hidden ending code after the first occurrence of the entry, if necessary.

5. Click an insertion point in front of the first letter of the last occurrence of the entry.

6. Choose **Hidden** from the Format menu or press **Shift-Command-X**.

7. Type **.i)**. (Again, don't insert a space after the second period.)

8. Insert a hidden ending code, if necessary.

If you don't want to include all the pages on which the entry appears, you can mark the first and last occurrences of the word for each series of pages you want to use.

When you compile an index with extended entries, Word automatically eliminates any redundancy. No matter how many times you have marked the same entry, the program lists the entry only once, followed by the pages on which the entry appears. Word separates consecutive page numbers with a hyphen, and intermittent page numbers with a comma.

Suppose, for example, that you discuss the subject of *trade winds* on pages 20 through 25, and the words appear on each of those pages. You can mark the first occurrence of the entry on page 20 with the *.i(.* code and the last occurrence on page 25 with the *.i).* code. Word compiles the entry in the index as *trade winds 20-25*. If the words *trade winds* appear only on pages 20, 23, and 25, you mark the first and last entries the same way. However, Word compiles the entry as *trade winds 20, 23, 25*. If the entry appears on pages 21, 22, 23, and 25 (in other words, on both consecutive and intermittent pages), Word compiles the entry as *trade winds 21-23, 25.*

Cross-Referencing Index Entries

You often can list a particular subject in an index in more than one way. To help readers find what they're looking for, you can cross-reference a subject by listing other words under which readers are likely to look for this information. For example, suppose that you have written a report discussing how your company can maintain a competitive edge in international markets. The report includes a number of references to agencies and often uses their acronyms instead of their full names. You could create the following cross-references in the index, in anticipation of the fact that readers might look for information under the acronyms rather than the full names:

Occupational Safety and Health Administration (OSHA), 5-9, 42, 63
OEEC. *See* Organization for European Economic Cooperation
Office of Management and Budget (OMB), 10-12
Office of Surface Mining Reclamation and Enforcement, 24
OMB. *See* Office of Management and Budget
OPEC. *See* Organization of Petroleum Exporting Countries
Organization for European Economic Cooperation, 1-4, 20, 58
Organization of Petroleum Exporting Countries, 23-27
OSHA. *See* Occupational Safety and Health Administration

You may prefer to duplicate the page numbers under each entry or to list the most important page numbers and include *See also* cross-references, such as those shown below:

Occupational Safety and Health Administration (OSHA), 5-9, 42, 63
OEEC, 1-4. *See also* Organization for European Economic Cooperation
Office of Management and Budget (OMB), 10-12
Office of Surface Mining Reclamation and Enforcement, 24
OMB, 10-12
OPEC, 23-27
Organization for European Economic Cooperation, 1-4, 20, 58
Organization of Petroleum Exporting Countries, 23-27
OSHA, 5-9. *See also* Occupational Safety and Health Administration

To create an index entry that includes a cross-reference, do the following:

1. Insert the appropriate hidden beginning code in front of the entry.

2. Click an insertion point immediately after the last letter of the entry.

3. Choose **Hidden** from the Format menu or press **Shift-Command-X**.

4. Type # (a pound symbol) followed by the cross-reference text and then the ending code.

For example, the last entry in the partial index shown previously for the competitive-edge report would appear as follows in your text (formatted, of course, as hidden text):

.i.OSHA#*See also* Occupational Safety and Health Administration;

You could add this *See also* note to every occurrence of *OSHA* on pages 5 through 9, or you could include the note only in the first occurrence on page 5 and the last occurrence on page 9. Remember, if you want words that don't appear in the text to appear in the index, format them as hidden text next to the entry to which they apply.

Compiling the Index

Once you finish marking your index entries, you are ready to compile the index. Before choosing the Index command, make sure that you have toggled off the Show Hidden Text option in the Preferences dialog box so that Word doesn't include hidden text when paginating the document.

Compiling an Index for Individual Documents

You can compile an index for individual documents or for a series of linked documents as well. The procedure is basically the same for both.

To compile the index for a single document, carry out the following two steps:

1. Choose **Index** from the Document menu.

Word displays the dialog box in figure 18.4. For now, accept the default Nested setting.

Fig. 18.4

The Index dialog box.

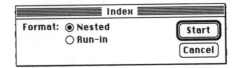

2. Click **Start**.

If this is the first time you've compiled an index for this document, Word automatically adds the index to the end of the document, inserting a section break before the index. In the index for the sample paragraph shown in figure 18.5, all entries occur on page 1 because the document is only one page long. In a real document, the page numbers would vary according to the locations of the entries within the document.

Fig. 18.5

The index compiled with the Nested *option selected.*

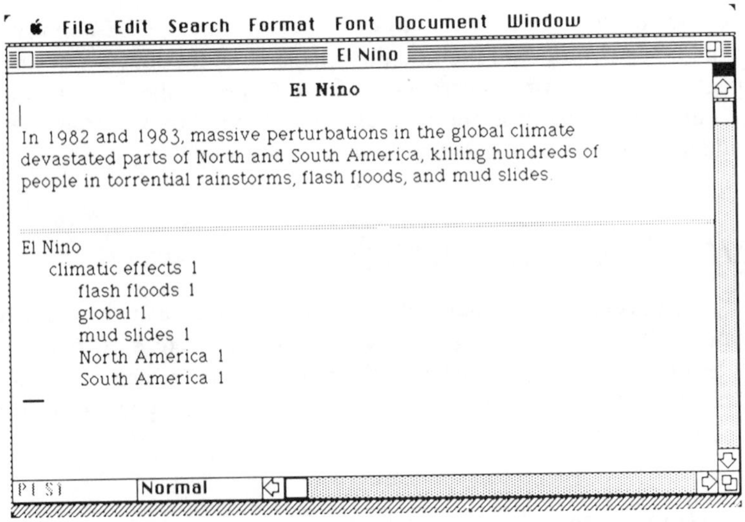

     File   Edit   Search   Format   Font   Document   Window

     El Nino

     El Nino

In 1982 and 1983, massive perturbations in the global climate devastated parts of North and South America, killing hundreds of people in torrential rainstorms, flash floods, and mud slides.

El Nino
    climatic effects 1
        flash floods 1
        global 1
        mud slides 1
        North America 1
        South America 1

P1 S1   Normal

The Index dialog box gives you the options of formatting the index with either nested subentries or run-in subentries. Selecting the Nested option (the default setting) causes Word to put each subentry on a new line under the main entry while indenting the subentry 0.25 inch from the previous entry. The sample index you have just compiled uses the nested format. Selecting the Run-in option causes Word to list subentries one after another on the same line while inserting a comma between the subentry and its page number(s) and a semicolon between one subentry and another. Figure 18.6 shows how the index for the El Niño document looks if you select Run-in instead of accepting the default Nested option.

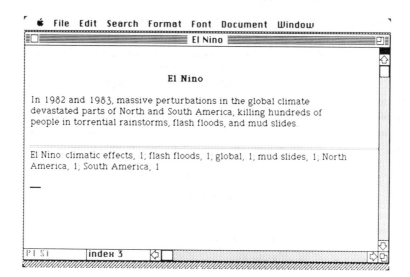

Fig. 18.6

The index compiled with the Run-in *option selected.*

Before compiling the index, Word checks to see whether an index already exists. If you previously have created an index for this document, the program displays an alert box that asks if you want to replace the existing index with the new one. You click Yes to replace an existing index or No to append the new index to the document and retain the existing index.

After compiling the index, you can move it elsewhere in your document by selecting and cutting and pasting the index, just as you would any other text. If you later choose the Index command and specify that the new index should replace the existing one, Word updates the index in its current location. If you specify that the new index should not replace the existing one, Word tacks the new index onto the end of the document, leaving the existing index wherever you have moved it.

If one or more of your entries is missing from the index, check to make sure you correctly used the beginning and ending codes. Did you leave a space after the second period? Does the entry have an ending code? Did you use hidden text?

Compiling Indexes for Linked Documents

To create an index for a series of linked documents, you must first mark all the entries in all the documents, just as you would when indexing a single document. As you work with each document, choose Page Setup from the File menu and check that the name of the next document appears in the Next File box and that the Start Page Numbers at box is blank for all documents except the first. Then when Word compiles the index, this precaution ensures that the program handles the documents in the correct order and that the page numbers are consecutive across documents.

To compile the index for a series of documents, do the following:

1. Open the first document in the series or, if the document already is open, make sure its window is active.

2. Choose **Index** from the Document menu.

3. Select **Nested** or **Run-in**.

4. Click **Start**.

Word automatically collects the marked entries from each document, adds page numbers, alphabetizes the entries, and inserts the index at the end of the last document.

You can move the index elsewhere in the series by using standard cut-and-paste methods. If you later re-index the series of documents, Word automatically replaces the index in its new location.

Formatting Index Entries

Most words you mark as index entries will be lowercase, and, unfortunately, Word provides no quick way to capitalize the first letter of main entries. You manually can capitalize the first letters as part of the editing process, or you can insert the entry word with an initial capital letter (formatted as hidden text) in front of the index entry itself. For example, adding *.i.Global* in hidden text in front of the word *global* tells Word to list the entry as *Global* rather than *global* in the index.

Most of the formatting you apply to index entries can be done more automatically, however. You can apply different character or paragraph formats in the usual way by choosing Character or Paragraph from the

Format menu and selecting the options you want. For example, if you wanted to make *El Niño* italic to reflect its foreign origin, you could format the words with the italic style once the index was compiled.

Changing Formatting by Changing a Style Sheet

Word's default style sheet includes seven automatic styles for index entries: Index 1 through Index 7. As you mark index entries in a document, Word adds the default style for that level of entry to your document's style sheet. The program determines the entry's correct level from its punctuation.

For example, Word applies the default Index-1 style to entries bracketed only by beginning and ending codes (*.i.* and a semicolon, end-of-line, or paragraph mark) and prints these entries flush with the left margin. When Word encounters a colon within the coding for an entry, the program automatically assigns the default style for the appropriate level, depending on the number of colons. For example, Word would assign the Index-3 style to the entry *.i.Ships:sailing:Golden Hind;* because the entry's coding has two colons.

When you select the Nested option in the Index dialog box, each level below Index 1 is indented 0.25 inch from the previous level. Thus, Index 2 is indented 0.25 inch from the left margin; Index 3 is indented 0.5 inch; and so on.

You easily can change index formatting by changing the entries in Word's default style sheet. By default, the program formats Index 1 through Index 7 as normal text. You can change the text style for any index level, however, by choosing Define Styles from the Format menu and defining new formats. For example, if you want to make all main entries italic, you would choose Define Styles (see Chapter 9) and change the character format for Index 1 from normal to italic.

Changing the Formatting of Page Numbers

Another way to customize an index's appearance is to make the page numbers bold or italic. You might, for example, want to make all main-entry page numbers stand out by formatting them differently from sub-entry page numbers.

To make index page numbers bold or italic, do the following:

1. Click an insertion point in front of the entry you are indexing.

2. Instead of typing the usual beginning code (*.i.*), type a hidden *.ib.* or *.iB.* if you want the page numbers to be bold or type a hidden *.ii.* or *.iI.* if you want them to be italic.

3. Follow the index entry with a hidden semicolon if necessary.

Of course, you will want to store these beginning codes in the glossary if you anticipate using bold or italic page numbers frequently.

Most computer-generated indexes require considerable editing. Often, the logic of some entries may not be apparent when you see them in the index rather than in context. To overcome any shortcomings, you can edit an index just as you would any other document. Remember, you lose any changes you have made if, later, you change your document and use the Index command again; therefore, wait until your document is in its final form and then alter your index.

Sometimes, books are judged by the quality of their indexes, and when producing any long document, you would be wise to give some thought ahead of time to the kind of index that would be most useful to your readers. The discussion in this chapter necessarily has taken a simple approach to what can be a very complex topic.

If you are unfamiliar with indexing conventions, we suggest you consult a good style manual, such as *The Chicago Manual of Style*, before creating your first index. Because computer-generated indexes are relatively new, however, even the most recent edition of *The Chicago Manual of Style* recommends using index cards or slips of paper to create an index. You don't need these paper items if you use Word's indexing feature. The examples in the manual of how to classify and cross-reference information are nevertheless relevant to electronic indexing and are often helpful guides for deciding what to include and how to organize the entries.

Creating a Table
of Contents

Usually, a table of contents appears at the beginning of a document and is a simple list of headings, subheadings, and page numbers. Creating a table of contents manually isn't a particularly difficult task, but the process can be tedious, taking up time most of us would rather spend in other endeavors.

With Word, Version 3, you now can compile and update a table of contents automatically, using the Document menu's Table of Contents command. Word offers two methods for compiling a table of contents. If you have created an outline for a document, you can have Word compile a table of contents from the outline's headings and subheadings. Otherwise, you can mark the entries you want to appear in the table of contents with codes similar to those you use for indexing. You then can have Word compile the table from the coded entries.

Regardless of the method you use, Word adds page numbers to the entries and inserts the table of contents as a separate section at the beginning of the document.

Just as with indexes, you can compile a table of contents for a series of linked documents. Word searches through each document in succession and, depending on the method you have selected, compiles the table of contents from either outline headings (if all the documents have been outlined) or coded entries. You have to select one method or the other for all the documents; you cannot compile a single table of contents for linked documents if some documents have outline headings and others have coded entries.

Creating a table of contents is similar to creating an index. We do not repeat in this chapter the information we discussed in detail in the previous chapter; therefore, if you have read Chapter 18, you have a head start in honing the skills you need to create informative tables of contents for your documents.

Using Outline Headings

If you have outlined a document by using the Document menu's Outlining command (see Chapter 17), then converting the outline to a table of contents is simple.

Before compiling a table of contents, be sure to conceal any hidden text in the document by toggling off the Show Hidden Text option in the Preferences dialog box. You don't want Word to include hidden text when calculating page breaks because the extra text can cause the page numbers to be inaccurate. After you have compiled the table of contents, you can redisplay the hidden text.

To use an existing outline to compile a table of contents with page numbers, do the following:

1. Choose **Table of Contents** from the Document menu.

Word displays the dialog box shown in figure 19.1.

Fig. 19.1

*The Table of
Contents dialog
box.*

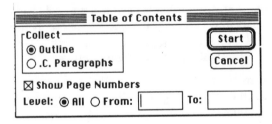

2. Accept the default **Outline** option.

3. Accept the default **Show Page Numbers** option.

You can click this option to deselect it if you prefer not to include page numbers.

4. If you don't want all the heading levels to be included in the table of contents, click the **From** button and type the levels you want in the From and To boxes.

For example, you might type *1* in the From box and *3* in the To box to include first-, second-, and third-level headings in the table of contents.

5. Click **Start**.

Word compiles the table, adds page numbers, inserts dot leader characters between the entries and the numbers, and inserts the table at the beginning of the document, with a section break after the table (see fig. 19.2).

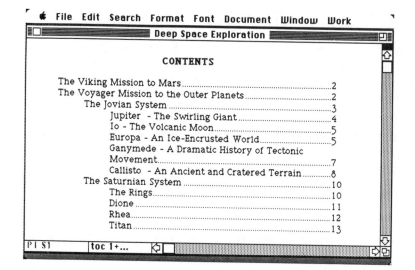

Fig. 19.2

A table of contents compiled from an outline.

As you can see in figure 19.2, each table entry begins on a new line, and dot leader characters separate the heading from the associated page number. If you have chosen Show ¶, you see a paragraph mark ending each entry. Because the table is in a separate section, you can change the table's page-layout and page-numbering systems independently of the rest of the document.

You also can edit the table of contents as you would any other text. However, if you later recompile the table, Word cannot include your changes. You will have to edit the individual entries and their page numbers all over again.

Once you have compiled a table of contents for a particular document, choosing Table of Contents again causes Word to display a dialog box asking whether you want to replace the existing table. Clicking Yes updates the table, and clicking No inserts the new table of contents at the beginning of the document, preceding the existing one.

The only way to merge a new table of contents with an old one is manually. For example, if you have compiled one version from an outline and another from coded entries, you might want to combine them to produce a comprehensive table. However, think twice before you manually combine tables of contents or do extensive editing. All your work will be wasted if, later, you have to update the table.

Using Coded Entries

Suppose that you want to create a table of contents for a document that has not been outlined. You need to insert special beginning and ending codes around each of the entries you want to include in the table, in much the same way as you mark index entries. And, as with index entries, you format the codes as hidden text.

Because you have to use hidden text repeatedly when you create table of contents entries, you may want to add the Hidden option from the Character dialog box to the Format menu.

To add the Hidden option to the Format menu, do the following:

1. Press **Command-Option-+**.

Use the + at the top of the main keyboard, not the one from the numeric keypad (but do not press Shift).

2. Choose **Character** from the Format menu.

3. Click **Hidden** in the Character dialog box.

4. Click **OK** to close the Character dialog box.

The Hidden style appears at the bottom of the Format menu, and you now can choose Hidden whenever you want to create hidden text.

To designate a table of contents entry, precede the entry with *.c.* or *.c1.* if the entry is a main entry, *.c2.* if the entry is a subentry, and so on, up to *.c9.* for ninth-level entries. You follow the entry with either a semicolon, an end-of-line mark (Shift-Return), or a paragraph mark. Use the semicolon if the entry does not end the line or paragraph. You always must format the beginning code as hidden text. You need to hide ending semicolons only if you don't want Word to print them.

Before you start marking table of contents entries, make sure that the Show Hidden Text option is turned on in the Preferences dialog box so that you can see the formatted entry codes. Before compiling the table, you need to turn off the option again. Otherwise, Word includes the hidden text when the program calculates page breaks.

To mark the beginning and end of a main table of contents entry, do the following:

1. Click an insertion point in front of the first word of the entry.

2. Choose **Hidden** from the Format menu or press **Command-Shift-X**.

3. Type **.c1.** (Don't insert a space after the second period.)

4. If an end-of-line or paragraph mark does not immediately follow the word or words to be indexed, click an insertion point at the end of the index entry and insert a semicolon.

5. If you inserted a semicolon, select it and choose **Hidden** from the Format menu.

Repeat this process for each entry, substituting appropriate subentry beginning codes (*.c2.*, *.c3.*, and so on) for *.c1.* when appropriate. If you want to insert the same code a number of times in succession, insert the code once and then press Command-A (Word's repeat key) after clicking an insertion point wherever you want that same code to appear.

As when you're indexing, you can speed up coding by making glossary entries of the table of contents codes. Then, rather than typing the codes each time and formatting them as hidden text, you quickly can insert the codes from the glossary wherever needed. (See the section titled "Using the Glossary To Mark Index Entries" in Chapter 18 for details.)

If you want to create a table of contents entry from text that does not actually appear in the document, choose the appropriate location and insert the entry in hidden text, bracketed by hidden beginning and ending codes. Figure 19.3 shows the coding for two entries for a table of contents similar to the one in figure 19.2. The first coded entry does not actually appear in the text.

When you finish coding your table of contents entries, you are ready to compile the table.

Fig. 19.3

*The coding for
two table of
contents entries.*

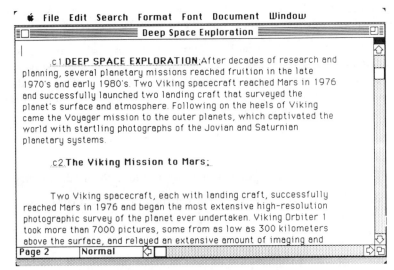

To compile a table of contents with page numbers from marked entries, do the following:

1. Choose **Table of Contents** from the Document menu.

Word displays the Table of Contents dialog box.

2. Click the **.C. Paragraphs** button in the `Collect` section to tell Word you are using codes to mark the entries.

3. Accept the default **Show Page Numbers** option.

You can click this option to deselect it if you prefer not to include page numbers.

4. Click **Start**.

Word may take a few minutes to compile the table, especially if the document is long or you are working with a series of linked documents. When the program has finished, the table of contents looks like figure 19.4. Notice that the first entry is the one inserted entirely in hidden text in figure 19.3.

Word inserts the paginated table of contents at the beginning of the document or at the beginning of the first document in a series of linked documents. You now have the same editing options as you have with tables of contents compiled from outlines—and the same cautions apply.

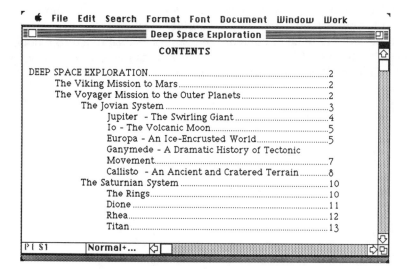

Fig. 19.4

A table of contents compiled from coded entries.

Window contents:

```
 File  Edit  Search  Format  Font  Document  Window  Work
```

Deep Space Exploration

CONTENTS

P 1 S 1   Normal+...

Formatting Tables of Contents

Word applies an automatic style from the default style sheet to each level of entry in the table of contents. These styles, called toc 1 through toc 9, are formatted as normal text. Each level is indented 0.5 inch more than the previous level. The toc 1 style is flush-left; toc 2 is indented 0.5 inch; toc 3 is indented 1 inch; and so on. The styles also include a left-aligned tab stop at 5.75 inches and a right-aligned tab at 6.0 inches.

You can change the format of any of the table of contents entries by applying character or paragraph formatting directly to the text or by redefining the automatic styles in the Define Styles dialog box. For example, if you want main entries to appear in bold capital letters, you can redefine toc 1 to include this character formatting. If you want to redefine one of Word's automatic table of contents styles for all subsequent documents, click the Set Default button after choosing the desired character and paragraph formats. (See Chapter 9 for more information about changing styles.)

As we said at the beginning of the chapter, creating a table of contents manually is not a particularly difficult task, but it is a tedious one. Because making a "road map" for your documents is easy with Word, however, you probably will be more likely to consider creating a table of contents. Like an index, a table of contents adds a professional touch to a document by giving readers an overview of the information you are presenting and directing them to items of specific interest.

Creating Footnotes

Our perspective on footnotes often depends on whether we are reading them or writing them. To an inquisitive reader, footnotes can be a wonderful surprise—a windfall of information uncovered by someone else. Sometimes, reading expansive footnotes can be like listening to a good debate—the main text presenting one point of view and the footnotes the other. At other times, however, footnotes can seem more trouble than they're worth. Probably only a few of us take the time to read footnotes in foreign languages, for example, and ignore references in Serbo-Croatian even though the references may establish the authenticity of the research or its conclusions.

From the writer's perspective, rounding up or keeping track of footnotes tends to be about as rewarding as shepherding a flock of frightened sheep for their annual shearing. In the constant jostling, one or two critters always dart away, threatening to take the rest of the group with them. Losing track of one or two footnotes has the potential for similar confusion—you can sometimes spend hours trying to figure out which footnote goes with which reference in the text.

As we create larger and more complex documents, the process of creating, positioning, and keeping track of footnotes becomes correspondingly more complex. For one thing, footnote styles vary greatly, and each academic discipline or professional field tends to prefer the use of one style over another. Sometimes, footnote references have to be specific symbols, and the footnotes themselves have to appear at the bottom of the same page as the reference. At other times, footnote references have to be numbers, and the text of the footnotes has to appear at the end of the document. Is it any wonder that, unless we are part of the worlds of academic treatises and government reports, many of us avoid using footnotes altogether?

Now, Word makes the entire footnote process manageable. With Word, you can create footnotes and mark their associated footnote references as you type your document or after you have finished typing it. You can specify a footnote reference symbol or allow the program to number automatically the footnote references, starting with number *1*.

To accommodate the range of footnote styles you may need to use, Word provides a wide variety of footnote formats from which to choose. Three automatic footnote sequencing schemes number footnotes by page, by section, or with one continuous sequence throughout a document. All you need to do is specify the starting footnote number and the numbering scheme in the document's Page Setup dialog box. The Page Setup dialog box also gives you control over where a footnote is printed: on the page containing the footnote reference or at the end of a section. Word automatically maintains the correct sequence even if you move, add, or delete footnotes.

Because Word facilitates the positioning, editing, and moving of footnotes, those of you who have shied away from footnotes may reconsider using them to add weight to your arguments. To get you started, this chapter shows you how to create footnotes quickly and how to revise them as you change a document. Then we demonstrate some of the finer points of formatting footnotes so that you can give your footnotes a professional look.

Inserting Footnotes

Word makes inserting footnotes into a document a much more streamlined process than ever before. In fact, the only things the program cannot do for you are write the footnote text and insert the footnote references in their correct locations in the document. To show you that using footnotes is easy, we're going to add footnotes to the sample document shown in figure 20.1. You can type this document and follow along with the exercises, or you can practice with a document of your own.

To add footnotes to a document, do the following:

1. Click an insertion point in the place where you want to add the first footnote reference mark.

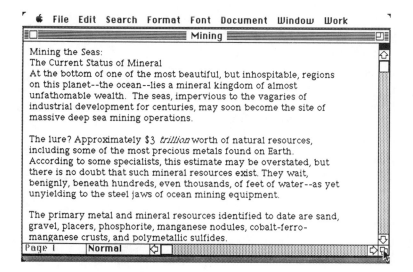

Fig. 20.1

*The sample
document
before inserting
footnotes.*

In the sample document, click an insertion point after the period following the word *Earth* in the second paragraph.

2. Choose **Footnote** from the Document menu or press **Command-E**.

Word displays the dialog box shown in figure 20.2.

Fig. 20.2

*The Footnote
dialog box.*

3. Click **OK** or press **Return**, to leave the Auto-numbered Reference option checked.

Word splits the document window. Recall that when you split the window by dragging the split bar down, each window contains a copy of the document on which you are working. In this case, the upper window displays the document and the lower window displays the footnote area. The number *1*—the first footnote reference—is currently in the footnote window, which is active (see fig. 20.3).

Fig. 20.3

The split window with the document text above and the footnote area below.

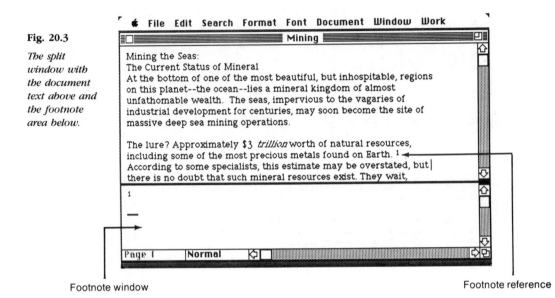

Footnote window   Footnote reference

4. Type the text of the footnote.

If you're working with the sample document, type *Insight, April 7, 1986.* This footnote is the source for the *$3 trillion* statistic.

5. Press **0** on the numeric keypad, press **Command-Option-Z**, or simply click in the document window to return to the document.

6. Repeat Steps 1 through 5 a few times to add more footnotes.

For this example, randomly pick two places in which to insert two more footnote references. Notice how Word automatically numbers the footnote references sequentially.

7. When you have finished adding footnotes, close the footnote window by dragging the split bar either back to the top of the window or below the bottom of the window.

You also can toggle the footnote window open and closed by pressing Shift-Command-Option-S.

Now that you have had an overview of the footnote process, take a closer look at the Footnote dialog box.

Examining the Footnote Dialog Box

The Footnote dialog box (see fig. 20.2) allows you to select both the mark that Word inserts into the text as the footnote reference and the line or other *separator* that the program uses to set off the footnotes from the main text of the document.

Selecting Reference Marks

The easiest method for inserting footnote references is to let Word automatically insert them. If you accept the default Auto-numbered Reference setting, Word automatically inserts a sequential, superscripted arabic number (starting with *1*) at the current insertion point. If you prefer to use a symbol (an asterisk, for example) as a reference mark, type that symbol in the Footnote Reference Mark box. This box, which accommodates up to 10 characters, gives you a great deal of flexibility in designing reference marks. Supplying your own reference mark automatically deselects the Auto-numbered Reference option.

NOTE: In some scientific fields, writers identify sources within the text with author/date citations that reference an alphabetic list at the end of the document. These citations aren't footnote references per se because the actual sources are not listed sequentially. To use this type of reference, you have to type the citations as regular text instead of using the Footnote command.

Selecting Footnote Separators

The Footnote Separators area at the bottom of the Footnote dialog box contains three buttons that define how Word separates the footnotes from the text. Unless you specify otherwise, Word draws a 2-inch line below the main body of text on a page; the line separates the text from the first footnote. If a footnote extends beyond the bottom of the first page and carries over to the next page, Word draws an 8-inch continuation separator on the second page and gives you the option of inserting a continuation notice at the bottom of the first page.

Clicking one of the three Footnote Separators buttons produces a window similar to that used for headers and footers. Figure 20.4 shows the window displayed when you click Separator.

Fig. 20.4

*The Footnote
Separator
window in
which you can
design a line to
separate
footnotes from
the text.*

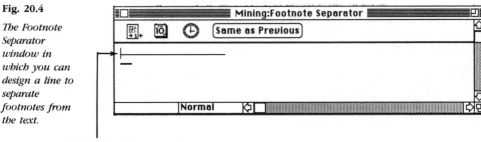

Default footnote separator

The windows for the three buttons are similar; only the title and the default entry in the text area differ. Otherwise, the windows all include dynamic page number, date, and time icons and a Same as Previous button. The Same as Previous button restores the separator to the default 2-inch line or to the style used in the previous footnote (if that style is not the default). This button is selectable only when the default separator style is not in effect.

When you click Separator, the entry in the text area of the Footnote Separator window is the default separator, a 2-inch line. You can change the separator to a line composed of other characters, such as dashes or asterisks, or you can enter any combination of text and graphics. Whatever you enter in the window is used to separate footnotes from the text.

When you click Cont. (Continuation) Separator, the entry in the text area is the default 8-inch line used when the text of a footnote runs to the next page. As with the normal separator, you can make this line practically anything you like.

You click Cont. (Continuation) Notice when you want to add a note, such as *continued* or *see next page*, at the end of the first page of a footnote that is longer than the page. You probably will not use the Cont. Separator or Cont. Notice options much, because footnotes seldom run over to the next page.

Figure 20.5 shows three footnotes for the sample document as they appear in the Page Preview window. Currently, the default 2-inch separator is in effect. For practice, you are going to change the style of the separator.

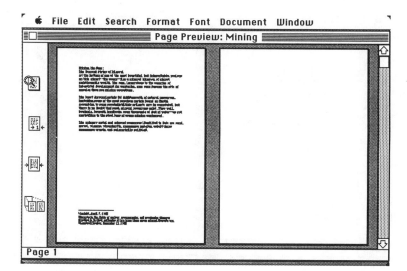

Fig. 20.5

*The sample
document, with
footnotes, in the
Page Preview
window.*

To change the separator, do the following:

1. Choose **Footnote** from the Document menu or press **Command-E**.

2. Click **Separator**.

3. Double-click the default separator to select it.

The 2-inch separator is highlighted.

4. Type whatever characters you want for the new separator.

In this case, type about 20 asterisks. The highlighted original separator disappears as soon as you enter the new characters. You also can include the date, time, and page number icons in the separator.

5. Click the Separator window's close box.

6. To see the effect of your change, choose **Page Preview** from the File menu.

Figure 20.6 shows the new separator in the Page Preview window.

7. Repeat the process until the separator looks the way you want it.

If you decide you like the default footnote separator better than your modified version, you can return to the default by clicking Separator

Fig. 20.6

The sample document after you have changed the footnote separator.

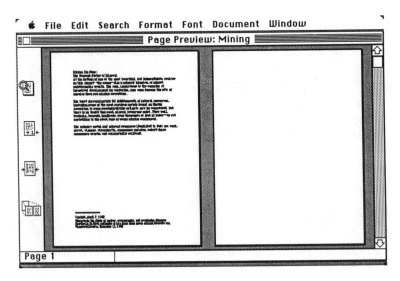

in the Footnote dialog box and then clicking the `Same as Previous` button in the Footnote Separator window.

You can use these same techniques to modify the settings in `Cont. Separator` and `Cont. Notice`. You also can apply character and paragraph formatting to the separators and the continuation notice.

Reorganizing Footnoted Text

We seldom start a report, article, or research paper at the beginning and proceed, in an orderly fashion, right through to the end. Usually, we first write the section we know the best and add new sections as we gather the relevant information. Often, we wait until everything else is done before writing the introduction. This process can involve hours of ordering and reordering the text and its attendant footnote references as well as keeping track of which footnote belongs to which reference.

Provided you have created footnotes with the `Auto-numbered Reference` option checked, Word greatly simplifies this ordering process by automatically renumbering footnotes and their references whenever you rearrange your text. You can move and edit footnotes as effortlessly as you move or edit any other part of the text. As you add footnotes and move or delete sections of text containing footnote references, Word renumbers the footnotes so that they remain sequential.

To see Word in action, select the entire sample document and copy the text several times beneath the original copy. As you paste in each copy, Word renumbers the footnotes in the copy to continue the sequence of those in the text above.

Deleting Footnotes

To remove a footnote, simply delete the footnote reference from the document's text. Word deletes the corresponding footnote from the footnote window. If you try to delete the footnote directly from the window rather than deleting the footnote reference from the text, Word displays the warning in figure 20.7.

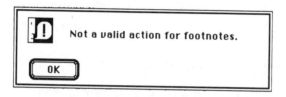

Fig. 20.7

The alert box displayed when you try to delete a footnote from the footnote window.

Try deleting one of the footnotes from the sample document to see just how easy the process is. You don't have to open the footnote window to delete a footnote, but if you open the window now, you can watch the footnote disappear.

Do the following to delete a footnote from your document:

1. In the text of your document, select the footnote reference for the footnote you want to delete.

If you double-click the footnote reference to select it, Word also selects any following punctuation mark and space. To avoid selecting these extra characters, drag through the footnote reference.

2. Choose **Cut** from the Edit menu or press **Command-X**.

Word deletes the footnote reference and its footnote and instantly re-numbers the references and footnotes that follow the deleted ones.

NOTE: If you don't want to insert the footnote elsewhere, simply select the footnote reference and press the Backspace key instead of choosing Cut.

Moving Footnote References

Moving a footnote reference so that its footnote applies to a different part of the text is a simple matter of cut and paste.

To move a footnote reference, do the following:

1. Select the footnote reference you want to move.

2. Choose **Cut** from the Edit menu or press **Command-X**.

3. Click an insertion point after the text to which you want to attach the footnote.

4. Choose **Paste** from the Edit menu or press **Command-V**.

When you paste the footnote reference back into the text, Word renumbers that reference and all the other references that have been affected by the move.

Duplicating Footnotes

If you copy rather than cut a footnote reference, Word renumbers the reference when you paste it back in the text and duplicates the footnote with its new number in the footnote window. If you know you are going to use the same footnote in several places, you might want to make the footnote a glossary entry so that you can insert the footnote quickly wherever you need it, rather than having to search the text for the reference each time you need it.

To store a footnote in the glossary, do the following:

1. Select the footnote reference in the document.

In this case, select a footnote reference corresponding to the *Insight, April 7, 1986* footnote you created earlier.

2. Choose **Glossary** from the Edit menu or press **Command-K**.

3. Type a name for the footnote.

For this example, type *In*.

4. Click **Define**.

The program inserts the name of the footnote in the Glossary (see fig. 20.8).

5. Close the Glossary dialog box by clicking its close box.

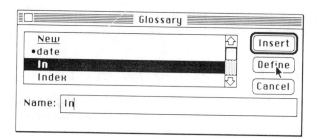

Fig. 20.8

*The Glossary
dialog box after
you have
defined a
footnote as a
glossary entry.*

To insert a footnote from the glossary, do the following:

1. Click an insertion point in the text where you want the footnote reference to appear.

2. Press **Command-Backspace**.

The word Name appears in the page number area in the lower left corner of the window.

3. Type the name you assigned to the footnote and press **Return**.

In this case, type *In*.

If you insert the footnote into a document that has the same numbering scheme as the document from which the glossary entry was created, Word integrates the footnote into the receiving document's numbering sequence. However, if you insert the footnote into a document that uses a different scheme, the original footnote number, letter, or symbol is retained, and you have to change it manually.

Formatting Footnotes

As you have seen in previous chapters, Word gives you a great deal of control over the appearance of text. However, the program usually doesn't force you to take control. With most formatting options, Word implements a default selection if you take no action. The formatting of footnotes is no exception.

Word has built-in styles for both footnote references and footnotes. By default, references are 9-point, superscripted numbers; and the footnote text is 10-point. Two methods are available for changing these default styles: you can apply character or paragraph formatting to individual footnotes, or you can modify the styles in the current document's style sheet to change all footnotes automatically. If you choose to modify the style sheet, you have the additional option of applying the new styles only to the current document or of making them the default styles for references and footnotes in all future documents.

Applying Formatting Directly

You can apply any of Word's character and paragraph formatting to footnotes by using the same techniques you would use with any other text. Although you obviously cannot apply paragraph formatting to footnote *references*, you can apply character formatting to them.

To change the character format of text in a footnote, do the following:

1. Press **Shift-Command-Option-S** to open the Footnote window if it is not already open.

2. Select the text to be formatted.

For this example, select the word *Insight* from the sample footnote.

3. Choose **Character** from the Format menu or press **Command-D**.

4. Click the options you want to apply to the selected text.

In this case, click the Italic box in the Character Formats area.

5. Click **OK** or press **Return**, to apply the formatting and close the Character dialog box.

Figure 20.9 shows the *Insight* footnote with its new formatting.

You follow a similar procedure to change a footnote's paragraph formatting by choosing Paragraph instead of Character from the Format menu.

Altering Footnote Styles

When you create a footnote, Word automatically adds default footnote reference and footnote styles to your document's style sheet. To take a quick look at these styles, do the following:

1. Choose **Styles** from the Format menu.

The dialog box in figure 20.10 appears, displaying the three styles used in the sample document—footnote reference, footnote text, and Normal—listed in alphabetic order. The style for the text element that contains the insertion point has a check mark next to the style, and the style's description appears at the bottom of the dialog box.

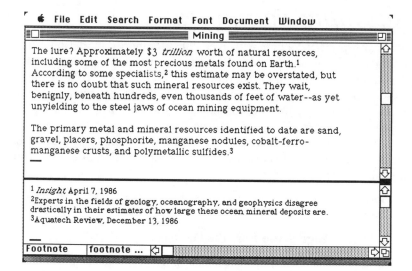

Fig. 20.9

The Insight *footnote with italic character formatting.*

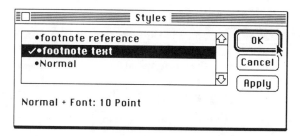

Fig. 20.10

The Styles dialog box for the sample document.

2. Click **footnote reference**.

A description of this style now appears at the bottom of the dialog box.

3. Click **footnote text** and **Normal**, to see their style descriptions.

4. Click **Cancel** to close the Styles dialog box.

You can change the style for footnotes and footnote references by choosing Define Styles from the Format menu and assigning new styles. For example, if you wanted to make all footnotes italic, you would choose Define Styles and change the character format for footnote text from normal to italic (see Chapter 9 for more information).

Positioning Footnotes

When you print a document that contains footnotes, by default Word automatically places each footnote at the bottom of the page containing the corresponding footnote reference. However, you can control where Word prints footnotes by changing settings in the Page Setup dialog box. As an alternative to printing footnotes at the bottom of the page on which their references appear, you can print them directly beneath the last line of text on the page, at the end of the section, or at the end of the document. Footnotes printed at the end of a section or a document are called *endnotes*.

To position footnotes beneath the last line of text on a page, do the following:

1. Choose **Page Setup** from the File menu.

Word displays the dialog box shown in figure 20.11. In the bottom half of the dialog box is a Footnotes at setting with three options: Bottom of Page, Beneath Text, and Endnotes. Bottom of Page is the default setting. Note that you also can specify the starting number for footnotes in this dialog box.

Fig. 20.11

The Page Setup dialog box.

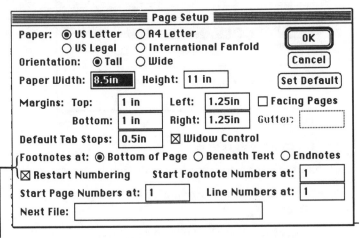

Footnote options

2. Click the **Beneath Text** button.

3. Click **OK** or press **Return**.

The Beneath Text option is useful when footnotes will be printed on a page not full of text—such as the last page of a section of a report. The footnotes will appear immediately below the last line of text instead of at the bottom of the page.

To position footnotes at the end of each section (or at the end of a single-section document), do the following:

1. Choose **Page Setup** from the File menu.

2. Click the **Endnotes** button.

3. Click **OK** or press **Return**.

Word automatically selects the Include Endnotes option in the Section dialog box. (You can verify this by choosing Section from the Format menu.)

The program now will print all footnotes referenced in each section at the end of that section.

If your document contains more than one section and you want to position footnotes at the end of the entire document, do the following:

1. Choose **Page Setup** from the File menu.

2. Click the **Endnotes** button.

3. Click **OK** or press **Return**.

4. For all but the last section in the document, deselect the **Include Endnotes** option in the Section dialog box.

Word now will print the footnotes for each section at the end of the section for which the Include Endnotes option still is selected.

Beneath Word's deceptively simple exterior lurks a powerful word processor, ready to respond to your every need. As you have learned, you can create simple documents without tapping this extra power—just as you can drive a Ferrari to the corner market to pick up a loaf of bread and a dozen eggs. But if you believe in pushing a performance machine to its limits, then you will want to delve deeper into Word's capabilities.

With a little imagination and practice, you soon will be producing polished work rivaling that of publishing professionals.

A

Using the Apple Extended Keyboard

The standard keyboard for the Macintosh II and Macintosh SE personal computers consists of a typewriter-style layout, a numeric keypad, and cursor keys. A variation of this standard keyboard has what some people call a Cyclops key above the top row of number keys. If you are using version 4.1 of the Macintosh operating system, this Cyclops key powers your computer on and off.

The Apple Extended Keyboard is an alternative keyboard for Macintosh II or Macintosh SE computers. The Extended Keyboard has 15 function keys, a numeric keypad, four cursor-movement keys arranged in a T-style layout, and six cursor-control keys. This keyboard, shown in figure A.1, is ideal for use with complex programs, such as Microsoft Word, that take advantage of function-key shortcuts to speed operations and cut down on file-handling time.

Table A.1 lists the ways that Microsoft Word, Version 3, takes advantage of the additional keys on the Extended Keyboard. Versions of the program above level 3 may add even more capabilities.

Fig. A.1

The Apple
Extended
Keyboard

Table A.1
Word's Function-Key Support for the Apple Extended Keyboard

Function Key	Support
F1-F2	Not yet supported
F6	Moves the selection directly to a destination, bypassing the Clipboard (Command-Option-X)
F7	Copies the selection directly to a destination, bypassing the Clipboard (Command-Option-C)
F8	Copies the formats of the selection directly to a destination (Command-Option-V)
F9-F10	Not yet supported
F11	Scrolls up one line without moving the insertion point (Command-Option-[)
F12	Scrolls down one line without moving the insertion point (Command-Option-/)
F13-F15	Not yet supported
ESC	Exits the current function (Command-.)
HELP	Accesses quick information (Comand-?)
DEL	Deletes the character to the right of the insertion point (Command-Option-F)
HOME	Moves the insertion point after the last character at the end of the document (Command-3 on keypad)
PAGE UP	Moves the insertion point up one screen (9 on keypad)
PAGE DOWN	Moves the insertion point down one screen (3 on keypad)

INDEX

D

E

I

J-K

N

T

More Computer Knowledge from Que

SELECT QUE BOOKS TO INCREASE
YOUR PERSONAL COMPUTER PRODUCTIVITY

Using Dollars and Sense

by John Hannah

Written for users of Apple II and Macintosh computers, *Using Dollars and Sense* helps you gain effective use of the popular financial management program. This book shows you how to track your accounts, determine your net worth, and estimate your tax liability at any time of the year. Hands-on hints and examples of business applications will help you better use Dollars and Sense to manage your personal and business finances. Get the maximum return on your software investment with *Using Dollars and Sense*!

Excel Macro Library

by Mary Campbell

Extend the capabilities of Excel on your Macintosh with Que's *Excel Macro Library*. This book shows you how powerful macros can simplify tedious tasks by assigning several commands to a few simple keystrokes. Use this book's library of practical, ready-to-use macros in your Excel spreadsheets, or learn to create customized macros that meet your specialized needs. Use the *Excel Macro Library* to master the techniques for creating efficient, timesaving macros. Companion software, containing the macros discussed in this book, is also available.

Using Excel

by Mary Campbell

A comprehensive reference, *Using Excel* offers a thorough examination of Microsoft's powerful Macintosh spreadsheet. This book presents the features of Excel in a logical manner with clear, easy-to-understand examples. You will learn how to navigate through the Excel worksheet, use windows, set up a database, create graphs, and develop timesaving macros. Methods of transferring information between Excel and other programs are also discussed. Use Que's *Using Excel* to progress from simple program installation to advanced application design.

Using Microsoft Works

by Ronald Mansfield

Microsoft Works is the program for the Macintosh that combines word processing, database, spreadsheet, and communications into one easy-to-use package. *Using Microsoft Works* is the book that makes Works easy to learn and easier to use. Combining Quick Start tutorials with more advanced tips and techniques, *Using Microsoft Works* shows you both basic and advanced features of each of Works' four applications. After you've conquered the individual modules, you'll learn how to copy and merge data between applications, and how to exchange information with other products. Whether you are a Works novice or an experienced Works user, *Using Microsoft Works* is the book for you!

REGISTRATION CARD

Register your copy of *Using Microsoft Word: Macintosh Version* and receive information about Que's newest products. Complete this registration card and return it to Que Corporation, P.O. Box 90, Carmel, IN 46032.

Name _____ Phone _____

Company _____ Title _____

Address _____

City _____ ST _____ ZIP _____

Please check the appropriate answers:

Where did you buy *Using Microsoft Word: Macintosh Version*?
- ☐ Bookstore (name: _____)
- ☐ Computer store (name: _____)
- ☐ Catalog (name: _____)
- ☐ Direct from Que
- ☐ Other: _____

How many computer books do you buy a year?
- ☐ 1 or less
- ☐ 2–5
- ☐ 6–10
- ☐ More than 10

How many Que books do you own?
- ☐ 1
- ☐ 2–5
- ☐ 6–10
- ☐ More than 10

How long have you been using Microsoft Word?
- ☐ Less than six months
- ☐ Six months to one year
- ☐ 1-3 years
- ☐ More than 3 years

What influenced your purchase of *Using Microsoft Word: Macintosh Version*?
- ☐ Personal recommendation
- ☐ Advertisement
- ☐ In-store display
- ☐ Price
- ☐ Que catalog
- ☐ Que postcard
- ☐ Que's reputation
- ☐ Other: _____

How would you rate the overall content of *Using Microsoft Word: Macintosh Version*?
- ☐ Very good
- ☐ Good
- ☐ Not useful
- ☐ Poor

How would you rate the *command reference chart*?
- ☐ Very good
- ☐ Good
- ☐ Not useful
- ☐ Poor

How would you rate *Part II: Adding to Your Repertoire*?
- ☐ Very good
- ☐ Good
- ☐ Not useful
- ☐ Poor

How would you rate *Part III: Using Advanced Features for Long Documents*?
- ☐ Very good
- ☐ Good
- ☐ Not useful
- ☐ Poor

What do you like *best* about *Using Microsoft Word: Macintosh Version*?

What do you like *least* about *Using Microsoft Word: Macintosh Version*?

How do you use *Using Microsoft Word: Macintosh Version*?

What other Que products do you own?

What other software do you own?

Please feel free to list any other comments you may have about *Using Microsoft Word: Macintosh Version*.

_____

_____

_____

_____

_____

FOLD HERE

Place
Stamp
Here

Que Corporation
P.O. Box 90
Carmel, IN 46032

ORDER FROM QUE TODAY

Item	Title	Price	Quantity	Extension
185	Excel Macro Library	$19.95		
182	Using Dollars and Sense	16.95		
198	Using Excel	19.95		
106	Using Microsoft Works	18.95		

Book Subtotal	
Shipping & Handling ($2.50 per item)	
Indiana Residents Add 5% Sales Tax	
GRAND TOTAL	

Method of Payment:

☐ Check   ☐ VISA   ☐ MasterCard   ☐ American Express

Card Number _____ Exp. Date _____

Cardholder's Name _____

Ship to _____

Address _____

City _____ State _____ ZIP _____

If you can't wait, call **1-800-428-5331**, ext. 888 and order TODAY.

All prices subject to change without notice.

FOLD HERE

_____

_____

_____

_____

Place
Stamp
Here

Que Corporation
P.O. Box 90
Carmel, IN 46032

Here's a tiny sample of the kinds of articles you'll read in every issue of *Absolute Reference*:

Discover the incredible power of macros—shortcuts for hundreds of applications and subroutines.

- A macro for formatting text
- Monitoring preset database conditions with a macro
- Three ways to design macro menus
- Building macros with string formulas
- Having fun with the marching macro
- Using the ROWs macro
- Generating a macro for tracking elapsed time

New applications and new solutions—every issue gives you novel ways to harness 1-2-3 and Symphony.

- Creating customized menus for your spreadsheets
- How to use criteria to unlock your spreadsheet program's data management power
- Using spreadsheets to monitor investments
- Improving profits with more effective sales forecasts
- An easy way to calculate year-to-date performance
- Using /**D**ata **F**ill to streamline counting and range filling

Extend your uses—and your command—of spreadsheets.

- Printing spreadsheets sideways can help sell your ideas
- How to add goal-seeking capabilities to your spreadsheet

- Hiding columns to create custom worksheet printouts
- Lay out your spreadsheet for optimum memory management
- Toward an "intelligent" spreadsheet
- A quick way to erase extraneous zeros

Techniques for avoiding pitfalls and repairing the damage when disaster occurs.

- Preventing and trapping errors in your worksheet
- How to create an auditable spreadsheet
- Pinpointing specific errors in your spreadsheets
- Ways to avoid failing formulas
- Catching common debugging and data-entry errors
- Detecting data-entry errors
- Protecting worksheets from accidental (or deliberate) destruction
- Avoiding disaster with the /**S**ystem command

Objective product reviews—we accept *no advertising,* so you can trust our editors' outspoken opinions.

- Metro Desktop Manager
- Freelance Plus
- Informix
- 4Word, InWord, Write-in
- Spreadsheet Analyst
- 101 macros for 1-2-3

Mail this card today for your free evaluation copy or call 1-800-277-7999.

BUSINESS REPLY MAIL
FIRST CLASS PERMIT NO. 278   CARMEL, IN

Postage will be paid by the addressee

THE JOURNAL FOR 1 2 3 AND SYMPHONY USERS

Que Corporation
11711 N. College Avenue
Carmel, Indiana 46032-9903